GW00367316

STRATEGIC
SURVEY
1999/2000

Published by
OXFORD
UNIVERSITY PRESS
for
The International Institute
for Strategic Studies
Arundel House
13–15 Arundel Street
London WC2R 3DX
United Kingdom

Strategic Survey 1999/2000

Published by
OXFORD
UNIVERSITY PRESS

for

The International Institute for Strategic Studies

Arundel House, 13–15 Arundel Street,
London WC2R 3DX, United Kingdom

Director .... Dr John Chipman
Editor .... Sidney Bearman

Assistant Editor:
  Maps .... Dr Mats R. Berdal
Managing Editor .... Susan Bevan
Research Assistant .... Ellen Peacock

Project Manager,
Design and Production ...... Mark Taylor

This publication has been prepared by the Director of the Institute and his Staff, who accept full responsibility for its contents, which describe and analyse events up to 30 March 2000. These do not, and indeed cannot, represent a consensus of views among the worldwide membership of the Institute as a whole.

First published .... May 2000

ISBN 0-19-922475-7
ISSN 0459-7230

© The International Institute
for Strategic Studies 2000

Strategic Survey (ISSN 0459-7230) is published annually by Oxford University Press.

Payment is required with all orders and subscriptions. Prices include air-speeded delivery to Australia, Canada, India, Japan, New Zealand and the USA. Delivery elsewhere is by surface mail. Air-mail rates are available on request. Please add sales tax to prices quoted. Payment may be made by cheque or Eurocheque (payable to Oxford University Press), National Girobank (account 500 1056), credit card (MasterCard, Visa, American Express, Diners, JCB), direct debit (please send for details) or UNESCO coupons. Bankers: Barclays Bank plc. PO Box 333, Oxford, UK, code 20-65-18, account 00715654.

Claims for non-receipt must be made within four months of dispatch/order (whichever is later).

Please send subscription orders to the Journals Subscription Department, Oxford University Press, Great Clarendon Street, Oxford, OX2 6DP, UK. *Tel* +44 (0)1865 267907. *Fax* +44 (0)1865 267485. *e-mail* jnl.orders@oup.co.uk

Strategic Survey is distributed by Mercury International, 365 Blair Road, Avenel, NJ 07001, USA. Periodical postage paid at Rahway, New Jersey, USA, and additional entry points.

US POSTMASTER: Send address corrections to *Strategic Survey*, c/o Mercury International, 365 Blair Road, Avenel, NJ 07001, USA.

Abstracted and indexed by: Reasearch Base Online, PAIS.

PRINTED IN THE UK by Bell & Bain Ltd, Glasgow.

Contents

List of Tables, Figure and Maps

Perspectives

A S THE NEW MILLENNIUM ROLLED IN, the world was sandwiched between enduring conflicts that had their roots in earlier centuries and a number of strategic tendencies that reached out into the twenty-first century. The US, the world's most powerful nation, found itself caught between the two. On the one hand, because of the unique role it had been constantly called upon to play as mediator or prodder, it found itself mired in the detritus of the twentieth century. At the same time, as it led the world in technological innovation, it was involved, as no other nation was, in creating the matrix for the new century. As the dynamic force behind globalisation, the extraordinary explosion of information technology and, more often than not, the development of a new view of international humanitarian laws, the US was playing a role that no other nation could play. Too often it stumbled; but this was hardly surprising in the face of the new, revolutionary developments that were beginning to characterise the new millennium.

As the 1990s slid to a close, hopes had been raised that many of the intractable problems that had hung on for years might be near resolution. Reality soon intruded. As the decade dragged on, intransigent ethnic, religious and historical enmities shattered that comfortable illusion. India and Pakistan began 1999 making pleasant sounds to each other; the Indian prime minister even visited Pakistan, travelling on the first bus to open a new route between the two countries. With the election of Ehud Barak in Israel, hopes for the Israeli–Arab peace negotiations looked up, in both their Palestinian and Syrian modes. The Northern Ireland peacemakers struggled towards what looked like a wonderful resting place, more than half-way up the mountain. Amid the jubilation that followed the NATO victory in Kosovo was the feeling that a true settlement could not be far behind. China and Taiwan seemed to have moved beyond their 1996 semi-battle in the Taiwan Straits, and were meeting on questions of trade, investment and tourism. Yet, none of the hope embodied in these situations lasted beyond the initial stages, and each had the taint of failure about it.

While much went wrong during the year, there was also much that went right. With the notable exception of Japan, the economies of the stricken East Asian nations continued their rapid recovery from the financial crises that had so rocked them. The economies of the industrialised West, led by the booming US, held firm. Whether through foresight and remedial action, or because the problem was more hype than reality, the widely anticipated global computer disruption at the end of 1999 did not materialise. The major computer users spent billions of dollars to ensure that there would be no unexpected glitches; even if the fears that occasioned their expenditure were not fulfilled, these billions were far from wasted. Businesses and countries alike have vastly improved their information-technology capabilities, giving them a competitive edge that those who did not follow suit will be hard pressed to overcome. Yet, the litany of failure that characterised the year should prevent complacency. Without tender care and constant attention, every circumstance that now appears to be a cause for rejoicing can all too easily turn to dust.

Dreams Deferred

The list of situations turned sour was a lengthy and sad one, even if it was somewhat familiar. India and Pakistan had begun 1999 with an encouraging agreement reached between their prime ministers at Lahore. This crashed in early May, when Pakistan encouraged and supported an attempt by Islamic 'freedom fighters' to gain a foothold in Indian-held Kashmir. The leader of the army coup that toppled Pakistani Prime Minister Nawaz Sharif some six months later had clearly been behind this action, a guarantee that any vestige of goodwill between the two countries would not be recovered quickly. By the end of the year, tensions were higher than they had been since their 1971 war, and worries that these two powers, recently armed with nuclear weapons, might come into conflict again agitated international chanceries.

Northern Ireland's Good Friday Agreement – the long-time poster child of conflict mediators – stumbled during 1999, but recovered its balance in time to allow the establishment of a power-sharing government at Stormont by the year's end. Less than two months after Unionists and Nationalists had arranged themselves with smiles around the same table, however, the unanimity was gone. It foundered on the customary mistrust that has bedevilled every effort at reconciliation. The refusal of the Irish Republican Army (IRA) to give up any arms at all, and the Unionists' insistence that they were led to believe the IRA would do so, left the British government with little choice but to dismantle this latest effort at power sharing and once again take up the mantle itself. While the cease-fires hold, it is possible that some different approach may be found; but it is hard to be confident, for it will take statesmanship that has been all too rare in this conflict.

NATO's famous victory in Kosovo, celebrated for its unprecedented success in air-power and smart munitions, has begun to look dodgy. The Albanian refugees returned and immediately turned on the Serbs, trying to treat them to the same fate that, courtesy of Western power, they themselves had barely escaped. Slobodan Milosovic is still in power, still stirring the witches' brew of ethnic hatred. NATO has not provided the requisite number of troops, and the allies are squabbling over who is to supply how much money, arguing over what has happened to the unfulfilled promise of police support, and lacking coordination and overall plans. NATO had obviously not correctly judged the desire for revenge that now affects all sides in this battle-scarred land. The Alliance cannot now afford to sit back and rest on its laurels if it is to avoid seeing its victory dissolve into defeat.

The stable relationship between China and Taiwan has for decades rested on their ability to maintain complete ambiguity regarding the question of the island's sovereignty: both agreed that there was one China, but disagreed over how Taiwan fitted into it. That ambiguity leached away during 1999, creating the most dangerous security flashpoint in Asia, one that could all too easily get out of hand. There has never been any doubt that Taiwan's leaders lacked interest in accepting Beijing's embrace. With the advent of a robust democratic system on Taiwan there is now no doubt that its citizens look upon such a development with equal horror.

In mid-1999, President Lee Teng Hui drove beyond the limits established as acceptable by Beijing when he declared that relations between the two should henceforth be conducted between equals, as 'a special state-to-state relationship'. This declaration, close to a demand for recognition of independence without actually saying it, was anathema to China. Beijing's riposte, embedded in a carefully drafted 11,000-word White Paper, was to reiterate adamantly that Taiwan was merely a province of China, and to threaten unequivocally that, if Taiwan continued indefinitely to refuse to open unification negotiations, China would use force to get the result it desires. The threat was intended to affect the March 2000 Taiwanese presidential election, but it went beyond that to lay the foundation for an early resumption of negotiations. However, since the election resulted in the leader of the pro-independence party becoming president, the value of strategic ambiguity as a guide to Taiwan's status is fast dwindling. Without great care, this volatile situation could explode, dragging the US, which continues to support Taiwan, into direct conflict with China.

While the US has been exercising its influence behind the scenes to dampen any possibility of an irrevocable act by either China or Taiwan, it has taken centre stage in the effort to keep the peace negotiations in the Middle East alive and vibrant. Barak's announced timetable for positive results in both the Palestinian and Syrian talks was certainly welcome, if perhaps a little too ambitious. Expectations of early success have been shredded by suspicions among all parties involved that movement will result in loss for themselves. Although the leaders and negotiators are willing to seek sensible compromises, they must continually look over their shoulders at strong domestic opposition. Without the forceful prodding of the US, all negotiations would now be stalemated. But the US can not force the last stage. The major Middle East players must themselves recognise that this is not a zero-sum game; each will gain immeasurably if agreement can be reached. Certainly, such an agreement will need to be followed by positive actions to ensure a secure peace and the possibility of attendant prosperity, but the initial step must first be taken.

Is There a Superpower?

The inability of the US to move Middle Eastern countries in the direction it wishes is not the only failure which prompts questions about the real power it can bring to bear in today's world. Despite all its military and diplomatic pressure, Saddam Hussein is still in charge in Iraq, and is still thumbing his nose at the US. Efforts to recreate an effective monitoring and verifying regime, which could prevent his attempts to develop weapons of mass destruction and missiles capable of spreading his influence in the neighbourhood, have been stymied in the UN by France and Russia. Europe has begun to create the European Security and Defence Identity (ESDI) that the US has considerable misgivings about. The best the US has been able to do is to express concern quietly, while Europeans, led by France and the UK, go their own way.

In areas where the US feels strongly that certain defence efforts must be made, it finds itself alone with its worries and proposed solutions. Washington is certain that a limited National Missile Defence (NMD) and shared Theater Missile Defence (TMD) system are essential to ensure full protection for itself and its allies from the threat of rogue-nation missiles and possible nuclear attack. Not only does the US find itself criticised by Russia and China, which feel that this defensive effort is directed against themselves, but its NATO allies are reluctant to endorse the US premises. Many of them feel that NMD is an unnecessary, destabilising move to counter an exaggerated threat. The strength of feeling in the US is so great, however, that it is not a question of whether the US will construct a limited NMD system, but when. European fears of US unilateralism, inaccurate in almost every other case, will probably be vindicated in this instance.

In international economic matters also, US-government wishes are thwarted. Partly because of poor preparation, but partly because of vehement and vocal opposition by a strange assortment of protesters – union members, left-wing intellectuals, environmentalists, right-wing ideologues and just plain, permanent, professional protesters – the US agenda for the World Trade Organization (WTO) general session in Seattle was disrupted. Nor can the US always win its way with regard to the leadership of such international organisations as the International Monetary Fund (IMF). Having vetoed one German candidate, it was forced to accept another, despite the misgivings which it shared with many third-world nations. It is true, but not necessarily right, that the head of the IMF has traditionally been a European. If a better candidate appears, even if he or she is an American, logic and good sense dictate that the candidate should be chosen. That this does not happen is another measure of US unwillingness to assert the overwhelming strength that it is all too often condemned for using.

Is the US, then, a weak and pathetic giant, as former President Richard Nixon once fretted? Not when it chooses to act. In Kosovo even more than in the 1991 Gulf War against Iraq, the imbalance of power among the NATO allies was striking. The US Air Force flew not many more than 50% of the missions, but dropped the vast majority of the munitions and provided some two-thirds of the aircraft. Most of the smart weapons, cruise missiles and air transport was supplied by the US, even when they were used by the 12 other NATO nations involved. The asymmetry has shown up a dangerous gap in the ability of the allies to synchronise their efforts. Increases in defence spending by the European allies will be necessary to close this gap, but unfortunately there is little sign that the message will be heeded.

It is not comparative capabilities that call US strength into question. It is how those capabilities are used – or, more often, not used. As a presidential candidate, Bill Clinton made much of then President George Bush's lack of vision in foreign affairs. As president, once the US was thrust forward as the 'last superpower', Clinton has shown no more grasp than his many critics of how to shape the international order. His approach to foreign problems has been mostly reactive; all too often, action has been delayed until the breaking point, when disproportionate means were then thrown into the breach. Now a lame duck president – his influence diluted by his bitter feuding with a Congress frustrated by its failure to impeach him for lying about his predatory sexual nature – he heads an administration that cannot be expected to launch the significant foreign-policy initiatives that might help to delineate a friendlier, warmer international environment. More's the pity.

But Efforts Are Being Made

Like-minded nations are hesitantly moulding a different world. Both the intervention in Kosovo for humanitarian reasons, and the activities of international courts dealing with humanitarian offences, pointed to the quickening evolution of a body of international humanitarian law. This law is certain to have a growing impact on the conduct of nations, for it is creating a body of precedents which indicate when the UN, and nations generally, can intervene in another state's affairs to prevent violations of basic humanitarian norms. It has further clarified the proposition that no one, not even a former head of state, is immune from prosecution by the international community for actions taken while they were in charge.

All are not wedded to these far-reaching new attacks on the idea that a sovereign state has an absolute right to act at home as it wishes. Some are adamantly opposed. China stands out in this regard. As a nation with one of the worst records of human-rights abuses, and with a government whose autocratic self-righteousness is unmatched in today's world, it correctly fears that it could be called before some bar of justice in the near future for acts committed, or indeed for acts which it has failed to commit. Many developing countries – and Russia on some occasions – are also exceedingly wary. Russia would countenance actions taken with the blessing of the UN Security Council, as its power of veto would protect it. It probably would have joined China in vetoing the Kosovo action if NATO had not carefully avoided the Security Council before enforcing its will against Serbia.

The humanitarian principle is firming up. That does not mean that even its most vocal advocates will encourage its use under most circumstances. The disproportionate force that Russia has used against Chechnya, and particularly against Chechen civilians, might well bring it within the bounds of the new law if other political considerations did not weigh more heavily. The reluctance of outside nations to intervene in East Timor without agreement from the Indonesian government, despite the obvious and massive transgressions there by the Indonesian armed forces, underlined the brakes that exist on the new humanitarian concept. Its existence and its availability for use cannot be doubted, however.

The successful use of force, even if now legitimised, is not enough. Force used to right an obvious wrong must be followed up by actions that will ensure that the Kosovo War had a purpose. NATO and the UN must create viable and humane politics and economics in Kosovo, not only for those in whose name the force was used, not only because their own credibility is still being tested, but also to validate the humanitarian concept. Years from now, if anarchy and crime rule in Kosovo – as they may well do unless the UN authority now established there receives more of the promised aid that is sadly lacking – hopes of a more humane world, prepared to exercise the right of humanitarian intervention, will fade. NATO's leaders should push this thought of the future to the forefront and abandon any notion that it has already done more than enough.

That General Augusto Pinochet was allowed to return to Chile without having to face justice in a Spanish court did not abrogate the principle that international criminal law has now become universally applicable. His release was allowed on technical medical grounds. No brutal dictator, unless suffering from senile dementia and thus unable to understand or react to the charges that can be brought by any national court, should take comfort from Pinochet's return home. Chad's exiled dictator Hissène

Habré, for example, has been charged by a Senegalese court with torture and killings. This encouragingly rapid follow-up in an African nation of the principle established by the Law Lords in England is a happy expansion of the idea that in a humane world no one should be considered above the law.

Those who do the actual deeds ordered by the Pinochets and Habrés are also finding that it is more difficult to hide or to avoid punishment. The International Criminal Tribunal for the former Yugoslavia (ICTY), established in the Hague in 1993, has slowly gathered momentum. In the most significant case to date it nailed its highest ranking suspect when it sentenced Croat General Tihomer Blaskic to 45 years in prison for torture and killings. The number of indicted individuals has recently increased significantly, and more suspects are being arrested and charged. The tribunal's activities may not deter all future inhumane behaviour, but it shines out as a testament to the international community's willingness to hunt down and jail offenders of all ranks. It is unfortunate that the tribunal established to try crimes in Rwanda has not pursued its mandate with greater zeal.

Both these tribunals have single mandates only, and cannot be used to try those charged with humanitarian offences committed anywhere beyond their own jurisdiction. To remedy this defect, the Court of International Justice (CIJ) was established at a 1998 meeting of 160 nations in Rome. This will sit permanently and its writ will run world-wide. Surprisingly, there are two important hold-outs: the US and China, an unlikely alliance on a human-rights issue. Beijing's reluctance is not hard to fathom. The US refusal to join in what would appear to be a natural cause for it revolves around a fear in the Pentagon that any number of countries would be eager to condemn US troops engaged in conflict abroad on little or no evidence of wrongdoing.

There is little chance that such charges would result in hauling US personnel before the CIJ – the founding charter carefully stipulates that no citizen of a country would be liable before this court if he was arraigned in his nation's courts and if those courts were known to be free and unprejudiced. The US should therefore join with the rest of the world to ensure the CIJ is set up and working effectively. It could be a Yugoslav Tribunal writ large; its range would be wide, and in time it could deter some from joining in the brutality that is all too often seen around the world at present.

Non-governmental Patterns

The US and China are also allied in a more positive relationship, the effort to bring China into the WTO. There would be membership benefits for China, of course, but there would be even more for the rest of the world.

WTO membership would require China to abide by the legal restrictions under which all Western nations trade; it would force the country to make available information it now keeps from its own people as well as the rest of the world; it would integrate the country more closely to the globalised world economy; and, by creating new skeins of interdependence, it would invigorate conditions that could liberalise economic and political life at home. Clinton, followed by the EU, was right to champion its cause.

It took Clinton and the US considerable time to get to this proper juncture. Thirteen years of hard bargaining to ensure that China understood, and was willing to abide by, the need to operate on a free and open-market basis, was almost jeopardised in summer 1999 by Clinton's kow-towing to the contrary views from the labour unions, the traditional source of much Democratic Party support. It was an uproar of protest from concerned businesses that tipped the balance back and allowed Clinton to accept the concessions which the Chinese were offering. By any standard, this is the wrong way to do business.

Having surmounted that self-inflicted obstacle, Clinton faced another in the Congress. To ensure that China will give the US the low-tariff benefits it has agreed, the US must make available reciprocal normal trading tariffs to the Chinese on a permanent basis. Congress has regularly voted such a trade status each year, on the basis of a review by the White House of China's human-rights record. It has therefore always been a dicey affair, subject to the whims of individual congressmen at any given time. The same unusual bed-fellows (environmentalists and trade union-ists; Greenpeace and right-wing ideologues; left-wing intellectuals and professional agitators) are gearing up to pressure Congress on this issue, as they did in Seattle. They believe that their invasion of Seattle trashed the last meeting of the WTO, and that a concerted campaign against the organisation will effectively destroy their real target – the globalised economy – which they condemn for all the sins they can think up.

But the globalised economy does none of the things such protestors fear. The extraordinary wealth that Americans enjoy is a result of the integration of free-trade economies; rather than stealing jobs in the US, as the trades unions claim, the globalised economy has created them. Developing countries have not backed this retrograde movement because they expect to benefit from free trade; ultimately their poor will suffer not from globalisation but from a successful attempt to cripple it. In many areas it has been a boon for the environment, not an enemy. Free trade helps competition to develop; it is not there solely to strengthen multi-national corporations The trouble with the list of evils recited by the protestors is the impact which it makes with a public that at best does not understand what globalisation is, or what benefits it brings, and is therefore apt to accept and act on such criticisms.

Although governments have been unable to shape the world of today, globalisation, without conscious planning, has been helping to provide some shape. Greater integration of economies brings greater interdependence. Freer trade tightens economic bonds, which in turn aids stability. Regulation of world markets is a necessity for this structure to work properly, and the WTO is necessary in order to monitor the enforcement of rules on which governments agree. The US Congress has a duty to stand up for intelligence in the face of this new 'know nothing' movement. It should not shirk that duty. The G-8 group of leading industrialised countries, which will meet in July, must also find a way to make globalisation a less threatening phenomenon.

Governments do not need, nor should they try, to regulate the second powerful force which is unconsciously shaping today's world, and tomorrow's. Words like 'revolution' are often misused, but it is no exaggeration to note that the world is now being swept along by a true revolution, based on the rapid spread of electronic information technology. The free and rapid spread of information, the result of the electronics revolution, is having and will increasingly have, a profound effect on the state, on how the world does business, and on how it fights its wars. Since this is a true revolution, exactly how it will work out cannot yet be foreseen. But there are clear directions that can be discerned.

The information revolution tends to reduce the ability of an authoritarian state to control its populace. The easy availability of knowledge undercuts repressive mechanisms and empowers people. Insofar as a state wishes to be part of the global economic upsurge, it must allow its businesses, its scientists and eventually its ordinary citizens to have access to the Internet. China's efforts to find a way to use information technology while at the same time restricting its impact on the populace is a clear testimony to the dangers such technology holds for an authoritarian regime. Those efforts cannot succeed; short of barring any access, which would create unacceptable restrictions on its economy and scientific innovation, there is no way to prevent information from going where the state does not want it to go.

The development and expansion of the Internet will also suck all businesses, domestic and global, into its maw. As *The Economist* pointed out, more and more businesses will perforce become Internet businesses until they all are Internet businesses, just as all businesses became telephone businesses once that vital instrument became ubiquitous. It is no longer a luxury to have a website to which customers can connect – it is a necessity that customers will soon insist on. The ease of communication will benefit those that seize its promise, and will tie the global economy into a tighter web. Since globalisation pays dividends in terms of jobs and wealth, the combination of a burgeoning electronic world with an integrated world economy can only be considered a positive development.

There are obvious downsides to information technology. Just as it is difficult to stop people from reading what is being sent cheaply through cyberspace, so is it difficult to monitor what is being sent. Misinformation vies for attention with truth. Even accurate information can be dangerous: teaching irresponsible people how to make bombs efficiently, or where to acquire weapons, cannot be considered useful. Yet, on balance, what appear to be the more important trends of the Internet seem certain to bring profound, and mostly positive, changes in the way humankind manages its affairs.

In the ten years since the Soviet Union dissolved, statesmen have had little success in managing the shapeless international community that was left in its wake. It may be, however, that this is no great loss. There are times when inaction pays far greater dividends than action. The inaction required at the moment is to avoid stultifying the two forces that are revolutionising our times. They do not need the heavy hand of control: they will flower best in freedom. Although politicians are generally people of action, who find it difficult to do nothing, they would be well advised to recognise that these new forces will help to bring about a better future if nothing is done to impede them.

Strategic Policy Issues

The NATO Capability Gap

Operation Allied Force, the 78-day air war against Serbia in March–June 1999, was a clear victory for NATO. This was the Alliance's second combat operation in its 50-year history (the first was the less intense air operation in Bosnia during summer 1995). The massive air-strikes, coupled with the possibility of a NATO ground attack and the withdrawal of Moscow's support for Belgrade, compelled Slobodan Milosevic to withdraw the Yugoslav army from Kosovo and accept the presence of 52,000 NATO troops in the province. At the same time, however, the war revealed a disturbing disparity in the capabilities of NATO members, which could seriously affect the future effectiveness of NATO forces. Bridging the gap will take considerable effort, determination and money. As all three seem to be lacking at present, the gap threatens to grow rather than diminish.

The US, and Then the Rest

During the short Kosovo War, NATO aircraft flew just over 38,000 sorties against targets in Serbia, including 10,424 strike missions expending over 23,600 munitions. All 19 NATO members participated in one form or another, but the United States played the dominant role. It paid roughly 80% of the cost of the air campaign and supporting-force deployments, with France and the UK contributing much of the balance. The navies of nine NATO members participated, but the US provided the vast majority of carrier, air and cruise-missile assets. The US supplied 650 of the 927 aircraft that participated in the air campaign: the remainder came from Belgium, Canada, Denmark, France, Germany, Italy, Netherlands, Norway, Portugal, Spain, Turkey and the UK. US aircraft delivered more than 80% of all ordnance, flew 52% of all strike missions and performed just over 70% of all support missions. The United States was the only member to contribute long-range bombers. The two-dozen or so B-52, B-1 and B-2 bombers that participated in *Allied Force* only flew about 320 sorties, yet they dropped roughly half of the bombs and missiles used during the war.

The war also revealed the difficulties inherent in waging war as a coalition. Throughout the campaign, NATO employed a cumbersome command-and-control system. As a result, gaining approval to strike a given target often took some time. Moreover, there was an understanding that the main nations would consult on targets, and such consultations were not always effective. Nor did NATO actually control all the assets used in the air campaign. The US planned the employment of F-117 *Nighthawk* attack aircraft, B-2 *Spirit* bombers, and Tomahawk Land-Attack Missiles (TLAMs) separately from NATO.

Operation Joint Guardian, NATO's subsequent peacekeeping operation in Kosovo, revealed additional problems. While both the United States and its NATO allies were able to deploy a large air armada to bases on the periphery of the Former Republic of Yugoslavia, moving and sustaining ground forces proved more challenging. To many reformers both inside and outside the US Army, the problems the service encountered while trying to deploy a regiment of AH-64 *Apache* attack helicopters and support units have come to symbolise its inability to respond rapidly to crises across the globe. During the war, the US Army lacked units light enough to move quickly yet heavy enough to strike hard. This shortfall has prompted Army Chief of Staff General Eric Shinseki to reconfigure two brigades into mobile, lethal units capable of deploying anywhere in the world within 96 hours.

NATO's European members face even greater challenges. NATO Secretary-General Lord Robertson has noted that NATO's European armies struggled to deploy 40,000 troops to Kosovo, a mere 2% of their combined total of about two million. Those armies still look much as they did during the Cold War, designed to defend Western Europe against the Warsaw Pact's armoured forces. Many lack the mobility necessary to deploy quickly outside their own borders. They also lack the logistical support to sustain combat operations. If NATO is to respond effectively to future Kosovos, European armies must embark on the sort of fundamental restructuring that the US Army is only now beginning. The organisational, fiscal, and bureaucratic barriers to such a transformation are, however, formidable.

The transatlantic capability gap is most pronounced in cutting-edge areas of warfare, such as precision strike, command-and-control, and intelligence, associated with the emerging Revolution in Military Affairs (RMA). Even before Kosovo, defence analysts on both sides of the Atlantic worried that US programmes to incorporate information technologies into the armed forces would outpace the efforts of other Alliance members. Their fears were confirmed: throughout the war, the US's allies lacked the equipment necessary to gather detailed intelligence, strike targets with precision and sustain their forces. Even as the United States invests in a new generation of military technology, many allies continue to fall behind. European defence spending in 1999 was roughly half that of the US, and their military research and development spending was just one-quarter of

US levels. The US spent $47 billion on procurement; European states spent $28bn.

There was a widespread use of precision-guided munitions (PGMs) during *Operation Allied Force*. Less than 8% of the munitions used in the Gulf War had been PGMs; in *Allied Force* they made up 35% of the 23,600 bombs and missiles that were used. The US air forces used a far larger number of PGMs than their European and Canadian counterparts. While British aircraft, for example, flew more than 1,000 strike missions, three-quarters of the munitions they dropped were unguided. And even though European aircraft sometimes flew half of the Alliance's strike sorties, the US had to supply them with weapons. Only the US and the UK possess the *Tomahawk* cruise missile, which allowed NATO to strike high-value targets in all types of weather without risking pilots' lives. The United States launched well over 90% of the cruise missiles in the campaign: Britain launched 20 *Tomahawk* land-attack missiles (TLAMs) from HMS *Splendid*, whereas the US launched 240 TLAMs from submarines and ships and 60 air-launched cruise missiles from bombers.

PGMs – particularly those which rely on laser-designation or employ optical guidance – were no panacea. Adverse weather conditions over Serbia frequently prevented air strikes from being launched. In other cases, the Alliance's rules of engagement prevented aircraft from dropping their ordnance. One of the most useful munitions of the war was the US Joint Direct Attack Munition (JDAM), a Global Positioning System (GPS)-guided weapon capable of attacking targets in all types of weather. Unlike laser- and television-guided bombs, fog clouds and rain did not hamper the JDAM.

The widespread use of PGMs during the war led to concern in Washington that the US inventory was growing dangerously low, and the US armed forces have stepped up their efforts to replenish stocks. NATO's European members are emphasising their own acquisition of PGMs. Britain and France, for example, will soon deploy the stealthy *Storm Shadow* land-attack cruise missile, while France will field the stealthy *Apache* air-launched and *Scalp* strategic land-attack cruise missiles. These developments will significantly boost the coalition's long-range precision-strike capability.

A further shortfall involved transporting troops and equipment to the theatre of operations, one that has prompted NATO to explore the further use of commercial air- and sea-lift for contingency operations. In addition, Germany has proposed the formation of a European mobility command to centralise European NATO's mobility assets, including the proposed future European large transport aircraft (FLA). The Alliance is also in the process of forming a Multinational Joint Logistics Center to allow it to deploy assets more effectively. Britain, for its part, plans to lease American C-17 transport aircraft to augment its airlift capability.

Secure communications equipment was another conspicuous deficiency during the air campaign. Because some of the European allies' aircraft lacked the ability to encrypt their communications, Serb armed forces were able to monitor transmissions, thereby compromising the operational security of the air campaign. British and French aircraft also lacked reliable identification-friend-or-foe (IFF) systems. The US, British and French governments have all now identified the acquisition of secure communications equipment as a top priority. NATO is also developing architecture for a modern Alliance-wide communications network.

During the Kosovo War, the Alliance was highly dependent upon the United States for airborne and satellite imagery, underlining the gap that exists within NATO regarding intelligence collection, analysis and dissemination. France is the only other NATO member that operates a reconnaissance satellite, and its capabilities are limited compared to American platforms. Moreover, European air forces contributed few of the reconnaissance aircraft used in the air war and lacked platforms comparable to the U-2 and Joint Strategic Airborne Reconnaissance System (JSTARS) aircraft. This shortfall has reinvigorated NATO's Alliance Ground Surveillance (AGS) programme, which envisions fitting unmanned aerial vehicles (UAV), helicopters and jet aircraft with ground-surveillance radar to give them a JSTARS-like capability. The system will not be fielded, however, until the second half of this decade. UAVs were employed for reconnaissance, surveillance and target acquisition throughout the war. While 15 of the drones crashed or were shot down, they proved valuable for locating Serb forces and assessing bomb damage. The US, UK and France are all stepping up their efforts to acquire UAVs.

The Kosovo War also highlighted the need for both the US and European NATO members to procure additional electronic warfare assets. Throughout the air campaign, NATO relied upon US electronic warfare systems – particularly RC-135 *Rivet Joint* aircraft – to jam Serb air defences. The US Air Force's decision to retire its EF-111 electronic warfare aircraft and rely upon an ageing fleet of Navy and Marine Corps EA-6B *Prowler* aircraft came back to haunt it, as these aircraft were stretched to their operational limit. Electronic warfare is thus receiving renewed emphasis on both sides of the Atlantic.

But NATO also faces a more subtle capability gap. The US armed forces are committed – at least rhetorically – to transforming themselves through the rapid adoption of advanced information technology to achieve an RMA. Each of the services is pursuing initiatives to acquire cutting-edge technology and develop innovative operational concepts and organisations. European armed forces have been much more reluctant to embrace war in the information age. As the US armed forces accelerate their transformation, the transatlantic gap will widen. Divergent approaches to the emerging RMA may hamper the Alliance's operational effectiveness.

While American efforts to exploit the information revolution promise discontinuous increases in military effectiveness, they may also render more difficult operations with other NATO members not similarly equipped.

These disparities threaten to hamper NATO's ability to operate effectively. Failure to achieve a more equitable distribution of labour across the Atlantic may limit Europe's ability to act, with or without the US. Similarly, a growing perception in the United States that Europe is unwilling to shoulder its fair share of the transatlantic defence burden may fuel resentment and limit US willingness to intervene in future European contingencies.

Tackling the Problem

NATO has taken a number of steps to bridge the capability gap. At the Alliance's April 1999 summit in Washington DC, members launched the Defence Capabilities Initiative (DCI) to enhance allied military capabilities in five key areas: deployability and mobility; sustainability and logistics; effective engagement; survivability of forces and infrastructure; and command-and-control and information systems. The initiative's goal is to strengthen NATO by pooling resources and rationalising capabilities. Italian Prime Minister Massimo D'Alema, for example, has noted that while NATO's defence spending is more than 60% of that of the US, it yields only 10% as much capability, either because European states are not buying the latest technology or because they are duplicating existing capabilities. In some cases, addressing this problem may require increased spending by some or most European nations; in others, it may demand the more efficient use of resources.

Individual NATO members are also re-evaluating their defence requirements. France is moving towards an all-professional army; Italy and Spain are expected to follow soon. The British Ministry of Defence is examining ways to improve the UK's capability to launch all-weather stand-off attacks against a variety of targets. It is also exploring options to modernise its communications and information systems. Germany plans to improve its reconnaissance capabilities and acquire wide-body transport aircraft to improve the mobility of its forces. France and Germany have agreed to share the costs of the *Syracuse III* military communications satellite, which will go into orbit in 2003.

Yet, despite the attention the capability gap has received on both sides of the Atlantic, there is little sign of an effective attack on it. Part of the problem is the disparity of available funds. The US spent $283 billion on defence in 1999. The European members of NATO spent a combined total of $174bn, and many NATO allies are cutting their defence expenditure (in NATO Europe it has fallen 22% in real terms since 1992). Moreover, much

Strategic Policy Issues

of what is spent by European governments goes not towards new technology or better training, but towards the costs of short-term conscripts, pensions and infrastructure.

Sustaining defence expenditures is a major challenge, especially for countries such as France, Germany, Italy, the Netherlands and Spain that have yet to meet the Maastricht Treaty's criteria for government debt. While there are several avenues open for these states to realise efficiencies in defence spending – such as reforming their procurement systems, cutting the size of their armed forces, and eliminating excess infrastructure – each brings with it significant domestic political hurdles.

Economic factors further complicate efforts to address the transatlantic capability gap. The weak euro has made American military technology more expensive in Europe and increased the competitiveness of European defence exports, giving European governments an incentive to prioritise exports over procurement. (The US, however, has traditionally been reluctant to purchase European defence technology.)

NATO and ESDI

The European Security and Defence Identity (ESDI), the European Union's effort to create a military force separate from NATO, has complicated the issue. At the EU's Helsinki summit on 10 December 1999, members approved the formation of a rapid-reaction corps of up to 60,000 soldiers – roughly three divisions – by 2003. The force, which would operate under the direct control of the EU, would be on standby to conduct humanitarian and peacekeeping missions, as well as non-combatant evacuation operations. Members also approved the formation of command and planning staffs, intelligence centres, and decision-making and deployment apparatuses. The French government has emphasised the need for Europe to be able to handle future Kosovos without the United States. But an independent capability to conduct high-intensity combined-arms operations remains a distant possibility at best.

The advent of the ESDI has sparked considerable transatlantic debate. In the US, many fear that it will draw money away from NATO by duplicating existing capabilities and impeding efforts to modernise and rationalise the Alliance. Many Europeans believe, on the contrary, that a stronger, more united European military will strengthen NATO, playing an important role in situations where NATO cannot or will not act. Some go even further, portraying the ESDI as the vanguard of a unified European military. They hold that although the US complains that Europe is not doing enough, it objects to any European efforts to do more.

The ESDI is on balance a positive development. A 60,000-man force, if properly trained and equipped, can serve a useful role in handling peacekeeping and peace-enforcement missions. If the transatlantic capabilities gap is to narrow, however, more is needed. But it is unlikely that NATO's European members will increase their defence budgets, and economic pressures will, if anything, make it more difficult for European states to sustain even their current level of spending. Nor is it likely that the US will retard its modernisation efforts to keep pace with NATO as a whole, as such a move would rob the Alliance of valuable capabilities. Given these realities, the best that can be expected for the foreseeable future may be an effort to cope with the gap.

The overarching goal of NATO efforts should be to ensure that NATO as a whole can exploit the potential of emerging ways of war associated with the RMA. To realise this vision, NATO's European members will need to develop capabilities sufficiently compatible with those of the US to allow them to perform meaningful, mutually supporting combat and peacekeeping roles and missions. Perhaps the best way to do so within existing and anticipated resources would be to implement a robust programme of combined experimentation and training. A NATO-wide programme might utilise war games, simulations and exercises to investigate innovative concepts of operations, explore new organisational arrangement for crisis management and waging regional conflicts, and examine command-and-control arrangements to allow the Alliance to perform more effectively in future contingencies. Experimentation with advanced command-and-control and intelligence, surveillance and recon-naissance systems and doctrine is particularly important. The Alliance should also emphasise combined training that exploits lessons learned from recent coalition operations in Bosnia and Kosovo. Failure to capitalise on the experience could lead to a widening of the capability gap and ultimately to a two-tiered Alliance, a situation that is neither desirable nor workable.

The Shifting Sands of Sovereignty

Debates about the legitimacy and practicability of humanitarian inter-vention were sharply focused in 1999 by NATO's campaign in Kosovo, the UN's intercession in East Timor, and the contrast of both with the lack of outside interference with Russian actions in Chechnya. These cases were, of course, different in important respects. Firstly, while Kosovo is still undeniably part of Yugoslavia, and Chechnya (despite an assertion of *de facto* independence) is part of the Russian Federation, East Timor was never legally incorporated into Indonesia. Secondly, the intervention force entered East Timor only after authorisation from the Security Council and with the consent of Indonesia, while NATO action in Kosovo was without a UN mandate. The Security Council had, however, condemned Yugo-slavia's human-rights abuses in the province. Military intervention in Chechnya was never a political or practical possibility.

Despite the differences, the three cases prompt a number of similar questions:

- When, if ever, is outside intervention (especially military intervention) in a state justified on humanitarian grounds?

- Who has the right to intervene, when and how?

- Most difficult of all: how should intervention be followed up?

The importance of these questions was highlighted by UK Prime Minister Tony Blair's call for a greater degree of humanitarian activism in his 22 April 1999 speech at the Economic Club of Chicago, and by the damning, and more significant, UN report, published on 15 December 1999, on the consequences of non-intervention in Rwanda in 1994.

In examining how the concept of humanitarian intervention will develop in the next few years, it should be remembered that such action is not necessarily armed. Less dramatic moves, such as the imposition of economic sanctions or the prosecution of individual offenders, may sometimes be more effective.

The Legitimacy of Humanitarian Intervention

Critics of humanitarian intervention tend to attack it on one, or sometimes both, of the following grounds:

- It represents an assault upon the principle of state sovereignty.

- The potential for abuse creates a greater threat to international peace than the commission of atrocities within a state.

Neither criticism is as potent as it once was.

State sovereignty – though still far more important in international law, and exercising a more powerful influence on international opinion than is sometimes recognised – is not an absolute concept. Since the Second World War, if not before, it has been nonsense to suggest that states have a sovereign right to behave as they wish within their own territory. The United Nations Charter balances the right of states to their independence against the need to maintain international values and to promote human rights. The acceptance by states of human-rights obligations, of arms controls and of the UN Security Council's authority has limited the concept of sovereignty in numerous ways. Sovereign rights do not extend, for example, to committing torture, genocide or 'ethnic cleansing' or to disobeying binding Security Council decisions. While that has been the case for several decades, the implications have only recently become widely appreciated: if a state breaks international law, even if it does so only within its own territory and at the expense of its own nationals, that is a matter of international concern. As then UN Secretary-General Boutros Boutros-Ghali wrote in 1992 in his memoirs, *An Agenda for Peace*, 'the time of absolute and exclusive sovereignty ... has passed; its theory was never matched by reality.'

Since those words were written, there has been a dramatic increase in the international community's willingness to limit individual states' freedom of action within their own territories. One development has been the arraignment of individual offenders under international legal authority. The Security Council has established criminal tribunals for the Yugoslavia and Rwanda, in 1993 and 1994 respectively, with jurisdiction over crimes against humanity and war crimes, even those committed in civil wars. The Rome Statute of the International Criminal Court, adopted in 1998, will in time create a standing international tribunal where such crimes will be tried. In other cases there has been a greater willingness to make existing institutions or jurisdictions a reality. Thus, the prohibition of torture was well established by the 1970s and the Torture Convention provided for the trial of state torturers before the courts of other states during the 1980s. However, the significance of that development only became clear with the British courts' decisions in the case of Chile's General Augusto Pinochet in 1998–99. While such measures are far less serious than military action, they demonstrate, as then UN Secretary-General Javier Perez de Cuellar suggested in 1991, that 'the principle of non-interference with the essential domestic jurisdiction of states cannot be regarded as a protective barrier behind which human rights could be massively or systematically violated with impunity.'

The second argument against humanitarian intervention, based on the risk of abuse and the threat it may pose to international peace where military action is involved, is perhaps more telling. Humanitarian intervention on behalf of German minorities in neighbouring states was claimed by Hitler to justify his aggression. Throughout the Cold War, avoiding nuclear conflict was a higher priority than championing human rights. However, the end of the Cold War has greatly reduced the risk of humanitarian intervention leading to major conflict. NATO's intervention in Kosovo, although opposed by the Russian Federation and China, never threatened to escalate into an international confrontation. The end of the Cold War has also unlocked some of the Security Council's potential as an authoritative judge of when the claim of humanitarian intervention is justified, thereby reducing the risk of abuse..

These dangers have not been completely removed, however. Intervention in Kosovo did not pose the risk of wider international conflict, but military intervention in Chechnya or Tibet would do so. That does not affect the legal position – what has developed in international law is a right to intervene, not a duty – but it does mean that the risk of causing a wider conflict is likely to continue limiting when and where intervention will occur. Nor is the risk of abuse entirely eliminated. Such risk is, however, inherent in any rule of law permitting the use of force. The right of self-defence has been abused on numerous occasions, yet it has never been suggested that the international community could or should deny that prerogative.

Who has the Authority to Intervene ?

Where humanitarian intervention involves military force, the debate has tended to be about whether Security Council authorisation is required. The United Nations Charter gives the Council power to take enforcement action (including the power to take, or to authorise others to take, military action) only when there is a threat to international peace and security. However, the Council has repeatedly held that the humanitarian situation inside a state may become so serious that it poses such a threat. Where massive or systematic human-rights violations within a state spill across its borders, the threat to international peace is evident. In recent years, however, the Council has gone further, and considered that international peace was endangered in cases where there was little or no trans-border element. For example, in December 1992, the Council determined in its Resolution 794 that 'the magnitude of the human tragedy caused by the conflict in Somalia … constitutes a threat to international peace and security'. On that basis, the Council authorised the US to take military action in Somalia, and similarly in Haiti in 1994, and, though the position was more complex, with the UN Intervention Force in Bosnia-Herzegovina in 1995.

In recent years, the international community has widely accepted that the Security Council can engage in humanitarian intervention on this basis, although some states, notably China and India, continue to express grave reservations. In practice, if the situation demands military action which might be resisted, the Council has not attempted to take the action itself, but has authorised others to do so on its behalf. Thus, NATO conducted air operations over Bosnia-Herzegovina under a Council mandate, and a US-led force intervened in Somalia.

The Council's power to act is, and is likely to remain, subject to a number of practical limitations:

- its freedom of action is always subject to an actual or threatened veto, as was the case with military action in Kosovo;

- the Security Council has no forces of its own, and while it can authorise member states to use force, it has no power to compel them. Humanitarian intervention by the Council is therefore dependent upon those States with the necessary military capability being willing to employ it; and

- the UN continues to work on a consensual basis wherever possible, and, before authorising deployment of force in a state, will usually try to secure agreement from its government and sometimes from other parties as well.

This last consideration is not necessarily a weakness, so long as the Council remains prepared to take military action without consent in those cases where a humanitarian emergency exists and consent is nonetheless refused. In East Timor in October 1999, for example, the Council had the legal right to intervene whether the Indonesian government consented or not, but obtaining that consent had important practical advantages, not least in minimising the risk to the intervention force, and thus making it easier to obtain troop contributions. Those advantages have to be set against the consequences of the delay which obtaining consent necessarily entailed.

Intervention without a Security Council mandate, such as NATO's campaign in Kosovo between 24 March and 10 June 1999, does not enjoy the same degree of international acceptance as where there is UN sanction. The Kosovo operation, however, was by no means the only instance of humanitarian intervention under those conditions during the 1990s, although it involved by far the most extensive use of force. The initial action taken by the Nigerian-led Economic Community of West African States (ECOWAS) in the 1990 Liberian civil war relied for its justification largely on the claim of a humanitarian crisis, and did not receive any authority from the Security Council until late 1992. The Western intervention in northern Iraq in 1991 and the imposition of the ' no-fly zone' in southern Iraq the following year were justified by the UK on the basis that there was a customary right under international law to take action in a case of extreme humanitarian need. The same justification was advanced by the UK government during the Kosovo operation. There is, however, undoubtedly room for debate about the legality of humanitarian intervention without an express Security Council authority. The more soundly-based view, even before Kosovo, was that such action is lawful only when it is taken to prevent an imminent humanitarian catastrophe threatening international peace and security, which the Security Council is unable to prevent.

There were two particularly important features of the Kosovo campaign. First, NATO's assertion of a right to act based on the humanitarian crisis in the province attracted a remarkable degree of support. A Russian proposal to condemn NATO's action was defeated in the Security Council by twelve votes to three. Those voting against the draft resolution included Argentina, Bahrain, Brazil, Gabon, Gambia, Malaysia and

Slovenia, as well as the NATO states. Once Belgrade agreed to withdraw its forces from Kosovo in June 1999, the Security Council embodied the terms of the agreement in Resolution 1244. This effectively authorised forces from the NATO states to take control of Kosovo and then to work alongside the UN administration created to govern the province. It is difficult to reconcile that decision with the view that NATO had committed an illegal act of aggression.

Secondly, although the Security Council did not mandate NATO's action, this was not a case of unilateral action taken without any reference to the UN. As early as March 1998, the Security Council had condemned the Serbian government's repression of Kosovo's civilian population and recognised, in Resolution 1160, that the situation created by that repression and by the reciprocal violence of the Kosovo Liberation Army (KLA) constituted a threat to international peace and security. That view was repeated in Resolution 1199, adopted six months before the NATO action began, in which the Council expressed its alarm at 'the impending humanitarian catastrophe' in Kosovo and emphasised the need for action to prevent it happening. The Council repeatedly affirmed the existence of a humanitarian emergency, and the Belgrade's responsibility for creating it. The Council's role in establishing the settlement after the conflict is also significant.

Kosovo thus constitutes a highly significant precedent, which establishes more firmly in international law the right to intervene on humanitarian grounds, even without an express mandate from the Security Council. The case confirms, however, that this right is exceptional. The NATO states' positions, and other governments' reactions, suggest that military intervention for humanitarian purposes without UN sanction is lawful only when:

- a grave emergency threatens widespread loss of life;

- that emergency's existence is authoritatively confirmed; and

- action by the Security Council is blocked by the veto (or the threat of a veto).

Kosovo also demonstrates NATO's willingness to take military action under circumstances where it would not have done so before. Although some critics saw the operation as undermining the Security Council's effectiveness, that criticism is misplaced. The Council could not have dealt effectively with the Kosovo situation because, by March 1999, it was unlikely that anything but military action would have been effective, and Russia had made clear that it would veto a resolution providing for such action by the UN. On the contrary, by emphasising that, in an extreme case, there is a right of humanitarian intervention outside the Security Council, the Kosovo episode has probably made it easier for the Council to act in future humanitarian emergencies. A permanent member that is inclined to veto such action will fear that other states will take the initiative outside the Council framework, in an even less palatable way

The Means of Intervention and the Aftermath

The humanitarian intervention in Kosovo is unique in its use of air power as the principal means of enforcement. In previous interventions, such as in Iraq, Somalia and Liberia during the 1990s, the force used was, at least initially, very limited and intervention was largely through the deployment of ground forces. In Kosovo, the early use of ground forces was ruled out. Moreover, air power was used not so much to defeat the Yugoslav forces, which were carrying out the atrocities in Kosovo, as to bring about a change of policy in Belgrade

This course of action aroused controversy over both its effectiveness and its legitimacy. The question of effectiveness is debatable. The Milosevic government did back down in the end, but it seems likely that it was more a combination of the effects of the bombing, the diplomatic initiatives and the possibility of a land offensive than the bombing alone that brought about a change of policy. The legitimacy of using air power as a means of humanitarian intervention is equally debatable. When force is used for humanitarian purposes, as when it is used in any circumstances, the degree and kind of force employed must be reasonably proportionate to the result sought. That does not mean that an air operation is inevitably unlawful. In Kosovo, no other means were available to NATO in March 1999, but it will probably prove an exceptional case. Additonally, the fact that force is used for humanitarian purposes does not remove or qualify the users' duty to comply with the laws of armed conflict. In particular, like any state resorting to force, those who intervene have a duty to direct their attacks only against military objectives (though these are widely defined) and to take all reasonable steps to avoid civilian casualties and damage. Compliance with these requirements is a matter of first importance in law, but may well cause difficulties when force is used to exert pressure on a government, since a highly significant political target may not be a military objective.

Perhaps the most difficult question arising from the Kosovo case is: what should happen after humanitarian intervention? The action's immediate objective is, of course, to halt and, so far as possible, reverse the effects of humanitarian abuses, but the next steps are not always clear. Since humanitarian intervention is usually prompted by the abuses committed by an existing government (or, as in Somalia, because of the collapse of government), the intervention force cannot usually simply withdraw and leave that government to re-establish itself. This was not a problem in East Timor because the United Nations had already insisted that the territory must become independent if the population voted for this in a referendum. In Kosovo, however, there had been no such decision and the international community's initial goal had been to restore autonomy to the province. The NATO intervention succeeded in ensuring that the Kosovar majority could return home and reversed the effects of ethnic cleansing. That left, however, an immediate problem of how to protect what remained of the Serb minority in the province and a longer-term question about Kosovo's future.

The UN has attempted to solve the immediate problems by establishing a civil administration in Kosovo and, in effect, placing it under a form of international trusteeship, while using the NATO-led Kosovo Force (KFOR) to try to protect the remaining Serb population. The longer-term future, however, remains uncertain, as does the future of the protected Kurdish area in northern Iraq. That raises difficult questions about UN willingness to preside over the secession of part of a state, something it has generally set its face against in the past.

Developing Law

The events in Kosovo and East Timor suggest that humanitarian intervention is now established as an important feature of international relations. The evolving right to intervene does not in itself mean that governments will avail themselves of this right and it is unclear that politicians will turn to it with zeal unless there is real public pressure to act. There remains a firm preference for obtaining Security Council authorisation, even if (as was the case in both Kosovo and East Timor) the forces involved operate under national or alliance command and control, rather than being directly answerable to the Security Council or the Secretary-General. Kosovo, however, makes clear that in extreme cases, action is possible without a specific Security Council mandate, although that continues to arouse considerable disquiet, even outright opposition, in some quarters. What happens in the aftermath of an intervention will inevitably vary from case to case, but the extent to which the UN and KFOR succeed in providing satisfactory answers in Kosovo during the next two years will be of the utmost importance. Success is a powerful impetus to evolution, as much in international relations as in biology.

The Evolution of International Criminal Law

Developments in international criminal law during the 1990s had implications for the conduct of armed forces that are likely to have an increasing impact. The large body of 'international humanitarian law' – encompassing both the law of armed conflict and certain aspects of human-rights law – has become more specific, not only about the obligations to be observed by governments and armed forces, but also about implementation. A key development is the unambiguously clear identification of certain violations as international crimes, which states and international organisations have a responsibility to take action against; and in respect of which no-one, not even a head of government or state, can claim absolute immunity.

The four most conspicuous symbols of this new concern with implementation emerged in the space of six years:

- in 1993, the UN Security Council established the International Criminal Tribunal for the former Yugoslavia (ICTY);

- in 1994 the International Criminal Tribunal for Rwanda (ICTR) was set up by the Council;

- in 1998, the Rome Statute of the International Criminal Court (ICC) was concluded (it is not yet in force); and

- in 1999 the UK House of Lords reached the decision in principle that former Chilean President Augusto Pinochet could be subject to proceedings as a result of an extradition demand from Spain. The extradition demand concerned practices associated with internal repression in Chile after he came to power in 1973.

These developments raised hopes that the extremes of brutality that had characterised so many of the twentieth century's internal and international conflicts could at last be effectively addressed. They reflected a strong belief that punishment would deter violations, but they also raised some doubts. They confirmed that, in conducting diplomacy in the post-Cold War era, states were often more able to agree on judicial procedures than on substantive policies for addressing conflicts. Further, these developments raised complicating questions for the conduct of international politics:

- Does the effectiveness of international criminal law depend upon major powers being willing to use their political and military influence to ensure the arrest of suspects and the efficient operation of judicial procedures? (One related issue on which

Strategic Policy Issues

there has been a conspicuous absence of international agreement, the so-called right of humanitarian intervention in cases of mass violations of human rights, is considered in a separate article in this volume.)

- Would the emphasis on implementing fundamental norms cause new tensions and suspicions in inter-state relations? Might major powers find themselves becoming chronic critics of the conduct of wars in which they had no direct interest?

- Might political and military leaders from many countries be at risk of arrest and trial if they travelled to a foreign country with a zealous prosecutor?

- Would states become reluctant to use military force generally, even when its application was important in the cause of international peace and security, for fear that their armed forces or their governments might become subject to prosecution?

- How capable are courts of making judgements about the role of force in international relations, and about events occurring in the midst of armed conflicts? Can courts second-guess decisions which had to be taken in difficult circumstances, in situations where normal law and order has broken down, and on the basis of imperfect information?

- Would these legal developments make it impossible to incorporate amnesties – an ancient and important instrument of statecraft – as one component of peace agreements?

These questions about the developing international norms and procedures can only be answered by events. The new developments may be problematic, but there is no turning back. The pressures that resulted in the unprecedented emphasis on implementation were strong. A particular spur was awareness that arrangements for implementing legal norms were inadequate.

Changes in the Laws of War

The horrors of the dictatorships and wars of the twentieth century exposed as hollow the optimistic assumption of early agreements on the laws of war (for example, the 1899 and 1907 Hague Conventions and Declarations) that governments could be trusted to ensure that their armed forces would act in a disciplined, restrained and professional manner. Since 1945, there has been a definite movement – albeit sometimes slow and undramatic – towards a system of international criminal law affecting the activities of states and armed forces.

At the end of the Second World War, through the International Military Tribunals at Nuremberg and Tokyo, the Allies sought to overcome the weaknesses of existing law by establishing an international judicial procedure, and also by advancing the notion of 'crimes against humanity'. This category of crime can include acts committed by a government against its own citizens, and even some acts committed in peacetime. These tribunals were often criticised as 'victor's justice', but the fact that they were supported by victorious military powers at least meant that those indicted could be brought before the court and tried. Whatever the criticisms, the tribunals established important principles, including that individuals have responsibility for their actions, and that obedience to superior orders is not an adequate defence against criminal charges. The Nuremberg precedent was cited in virtually all subsequent attempts to develop international judicial mechanisms to prosecute war crimes and crimes against humanity.

Since Nuremberg, agreements on the laws of war have placed much emphasis on implementation. Precise definitions of certain conduct as criminal, and detailed provisions for investigation and punishment, have formed a natural part of this development. However, many such treaty provisions have in practice been ignored. For example, the four 1949 Geneva Conventions (which address protection of war victims) stipulate that all the 188 states which are parties must either prosecute those suspected of grave breaches, or else extradite them. Very little action has resulted.

Supplementing the 1949 Geneva Conventions, the 1977 Geneva Protocol I (which addresses international armed conflict, and to which 155 states are parties) adds further specificity to the provisions regarding repression of breaches. Aspects of implementation have also posed problems with this agreement. Article 90 of Protocol 1 provides for the establishment of a permanent commission to enquire into any facts alleged to be a grave breach. The International Humanitarian Fact-Finding Commission was duly set up in 1991, yet not one of the numerous subsequent problems has been referred to it. The Commission's relevance is called into question by the fact that, in the years since it was established, the UN Security Council has developed *ad hoc* mechanisms for investigating violations and taking any necessary action, most notably in connection with events in the former Yugoslavia and Rwanda.

In the 1990s, new treaties on the laws of war have placed much emphasis on penal sanctions in the event of violations, and also on the application of international rules, not just to inter-state wars, but also to civil wars. Provisions reflecting these concerns may be found, for example, in the two main agreements on land-mines: the 1996 Amended Protocol II to the 1980 Certain Conventional Weapons (CCW) Convention; and the 1997 Ottawa Convention on the Prohibition of Anti-Personnel Mines.

Strategic Policy Issues

Further evidence of these concerns is the 1999 Second Hague Protocol for the Protection of Cultural Property, which is not yet in force. A principal purpose of states in negotiating this agreement was to reinforce existing provisions for investigation and punishment, especially after rules against attacks on cultural property were evidently violated in a number of wars in the 1980s and 1990s. Dubrovnik in 1991 led directly to The Hague in 1999.

Human Rights Law

The new emphasis on implementation, including in civil wars, has not only involved the laws of war. It has also affected the development of human-rights law. Since law in this area has its origins in the events surrounding the Second World War, its involvement in certain issues relating to war, as well as to dictatorship, is not surprising. At least one agreement in the human-rights field, the 1948 Genocide Convention, can be regarded as being part of the laws of war. Certain other human-rights agreements are applicable to armed conflict. For example, Article 2 of the 1984 UN Convention on Torture specifies that neither war nor any other exceptional circumstance can be invoked to justify torture.

Human-rights law has particular application to acts of violence committed by governments against their own citizens. It was human-rights instruments, including the 1984 Torture Convention, that constituted the main basis for the March 1999 decision by the UK House of Lords that Chile's General Pinochet was in principle extraditable to face charges in Spain. The obvious immediate consequence of the episode, that in future few ex-dictators with skeletons in their cupboards would be able to travel widely, only concerned that relatively restricted group. However, the case also exposed other concerns about the growing reach of international criminal law. Generally, and particularly in Chile, it raised the question of whether a national amnesty concluded at the end of an internal conflict or period of dictatorship can have any application outside the country concerned. The Spanish government had had some reservations about the prospect of an eventual trial of Pinochet in Spain, both because Chileans might accuse Spain of resuming its old colonial role, and because Spain, in its notably successful transition to democracy following Franco's death in 1975, had largely avoided such legal investigation of its own past. In the US, there was unease that a trial would focus public attention on the history of American support of Pinochet, including at the time of the 1973 coup which installed him in power. Notwithstanding these concerns about the Pinochet affair, and regardless of its eventual outcome, the House of Lords' decision-in-principle was a landmark in the movement towards the concept that international criminal law is universally applicable. It also demonstrated the considerable potential role of national courts (as distinct from international tribunals) in that movement.

Human-rights law also impacted on situations involving armed conflict. In the past, one of the many side effects of the inter-state character of the laws of war was that there was a complete absence of formal procedures for individual legal redress. If violations occurred, it was for governments to take action: the individual may have been the object of the law, but was not in any meaningful sense its subject. This situation has changed. Under several national and regional legal systems – including those of Israel, Japan, the US, and the regional intergovernmental human-rights bodies of the inter-American system and of Europe – there has been a growing tendency for individuals to bring issues arising from armed conflicts and occupations before the courts. This is mainly, but not exclusively, because of the development of human-rights law.

Various international human-rights instruments allow scope for individual redress, whether through a right of individual petition or complaint, or through the right to bring cases. Some have involved the right to life. Although this right is inevitably subject to certain limitations in times of war and civil war, its existence can provide a basis for those whose rights have been undermined (or their surviving relatives) to argue that an armed force acted recklessly. This was the basis of the claims, in the case of *McCann and Others* v. *The United Kingdom*, which followed the British Special Air Service killing of three Irish suspects in Gibraltar on 6 March 1988. The European Court of Human Rights, in its judgement delivered on 27 September 1995, found that there had been a breach of Article 2, on the right to life, of the European Convention on Human Rights. However, the Court dismissed the applicants' claim for damages because the three people killed had been preparing an explosion. The British government of the time, in its instant and touchy reaction to this judgement, showed marked hostility to the whole idea of UK military actions in the long and difficult Northern Ireland conflict being subject to European court decisions; but it did not challenge the judgement's legal validity.

In short, two streams of law – the laws of war and human-rights law – had begun to merge in the 1980s and 1990s, at least insofar as both played a major part in developing an international focus on formal legal responses to violations in armed conflicts.

Late Twentieth-Century Conflicts

These legal developments were buttressed by certain aspects of conflicts during the past 20 years that pointed to the need for new instruments of international action to stop violations. Three such aspects help to explain why the issue of implementing the laws of war has become so central in international diplomacy.

Firstly, existing rules have been broken more seriously and more frequently than in earlier decades. Infractions have included:

- Iraq's use of chemical weapons during the 1980–88 Iran–Iraq war;

- systematic attacks on civilian populations and cruelty to detainees in the conflicts in former Yugoslavia starting in 1991;

- Somali factions' attacks on civilians and interference with relief efforts between 1992 and 1994;

- genocide in Rwanda in 1994; and

- the indiscriminate use of anti-personnel land-mines, causing huge casualties (mainly of civilians) during and after wars.

Secondly, some, but not all, of the atrocities of the 1980s and 1990s have been in conflicts with a civil-war dimension. Such wars are often more bitter than international conflicts: they frequently involve deliberate targeting of civilians, and a winner-takes-all mentality. Before the 1990s, the rules formally and indisputably applicable to civil wars were relatively few. They included the 1948 Genocide Convention; common Article 3 of the 1949 Geneva Conventions; and the 1977 Geneva Protocol II. There were various attempts to overcome the inadequacies of these rules during the 1990s. In the cases of Former Yugoslavia and Rwanda, the UN Security Council has proclaimed, or implied, that a wide range of the rules of humanitarian law are applicable to civil wars – thus seeking to reduce somewhat the significance of whether particular conflicts, or aspects of them, are to be deemed internal or international.

Thirdly, in many of the atrocities of recent years it has not been seriously difficult to establish what the law is, or even what the facts of the particular case are. Nor has the critical issue generally been whether a belligerent state (or non-state entity) has indicated adherence to particular treaties, or is bound anyway by basic universally applicable customary rules. The most critical issue has been what to do when, despite the existence of rules, and the clearest possible warnings that they must be implemented, states and non-state bodies persistently violate them, and then refuse to investigate and punish those responsible.

Establishment of Tribunals

All these aspects of conflict in the past twenty years have exposed the inadequacy of the traditional reliance on the belligerents themselves to ensure implementation of fundamental norms. International or supra-national enforcement is clearly needed. Since the Iran–Iraq War, the UN Security Council has assumed an unanticipated role in investigating violations and in implementing international humanitarian law. Although the United Nations as a wartime alliance was involved in war-crimes issues, this expanded role was not foreseen in its charter. Several laws-of-war treaties, as well as those in the field of arms control and disarmament, have progressively increased the UN's enforcement role. Further, the Security Council's general responsibility for international peace and security gave it a responsibility to address violations of international criminal law.

The Security Council's involvement in such crises has followed a common pattern. First, the Council has asserted the applicability of rules governing international armed conflict, and pressed belligerents to comply with their obligations under humanitarian law, for example, in Council Resolutions 764 of 13 July 1992 and 771 of 13 August 1992, dealing with former Yugoslavia. This puts Council members on a moral escalator: entreaties have to be followed by action of some kind. Thus the London Conference on the Former Yugoslavia of 26–27 August 1992 – a joint European Community–UN initiative – decided to 'take all possible legal action to bring to account those responsible for committing or ordering grave breaches of international humanitarian law'. Security Council Resolution 780 of 6 October 1992 asked the Secretary-General to establish an impartial Commission of Experts to examine evidence of grave breaches. Then, in decisions of February and May 1993, the Council set up the International Criminal Tribunal for the Former Yugoslavia (ICTY). The process was influenced by the political and moral pressure, strong in many countries, to take some action regarding Yugoslavia, and by the lack of agreement about what else could be done. At that time, the international community was conspicuously unable to agree on any major intervention or other decisive action, and establishing the Tribunal was one of the few options left.

The Yugoslav Tribunal was inaugurated in The Hague in November 1993. Although it follows the principles of the Nuremberg and Tokyo tribunals, it differs from them in certain key respects, including:

- it was concerned with punishing those on all sides;

- the conflicts were ongoing at the time it was set up; and

- the death penalty was explicitly ruled out.

Despite hopes that the Tribunal's establishment would deter further war crimes, some of the worst offences committed in the former Yugoslavia occurred after it was in action. Its first trial began in May 1996. In several cases, the court heard complex arguments about whether, in particular phases, the war in Bosnia was or was not international - a seemingly arcane issue related to whether the full range of law relating to international armed conflict applied.

In both the pre- and the post-cease-fire phases of the war in Bosnia and Herzegovina, the UN, NATO, and the Western powers generally, faced harsh choices about the extent to which they should pursue the war-crimes issue. The 1995 Dayton Peace Accords, in Article IX of the General

Strategic Policy Issues

Framework Agreement, obliged each party to cooperate in the investigation and prosecution of war crimes and other violations of international humanitarian law. In the early post-Dayton phases, the NATO-led international forces in Bosnia, the Implementation Force (IFOR) and the Stabilisation Force (SFOR) were reluctant to arrest indicted individuals for fear of endangering a fragile settlement. Once the peace had begun to consolidate, however, the forces became bolder. Overall, the numbers of indicted individuals brought into ICTY custody increased impressively in 1996–99. This was largely the result of increased US willingness to support action, re-confirming the importance of the relation between law and power.

The International Criminal Tribunal for Rwanda (ICTR) also demonstrated that link's importance. Like the Yugoslav tribunal, it was created by the UN Security Council, following a period of indecision about what to do in an ongoing crisis. After the tribunal was established in 1994–95, it proved possible to arrest the leading perpetrators of genocide in Rwanda because they had been defeated militarily in July 1994, thus ending their reign of terror in the country. Some suspects were handed over to the ICTR by the states to which they had fled. The court's verdict on Jean-Paul Akayesu on 2 September 1998 was the first-ever conviction by an international court for the crime of genocide. However, the operation of the ICTR exposed problems in the international administration of justice. In particular, there were numerous well-substantiated complaints about its inefficiency; it was an odd anomaly that those found guilty by the Tribunal could not be sentenced to death, whereas others tried by the successor regime in Rwanda itself could be, and in some cases were. The Rwandan national courts detained far more genocide suspects for trial than did the ICTR.

The International Criminal Court

The establishment of the two *ad hoc* tribunals for Yugoslavia and Rwanda, coupled with continued international preoccupation with international crimes generally, reinforced the pressures to create a permanent international criminal court. This project, which had been proposed at the UN as early as 1947, had occasionally re-surfaced in the intervening years, and again came under active consideration in 1993. In June–July 1998, delegations from 160 states met in Rome (along with observers from 135 non-governmental organisations) and adopted the Rome Statute of the International Criminal Court. Part 2 of this treaty contains a detailed description of three categories of crime with which the ICC is to be concerned: genocide, crimes against humanity and war crimes. (The crime of 'aggression', historically very hard to define, was left to be the subject of future provisions.)

Hailed by many as a milestone in the development of international legal restraints on conflict, the Rome Statute marked, at best, the beginning of what will be the long process of bringing the International Criminal Court into an effective existence. The first and most conspicuous problem was that many important states, including China, Russia and the US, refused to sign the statute.

The US opposition, in a reversal of its earlier support for the idea, raised questions about whether the ICC would have sufficient power to operate effectively. The fundamental concern was that US forces deployed in a wide range of global situations might face unfounded or politically motivated prosecutions. Although the statute's detailed terms contain safeguards against such an eventuality, Washington still fears it. It was part of the larger problem of US nervousness about committing itself to several laws-of-war agreements in the past 25 years, including the 1977 Geneva Protocols and the 1997 Ottawa Land-mines Convention.

Whatever the US fears, the impact of international legal norms on US forces has often been positive. In both the 1991 Gulf War and the 1999 war over Kosovo, the US, though not a party to 1977 Protocol I, observed many of its provisions – because of their customary law status, because it was policy to support them anyway, or because Washington needed to harmonise targeting and other matters with allies. Experience in the Gulf War and in Kosovo suggested that these provisions represented a useful set of guidelines for professional conduct. In Kosovo, the US, having campaigned diplomatically against the ICC for the previous six months on the grounds that US forces' actions should not be subject to a foreign prosecutor and tribunal, chose to wage war in the one part of the world where ongoing war was subject to such a tribunal, the ICTY. On 27 May 1999, the ICTY indicted Yugoslav President Slobodan Milosevic for Serb actions in Kosovo, which does not appear to have had the feared effect of increasing his intransigence. On 1 February 2000, ICTY Chief Prosecutor stated that there was no evidence that NATO's bombing campaign had violated international treaties on the conduct of war. It remains to be seen whether this experience will ease US concerns about the proposed ICC.

The Rome Statute faces other potential hazards. Its entry into force requires 60 ratifications – an unusually high threshold for a treaty on international humanitarian law. By the end of January 2000, it had been signed by 93 states, but only ratified by six (Fiji, Ghana, Italy, San Marino, Senegal and Trinidad). The slow pace is not surprising. Most states, before committing themselves, will have to pass complex domestic legislation to ensure that all the crimes identified in the statute are also crimes under national law. In addition, they will have to provide significant financial support for the Court once it exists. Finally, they will need to be confident that the ICC has sufficient support to be effective.

There is No Turning Back

The developing body of international criminal law and institutions presents serious problems for strategic decision-making and military practice. As shown by the detailed reasoning behind the 1996 Advisory Opinion of the International Court of Justice on the subject of nuclear weapons, there are some issues on which international lawyers and strategic analysts have separate and largely unrelated modes of thinking, with little attempt on either side to bridge the gap. The experiences and challenges of the last decade of the twentieth century and the first of the twenty-first are forcing the law into an improbable but close partnership with strategy. The ancient and enduring issue of the relation between power and law has taken important and problematical new turns.

It will probably be many years before the International Criminal Court can come into being. Although many European countries are moving rapidly to ratify the Rome Statute, finding the bulk of the 60 ratifying countries will be a daunting task. And, even after ratification, how much the court will be able to effect changes will be open to doubt.

The Pinochet decision, however, has had an immediate effect. Even while the British courts were still wrestling with the problem of whether Pinochet should be excused from trial in Spain on medical grounds, a Senegalese court indicted Hissène Habré, the exiled former dictator of Chad, on charges of torture. The case against Habré, who has been living in the Senegalese capital Dakar since he was overthrown in 1990, has been brought by international human-rights groups and survivors of his reign of terror. He was placed under house arrest and, even if a trial does not ensue, this first application of the precedents established in the Pinochet case – that former heads of state can no longer claim immunity from crimes against humanity committed under their rule in their own country – is a welcome indication of the extent to which international criminal law has evolved.

New Challenges to Defence Diplomacy

With the end of the Cold War, the emphasis of national-defence policy among NATO states shifted away from deterrence and territorial defence towards cooperative security. That shift resulted in an enlarged role for European armed forces and military establishments in supporting the foreign- and security-policy strategies of their governments. Increased direct contacts between the military establishments of NATO countries and Central and Eastern European (CEE) states represent one manifestation of this change. NATO military personnel are now involved in many programmes to support military reforms in CEE states, as well as in joint training and educational exchanges.

The 1998 UK Strategic Defence Review (SDR) identified this disparate but vital range of activities as one of the eight core missions of the UK's armed forces. The SDR christened these activities 'defence diplomacy', which it defined as follows:

> 'to provide forces to meet the varied activities undertaken by the MOD to dispel hostility, build and maintain trust and assist in the development of democratically accountable armed forces, thereby making a significant contribution to conflict prevention and resolution.'

Defence diplomacy will probably be increasingly reflected in NATO activities under the Alliance's present Secretary-General Lord Robertson, a strong proponent of the concept in his former position as UK Secretary of Defence. Yet unless there are significant changes in approach, the idea could be consigned to history as a well-meaning but ineffective diplomatic instrument.

How it Operates

The UK SDR officially recognised what many NATO states had been doing through their bilateral military-cooperation programmes with Russia and the CEE states since the early 1990s. With the 1988 meeting in Bern of then US Secretary of Defense Frank Carlucci and his Soviet counterpart, Marshall Dimitri Yazov, the US and Russia had opened bilateral military exchanges. In 1992, these exchanges moved from careful oversight at the highest political and military levels to routine programmes involving interactions between junior and mid-grade officers.

In 1996, then US Secretary of Defense William Perry introduced the term 'preventive defence' to characterise this programme and to delineate one of the key directions in which US defence policy was heading. According to Perry, the end of the Cold War had made it possible to use preventive defence as a first line of defence, deterrence as a second and military conflict as the third, and last, resort. The new concept included two dimensions – preventing the emergence of new threats to US vital interests (such as would be posed by a proliferation of nuclear, chemical and biological weapons), and engaging military and defence establishments around the world to further the spread of democracy and to enhance trust and understanding between nations.

Similarly, in 1990–93, Germany had provided $8 billion in assistance to the Russian armed forces during their withdrawal from East Germany. Subsequently, in its 1994 Defence White Paper, Germany listed military-political cooperation with CEE states among the core missions of its armed forces. Germany's particular circumstances gave it a significant advantage in the emerging military programmes with Central European states. Its geographical position, bordering Poland and the Czech Republic and close to the Baltic States, made it a natural partner. Its successful introduction of principles of civilian control over the military in developing its armed forces after the Second World War provided a positive model, as did its view of the armed forces as primarily a tool of security, rather than defence, policy. Germany could also offer valuable advice on military reform based on its experience of successfully incorporating parts of the East German armed forces and their equipment into the West German Army.

France and the UK have also been engaged in active military-to-military programmes in Central Europe. Already experienced in supporting democratic transition among the armed forces and governments of their former colonies in South Asia and Africa (including civil–military relations and institution-building), military advisers have assisted Central Europeans in reorganising their defence ministries, developing new defence budgets and providing training for their officers in European military schools. The UK Royal Navy already had a long tradition of conducting friendly port calls, and the UK Ministry of Defence offered extensive programmes in language training to the CEE militaries.

Proponents of defence-diplomacy activities argue that Europe's new security environment provides a rationale for military-to-military cooperation programmes distinct from the Cold War-era military-assistance programmes. The latter supported geopolitical objectives in the US–Soviet rivalry over their global spheres of influence. For the West, this meant that military assistance was often provided to regimes whose commitment to democratic transition was questionable. Moreover, such assistance – in terms of both training and military supplies – often contributed to regional instability and provoked new conflicts.

Defence diplomacy, on the other hand, seeks to extend understanding and trust towards countries in transition to democratic government. By ensuring that the CEE states develop effective and democratically accountable armed forces in cooperation with their neighbours and even old adversaries, it is intended to prepare them for integration into European and transatlantic institutions. Proponents argue that defence diplomacy is the most efficient and cost-effective policy for preventing conflicts today, and for helping to prevent countries from becoming adversaries tomorrow.

The Cost of Defence Diplomacy

A widely held myth is that defence diplomacy is the cheapest way to strengthen European security. Indeed, its proponents like to argue that it can fulfil its major goals with very little investment. But, of course, it has its costs. Although funding allocated to military assistance by key NATO members has declined since the end of the Cold War, the US and Western European governments continue to spend substantial sums to support defence-diplomacy activities, both within the Partnership for Peace (PFP) and bilateral programmes. Central European states also spend large amounts to implement what NATO regards as defence-diplomacy commitments: a transition to professional armed forces, development of national ministries of defence and military educational institutions, funding for joint exercises, and participation in joint peacekeeping operations in the Balkans.

Such activities glean further support from another major myth about defence diplomacy: that CEE states' efforts at military reform will enhance their chances of NATO membership or, failing that, at least will ensure NATO assistance should any threat to their security emerge. Yet these assumptions are increasingly challenged by NATO policy. At the April 1999 Washington summit, NATO did reaffirm its commitment to an open-door policy on enlargement and even developed a Membership Action Plan for advancing towards membership. But NATO leaders never fail to stress that any decisions on future membership will be made on a case-by-case basis.

The decisions will clearly not depend solely on a country's ability to meet NATO criteria – political and security considerations will also be taken into account. In addition, NATO has not developed a strong consensus to move speedily towards announcing a second wave of candidate countries. For CEE states, the cost of defence diplomacy began to increase once it became clear that the chances of integration into European institutions would be better met through EU membership, which requires increased spending on economic restructuring rather than on defence.

Table 1 NATO spending on PFP activities

(BFr '000)	Military Committee Budget	PFP cost	Civil Committee Budget	PFP cost	Total PFP spending
1996	1,100,207	12,102,	520,849	5,729	17,832
1997	2,095,626	23,052	540,010	5,940	28,992
1998	2,299,751	27,597	703,528	8,442	36,039
1999	2,140,266	27,823	1,059,059	13,768	41,591
2000	2,602,476	33,832	1,193,065	15,510	49,342

Source NATO

Strategic Policy Issues

The cost is also rising for Western Europeans. Defence-diplomacy activities may impact on their operational readiness, just as the European Security and Defence Identity (ESDI) and Balkan peacekeeping operations impose new burdens both on their defence budgets and on manpower availability. Moreover, the new phase of defence-diplomacy activities announced within the enhanced PFP programme focuses on enhancing

Table 2 UK Defence Assistance Fund for Central and Eastern Europe

Year	1994/95	1995/96	1996/97	1997/98	1998/99
Amount	£0.5m	£0.3m	£0.3m	£3.953m	£3.69m

Distribution of Defence Assistance Fund allocations

Country	Overseas personnel trained in the UK	MoD subsidy(£)
Albania	6	52,000
Baltic States	–	106,000
Belarus	3	28,000
Bosnia Herzegovina	–	10,000
Bulgaria	10	158,000
Croatia	–	18,000
Czech Republic	46	336,000
Estonia	7	66,000
Georgia	6	113,000
Hungary	36	194,000
Latvia	10	132,000
Lithuania	13	129,000
Macedonia	6	49,000
Moldova	3	30,000
Poland	40	132,000
Romania	54	318,000
Russia	10	1,107,000
Slovak Republic	18	187,000
Slovenia	9	141,000
Ukraine	47	389,000
Uzbekistan	–	3,000
Total	324	3,698,000

Note   UK MoD subsidy includes language training, resettlement assistance (Russia/Ukraine), equipment grants, seminars etc.

Source   UK Ministry of Defence Performance Report 1998/99.

interoperability and developing modern armed forces in partner states. This requires more costly assistance to modernise their weapon systems.

Is it Effective?

These costs must be taken into account when assessing the benefits and overall effectiveness of various defence-diplomacy efforts. European defence-diplomacy activities during the 1990s can be judged within four categories:

- establishing direct military-to-military contact (seeking to build understanding and trust through the human dimension);

- promoting democratic transition (civil–military relations, civilian control, defence management and accountability);

- enhancing interoperability (of exercises, doctrines and equipment); and

- supporting hard-security objectives (non-proliferation and arms control).

Military-to-Military Contact

Military-to-military contact is one of the most widely used components of defence diplomacy, absorbing a large part of allocated funds. Activities include high-level visits, medium- and junior-level military exchanges, exchange of interns and liaison missions on bilateral or multilateral NATO levels, educational exchanges, information sharing, academic conferences and political–military consultations within NATO structures such as the Euro-Atlantic Partnership Council. In the past, these activities were included as part of the confidence-building measures adopted by the signing of the Conference on Security and Cooperation in Europe (CSCE) at Helsinki in 1975. Their objective is to enhance trust and understanding, and to introduce what is often referred to as 'interoperability of minds' but what the UK SDR calls 'disarmament of the mind'.

It is clear that military-to-military contact has had a strongly positive effect on enhanced relations between NATO states and those countries in Central Europe recognised as viable candidates for NATO membership. But there is significant doubt about the effectiveness of such exchanges with countries unlikely to be accepted into the Alliance in the near future (such as Ukraine, Central Asian states and the Trans-Caucasus states), with Central European states that do not aspire to membership, or with Russia.

These exchanges are often criticised as 'military tourism', on which the CEE states spend a great deal of money which could be better invested in strengthening and upgrading their armed forces. Moreover, many CEE officers educated in Western military academies face grave difficulties in translating their new knowledge into national military reforms because the political and operational requirements in their home countries differ so radically from those of NATO members. In more extreme cases, as in Russia or other newly independent states (NIS), these officers are less likely to be promoted because they are regarded as representing a threat to their superiors who do not share a vision of radical military reform. Most Russian officers educated in US military academies soon leave military service because they are viewed with suspicion by their colleagues, and because they soon realise that their new skills can be used for much more attractive compensation in a civilian capacity. Those who stay often find themselves forced into military intelligence, thus creating security problems for their former host countries.

Critics also emphasise that the primary task of active military personnel is to defend their country and implement security policies outside their territory. Even if they develop personal ties with a foreign counterpart, this should not stop them from going to war against former colleagues if political authorities order it. Such critics hold that it is at best naïve, at worst misleading, to think that investing in greater military-to-military understanding can effectively prevent conflicts.

This was clearly demonstrated when a Russian brigade raced to seize Pristina airport in Kosovo ahead of NATO forces. Not only were members of this brigade serving side by side with their NATO counterparts in Bosnia, but the brigade was led by General Viktor Zavarzin, the Russian military representative at NATO headquarters. Supporters of defence diplomacy can argue that Zavarzin's background enabled him to establish a friendly dialogue with Kosovo Force (KFOR) commander General Michael Jackson, and prevented escalation of NATO–Russia tensions. But it was clear that Zavarzin was implementing orders from the Russian political leadership, which sought to avoid direct military confrontation with NATO.

While military-to-military contacts constitute an important element of confidence-building, they require a basic level of understanding and important shared national interests to make a real difference. Exchanges are expensive, while producing only marginal impact on the security perceptions within the CEE states. They are therefore likely to be welcomed and funded only so long as NATO's open-door policy on future enlargement remains credible.

Promoting Democratic Transition

Promoting democratic transition is an important task for defence diplomacy as defined by most NATO states. It is also closely related to military-to-military contact, as it is usually undertaken by military and civilian advisers from NATO states through short-term events, such as conferences and briefings, or longer-term in-country missions. NATO's military advisers work in practically all the CEE states giving help in the following areas:

- developing legislation to support civil–military relations;
- reorganising the structure of their defence ministries and the training of civilian personnel;
- developing national military doctrines;
- setting up military colleges and educational establishments;
- organising retraining programmes for retiring military personnel; and
- restructuring defence budgets and the system for their preparation, adoption and politically controlling their implementation.

Advice from NATO states on these practical aspects of military reform has been very valuable to almost all CEE states. Many of them – particularly the newly independent states of the former Soviet Union – had no structure on which to create their own defence ministries and national armed forces. For others in Central Europe it was important quickly to develop a system of defence policy-making and civil–military relations compatible with other European states.

NATO countries responded quickly to their requests for help. Germany provided advice on civil–military relations, the UK on resettlement, defence management and budgets, France on developing legislation and on defence management. The Scandinavian states helped their Baltic neighbours to set up a military-education system, the Baltic Defence College, and joint units (Baltbat, Baltnet and Baltron), and also to develop national military doctrines. All these measures provided a major contribution to European security by allowing CEE states to take control of their armed forces quickly, and to determine basic principles for their functioning throughout the transition to democracy.

An important part of these activities was the interaction between the government agencies and civilian entities of the NATO states themselves. They included defence, foreign and economic ministries, agencies for international development, national parliaments, non-governmental groups and private companies. Such interaction has strengthened political oversight, created greater public support and enhanced the commitment of national legislatures to provide funds for these programmes. In the US and France, some military-assistance programmes were put under the authority of the State Department and the Ministry of Foreign Affairs respectively, and given a separate budget. Even though inter-agency involvement increased bureaucratic red tape and overhead costs, and slowed down the implementation of programmes, the benefits still outweigh the potential costs.

Once the basic groundwork for military construction was completed, however, the democratic-assistance programmes became less effective. It is far easier to draft and adopt laws on civil–military relations than it is to make good relations a norm in the society. In addition, the incentive for pressing ahead was closely tied to prospects for NATO membership. The Czech Republic, Poland and Hungary have done most in this area. Those countries which are not yet recognised as NATO candidates with a clear timetable for membership find it increasingly difficult to continue allocating time and resources to military-reform efforts when they have more pressing economic and social needs. In other countries, the development of new democratic systems worked against speedy military restructuring, as democratically elected parliaments could refuse to allocate the necessary funds for military budgets.

Assistance to Russia's armed forces was not similarly successful. Russia had inherited a developed defence-management and armed-forces structure; it felt that it had no need for basic advice, and regarded offers as humiliating to a former military superpower. Nor did it have an incentive to adopt Western systems, since it did not aspire to NATO membership. Western advice was viewed as an attempt to weaken and corrupt the Russian armed forces. Russia also suspected that NATO's democratic support programmes for other CIS states were primarily instruments to entice these states into NATO's orbit, thereby undermining their military cooperation programmes with Russia.

Towards the end of the 1990s, critics of democratic-assistance programmes also started to appear in CEE states. They argued that these, like many other forms of aid, are used primarily to provide financial support for NATO's military personnel, rather than providing the financial assistance urgently needed to upgrade the Central European armed forces. They resent the fact that experts and advisers who come to work in CEE agencies often have no understanding of the specific country's environment.

By far the most important reason why the CEE states continue to pay for such activities, despite severe financial constraints, is that they hope the exchanges will improve their chances of NATO membership. Yet, they have also come to believe that the decision on membership is made on political grounds, rather than on how well the different states meet individual membership criteria. This is clearest in the case of the Baltic States and Romania, where the drive to obtain NATO membership has forced them to raise their defence budgets and host many foreign experts, although their chances remain uncertain.

Enhancing Interoperability

Enhancing interoperability between NATO and the armed forces of partner states represents a more clearly defined, easily measurable and strategically important task for defence diplomacy. Activities under this heading include joint exercises, the establishment of permanent multi-lateral units, and NATO assistance to modernise military equipment.

The importance of joint military exercises in all areas, from search-and-rescue to peace-support operations, was clearly demonstrated during the Balkan crisis, the September 1999 Moscow terrorist bombings , and also in the aftermath of the August 1999 Turkish earthquake. The exercises not only contributed to quick and coordinated action within multilateral coalition operations such as the Bosnia Stabilisation Force (SFOR), the Implementation Force (IFOR) and KFOR, but they also improved the ability of the national armed forces and emergency services to address domestic crises. Practically all states, including Russia, have recognised the importance of these activities, and have participated in them either within the PFP or through bilateral military cooperation programmes.

Permanent multilateral units – inspired by a Franco-German initiative within NATO – have become a reality in all parts of Europe, often with the assistance, but without the direct participation, of Alliance states. The German–Danish–Polish Multinational Corps Northeast, formed in March 1999 and based in Szczecin, was the first such initiative among the CEE states. Ukraine and Poland established a joint peacekeeping battalion in 1998 and the three Baltic states formed the joint Baltic battalion, Baltbat in 1999. The Central Asian states formed a joint peacekeeping battalion in July 1996, and in July 1999, Azeri servicemen decided to participate in KFOR as part of a Turkish battalion. These activities not only enhance each

Figure 1 NATO PFP exercises, 1994–2000

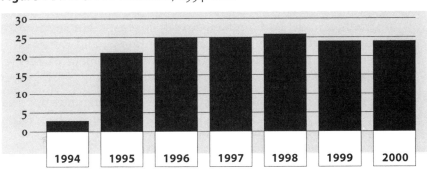

Source German MoD: Bestandsaufnahme

Strategic Policy Issues

country's ability to respond to crises by adopting a burden-sharing approach, but also significantly contribute to regional security.

Yet, joint exercises do not always enhance stability. In order to prevent one state from using them for its own narrowly defined political objectives, such exercises require detailed planning, transparency and understanding of the political environment in which they are taking place. *Sea Breeze-97*, the August 1997 Ukraine–NATO naval exercise off the Crimean coast, is the most prominent example of a flawed approach. Proposed by Ukraine, the scenario sparked off an uproar from Moscow and the majority of the Crimean population, and increased tensions in Ukraine–Russia and Russia–NATO relations.

Help with the modernisation of CEE equipment, particularly that relating to communications, is another important component of inter-operability activities within defence diplomacy. The limitations of such assistance are profound and are exacerbated by the failure of NATO states to meet interoperability criteria, even among themselves. In the West this failure is often attributed to countries needing to support their own national defence industries; in CEE states there are a number of more basic causes:

- modernisation is expensive, and funds for CEE military upgrades are not available from Western Europe and the US;

- the programmes often become a source of internal competition between NATO states, each seeking to promote its own national defence industry. The same is true of initiatives related to privatisation of defence-industry enterprises in CEE states;

- CEE modernisation programmes have been tainted by corruption scandals, which makes Europeans wary about offering assistance;

- CEE states do not have the necessary resources for new platforms. Essentially, they need support in upgrading Soviet-made equipment. The sole country experienced in providing such support is Germany, which inherited facilities and expertise for upgrading Soviet MiG fighter aircraft in East Germany. But German efforts require cooperation with Russia, and Russia is unwilling to participate in upgrading the equipment of new NATO members.

Another problem is that cooperative equipment programmes for the armed forces of Europe generally – such as the AN-70 transport aircraft – face active lobbying from the European defence industry, which regards such projects as potential competitors. Resistance of this kind led to declining interest in Russia–NATO interoperability programmes. Russia originally saw this as one of the key areas for cooperation with the

Alliance, and proposed a number of joint projects, including communications, personnel carriers and joint air-defence and air-traffic control systems. However, these projects did not move beyond feasibility studies, leading to disappointment and increasing Russian doubts about NATO's true commitment.

For these reasons, West European modernisation assistance has been implemented mainly through gifts of used equipment to individual countries such as the Baltic States, Georgia and Poland. However, such short-term solutions cannot contribute substantively to establishing interoperability with CEE armed forces, particularly as Western Europeans themselves are seeking to upgrade their equipment, and introduce new technology to meet their ESDI tasks.

One solution to the problems facing interoperability assistance would be for Western European states to support the concept of their CEE partners developing niche capabilities that could be effectively used in multilateral operations. This would require each partner country to determine the area in which it possessed unique strength – such as chemical warfare units in the Czech Republic or medical teams in Hungary. West Europeans could then provide modern equipment and training to strengthen these capabilities so that they are readily available for future coalition operations.

Supporting Hard Security Objectives

Supporting hard security objectives such as non-proliferation and arms control is a highly important defence-diplomacy task. Unfortunately, it does not receive the attention and support it deserves, particularly among European NATO members. The bulk of these programmes were originally directed towards assisting Russia to eliminate nuclear, biological and chemical weapons inherited from the Soviet Union. As Russia–NATO relations deteriorated, assistance programmes to Russia became increasingly difficult to implement. Moreover, these issues were traditionally addressed in a bilateral US–Russia context, and therefore it was expected that the US would continue to take responsibility for their implementation.

The US does continue to take the lead in such assistance through its Cooperative Threat Reduction (CTR) programme. This provides funding and expert advice to help Russia comply with arms-control agreements and to dismantle its nuclear warheads, to reprocess nuclear fuel from its submarines and to reduce its fissile-material stockpiles. The US has spent over \$3bn on such programmes since they started in 1994, and is planning to spend another \$4.5bn in the years 2000–05. The programmes, divided between the Pentagon, the Department of Energy and the State Department, have run into difficulty, however. Corruption in Russia, Russia's nuclear cooperation with Iran, its progressively more anti-US

Strategic Policy Issues

foreign policy, and its reluctance to provide access to US contractors or to indemnify them against liability for accidents have all prompted a growing reluctance in the US Congress to allocate funding, even for a programme which has a direct impact on US security interests.

In order to compensate for declining US support, European nations need to increase the amount that they are willing to provide. Many European states have already taken responsibility for some projects, such as the construction of chemical-weapon reprocessing facilities, providing containers for transporting Russian nuclear materials, conducting conferences on export-control policies and providing support for reprocessing

Table 3 US proposed Expanded Threat Reduction Initiative (ETRI) funding summary

(US$ billions) Agencies	Total Funded FY1992–99	Total FY2000	ETRI budget request FY2000–04
Department of Defense	2.06[1]	0.47	2.46
Department of Energy	0.95	0.24	1.32
State Department	0.08	n/a	0.74
Total	3.09	n/a	4.52

Note   [1] Does not include all Cooperative Threat Reduction programmes.
Source   Expanded Threat Reduction Initiative (ETRI) report, prepared by the Office of the Coordinator of US Assistance to the Newly Independent States

Table 4 CTR Achievements – Russia, Ukraine, Belarus, Kazakstan

Project	Current	2003	2005(final)
Warheads deactivated	4,854	7,404	8,515
ICBMs destroyed	372	769	977
ICBM silos eliminated	351	436	598
ICBM mobile launches destroyed	0	175	288
Bombers destroyed	52	95	96
SLBM launchers eliminated	160	564	652
SLBMs destroyed	30	565	645
SSBNs destroyed	12	15	31
Nuclear test holes, tunnels sealed	191	194	194

Source   Expanded Threat Reduction Initiative (ETRI) report, prepared by the Office of the Coordinator of US Assistance to the Newly Independent States submarine nuclear fuel in the Russian northern fleet. Such programmes, however, are still small when compared with US efforts.

Limitations and Challenges in the Next Decade

With the plethora of policy statements and attendant activities, the 1990s may well be remembered as the decade of defence diplomacy. But as Europe enters the new millennium, it faces a new political and security environment. Western Europeans initially gave the CEE states an emotional welcome as new members of a united and democratic continent. But this is increasingly giving way to scepticism about the timescale of political and economic transition and the price that Western Europeans have to pay to support integration.

With the next phase of NATO enlargement on hold, the focus has shifted to EU enlargement and many of the CEE states have found it difficult to sustain public support for increased defence spending. Military restructuring is therefore likely to move to a much lower priority on the list of national reform objectives. The CEE states are now completing the first basic stage of such restructuring – many have established defence ministries, reorganised their force structure, hired new personnel, adapted defence doctrines and passed the necessary legislation to support basic democratic principles of civil–military relations. The next phase of restructuring is likely to concentrate on a new set of problems related mainly to procurement and weapon systems modernisation. Unlike the basic restructuring stage, the next phase will require substantial additional financial resources from the NATO states.

This comes at a bad time since Alliance members are trying to restructure their own military forces. The EU decision to enhance European defence capabilities within the ESDI will undoubtedly put new strains on the amount they will be able to spend on defence diplomacy. Moreover, the ESDI is likely to produce new strains in the transatlantic debate on burden sharing, with the US insisting that Europeans must do more to guarantee security on the continent, including providing assistance to CEE states. Moreover, increasingly tense relations with Russia following NATO's intervention in Kosovo and Russia's ferocious campaign in Chechnya not only will strain NATO–Russia relations, but is also likely to increase Russia's opposition to NATO's military assistance to its neighbours.

Defence-Diplomacy Strategies for the Next Decade

In light of the recognised deficiencies of some of its strategies, and the new political and military challenges within Europe, the concept of defence diplomacy must avoid two dangers. On the one hand, it may be transformed from being a tool of preventive diplomacy and confidence-building to becoming a new source of tensions within NATO, between NATO states and their CEE partners, and between Russia and NATO, thus weakening rather then reinforcing security on the continent. On the other hand, there is a danger that, despite the strong rhetorical support for defence diplomacy, its role within NATO's policy will continue to decline. This will weaken the credibility of NATO's commitment to an integrated European security system, and force some Eastern European states to look for alternative ways to address their security concerns. To face these challenges, the concept of defence diplomacy needs to be rethought and restructured. In particular, its proponents must:

- *Break the link between defence-diplomacy cooperation and NATO enlargement.* This linkage created false expectations and encouraged CEE states to support programmes that did not offer clear benefits simply to enhance their chances in the race for NATO membership. As a result, many resources were wasted to only marginal effect. More emphasis should be put on bilateral and *ad hoc* multilateral military-cooperation programmes, and on encouraging more defence-diplomacy cooperation among CEE states. The experience gained by these states in their efforts at military restructuring could be shared for mutual benefit to a greater extent than at present.

- *Focus programmes on activities that offer concrete benefits to both CEE states and NATO.* Defence exchanges should continue, but they should move away from 'military tourism' towards specific long-term programmes, which contribute to developing interoperability of forces and doctrines. Military advisers of different countries should coordinate their activities more effectively to avoid duplication. Rather then inviting CEE students to Western military schools, viable educational institutions should be established in their own countries. More civilians should be engaged in the implementation of defence-diplomacy activities to create a body of political-military consultations and to integrate them more closely with foreign-policy priorities of both NATO and partner states.

- *Face up to the real costs.* For defence diplomacy to survive it must shake off the image of being a low-cost investment with a high return for European security. It must be recognised that military restructuring in CEE states, like economic and political reform, will take a long time, and these states do not have the resources to do the job on their own. Western Europeans should continue to provide assistance, both bilateral and institutional. The EU, the

European Bank for Reconstruction and Development and other independent financial institutions have a role to play in promoting civil–military relations, training a new generation of defence economists, helping to restructure defence budgets and supporting the integration of former military personnel into civilian society and civil economy. NATO assistance should be concentrated on supporting the most important new task for military reform in the CEE states – modernisation of their armed forces. This can bring real benefits for future multilateral coalition operations.

- *Give more priority to hard-security objectives.* Europeans should consider investing more money and effort to assist Russia with non-proliferation and nuclear security and safety objectives. A multilateral European programme similar to the US CTR programme is required. Continuing bilateral assistance in this area leads to duplication and inefficiency. The crisis in Russia–NATO relations means the EU must play a greater role in structuring such a programme; this could be an important element of ESDI.

- *Expand the range of participants.* The new pressures on European defence budgets necessitate the increased involvement of other agencies, including non-governmental and private actors. These can provide expertise at a lower cost and sustain public interest in defence-diplomacy activities. This will require greater coordination, but will ensure that defence diplomacy is better integrated with the other foreign and economic policies pursued by individual states.

If these measures could be set in motion, defence diplomacy would not only be able to survive its new challenges, but would provide a positive model for those other regions of the world which are similarly seeking to overcome historical divisions in favour of greater openness and engagement.

Arms Control: Unfulfilled Expectations

The debate in the US over the efficacy of arms control reached a turning-point in 1999. Putting years of calculated balance behind them, Senators voted in October not to ratify the Comprehensive Test Ban Treaty (CTBT). In so doing, they signalled the shift in their thinking away from arms control as a means of enhancing national and global security. The failure to ratify the CTBT is significant enough in itself, but the move coincides with a number of other policy decisions in both the US and Russia that could collectively represent a further decline in the role of arms control in shaping international security. This shift in attitude has important ramifications for attempts to promote world-wide confidence and improve security.

Nuclear Negotiations

There was a bad start to 1999 for nuclear arms control. In late 1998, the Russian *Duma* shelved hearings on the already fragile process of ratifying the Strategic Arms Reduction Treaty (START) II following the bombing of Iraq by the US and UK in response to Baghdad's refusal to allow the UN Special Commission (UNSCOM) to carry out inspections. In March 1999, when the *Duma* began preparing for a debate on START II legislation, proceedings came to an abrupt halt when NATO took action against Yugoslavia over Kosovo. With the loss of both of these opportunities for Russian ratification, START II has been languishing, awaiting a new political impetus from Moscow or Washington.

This may yet occur in 2000, driven by a combination of a change in the Russian political climate, concerns over Moscow's ability to maintain a strategic nuclear force even at the levels called for in START II, and presidential elections in both Russia and the US. Yet it is equally possible that START II may have bitten the dust for good – a casualty of worsening relations between the world's two largest military powers. Certainly, the agreement reached in Helsinki in March 1997 on beginning talks on START III before ratification of its predecessor has helped, but not enough as yet. Much depends on the Russian political process and a decision in the US on national missile defence (NMD) deployments. This is due in 2000 before the US presidential elections in November, but may be delayed until the following year.

The relationship between the US and China has fared little better. In early January 1999, a Congressional committee, chaired by Representative Christopher Cox, submitted its report, which claimed that espionage had provided China with highly sensitive information on US missile and nuclear-warhead designs. A few days later, US Defense Secretary William Cohen announced that the US would seek amendments to the 1972 Anti-Ballistic Missile (ABM) Treaty to permit its introduction of NMD. If changes could not be agreed with Russia, the US might exercise its right to withdraw from the treaty. The statement upset Moscow, but it nevertheless remains part of the dialogue between the two countries. China's reaction has been stronger. Despite US protestations, neither China nor Russia really believes that limited US national or shared theatre missile defences would be aimed solely at preventing an attack by a small state armed with weapons of mass destruction (WMD). Indeed, Chinese officials are far from convinced that the US would go to such expensive lengths to counter a vague threat from small states which could, in their view, be effectively dealt with in more conventional ways.

Tests of missile-defence interceptors took place in March, June and October 1999. Each sparked much controversy over whether the interceptors worked. At best, it appears that the technology needs considerable development before it becomes clear whether NMD could work with any efficiency. Despite these doubts, the issue of missile defences is at the heart of the debate over arms control. The ABM Treaty acknowledged the relationship between the offensive and defensive strategic systems of the US and the Soviet Union. As a concept, nuclear deterrence between the US, Russia and China relies on the mutual vulnerability of strategic nuclear forces. If one state becomes much less vulnerable than the other, deterrence can break down. There is, however, one way in which defences can be seen as an aid to strategic stability. When nuclear weapons are being reduced to very low levels, missile defences could act as a hedge against breakout or cheating on a process of reductions, thus enhancing stability. At high levels of weapons, however, defences are more likely to induce force enhancements and encourage a potential first strike posture.

By the end of 1999, Russia was publicly stating that amending the ABM Treaty was not negotiable, but privately analysts and officials believe that a deal over missile defences will be reached. This would trade deployment for reductions in strategic nuclear weapons to START III levels or even below; US technical assistance to Russia's national missile defences; increased involvement with the US and Europe; and various projects involving hard currency. On the other hand, Chinese officials are adamant, at least publicly, that any deployment of missile defences, whether national or theatre, will deal a severe blow to all future arms-control efforts, and badly damage US–China relations.

Other states are also concerned about missile defences. At the UN General Assembly in late 1999, France voted with Russia and Ireland in favour of a Russian resolution that the ABM Treaty should be preserved and complied with. The UK could play an important role in the overall bargain between Russia and the US, since radar and early-warning facilities in north-east England will have to be upgraded for a US NMD to work. The debate in NATO has already exposed the divisions between those countries which want greater reductions in nuclear arsenals, and those prepared to go along with missile defences because of their lucrative technical opportunities, whatever the implications for arms control.

NATO's military action in Kosovo became a focus for much that other states feared from US military dominance. Whatever the rights and wrongs of the action, the fact that Russia was not involved in the early policy decisions, the unfortunate bombing of the Chinese Embassy in Belgrade, and the hype surrounding so-called smart-bomb technology supplied anti-US factions in both Beijing and Moscow with an opportunity to strengthen their opposition to US missile-defence plans.

In other respects as well, nuclear matters have not had an easy ride. Although not directly linked to nuclear weapons, the leak at a nuclear power plant in Japan in July 1999 and the scandal over the failure to record safety data by British Nuclear Fuels (BNFL) when handling Japanese fuel in September have further increased anxiety in Japan. In August 1999, the Tokyo Forum on Nuclear Non-Proliferation and Disarmament (a Japanese follow-on to the 1996 Canberra Commission on the Elimination of Nuclear Weapons) reported its findings. The forum's report was pessimistic, and urged renewed efforts to stop a perceived decline in regional and international security.

The nuclear-weapon tests carried out by India and Pakistan in 1998 continued to reverberate, both regionally and internationally. In mid-1999, an expert panel established by the Indian government published a draft nuclear doctrine. The draft, which seemed to have swallowed the whole Western concept of nuclear deterrence, postulated a land-, sea- and air-based nuclear triad, resulting in the development and deployment of hundreds of nuclear weapons. Although the Indian government posted the draft doctrine on its website and asked the world for comments, it has become clear that New Delhi is far from comfortable with it, and is rethinking its approach.

Despite public and private statements that India would sign the CTBT, neither India nor Pakistan had done so by the end of March 2000. The US Senate's decision not to ratify the treaty has had a considerable impact on the debate in South Asia. Those opposing India's participation in the treaty have found themselves strengthened by the Senate's action, particularly since there are clear technical pressures to keep open the option to test. Indeed, should India test again, China would have a ready-made excuse for doing the same, thus blowing a hole in the CTBT – an outcome likely to be applauded by certain quarters in Washington and Moscow.

All of these developments occurred in the lead-up to the first Review Conference since the Nuclear Non-Proliferation Treaty (NPT) was extended indefinitely in 1995. In April 1998, the preparatory committee papered over deep cracks and agreed a document to go forward to the conference in 2000. As is normal, it said little of substance, but at least the political process could go ahead. However, as a serious review of the 1995–2000 period has to take place in 2000, there is little point in anything but brutal honesty. The nuclear non-proliferation regime has suffered serious set-backs:

- despite huge efforts by the International Atomic Energy Agency (IAEA) to bring into force an enhanced safeguards regime, the pace of ratification of the protocol is as slow as ever;

- confidence in the ability of the UN Security Council to deal effectively with Iraq's WMD is the lowest it has been since the end of the Gulf War in 1991;

- countries surrounding Iraq are increasingly nervous, and Iran at least may be developing nuclear weapons;

- dealing with North Korea is a painfully slow process;

- the nuclear-weapon states have signalled their strong opposition to any moves that might lead to a timed programme for eliminating nuclear weapons, despite their promises to the contrary in 1995;

- the US is likely to deploy limited NMD;

- Russia is considering redeploying and perhaps developing its tactical nuclear-weapon systems;

- China continues to increase its nuclear capability; and

- India and Pakistan are entrenching nuclear weapons within their military strategies.

For the time being, there seems to be little hope for nuclear arms control, and prospects for meaningful progress within the NPT are bad. The only chink of light could be ratification by the *Duma* of START II, progress on START III and agreement between the US and Russia on the ABM Treaty. The state parties to the NPT could agree a fudged document at the Review Conference in 2000. It seems more likely, however, that there will be no consensus on a final document, and that the conference, like most since the first in 1975, will end acrimoniously.

From the perspective of the treaties the situation is undoubtedly gloomy. But there have been positive developments in the sphere of practical action outside the treaties. In the midst of the NATO bombing campaign in Kosovo the US and Russia completed the negotiation of, and signed, a protocol establishing the Cooperative Threat Reduction (CTR) program for seven years. While progress has been slower than planned, a programme for the safe and secure dismantlement of nuclear weapons is steadily continuing. For the period 2000 to 2005, the US has allocated $4.2 billion for this activity. Some of these funds go towards the International Science and Technology Centre which sponsors non-weapons projects for scientists and engineers previously employed on weapon programmes. The EU and Japan also support this activity. Important non-proliferation programmes like these provide an excellent opportunity for Europeans in particular to make a substantial contribution to disarmament and stemming proliferation. Even a modest increase in the amount Europe spends on such activities could bring large security benefits.

Strategic Policy Issues

Conventional Forces

Despite the furore over NATO's action in Kosovo and the use of high-technology conventional weapons, the 1990 Conventional Armed Forces in Europe (CFE) Treaty was adapted as planned in November 1999. This marked the end of three years of negotiation on adjusting the treaty so that it better reflects the reality of European security today. The adaptation opens the treaty to states outside of NATO and the former Warsaw Pact. Each state now has individual ceilings allocated to it for armaments on a national and territorial basis, instead of allocating ceilings on the basis of group levels. The new ceilings also mean further conventional disarmament in Europe: 11,000 weapon systems – battle tanks, artillery pieces and combat aircraft – will be dismantled, thus cutting the number of conventional weapons in Europe by a further 10%. Considering the difficulties between NATO and Russia over Kosovo and the ABM Treaty, it is encouraging that adapting the CFE went as smoothly as planned.

Small arms moved up the arms-control agenda in 1999. Small arms are a major humanitarian issue, since they account for the vast majority of casualties in wars around the globe. It has been estimated that up to 500 million small arms, many of them left over from the Cold War, are in circulation. Some are now exacerbating conflicts in developing countries and ending up in the hands of terrorists and participants in organised crime.

In August 1999, planning for an international small-arms conference in 2001 got under way, with UN General Assembly resolutions and recommendations based on the report of the UN's Group of Governmental Experts on Small Arms. However, the purpose of the conference has not yet been clarified. The UN Expert Group on Ammunition and Explosives also completed its report to the General Assembly. It argued that controls on small arms cannot be achieved without controls on ammunition, and thus recommended the marking, stockpile management and destruction of surplus ammunition stocks world-wide.

Two new initiatives in 1999 considerably increased non-governmental (NGO) activity on small arms. The first, the International Action Network on Small Arms (IANSA), attempts to coordinate NGO activities aimed at measures to control the spread of small arms. The IANSA is based temporarily in London, but operates almost entirely over the Internet. The second, the Small Arms Survey based in Geneva, is an annual report on the proliferation and use of these weapons. Both initiatives, which bring together humanitarian organisations and disarmament groups, are working closely with like-minded governments and key UN organs to push for increased controls on small arms and the removal of surplus arms in post-conflict regions.

The 2001 conference is likely to lead to a number of negotiations and initiatives. NGOs play an increasingly important role in the debate over small arms and, as they were in the Ottawa process on landmines, they will be an important force in any official negotiations. This will be particularly true for humanitarian organisations working in regions of conflict and in post-conflict reconstruction. On 1 March 1999, the Ottawa Convention banning anti-personnel landmines entered into force. The first meeting of state parties was held in Maputo, Mozambique, on 3–7 May. One of the important features of the Maputo meeting was a decision to establish a programme of inter-sessional work in Geneva. Both governments and NGOs are participating in these meetings, which focus on mine clearance, victim assistance, stockpile destruction, mine-action technologies and the general operation of the Convention. Even states which have yet to ratify the Ottawa Convention have modified their behaviour in areas such as weapon sales and deployment strategies. Next on the agenda for the humanitarian groups behind the Ottawa process are cluster bombs and unexploded ordnance.

Chemical and Biological Weapons

The Organisation for the Prohibition of Chemical Weapons (OPCW) got into its stride in 1999, a year after the Chemical Weapons Convention (CWC) entered into force. Some 130 states have ratified the Convention. The OPCW has inspected over 70,000 tones of stockpiled chemical weapons, and eight million munitions and bulk containers. OPCW monitoring teams have verified the destruction of more than a million chemical weapons and 4,000 tonnes of chemical-warfare agents. In addition, all 60 of the thus-far declared facilities around the world producing chemical weapons have been inspected and sealed. Of these, 20 have been certified as destroyed, and five have been approved for conversion to peaceful purposes.

Although difficulties have been put in its path, the OPCW has begun inspecting industrial facilities throughout the world that produce, or consume, 'dual-use' chemicals. It will be slow work, for only a tiny fraction of such facilities can be inspected in the course of a year. The CWC inspection regime was also undermined by the reservations accompanying US ratification. If the US does not allow certain activities to be carried out on its territory, the OPCW cannot demand that other state parties allow them either. In addition, the US had not made its initial industrial declaration by the end of 1999. Once this is delivered, the volume of work of the OPCW will increase dramatically. A more serious concern than these technicalities is the refusal of key states in the Middle East to ratify the Convention.

Strategic Policy Issues

In Geneva, negotiations for an additional protocol to the Biological and Toxin Weapons Convention (BTWC), to establish a verification and confidence-building regime for the Convention, proceeded slowly. There are still deep divisions among the countries negotiating the protocol. Some wish to avoid a protocol altogether, citing doubts about its efficiency and cost, and fears about intrusive inspections and discrimination; others want a protocol at almost any cost.

Despite the publication in May 1999 of Russian scientist Ken Alibek's book *Biohazard*, which reported on Soviet and Russian non-compliance with the BTWC, fear of developments in biotechnologies and weaponry, particularly with the new genetic advances, does not seem to have had a significantly sobering effect on many of the state parties to the treaty. Alibek's book demonstrates clearly how a country can evade detection of a biological-weapon programme, even if intrusive verification procedures are in place. According to Alibek, Soviet scientists went to great lengths to conceal the extent of the country's programme during confidence-building exchange visits. Soviet scientists claimed that they did not believe that the US had stopped developing and producing biological weapons, until Alibek and his colleagues came to the US on an exchange visit. According to Alibek, they believed they were working on weapons to counter a supposedly superior, and still developing, US capability.

Books and papers published in 1999 on Iraq's biological-weapon programme also demonstrated the difficulty of creating a global monitoring regime. UNSCOM's executive chairman, Richard Butler, stepped down at the end of his term on 30 June 1999, and the transformation of UNSCOM into its paler shadow, the UN Monitoring, Verification and Inspection Commission (UNMOVIC), had not been completed by the end of 1999. The IAEA has since undertaken a routine inspection of a nuclear facility in Iraq, but UN inspections have not taken place since December 1998. By the time UNMOVIC inspections begin, Iraq may have enjoyed several years without in-country monitoring, time which it could have made very good use of.

March 2000 marked the twenty-fifth anniversary of the entry into force of the Biological Weapons Convention (BWC) – a treaty which has never had any verification provisions. Originally, negotiations on the verification protocol were to have been completed before the BWC's Review Conference in 2001. This looks increasingly unlikely because of delays in the negotiations, although a chairman's text – scheduled to be tabled in late March 2000 – might prompt a speedy end-game. This is important because, if the protocol is not agreed by the end of 2000, the newly elected US president may find it difficult to formulate a new and consistent policy, and achieve a finalised text before the review conference. Indeed, the incoming president's policy may be so different from that of the current administration that the protocol negotiations could be set back by years, or could even be put on hold.

Is There a Way Forward?

Future arms-control historians could look back on 1999 as a turning-point, where arms control either entered a long period of stagnation, or a period that provided a necessary catalyst for an entirely new approach. Much will depend on whether or not Russia decides to strike a deal with the US over the ABM Treaty. This could be a 'quick fix', in which Russia received some technological assistance with its own missile defences, achieved further reductions in nuclear arsenals and was given other sweeteners. Over the long haul, such a deal could mean greater gains for Russian security, but in the short run it might not appear so appealing to politicians facing an increasingly cynical electorate.

Multilateral arms control in Geneva, whether nuclear or biological, is hostage to the games being played between Russia and the US. This is little changed from the Cold War. Now, however, the role China has taken on as a blocker is increasingly important, and all other states have to take this into consideration. Other important players can exploit these differences for their own advantage in their regions, particularly in the Gulf and South Asia. There is a danger that some, particularly the Europeans, may become so obsessed with the treaties that they lose sight of the importance of supporting substantial activities outside of, but complementing, the WMD treaties. These include such efforts as the safe dismantling of nuclear weapons, and the economic and social adaptation of nuclear cities and military towns in Russia and other former Soviet states. Important expectations of the arms control process remain unfulfilled, but expectations must be realistic. They must take into account the security realities of various regions, as well as viewing soberly and pragmatically how much verification regimes can actually achieve.

The Americas

I T WAS ANOTHER EBULLIENT YEAR for the US economy. This went a long way to account for the equanimity with which Americans accepted the bad behaviour of their president, Bill Clinton, despite the Republican Party's best efforts to convince them that his sins warranted impeachment. If the economy holds up, and quiet reigns abroad, at least as far as the US is concerned, Vice President Al Gore, who clinched the Democratic Party nomination earlier than any non-incumbent has done before, should reap the benefit. His opponent, Texas Governor George Bush, who also grabbed the top prize early, is an attractive politician with an easier manner than Gore. It bids fair to be a very close race, and, because the primaries were bunched in the early part of 2000, an unusually long one, running from March to November.

A lame-duck president always has difficulties in advancing new initiatives, and Bill Clinton, opposed by a Republican-led Congress frustrated by its inability to puncture his popularity, will have more difficulties than usual. The Congress in 1999 refused his request to ratify the Comprehensive Test Ban Treaty, has pushed for a Taiwan Security Enhancement Bill that the White House feels will complicate its delicate relations with China, and can be expected to be obstreperous with regard to other foreign-policy issues. One area where the two have agreed is the provision of over a billion dollars in aid to Colombia's government and army to pursue their war on drugs. Colombia is one of the Andean countries that the US administration has singled out as causing great concern in Latin America.

Most of the Andean nations, and increasingly wide areas of Latin America as a whole, have slid away from the strong support for democratic traditions that helped to overthrow authoritarian regimes over the past two decades. There has been a backlash against the democratic regimes that have ruled since then. They are accused of being unable to deal with drugs, crime, poverty and social unrest. Instead, the leaders of many Latin American regimes have dipped into the public purse to enrich themselves. They are being replaced by charismatic leaders, dubbed 'neo-populists', who appeal directly to the most disaffected of the masses, and combine this with close ties to the military and business communities. They are prepared to ignore constitutional niceties to tackle corruption, poverty and inequality. This may be for the good. But their non-democratic behaviour raises serious questions about the costs society will pay and whether there will be much democracy left by the end of the next decade.

Map 1 The Americas

The US: Economic Power at Home, Restraint Abroad

For the US, 1999 was turbulent abroad and, compared to the previous year, mostly serene at home. The sex scandal that precipitated what some saw as an attempted Republican coup via impeaching President Bill Clinton rapidly receded from view. In the face of deep public mistrust resulting from their party-line attempt to convict the President of perjury, the Republican majority was eager to see the scandal fade. Despite the public's clear disapproval of his sexual peccadilloes, the President's job-approval rating continued to hover above 60% throughout the year, as voters attributed the remarkable persistence of the country's economic boom to administration policy.

On the other side of the Atlantic, however, US foreign policy elicited concurrent fears of isolation and unilateralism, embodied in French Foreign Minister Hubert Vedrine's diagnosis of *hyperpuissance* and the prescribed cure of containment. The apparent American excesses that stimulated these concerns did not, however, necessarily represent something new in the American approach to the world, or even a trend toward intensified self-absorption. They were more the aftershocks of a year of vicious infighting in American politics and idiosyncratic factors unlikely to reassert themselves in future years.

Two Cars in Every Garage, a Chicken in Every Pot

It was indeed an astonishing year for the US economy. Stock prices continued to rise, buoyed by the growth of highly valued and strongly capitalised Internet firms and a series of mergers in this and related industries, especially telecommunications, software development and entertainment. Unemployment, at 4.1% reached the lowest point in a generation. Household income and wealth rose for the seventh year of the Democratic administration. Setting aside the effect of volatile factors, such as the price of oil, which doubled during the year, little evidence of inflation could be detected, despite rocketing economic growth of 4.8% and 6.9% in the third and fourth quarters of the year. To reassure the markets, the Federal Reserve nevertheless increased interest rates four times during the year, but only by a quarter-point at a time.

Despite the large trade deficit, amounting to 4% of gross domestic product (GDP), caused by the coincidence of increased consumption by a roaring economy with depressed Asian demand, and a nagging concern that the economic expansion represented a bubble rather than a trend, Americans were robustly optimistic. Over 70% of them, according to

The Americas

mainstream polls, believed that their personal economic situation would improve in the coming years. This was markedly different from 1992, when the ratio was reversed. The sense of national wellbeing was enhanced by bipartisan calculations that there would be a budget surplus of almost $4 trillion over a ten year period. One -half of this figure represents a surplus in the Social Security Trust Fund, the national pension system which only two years ago appeared doomed to bankruptcy, just when the bulk of post-war baby-boomers were retiring.

Off to the Races

Thus, life at home for Americans was governed by a sense of relief at the evaporation of a sordid scandal and its dramatic political consequences, increased confidence in their government and a strong belief in their economic security. Policy issues were sparse because voters were essentially satisfied with their lot. Campaigns for the party nominations for the 2000 presidential election therefore focused on more inchoate conceptions of character. Fighting for the Republican nomination, Senator John McCain, a former Navy pilot, met with unexpected, if unsustainable, success by avoiding economics and focusing on campaign-finance reform, his own strong character forged in the cauldron of a North Vietnamese prison camp, and a commitment 'never to lie to the American people'. His claim to integrity, backed by military heroism, ignited the imagination of centrist and independent voters eager for political reform. Indeed, McCain's wildfire campaign might come to be seen as a transforming event for the Republican party, akin to Ronald Reagan's bitter and ideologically charged challenge to the party leadership in 1976, which culminated four years later in his election as President. If Texas Governor George W. Bush loses this presidential election, by the time the next comes around in 2004, the Republicans, like the Democrats in 1992, will have been in the wilderness for 12 years, and be shackled in voters' minds to an obsolete ideology, searching for a saviour and ripe for a transformation. Democrats are not immune from this nascent yearning for political renewal, as former Senator Bill Bradley's short-lived nomination challenge to Vice President Al Gore showed. Whatever the future may hold, foreign and defence policy issues have not been prominent in the current context, despite meaningful differences between the candidates.

Governor Bush, who ensured his status as the Republican nominee by defeating McCain in the 7 March 'Super-Tuesday' round of primary elections, has adopted the traditional, if relatively cautious positions on foreign affairs of preceding Republican presidential aspirants. He argues that the US should:

- regard China as a competitor, rather than a partner;

- intervene abroad in pursuit of strategic, rather than strictly humanitarian interests;

- maintain a strong defence;

- prepare to rely on American power to protect vital interests, rather than on unreliable multilateral bodies like the UN.

Bush has deplored what he sees as Clinton's disregard for vital alliances, which, he says, 'are not just for crises, summoned into action when the fire bell sounds'. Yet he also:

- advocated US withdrawal from the Balkans, leaving the work of peace building to the Europeans;

- rejected any suggestion that he would resubmit the Comprehensive Test Ban Treaty (CTBT) to the Senate for ratification; and

- advocated abrogation of the Anti-Ballistic Missile (ABM) Treaty if Russia does not agree to revisions necessary for US deployment of national missile defence (NMD).

He has not explained how these positions would be compatible with renewed attentiveness to the demands of alliance-management. One would expect these principles to be modified by the responsibilities of office and constraints imposed by a multi-polar world on unilateral instincts. Bush is unlikely to interfere with European Union efforts to build a military capability to implement its Common Foreign and Security Policy (CFSP), since the current administration has done the hard diplomatic work of aligning, to the extent possible, the aspirations of the European Security and Defence Identity (ESDI) with NATO needs and sensitivities. Bush's choice of advisors, almost all of whom were in his father's administration, or were among the more sturdily internationalist and prudent members of Reagan's second-term crew, reinforces expectations of the younger Bush's mainstream foreign policy. There is greater likelihood that he will fulfil his pledge not to resubmit the CTBT to the Senate, given the bipartisan opposition to it so evident in the current Congress. Bush's only comment on defence has been that US forces should exploit the so-called revolution in military affairs (RMA), yet he has not said he would increase defence spending or alter the Clinton administration's procurement priorities.

Vice-President Al Gore, who clinched the Democratic candidacy during 'Super-Tuesday' is likely to adhere to the broad contours of the Clinton administration's approach to foreign and defence policy:

- pragmatic participation in multilateral initiatives;

- humanitarian intervention and peacekeeping where costs are sustainable and public interest is high;

The Americas

- pursuit of arms-control agreements and broader non-proliferation agreements with Russia;

- engagement with China;

- support for free-trade agreements;

- continued strong presence in the Persian Gulf;

- use of American influence to hasten closure of the Arab–Israeli peace agreements; and

- continued expansion of the defence budget.

Given Gore's frustration with the Clinton White House decision-making style, which he is said to view as undisciplined, he would be likely to run a tighter ship, reaching decisions more quickly and systematically than his predecessor. He would also be likely to focus on transnational economic problems, 'geo-economics' in Gore's terms, with greater intensity than Clinton. Given what is known about the two candidates – their positions, temperaments, political histories and close advisors – America's friends and rivals should neither fear nor hope for a radical departure in US foreign and defence policy.

A Two-Front War

The relatively halcyon state of domestic economics and the post-Lewinsky White House was not matched abroad. The administration coped with a two-front war of attrition. In the rear it had to withstand a vengeful congressional opposition. On its flanks it had to deal with intractable regional problems threatening to spin out of control; multilateral initiatives that neared collapse; deeply troubled relations with Russia and China; and a Europe trying to be whole and free – of the United States.

The Home Front

Congress dashed, or circumscribed, the administration's plans in the important areas of arms control, defence policy, the UN, and the foreign-affairs budget. Rejection of the CTBT stood out as the most fundamental challenge by showing that politics, if they ever stopped at the water's edge, no longer did; and by revealing a profound loss of confidence in arms-control solutions to security problems.

As one participant observed, the Republicans failed to impeach the President for lying about his sexual relationship with Monica Lewinsky, so they impeached him on the CTBT. There is some truth in this. Senate Republicans had been preparing for months to ensnare the Democrats into a straightforward vote on the treaty that would result in its decisive defeat and a humiliating reversal for Clinton. They quietly enlisted arms-control experts and senior officials from prior administrations to lobby their colleagues against the CTBT. Democrats had meanwhile been casting about for a convenient issue with which to flog the majority; they settled on a demand that Senator Trent Lott, the Republican leader in the Senate, finally permit the languishing treaty to be brought to a vote, and threatened to obstruct the Senate agenda until he agreed. According to an administration official, the inflammatory demand and its personal attack on the majority leader was 'like poking a stick in the Republicans' eye'. The enraged Republicans, secure by then that they had more than enough votes to kill the treaty, sprang their trap. The Democrats, to the dismay of the White House, quickly accepted Lott's offer to put the treaty on the calendar for a vote, in return for the Democrats withdrawing their threat to impede the Senate agenda. A vote was scheduled virtually immediately, leaving the White House and treaty proponents in the Senate no time to lobby effectively for ratification, or even arrange for testimony in favour of the treaty.

The CTBT catastrophe, however, was not due entirely to political intrigue. Staunch Republican internationalists with a solid record of support for arms control joined the majority in rejecting the treaty. The CTBT was viewed by many as unverifiable, a threat to the reliability of the US nuclear weapons inventory, and at a more fundamental level, an outdated and irrelevant response to the looming problem of nuclear proliferation. Former CIA director Robert Gates called it a 'feel good treaty' that would please US allies, provide Americans with a false sense of security, and do nothing to constrain rogue states equipped with intermediate-range ballistic missiles, who would never agree to adhere to it. The débâcle signified an altered perception of the arms-control project and a preference for unilateral solutions. It was this emerging sentiment that had resulted in the legislation, signed by Clinton earlier in the year, requiring the administration to decide whether to deploy NMD by summer 2000.

The administration's reaction, in remarks by the President and Sandy Berger, his national security advisor, was to brand the Republicans as neo-isolationists, thereby deepening the underlying alienation between White House and Congress. Critics on the right and left rejected the label as politically motivated. In this embittered atmosphere, the administration brawled in the trenches with Congress over payment of contribution arrears to the UN. The administration had struck an agreement two years earlier with the congressional leadership that $926 million would be paid to the UN over a three-year period, provided the administration could certify that the UN had carried out specified reforms and placed an American appointee in an oversight position on the organisation's budget committee. The deal could not be sealed, however, because a single member of Congress, Chris Smith, Republican member for New Hampshire, with the acquiescence of his Republican colleagues, insisted that no funds could be spent on any programme that counselled women seeking abortion as a family-planning option.

The President, in view of key Democratic constituencies for whom women's 'right to choose' abortion was a profound interest, had refused for two successive years to concede and sign the legislation that would authorise appropriations for the repayment. In 1999, however, things changed. The White House now faced the imminent loss of the US seat in the General Assembly, mounting international charges of American unilateralism, and an undeniable financial crisis at the UN. Reluctant to lose the opportunity to compel badly needed organisational and fiscal reform at the UN, the White House agreed to a deal brokered by US Ambassador to the UN Richard Holbrooke. Under this the State Department would deduct a percentage of its contribution to the organisation's population programmes should recipient organisations provide abortion-related guidance. This ended the stand-off, but could not repair the corrosive effect it had had on executive–legislature ties in Washington, and in fostering perceptions abroad of American arrogance and irresponsibility.

The War Abroad

The UN was also the venue for the US battle to maintain sanctions on Iraq, reinsert weapons-inspectors into the country and, more broadly, sustain its policy of dual-containment. The battle was finally won, although it appeared to be a pyrrhic victory, since the UN Security Council resolution on inspectors received the votes of only two permanent members, the US and Britain. Russia and China abstained, as expected, but so did France, in a repudiation of the solidarity these three Principal Nations (P-3) had hitherto shown, and more broadly of the US stance on Iraq. The resolution's final draft represented such a departure from existing US preferences that the official justification for French abstention – that a residual phrase in the text, in Paris's view, would have justified continuing sanctions even after Iraq had met the resolution's requirements – seems less than satisfactory. In the end, Iraq rejected the resolution, and the status quo continued with more Anglo-American bombing and no inspections of Iraq's weapons sites. All that had changed was that France had demolished P-3 unity – and whatever deterrent effect that may have had on Saddam Hussein – and there was now a greater strain on the US–France relationship. Continued Gulf Cooperation Council support for America's position on Iraq, as expressed in the GCC's late-November summit in Riyadh, will undergird the status quo still more.

Dual containment also showed signs of wear in Iran's case, where Iranian activities under the former regime and the country's current transformation under President Mohammad Khatami combined to present the US administration with an insoluble dilemma. The problem from the past was Iran's complicity, according to the US, in the 1996 bombing of the Khobar Towers in Dhahran, Saudi Arabia, killing 19 US airman and injuring 500, including 240 US citizens. Evidence said to indicate that senior Iranian intelligence officials played a significant role had been provided by the Saudis to the US months before Washington was forced to publicise the new information during deportation proceedings for one of the Saudi suspects, Hani al Sayegh in October 1999. The administration, eager to stabilise US–Iran relations, had not wanted to disclose Iran's alleged role because the revelation would inevitably create domestic political barriers to *rapprochement*. When its hand was forced by Attorney-General Janet Reno's announcement of Sayegh's extradition to Saudi Arabia, the administration sought to turn awkwardness to opportunity by asking Khatami for Iranian assistance in the Khobar investigation. However, Tehran ultimately rejected the assertion of Iranian involvement and accused the US of manufacturing accusations to justify its continuing enmity to the Iranian revolution.

This exchange took place after nearly two years of halting steps by the administration to lower the temperature of the bilateral confrontation. Sanctions had been reduced during the previous year; Iranian sports and academic delegations had been admitted to the US; the State Department floated the reopening of the American consulate in Tehran; and both the President and Secretary of State Madeleine Albright made unambiguous public statements endorsing Iranian democracy and recognising the legitimacy of Iranian resentment of the West, especially the US. Washington saw these as important steps beyond which the US could not go until Iran softened its opposition to the Middle East peace process, halted its pursuit of weapons of mass destruction and curtailed its support for terrorism. US information indicating Iran's close involvement in the Khobar attack, the state's continued support for Lebanese Hizbollah – punctuated by calls for Israel's annihilation – and Tehran's demands for concessions far exceeding the limits of congressional tolerance made the administration's task in trying to improve US–Iran relations very difficult. In the wake of reformist gains in Iran's February 2000 parliamentary elections, this situation is increasingly frustrating for American officials who want to shed the burden of containment where Iran is concerned. In mid-March 2000, Secretary of State Albright announced a lifting of some sanctions against Iranian luxury goods, and an intention to settle outstanding Iranian assets frozen since the 1979 Revolution in the hope of interesting the Iranians in talks to improve relations. Iran welcomed her offers of positive actions, but Tehran immediately snubbed the idea of opening talks. Given this rejection, it appears that the US will be stuck with dual containment for the coming year.

The high hopes that caused Clinton to enthuse about meeting Israel's newly elected Prime Minister Ehud Barak for the first time on 15 July 1999 ('I feel like a kid with a new toy') have also dissipated. Throughout much of 1999, the President and Barak spoke often, sometimes daily, especially as Israel approached the 3–9 Shepherdstown meetings with Syria's peace team. Clinton also spoke in December 1999 to Syria's President Hafez Al-Assad, who reassured him that Syria was prepared to deal. The draft treaty text that the US team prepared for the instantly stalemated negotiators quickly found its way into an Israeli newspaper. Assad's retrograde riposte was published in a Lebanese newspaper almost immediately thereafter. A series of *Hizbollah* attacks against Israeli forces and their surrogates in southern Lebanon in February 2000, escalated by Israel into attacks against Lebanese infrastructure, further soured the mood of the parties, and diverted US attention from peace negotiations to stabilising the spiralling violence. Frustrated, the US has focused on ways in which it can help Barak win the referendum that he has promised to ratify agreement with Syria, should this ever come about. It has also shifted its attention to Barak's faltering negotiations with Palestinian Authority Chairman Yassir Arafat. In pursuit of the former objective, the White House is looking for ways to strengthen already intensive defence cooperation with Israel. The most likely arrangement will be a new memorandum of understanding which incorporates existing agreements, outlines new areas for defence-industrial cooperation, base improvements, and regular strategic consultations at senior levels. On the negotiations with Arafat, President Clinton, who hosted the Palestinian leader in February 2000, has tried to keep him focused on the costs of a delayed agreement, while pressing Barak to move quickly to transfer territory to Palestinian Authority jurisdiction.

US relations with Russia, China and its European allies were equally turbulent. Chief among the irritants was the President's impending decision on deploying an NMD system, designed to intercept a limited number of missiles launched deliberately or accidentally by a so-called rogue state – meaning North Korea, Iran, or Iraq. Russia, it is hoped, will ultimately agree to the ABM treaty revisions to permit deployment, out of fear that a Republican administration would be prepared to jettison the treaty in order to proceed with NMD. Although the administration anticipated an adverse Russian reaction, it failed to plan for strong opposition from US allies and China. The State Department believed that its threat briefings would convert the allies, while its assertions – contradicted by members of Congress – that China was not the target would mollify Beijing. These assumptions were wrong.

European governments were not convinced by demonstrations that Iranian and Iraqi missiles had the range to cover European capitals. They dismissed the threat because they did not acknowledge the possibility of conflicts in which missile attacks might occur. Nor did the allies understand why deterrence had suddenly dropped out of fashion in Washington: if 3,500 warheads and a secure second-strike capability would deter Russia, why could North Korea not be deterred with one or two warheads? From this perspective, the risk of rogue-state attack simply did not outweigh the dangers of provoking a transitional Russia, increasingly reliant on its strategic forces to guarantee its security. Not only was this destabilising, but to the allies it presaged US decoupling from its stake in European security.

European discomfort with America's dominating role in European security had been intensified by the way the US had dictated strategy in the March–June 1999 Kosovo war. The general complaint was that US obsession with avoiding American casualties militated in favour of strategic bombing, and therefore against planning for a ground war. The complaint was not entirely logical: only the British government had been willing to talk openly about a ground invasion; and there was merit in the White House argument that such talk threatened not only US participation but the fragile consensus among the 19 NATO members as well. Nonetheless, Paris, in particular, considered it a continuing anomaly that the rational response to European security challenges was constrained by political considerations in Washington. In Kosovo, Europeans had lacked the means to muster and deploy their own forces on the ground, and lacked the technological edge to participate in and thereby influence the execution of the air campaign. This deficiency was unacceptable and begged correction.

Sensitivities in Paris were no doubt already bruised by the hectoring of senior US officials determined to ensure that the language on ESDI at the EU's 10 December 1999 Helsinki summit was consistent with NATO interests, as spelled out in the April 1999 fiftieth Anniversary NATO Summit declaration, and took US concerns into account. These concerns were:

- NATO should be the first resort in a contingency;

- spending on force improvements and new procurement should be allocated first to obligations to NATO under the Defense Capabilities Initiative.

- there should be a guarantee that non-EU NATO members would not be frozen out of EU planning and military operations.

- a formal link should be established between EU headquarters and NATO headquarters in Brussels to ensure 'transparency' and to reassure apprehensive NATO members, especially the US and Britain, that the two alliances were not inadvertently crossing paths.

The first of these concerns, enshrined at the Washington NATO summit, was easy to meet, since NATO, for practical reasons, would have to be the first resort for years. The second concern is not pressing, in view of EU members' pessimism about prospects for raising more money for defence programmes. Even the incorporation of non-EU members would be manageable, despite German distaste for giving the Turks yet another claim on accession. Pressure for transparency, however, would certainly face French resistance, for Paris sees it as vitally important to seal off the EU headquarters 'to preserve the sovereignty of the organisation', a euphemism for 'keep American influence out'.

To China, engaged in deploying additional ballistic missiles opposite the 'renegade province' of Taiwan, the concept of NMD posed a direct challenge to its sovereignty over the island. This perception was reinforced by congressional statements that lumped China together with Iran, Iraq and North Korea as the targets of US missile defences. Beijing's harsh reaction, which included the threat to renege on its non-proliferation commitments to Washington, fuelled the mixture of anger and misapprehension that characterised 1999 in Sino-American relations.

Tensions were already high in the wake of US accusations in early 1999 of Chinese espionage over the past 20 years with regard to nuclear weapons, sharp disagreements over Kosovo and the inadvertent US cruise-missile attack against the Chinese embassy in Belgrade. Just when the Chinese reaction to that incident – the sacking of the US consulate in Beijing amidst orchestrated protests inflamed by wildly anti-American official rhetoric – had began to fade, Taiwan's President Lee Teng-hui threw a policy grenade into the mix in July 1999. He insisted that henceforth Taipei and Beijing should deal on 'a special state-to-state relations' basis. An angry US administration, concerned about existing tensions with Beijing, dismissed Lee's claim, reiterated the validity of the 'one China' formula, and counselled Chinese restraint. After strident Chinese attacks on the Lee formula, a disarming lull set in and it appeared all concerned were awaiting the outcome of the Taiwanese presidential elections on 18 March.

In February 2000, the highest ranking US delegation to visit China since Tiananmen spent two days seeking to advance the relationship between the two countries. Its immediate objective was to restore contacts between the US and Chinese militaries, but it had little success. Upon returning home, the delegates learned through the news media that China, without warning them, had threatened to seize Taiwan by force if reunification talks were delayed indefinitely. A senior Defense Department official warned China of 'incalculable consequences' if it were to use force, but the administration could think of nothing further to say, paralysed by uncertainty as to whether the Chinese statement was a vigorous formulation of a longstanding position, or a rejection of peaceful unification. The White House was also wary of how Congress would approach

China's joining the World Trade Organisation (WTO) and normalisation of its trade status; and to the Taiwan Security Enhancement Act (TSEA). This had been passed overwhelmingly by the House of Representatives but was simmering in the Senate, where cautious lawmakers, aware of its potentially incendiary effect on Beijing, kept it tied up in committee.

At the end of March 2000, it appeared that Congress would react to Beijing's failure to disclose its impending threat to Taiwan, either by rejecting China's trade status – a difficult course for politicians representing business constituencies aching for the opportunities of an open Chinese market – or passing the TSEA, which would confer political benefits on lawmakers, while bringing the US closer to confrontation with China. In either case, Congress seemed determined to demand new arms sales to Taiwan, including sophisticated items like *Aegis* destroyers, whose tracking and fire-control systems can be adapted to missile defense. The administration could influence the outcome, but its position was unenviable. It faced being forced to take a position that was certain to trample the sensitivities of one or more of the players. The State Department annual human rights report issued in February 2000, which excoriated China for widespread abuses, exemplified these dangers. From Washington's point of view, the situation was rapidly drifting out of control. The US is being pulled inexorably and unwillingly into the inherently unstable process of Chinese unification with the possibility of a sharp crisis in its relations with Beijing.

China–Taiwan was not the only conflict into which a reluctant administration was dragged. Pakistan's breach of the Kashmir Line of Control at Kargil which came to light in May 1999, immediately drew in the US. It played a key role in persuading then Pakistan President Nawaz Sharif to pull back the militants and in counselling Indian Prime Minister Atal Bihari Vajpayee not to succumb to pressure to cross the line of control. President Clinton took an especially tough line with Sharif when he met with him in Washington on 4 July 1999. The ensuing army coup, which brought General Pervez Musharraf to power in Pakistan, was both a nuisance and a relief. The likelihood that Musharraf had instigated Pakistan's bizarre adventure in Kargil was, of course, disquieting; but Sharif's incompetence and megalomania were corroding an already dangerously weak polity, whose disintegration would be disastrous. Clinton's decision in March 2000 to stop in Islamabad on his visit to India will not have been easy. The visit risked legitimising the coup and sanctioning Pakistan's nuclear option, but bypassing Pakistan would have inadvertently contributed to its isolation, weakened US influence over its strategic thinking and strengthened the hold of anti-western extremists on Pakistani politics. Clinton's talks in New Delhi aimed to persuade India that, with radicalism rising in Pakistan, the time for getting a durable deal on Kashmir is rapidly shrinking. He urged Vajpayee to abandon India's longstanding refusal to internationalise the dispute, and to involve outside mediation as its best hope to curb Pakistan and reduce the possibility that events will spin out of control. There was little likelihood that this argument would prevail.

Preparing for the Enemy Within ...

Just before Christmas 1999, Americans woke up to learn that a Muslim extremist had been arrested on the Canadian border at Port Seattle, Washington. He had attempted to enter the US with a carload of explosives. Within days, arrests of co-conspirators were announced in Canada, Vermont and New York. The would-be terrorists, according to investigators, were linked to Osama bin Laden, the renegade Saudi who lives in Afghanistan. At approximately the same time, Jordan announced the arrest of 13 bin Laden- affiliated operatives. What appeared to be an international plot to penetrate the US sparked recollections of the World Trade Center bombing in 1993 and triggered the largest manhunt in recent years. It also underscored the administration's concern with the domestic terrorist threat and the possibility that extremists would at some point use chemical, biological or nuclear weapons to achieve their goals. Within a month, the arrests were followed by a frivolous, but nonetheless skilled and comprehensive, disruption of commercial websites in the US. This appeared to be the work of hackers, but it reinforced fears that terrorists could mount a similar attack against critical infrastructure. These anxieties produced a counter-terrorism and cyber-security budget request for the next fiscal year of more than $12 billion. They also led the US to maintain its pressure on allies to cooperate in an effort to counter terrorism.

... And the Enemy Without

The administration submitted to Congress a budget for fiscal year 2001, which included a request for $277.5bn for defence. This was the first real increase in defence funding in many years. When it finally emerges from the appropriations process in the autumn, the allocation is certain to be closer to $300bn. The request differs from prior years in allocating $60bn to new procurement, which ground to a halt for much of the Clinton administration. The way a large part of this increase is spent will be shaped by the lessons of the Kosovo campaign and the need to provide the services with a greater capacity for rapid power-projection. The services will get large quantities of precision-guided munitions, high-altitude unmanned aerial vehicles, long-range stand-off munitions and another squadron of electronic-warfare aircraft.

The bulk of the increase will be dedicated to three new tactical aircraft: the multi-service Joint Strike Fighter; F-18 E/F *Super Hornets* for the Navy; and the F-22 *Raptor* for the Air Force. The Navy will get new *Virginia*-class attack submarines, the last of its big deck carriers and amphibious assault ships. The Air Force inventory of long-range, large capacity cargo and refuelling aircraft will be significantly enlarged. The Army, suffering for its absence from the Kosovo conflict, will get the smallest share of the increase and, predictably, will spend it to develop tactical vehicles and artillery that can be easily transported in large numbers by aircraft. The budget continues the perennial balancing act between funding the ability to participate in manpower- and lift-intensive humanitarian interventions and the need to absorb the RMA so as to fight major wars quickly and relatively bloodlessly. These improvements will cause US and European capabilities to diverge even more than they already have. The widening gap is certain to generate more tension within the Alliance and between NATO and the EU, as the latter tries to fulfil its Defence Capabilities Initiative commitments and put some flesh on ESDI's bones at the same time.

Hyperpuissance?

A review of the past year makes Hubert Vedrine's vexation about *Hyperpuissance* perplexing. It is true that a unilateralist tendency in American foreign policy, which tends to ebb and flow, has flowed a bit more than it did during the Reagan administration. Nevertheless, there is not much evidence of a conclusive shift. The vote on the CTBT could easily have gone the other way if the administration had been attentive, Senate Democrats had been less oafish and the political atmosphere had not been quite so fraught. The facts seem to contradict the notion that the treaty's rejection stemmed from a surging unilateralism rather than reflecting the periodic and unwelcome intrusion of US domestic politics into the realm of foreign policy. The delay in settling debt to the UN is an unfortunate result of the same phenomenon.

Nor does deployment of a limited NMD system against attack by rogue states necessarily signify a decisive turn to unilateralism. The truth is more complicated. The administration has sought, however ineffectually, to bring its allies under the same shelter and places a high priority on NMD being deployed under the aegis of the ABM Treaty. Indeed, the impact of a deployment on American arms-control commitments was one of the four criteria that Clinton set on which to base decisions on deployment. From the US perspective, its allies are refusing to acknowledge American threat perceptions, and are forcing it to remove the threat by adopting a unilateral approach that it would prefer to avoid.

Indeed, *hyperpuissance* seems curiously absent from the past year's record. In the Middle East and Persian Gulf, US objectives have been essentially thwarted. America lacks the power to pull Assad to the conference table or push Barak to halt settlement activity. On Iraq, France has fought the US to a stalemate that forecloses the possibility of continuing monitoring or verification. Containment of Iran has lost force through government-backed Elf Acquitaine and Royal Dutch contracts for oil-field development, which the US, despite the Iran–Libya Sanctions Act (ILSA) is powerless to stop. In Europe, ESDI proceeds apace, fundamentally unconstrained by the US, despite American fears of its long-term threat to NATO cohesiveness and effectiveness, let alone to American influence in Europe. In Asia, the US can neither compel Chinese restraint nor press Taiwan to pursue unification talks seriously. Even in the trade arena, US power seems distinctly circumscribed both by the WTO and the developing world's refusal to subscribe to the American agenda. On balance, the US, in its 1999 foreign and defence policy, looks more like a power which has had only modest success in defending its core interests than as an unconstrained power imposing its will unilaterally. Given that 2000 is an election year in the US, policy will inevitably be even more constrained than in 1999.

Latin America:
Whither Democracy at Century's End

The democratic euphoria that swept Latin America two decades ago has passed. At that time, when most countries in the region were governed by military rulers, there appeared to be a profound transformation taking place among their citizens: democracy, for the first time, mattered. Human rights mattered. Even the left, which had long disdained the seemingly empty processes of 'bourgeois democracy', after suffering under the extreme abuses of authoritarian rule seemed to revalue the ideas of civil liberties, due process, democratic checks and balances and basic rights. The wave of democratic transitions in country after country that dominated the 1980s seemed to confirm new and deep support for democracy. By 1990, only Cuba had not undergone a democratic transition.

Yet, only ten years later, democracy has taken an unexpected turn. The same citizens who threw out authoritarian military rulers through protest marches, plebiscites, elections, subversion, ridicule and other means, now began to embrace a host of new leaders, less committed to the niceties of democratic practices, but more committed to good governance, weeding out corruption, and addressing poverty and inequality.

Instability, Crisis and Voter Backlash

In December 1999, the two most powerful forces in Ecuadorian politics – the military and the powerful indigenous movement – joined forces and ousted the elected president. This event was the climax of days of demonstrations by the country's large indigenous population, protesting against another round of economic austerity measures and a proposal by President Jamil Mahuad to abandon the national currency, the sucre, in favour of the US dollar. The military, for its part, was angry over its declining power and the unfavourable resolution of a long-running border dispute with Peru. A three-man junta was initially established, comprising the head of the indigenous movement, the former chief justice of the Supreme Court and the head of the Army. After sustained US pressure and warnings that Ecuador would be isolated internationally, the army withdrew from the junta, and the former vice-president, Gustavo Noboa, assumed power.

In March 1999, Paraguayan Vice-President Luis María Argaña was assassinated. The finger of suspicion pointed to President Raúl Cubas Grau and his military patron, the defence minister and former general, Lino César Oviedo. Congress immediately began impeachment proceedings against the president, who had released Oviedo from imprisonment for an earlier coup attempt and resisted a Supreme Court order to return him to prison. Facing an imminent impeachment vote whose outcome was not in doubt, Cubas resigned on 28 March and fled to Brazil. At the same time, Oviedo escaped to Argentina. Luís González Macchi, the president of the Senate, was sworn in as the new president of Paraguay.

In Venezuela, President Hugo Chavez, the former lieutenant-colonel who had staged a coup in 1992 and then parlayed his popularity into an overwhelming electoral victory in the December 1998 presidential elections, quickly moved to consolidate his power. He backed a national referendum in April 1999 to convene a Constituent Assembly, and 81.5% of the people voted to re-write the Constitution. In special elections held in July, candidates from Chavez's movement won 120 of the 128 seats, underscoring the collapse of Venezuela's traditional parties and guaranteeing that Chavez would have a free hand in designing the new political system. The new assembly immediately declared its authority to assume congressional and judicial functions, effectively eliminating the two branches of government that still held pockets of resistance to Chavez's authority. The new constitution, completed in November 1999, called for congressional and presidential elections, concentrated power in the executive and created a special role for the armed forces in a broad range of policy areas, from security to education and development. In a special referendum held on 15 December 1999, the new constitution was massively endorsed. Chavez immediately began campaigning for re-election as president.

In Peru, President Alberto Fujimori announced his intention to seek a third term in office in elections scheduled for 9 April 2000. Fujimori, first elected in 1990, had shut down Congress in 1992, to the cheers of his countrymen. Under strong international pressure to return to democratic rule, Fujimori convened special elections for a Constituent Assembly in 1993 which produced a new constitution, allowing for two consecutive presidential terms and creating a strong executive.

In 1995, flush with the success of defeating the Shining Path guerrillas, Peru's extreme Marxist insurgents, and having successfully transformed the economy from one of hyper-inflation and negative growth to one characterised by low inflation and rapid growth, Fujimori won a second term with 65% of the vote. In 1994 and 1995, Peru's growth rates of 11% and 13% were among the highest in the world. Fujimori signed permanent peace treaties with Ecuador (following a brief border war), and with Chile (which had taken Peruvian lands at the end of the nineteenth century in the War of the Pacific). The two peace efforts put an end to over a century of conflict. Yet, despite his success, Fujimori insisted on harassing and undermining his opposition and, with the help of the military and intelligence service, on concentrating power in his office. During his second term, opposition media were shut down and the country withdrew from the Inter-American Court of Justice following an unfavourable ruling denouncing its human-rights abuses. Fujimori is expected to win the April election. His popularity has diminished just enough, however, for him to probably fall shy of the needed 50% and to be forced into a second round, the date of which would be announced within 30 days of the announcement of the official result.

In Guatemala on 26 December 1999, former leftist Alfonso Portillo, now allied with the former right-wing military dictator Efraín Ríos Montt, was elected as president in a two-man run-off. In the first elections since Guatemala ended its bloody civil war in December 1996, through UN-brokered peace negotiations, the people rewarded Ríos Montt's party, the Guatemalan Republican Front, with 63 of the 113 seats. Ríos Montt, barred from seeking the presidency because he had previously come to power through a military coup, was quickly elected president of the Congress. Ríos Montt headed a brutally repressive military government in 1982–83. His record is so soiled that he has been charged with massive human-rights violations, and may be indicted in international courts for crimes against humanity. In February 1999, the Guatemalan truth commission (euphemistically named The Historical Clarification Commission), established with the peace agreements, charged high officials of the era with 'crimes against humanity'. Although the commission did not name names, it is clear that it has implicated Ríos Montt. Ríos Montt and Portillo seem to be reaping the same populist trend that has been flowing through the body politic of so many other Latin American nations.

Most analysts believe that the Guatemalan electorate is tired of the continued corruption and mismanagement of the country. Despite the peace process and the end to the political violence, Guatemala has yet to gain any relief from grinding poverty, alienation and now soaring crime rates. Repeatedly, voters have expressed their distrust of the system. In a special plebiscite in May 1999, voters rejected central provisions of the peace process which had called for greater indigenous rights, human-rights legislation, military reform and state restructuring. How could this happen? It seems probable that, as many analysts have stated, the people did not reject the peace, but they distrust the politicians who brokered it.

The Rise of the Neo-Populists

The old authoritarians have not returned, and are not likely to do so. The new leaders have mostly assumed power through the ballot box. Chavez in Venezuela, Fujimori in Peru, and Ríos Montt in Guatemala have all been elected, though each has shown little patience with the niceties of constitutional rule. Chavez and Ríos Montt had previously taken part in military coups, one failed, one successful. Fujimori enacted a 'self-coup' when he unconstitutionally shut down Congress during his first period of office. Yet today each has a semblance of democratic credentials.

In many ways, the new crop of leaders resembles an earlier period of populist presidents who came of age in the first half of the twentieth century, a time of great social, economic and political tumult. Then, nation after nation began to modernise, urbanise and industrialise, and new leaders and parties emerged to incorporate the newly formed middle and working classes. They were led by charismatic individuals who opposed the old oligarchic parties and politicians, and sought to create a new mass following in the most modern sectors of the economy.

The present generation of Latin American leaders have been dubbed 'neo-populists'. Like the early populists, they have emerged at a time of great economic transformation and upheaval. They are charismatic and seek to appeal directly to the masses, bypassing the intermediate and mediating institutions of democracy. And, like the earlier leaders such as Perón in Argentina, Vargas in Brazil and Cárdenas in Mexico, the neo-populists challenge the established system. In the opening years of the twenty-first century, this means denouncing the corrupt parties and politicians of the last 20 years, many of whom have grown rich during the democratic transitions.

Instead of presiding over a state with a larger share of the national economy, these neo-populists are committed to the new rules of the game: privatisation, state down-sizing and foreign investment. In this sense, neo-populist refers to the neo-liberal economic prescriptions of the current period. Instead of working with the organised sectors of the middle and working classes, the neo-populists appeal to the most marginalised, disenfranchised and excluded sectors in both rural and urban areas. Yet, the new neo-populists often have key allies in the military and business communities, and have come to the fore amid great economic crisis and privation.

In the case of Ecuador, these marginalised sectors and their leaders have still have not reached the presidency. Yet, their political awakening, organising and mobilisation has led to the overthrow of the last two elected presidents, who were attempting to institute unpopular austerity measures. In 1997, Abdalá Bucaram, nicknamed *El Loco*, was forced from office after mass protests led Congress simply to remove him. In January 2000, after just 17 months in office, President Mahuad was overthrown by a short-lived junta that brought together a charismatic indigenous leader, Antonio Vargas, with the head of the armed forces. The junta was dissolved in less than a day, and Mahuad was replaced by his vice-president Gustavo Noboa. However, the new president must still reach out to these new restless and organised sectors or risk being overthrown himself. This tension between the 'old' Ecuadorian politicians and the newly mobilised sectors and their allies has led to a total of seven presidents taking office – on two occasions for a day or less – in the past three years.

Peter F. Romero, a former US Ambassador to Ecuador and Acting Assistant Secretary of State for Western Hemisphere Affairs observed, 'It doesn't take a clairvoyant to predict that democracy will wane in the face of economic privation. The region's outstanding record of democratisation since the apex of military rule some 20 years ago cannot be taken for granted'. Events in the last few years underscore that democracy is not just about elections and process. Citizens are saying through their votes that democracy must deliver, or they will support other options.

The most recent statistics on economic growth, poverty and corruption seem to bear out Romero's thinking. After a long period of renewed growth, the region has faced difficulties in the past few years. This is partly due to external factors such as economic recession in Asia, volatile financial markets and unpredictable commodity prices. However, other factors have also played a role – the internal politics of resource mismanagement, misallocation, corruption and the aftershock of absorbing one-off funds from privatisations, which led to a momentary increase in revenues but then left a gap which had to be filled from elsewhere. In 1999, according to the Economic Commission on Latin America, there was no growth in the region as a whole, compared with 4.3%, 6.6% and 3.4% in the previous three years. At the level of individual economies, there appears to be a correlation between neo-populism, political instability and the poorest economic performance. The Venezuelan and Ecuadorian economies each contracted by 7%, the worst records in the region; Argentina dropped 3.5%, Colombia by 5.0% and Paraguay by 1.5%. Peru grew by 3.0%, which might have contributed to Fujimori's re-election, and Guatemala showed 3.5% growth, but this did not lead the electorate to endorse the government.

Urban unemployment during 1999 followed similar patterns. Venezuela posted rates of 15.4%; Ecuador experienced 15.1%; Colombia, which remains mired in internal conflict, led the region with 19.8% urban unemployment.

Not all the News is Depressing: Democracy is Variable

Not all of Latin America's 35 nations have gone down the neo-populist path, and not all nations have embraced non-democratic solutions. The record from the past year provides important examples of democratic consolidation and reform.

Perhaps most striking is the case of Chile. Throughout 1999 and up to March 2000, former dictator and senator-for-life Augusto Pinochet was detained under house arrest in Britain, pending a decision on an extradition request by Spain, which wanted to bring him to trial for crimes against humanity. The detention seriously divided Chileans, and some thought that it might undermine the fragile democratic transition, which was based on an implicit pact between the new civilian leaders and the former military rulers. According to that pact, the military would cede power in exchange for certain concessions: amnesty; continued prerogatives within the new system, such as life-time senate seats for Pinochet and several of his supporters; and complete control over military budgets, promotions and most internal security issues.

For the most part, the new civilian leaders were prepared to honour these agreements and had done so since the initial transition to civilian rule in 1989. For example, although the nation is at peace, Chile's defence expenditure ranks first in Latin America in both per capita terms and as a percentage of gross domestic product (GDP), and fourth in absolute terms, after the giants, Argentina, Brazil and Mexico. The detention of Pinochet in London threatened to unravel this pact, leading to predictions of a new era of instability.

To widespread surprise, in 1999, when Chile staged its third presidential election since the transition, Pinochet was not a campaign issue. The two preceding elections had been won by a centre-left alliance forged by the Christian Democrats and the Socialists. In the first two post-transition administrations, the elected president had come from the moderate Christian Democrats. In 1999, the socialist candidate, Ricardo Lagos, won the internal primary, and he squared off in the general election against a young conservative and former Pinochet minister, Joaquin Lavín. Perhaps because of the uncertainty of electing a socialist, or because of the looming absence of General Pinochet, the first round of voting was unexpectedly close. Lagos received 47.96% to Lavín's 47.52%. Lagos went on to win the second round, and took office on 11 March 2000.

The occasion was historic. A week before Lagos took office, the UK released Pinochet on the basis that his declining health rendered him incapable of understanding the charges against him, or of defending himself. The general immediately returned to Chile and received a rousing welcome from his supporters, a fact that embarrassed both the newly-elected Lagos government and the British. Yet the ascension of a socialist to power 27 years after Pinochet overthrew Salvador Allende, the last socialist to reach power, underscored how much the country had indeed changed, both in the years since the democratic transition and even during the 18 months of Pinochet's absence. Lagos promised to continue the economic policies of recent governments, and to create more opportunities for those who have been left behind. As for Pinochet, Lagos declared that he would let Chile's judicial system decide the fate of the ex-dictator.

Elsewhere, Mexico is struggling through the early stages of its transition to democratic norms. The ruling Institutional Revolutionary Party (PRI) has governed without interruption for over 70 years. It has overwhelmingly dominated politics and has often resorted to fraud and violence to retain its grip on power. The party recognises, however, that it can no longer indulge in these practices. Instead it has been engaged in a drawn-out process by which both it and the country have been set on a path towards democracy. This has accelerated over the past six years.

Opposition candidates have taken office at state and local levels. They control the lower house of Congress and they count the mayor of Mexico City, Cuahtemoc Cárdenas, among their ranks. For the first time, the PRI broke with the tradition of allowing the president simply to choose his successor, in a process known as the *dedazo* or 'the big finger pointing'. Instead, the party held an internal primary. It was won, with 52% of the vote, by Francisco Labastida, the 'official candidate' backed by President Ernesto Zedillo. Rodrigo Madrazo came in second with 38%, but he did particularly well in the more rebellious and fractious southern states. Nevertheless, the fact that primaries were held at all was a significant step forward.

Current polls indicate that Labastida cannot be assured of the presidency, as could all his PRI-candidate predecessors. The opposition remains divided between the centre-left candidate, Cárdenas and the centre-right candidate, former Governor of Guanajuato State Vicente Fox.

Polls indicate that a united opposition ticket could defeat the PRI, yet Cárdenas and Fox are both unwilling to renounce their candidacies. Cárdenas has slipped badly in the polls, however, and some of his key supporters have openly endorsed Fox. The dynamic raises the possibility of a very competitive presidential election in 2000. But as long as Cárdenas stays in the race, the odds still favour Labastida.

In Argentina democratic norms held firm. Two-term president, Carlos Menem was ultimately unsuccessful in manipulating the Constitution to allow for a third successive term, as his counterpart Alberto Fujimori had done in Peru. Moreover, in elections held on 24 October 1999, Menem's Justicialist Party lost to a centre-left alliance headed by Fernando de la Rua. The ruling coalition which took power at the election, the *Alianza*, brings together the Radical Party and dissident Justicialists. It won a clear plurality in the Chamber with 124 deputies against 99 for the Justicialists.

The centrepiece of de la Rua's campaign was anti-corruption, a message which clearly struck a popular chord. The new government began to act both symbolically and substantively to change a political culture where government office was simply considered a 'spoil of war'. The president has attempted to sell off the presidential plane commissioned under the previous government, and makes a point of flying on commercial airliners. More importantly, once in power de la Rua moved smartly to expose corruption in high places, and Argentine investigators have initiated some of the biggest anti-corruption probes in Latin American history. One of the first targets was the Pensioners Health Care Agency, which was reportedly bilked of hundreds of millions of dollars during the previous decade.

The pilfering that became part of the large privatisation programme has also come under investigation, as have corrupt government contracts. De la Rúa has removed more than 1,000 intelligence officials who were involved in widespread extortion and smuggling. The Argentine experience may well have repercussions throughout the region, where corruption is embedded in the political culture. In a ranking of corruption produced by Transparency International, many Latin American nations fell to the bottom of the scale. Of 94 countries listed in order of corruption, the major Latin American nations were rated as follows: Ecuador 82, Venezuela 75, Colombia 72, Argentina 71, Guatemala 68, Mexico 58, Brazil 45, Peru 40, Chile 19. The United States ranked 18.

Beyond Democracy: The Drug War

The Drug War continues to create a disturbing backdrop to security and democracy issues in Latin America. The US Congress passed the Western Hemisphere Drug Elimination Act which has once again elevated and accelerated US efforts in the region to attack illicit drug production at its source. Over the last five years, the US has successfully implemented its 'airbridge strategy', which cut off much of the Bolivian and Peruvian coca fields from the cocaine refiners and drug barons in Colombia. Under this policy, radar were placed throughout the region and with their help the Peruvian and Colombian Armed Forces were able to down aircraft engaged in transporting drugs. As a result, coca production in Peru has fallen by 56% since 1995, and Bolivia has seen similar declines. Yet the policy has also contributed to a massive increase of coca production in Colombia, leading US policy-makers to develop a 'Southern Colombian Strategy'. Under this scheme, President Bill Clinton's administration requested a $1.6 billion aid package to support the Colombian government's anti-narcotics efforts.

The package, still not approved by Congress, would greatly expand US involvement in Colombia. With US aid the Colombian Armed Forces would more directly engage the guerrillas of the *Fuerzas Armadas Revolucionarias de Colombia* (FARC), the dominant political actors throughout most of the coca-growing region. Whether the US should expand its involvement with the Colombian Armed Forces, an army widely associated with human-rights violations, is a question being asked with increasing concern. Critics have also asked whether the United States should become more directly involved in a counter-insurgency war, when it has not yet fully identified the risks or even the goals of its involvement.

The ambiguous expansion of the US military role in Colombia also underscores the crisis that has afflicted this northern Andean country. Although most Central American guerrilla wars ended a decade ago, and drug production has been greatly scaled back in Peru and Bolivia, there has been a steady increase in both Colombia's internal conflict and its drug-producing capacity. Indeed, the concentration of the drug trade has further fuelled the nation's longstanding conflict, and led to further degradation of its political institutions.

President Andrés Pastrana Arango's government has attempted to create an integral approach, 'Plan Colombia', to solve Colombia's complex crisis. It is requesting international assistance to modernise the armed forces, improve their human-rights record, combat drug production and negotiate peace with the guerrillas. There are competing interpretations of how these objectives fit together. Pastrana argued at the outset of his term that negotiating peace with the guerrillas would be his first priority, and the key to achieving other goals – whether fighting drugs, developing the economy or improving human rights.

The government and FARC opened talks on 28 October 1999, after negotiating an elaborate agenda. What the impact of US military assistance will be, if it is approved, is moot. Some argue that it will strengthen the government's hand at the negotiating table, thus increasing the likelihood of success. Others argue that it could undermine negotiations by leading to an escalation of the fighting. And the government has yet to articulate a coherent policy about how it will confront the growing right-wing paramilitary forces, which most human-rights groups believe are responsible for over 70% of the human-rights violations in the country.

The Colombian economy, for decades one of the strongest in the region, is afflicted by the worst recession in over 60 years, adding to the government's woes. GDP dropped 5% in 1999 and, at 19.1%, the country now has the highest unemployment rate in the region. The idea of peace negotiations was to strengthen and expand democracy through political reform and national reconciliation. Yet the mounting violence and economic crisis seems to be pushing that goal further away, despite the efforts to reach a negotiated settlement.

Washington's largest aid programme in Latin America was directed towards Colombia, but the other nations in the Andean region also have become a source of growing US concern. In late March 2000, Thomas Pickering, the third-highest ranking member of the Department of State, toured the area to assess the situation and to inform individual governments of Washington's concern. With the partial exception of Bolivia, each is now run by neo-populists who head nations with varying degrees of economic, social and political unrest. Although no new plans have been announced beyond the large sums to be allocated to the Colombian military, the expressions of dismay now heard in Washington, combined with Pickering's trip, indicate that this region has risen to a higher priority on the US foreign-policy agenda.

The Fading Dream

With some notable exceptions, democracy in most Latin American countries has not delivered. Instead it has become associated with corruption, crime and violence. Over the past decade, the people's hopes that democracy would enhance and improve their lives have faded. As the decade reached its close, the embrace of democracy has been weakened. In countries such as Peru and Venezuela where neo-populist leaders have emphasised equality, direct participation and good governance over the institutions of representative democracy, the people have rewarded them with strong and enduring support. These leaders have not yet tipped over to the kind of authoritarian rule that the earlier democratic movement replaced. Yet their exercise of one-man rule raises questions concerning the cost that society will pay, and what kind of democracy will be in place in the region at the end of the coming decade.

Europe

L EADERS OF THE EUROPEAN UNION could look back on 1999 with considerable satisfaction. Under the firm leadership of its new president, Romano Prodi, the Commission recovered with aplomb from the scandals that had forced the mass resignation of its office holders in March 1999. The euro, after a year in use, showed that it could help to produce price stability and to knit those countries using it closer together. There was further movement towards enlargement – with Turkey at last given the go-ahead in December to apply for membership – and the EU also moved towards the development of a European rapid-reaction force. Some individual countries did not fare quite so well, however. Germany was rocked by money scandals, which affected former Chancellor Helmut Kohl and the Christian Democratic Union. In Northern Ireland in February 2000, a brave attempt to form a power-sharing government stumbled after less than two months because of the Irish Republican Army's failure to begin disarming.

In the Balkans, too, a promising development threatens to turn sour. NATO's March–June 1999 air campaign against Yugoslavia, combined with a threat of ground action and Russian pressure on Serbian President Slobodan Milosevic, forced him to remove Serb forces from Kosovo and allowed the Allies to escort Albanian Kosovars home. They had more difficulty, however, in ensuring peace in the province as the Albanians sought revenge for the mistreatment that they had suffered. Unless the Allied nations are prepared to devote more money, more personnel (particularly more police, judges and civil servants) and more effort to creating a new structure for the province's governance, their intervention may turn out to have been in vain. In the wider Balkan area, the situation looks far more promising; key problems are at last being addressed and there is a mood of renewed optimism.

There is also a changing mood in Russia. Much of this is due to ailing former president, Boris Yeltsin's decision to resign and make way for an early election. His choice of successor was the young, forceful former KGB operator, Vladimir Putin, who swept to victory in the March 2000 election. Putin's rise from obscurity to highest office was astonishing; little is known of his views, but his determination to crush the rebels in Chechnya boosted his popularity at home. The Russian people, beset for many years by erratic leadership, crime and a plunging economy were clearly looking for a strong hand at the helm. With Putin's election and some economic

Map 2 Europe

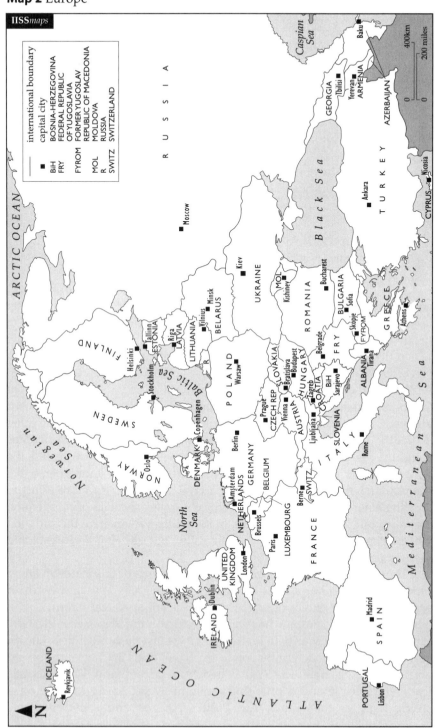

improvement, there are hopes that Russia is over the worst of its transition from Communism to free-market economics and democracy. This is also the fervent hope of the international community, for a stable Russia will help to secure a stable world.

Western Europe: Shadow and Substance

Western European politics were characterised by both scandal and success in 1999. In the EU as a whole, and in the individual member countries, achievements such as the unified action in Kosovo, improved economic indicators and progress on enlargement vied for the headlines with shadowy misdealing in the EU Commission and within major political parties of member states. When exposed to the bright glare of public scrutiny, these scandals had serious repercussions for the politicians involved, nowhere more so than in the EU's most populous state, Germany.

Country Focus: Scandal in the Federal Republic

Although Germany elected a new chancellor, Gerhard Schröder, in late 1998, moved to a new capital in Berlin in 1999, and took on the presidencies of both the EU and the Western European Union (WEU) for the first half of the year, the biggest story emerged only at the very end of 1999. Helmut Kohl, the respected elder statesman who had unified Germany during his 16 years as chancellor and 25 years as head of the Christian Democratic Union (CDU), became mired in a major party-finance scandal. He was not the only German politician to fall from grace in 1999. The Social Democratic Party (SPD) premier of the state of Lower Saxony, Gerhard Glogowski, was forced to resign after accusations that he inappropriately accepted free travel. SPD Federal President Johannes Rau stood accused of not always separating his public-office functions from those of his party and private life, and using state-owned companies as sources of funding for political activities. But the revelation of Kohl's illegal financial dealings overshadowed them all and was of far more than historical significance. It ended his party's year-long string of successes in state elections; it dashed expectations that the embattled SPD–Green coalition government would collapse and allow the CDU to rule again even before the next election; it allowed a woman and a former East German, Angela Merkel, to become the CDU's most likely future leader; and it exposed the party to mammoth fines that will endanger its solvency and its ability to fund future campaigns.

The scandal began in autumn 1999, when attorneys in Augsburg uncovered records hinting that the CDU had failed to declare significant donations. These were consequently illegal; according to German party-finance regulations, names of donors of more than DM20,000 have to be made available. Large amounts were involved: there was evidence of six-figure sums in Deutschmarks changing hands (sometimes in cash bundles carried in suitcases to one-to-one meetings). Indeed, a hastily arranged audit of the CDU's financial records for 1989–98 by accountants Ernst & Young, published on 20 January 2000, showed that nearly $6 million was not accounted for.

Considerable evidence suggested that Kohl was aware of the undeclared donations. Mere weeks after what amounted to a triumphant victory tour on 9 November 1999, to celebrate the tenth anniversary of the fall of the Berlin Wall, the former chancellor issued a terse statement to his party conceding that he had known about some illegal gifts. This provoked more bloodletting rather than stanching the flow. Critics noted that he only admitted to accepting about $1m of the questionable donations over the previous six years, though he had been party leader for over four times as long. The time frame was significant because German law does not require records to be kept for more than six years.

Kohl worsened the damage by refusing to identify the donors. He thereby exposed his party to endless speculation as commentators tried to guess whom they might have been, and what they had received in exchange. Kohl maintained that the donations had neither lined his own pockets nor influenced his political decisions, and he claimed that the funds had been distributed within the CDU. This claim also backfired because it immediately implicated nearly every senior party member during his leadership as a potential recipient of dubious funding. The former interior minister, Manfred Kanther, admitted to salting away more than DM30m in foreign accounts over 20 years. Prince Casimir Sayn-Wittgenstein, CDU party treasurer in the state of Hesse over the period 1976–98 tried, in a particularly bizarre move, to dismiss unaccounted sums as donations from Jews, a claim that was soon retracted.

As a result, the party lost the momentum it had gained through a series of election victories: in Hesse on 7 February 1999; in Brandenburg and the Saarland on 5 September; and in Thuringia and in local elections in North Rhine–Westphalia on 12 September. These victories had eliminated the SPD's majority in the *Bundesrat*, and the CDU appeared to be on an unstoppable roll to resuming national power. But the combination of the scandal and the unwillingness of the party and its leaders to reveal the truth torpedoed the CDU in opinion polls. The party leader, Wolfgang Schäuble, formerly one of Kohl's closest associates and one of the most admired politicians in the country, grudgingly conceded that his office had also received a bundle of cash, reportedly totalling $50,000, that was not subsequently declared. He resigned in the wake of the 15 February 2000 announcement that the CDU would have to pay roughly $21m in just the first of several fines. This was the highest penalty ever levied against a political party in Germany. Meanwhile the former defence minister, Volker Rühe, lost an election in Schleswig-Holstein on 27 February 2000 that he had been expected to win easily, and decided not to stand as a candidate to replace Schäuble. At the end of March 2000, it appeared fairly certain that Merkel would become the CDU's next leader.

The scandal was not without its beneficiaries. It could not have come at a better time for Schröder and the ruling SPD–Green coalition. The first year in power had been very difficult for 'red/green' politicians, whose electoral victory in September 1998 had surprised even them. The chancellor had at first blundered from one gaffe to another. For example, he allowed himself to be photographed for a fashion magazine wearing luxurious Italian suits as he simultaneously told his country to tighten its belt. Even worse than these errors of style was the sense that his government had little coherent vision. Comparisons with UK Prime Minister Tony Blair were misleading; unlike Blair, Schröder had failed either to modernise his party or to unite it firmly behind him before becoming chancellor.

Europe

Where the EU was concerned, Schröder achieved little with his bluster about Germany's need to pay less into EU funds and receive more. As a net contributor of $12.3 billion, five times more than any other country's contribution, Germany had hoped to reform EU farm policy and reduce regional spending, but it made little headway against French resistance. Schröder had to settle for a modest package of EU farm reforms at the 3–4 June 1999 Cologne summit. His loyalty to NATO in the Kosovo campaign, and his willingness to involve German forces in combat abroad for the first time since 1945 earned him, along with Defence Minister Rudolf Scharping and Foreign Minister Joschka Fischer, gratitude from their allies; but it caused friction with the left-wing elements of their respective parties.

Schröder did achieve some success in 1999. The powerful and ambitious finance minister, Oskar Lafontaine, resigned on 11 March 1999, after repeated disagreements with the chancellor over how to modernise Germany's economy. Schröder wisely used Lafontaine's departure to consolidate his control over the SPD. He took over as party leader and received an unexpected degree of support at the party congress in Berlin on 6–10 December. With the competent help of Lafontaine's replacement, Hans Eichel, Schröder introduced a long-overdue plan to curb spending. Given that debt servicing had become the biggest item in the budget after labour and social affairs, and that the national debt had risen to approximately 60% of Germany's gross domestic product (GDP), it was clear that some kind of austerity plan was needed. Eichel called for a

DM30bn reduction in planned government spending in the coming year. This faced ongoing opposition, not least from cabinet members whose competencies would be affected, but it was a step in the right direction, and received parliamentary approval on 27 November.

Which of Schröder's tendencies, reformer or compromiser, will dominate in the future remains to be seen. Germany, whose hourly labour costs are among the highest in the world, must modernise and deregulate its economy. However, a modest fall in unemployment at the end of 1999, coupled with the prospect of elections in North Rhine–Westphalia in May 2000, may diminish the government's enthusiasm for painful measures. At the end of 1999, it was easier to rejoice in the news that unemployment was down to 10.5%, and that year-on-year GDP growth reached 1.2% in the third quarter, than to focus on the work yet to be done.

Scandal Too in France

Like Germany, France received welcome economic news at the end of a year marred by corruption scandals. Indeed, the two issues were linked in the fate of Finance Minister Dominique Strauss-Kahn. On 2 November 1999, he unexpectedly resigned in the face of allegations that he had created false invoices to conceal payments he had improperly received in the mid-1990s. Ironically, Strauss-Kahn resigned just as he was receiving public accolades for his performance. An urbane and multilingual figure, he was credited with promoting cohesion within Prime Minister Lionel Jospin's coalition government, which brought together Socialists with Greens and Communists. Strauss-Kahn seemed to have the ability to convince the ruling leftists of the need to privatise state-owned firms and cut taxes, while simultaneously reconciling the business world to the left-of-centre government. Whether through luck or through his doing, France's economic indicators picked up noticeably while Strauss-Kahn was in charge, although growth was not as strong as in Portugal, Finland, Ireland, and Spain. By mid-year 1999, France's GDP was 2.1% higher than a year earlier. Consumer spending remained strong and industrial output was rising throughout 1999. Forecasts for 2000 predicted growth above 3%, with no prospect of serious inflation.

The heartening economic news provided distraction from the fate of French politicians either on trial or under investigation in 1999. The head of the Constitutional Court and former foreign minister, Roland Dumas was forced to take leave from his job after accusations that he had accepted massive bribes from the former state oil company Elf. The same company was accused of making illegal donations to the CDU in Germany, causing speculation about the extent of corruption under former president, François Mitterrand: to what extent had he 'funded' Kohl via the state oil company? Both Alain Juppé, the former prime minister, and Jean Tiberi, the mayor of Paris, were also under investigation. And former prime minister, Laurent Fabius, his social affairs minister, Georgina Dufoix and health minister, Edmond Hervé were charged with manslaughter and criminal negligence as part of a long-running scandal about HIV-contaminated blood. On 9 March 1999, Fabius and Dufoix were acquitted, and Hervé convicted, but not sentenced. Critics claimed the proceedings were biased and did not allow fair representation for victims. Finally, a best-selling book called attention to the deficiencies of the French justice system as a whole. A first-hand account by Dr Véronique Vasseur, former chief doctor at the Paris La Santé Prison, forced Justice Minister Elisabeth Guigou to admit that France's penitentiary system was sorely lacking. Conditions were often inhumane, with prisoners suffering from diseases caused by the lack of bathing facilities, high temperatures, and bedding full of lice and insects. The European Court of Human Rights criticised France for holding an estimated two-fifths to one-half of its prisoners without conviction, which was in turn a condemnation of investigating magistrates' ability to jail suspects indefinitely without trial. Such accusations undermined attempts by the French and the EU to promote human rights in would-be EU members such as Turkey. Yet, efforts to reform the administration of justice stalled when President Jacques Chirac delayed a parliamentary congress, scheduled for 24 January 2000, which was to have discussed a constitutional amendment. The issue remains one of the most pressing facing France's closely knit political élites.

As discouraging as this litany of scandal may seem, it also reflects a welcome vitality among investigating magistrates and attorneys. Corruption among EU member-state politicians was hardly new in 1999, but efforts to tackle it showed a new fervour. The same was true within the EU's own administration.

The European Union Doubts Its Own Commission

The EU showed unexpected alacrity in pursuing questions of corruption and fraud in 1999. The entire European Commission, along with its president, Jacques Santer, had to step down on 16 March 1999. The resignation followed the publication on the previous day of a 144-page report by an independent panel, which had been appointed by the European Parliament to look into accusations of 'sweetheart deals' with subcontractors, kickbacks, nepotism, and other forms of corruption. The report was devastating. In addition to details of widespread fraud and nepotism, it condemned the commissioners as a group for acting as if they were not accountable to anyone or anything. Criticism of the former French prime minister, Edith Cresson, was especially intense. In general, the report concluded, it was difficult to find anyone on the Commission 'who has even the slightest sense of responsibility'.

The report and the resignations clearly required swift damage control, and the EU's national leaders proved equal to the task. The 15 heads of government at the 24 March 1999 summit meeting in Berlin, unanimously agreed to invite the former Italian prime minister, Romano Prodi, to take over. The appointment of Prodi, who was renowned for streamlining Italian public finances in the past, ended the sense of crisis. He took over almost immediately, although he was not formally appointed president until 17 September 1999. Unfortunately, beyond choosing Prodi, little else of substance was achieved. The heads of government could not agree on other necessary reforms, whether they concerned agriculture or the running of the Commission. Nonetheless, they had at least solved the most pressing crisis facing the union.

Prodi's new commissioners included Neil Kinnock, one of four survivors from the previous administration, as vice-president in charge of reform. Kinnock hoped both to make the Commission more accountable, and to prepare it for the challenge of taking in around 13 new members in the coming decade. On 19 January 2000, Kinnock published a white paper on reforms. He called for:

- a thorough-going overhaul of the Commission's financial management;

- the creation of an independent auditing unit;

- the opening of a new disciplinary board with its own legal staff; and

- the establishment of an ethics committee.

The Commission declared on 9 February 2000 that decentralisation was one of its main long-term goals, and promised to yield some of its executive powers to EU governments. Coming on top of the progress made at the December 1999 Helsinki summit in increasing juridical cooperation and law enforcement within the Union, these measures conveyed a sense of renewed vigour.

Such a sense was more necessary than ever, because the 1997 Amsterdam Treaty came into force on 1 May 1999. Under its terms, Prodi enjoyed a much stronger position than his predecessors in dealing with member states over selecting and keeping commissioners. He could veto nominees he deemed inappropriate, and demote poor performers. However, he seemed unlikely to exercise either provision since the Commission he took over was generally better than its predecessor. Other key members included Pascal Lamy of France, in charge of EU trade policy; Günther Verhügen of Germany, overseeing enlargement; Poul Nielson of Denmark, focusing on development; and Chris Patten of the UK, as the point-man on external affairs. It briefly seemed that Patten might emerge as a 'commissioner in chief', effectively taking charge of formulating a common foreign and security policy. But it proved impossible to get other commissioners to agree to such a 'promotion'. Moreover, the announcement that Lord Robertson would be willing to serve as the next Secretary-General of NATO cleared the way for the incumbent, Javier Solana, to accept a post as 'high representative' for the EU in matters of foreign and security policy. The division of labour between Patten and Solana was not entirely clear, and Solana's portfolio soon proved to be a rival to Patten's. In practice, Solana, who reports not to the Commission but to the Council of Ministers, has focused on high-profile foreign-policy strategy and on enlargement, while Patten has devoted his attention to the EU's foreign-aid budget, estimated at $6bn a year.

The EU's Intractable Problem: Illegal Immigration

The need for an unexpected and speedy change in leadership after the Commission scandal distracted attention in spring and summer 1999 from substantive issues confronting the Union. These included the intractable problem of illegal emigration. *The Economist* magazine has estimated that, by late 1999, smuggling human beings into the EU had become a lucrative $3–4bn-a-year business, with some 400,000–500,000 illegal entrants annually. This placed a strain on the resources of the countries most heavily involved – mainly those bordering on Eastern Europe or with a coastline easily accessible from North Africa – and their electorates' concerns about immigration were reflected at the ballot box.

Anger manifested itself most notably in the success of Jörg Haider's Freedom Party in Austria. Haider's group took second place in national elections on 3 October 1999, after shrewdly capitalising not only on immigration but also on anti-incumbency issues. The latter proved to have enormous appeal in a country where the socialists, for example, had been in government for 30 years. When the centre-left Social Democrats and the centre-right People's Party failed to cobble together yet another coalition, the People's Party decided to take the previously unthinkable step of forming a government with the Freedom Party. By 3 February 2000, it was clear that Haider's party would become part of the new ruling coalition. Haider himself did not seek a position in the government, but it was widely assumed that he would be pulling the strings.

Remarks that Haider had made in the past that could be interpreted as pro-Nazi had awakened strong feelings both in Austria and abroad. Riots accompanied the formal ceremonies over the next few days, as Austrian President Thomas Klestil installed the new coalition in power. Police had to use tear-gas and water-cannons on crowds in Vienna. World reaction was also swift and negative. Austria's fellow members of the EU had, in an unprecedented move on 31 January, announced their intention to isolate Austria diplomatically within the Union, which they hoped would prevent the coalition's formation. The EU had never previously called a free election into question in this way. When the attempted deterrence failed, the 14 member-countries recalled their ambassadors, as did the US and Israel.

A Weak Euro: Cause for Concern?

Another issue exercising media commentators in 1999 was the declining value of the euro against the US dollar. Following its launch on 1 January 1999, it dropped steadily from its initial level of $1.17. At the turn of the year, it was fluctuating around parity. While no regulation required the euro to be supported above parity, this was nonetheless a psychologically significant barrier whose breach was painful, particularly for Germans, who had for many years been used to the D-Mark appreciating against the US currency.

However, the devaluation against the dollar belied the strengths of the Eurozone. As the euro fell, European exports became more competitive elsewhere. A year after the new currency's launch, inflation was not a significant threat in Western Europe, and commercial bond markets were thriving. Both France and Germany showed welcome signs of economic health, with unemployment declining and growth expected (France, in particular, hoped for a 3.5% rise in 2000). European Central Bank (ECB) chief, Wim Duisberg argued that his mission was to ensure stable prices within the Eurozone. He believed that this goal was being achieved, and there was therefore little need for a substantial rise in interest rates. However, the ECB did raise rates by a marginal 0.25% to 3.25% on 3 February 2000. By the end of its first year, the euro was a qualified success. However, by then the conflict had become apparent between, on the one hand, maintaining the new currency's strength relative to the dollar (to reassure the Germans) and, on the other hand, freeing Europe from the tight-money constraints required to maintain exchange-rate values around an overly strong D-Mark.

Edging towards Enlargement

The euro's weakness in relation to the dollar had no impact upon the EU's attractions to would-be members. Even as Britain continued to doubt the merits of adopting the new currency, several East European applicant-states were so eager to join the Union that they toyed with schemes to adopt the euro while still outside. Estonia had already worked out a method: it had tied its currency to the D-Mark in 1992, and was thereby voluntarily subjecting itself to ECB control.

Another eager applicant for EU membership received good news from the 10–11 December 1999 Helsinki summit. At the beginning of the year, it had seemed that the EU's relations with Turkey had hit an all-time low. Turkey was upset about the second-class status given to its application; about the EU's willingness to consider negotiations with the Republic of Cyprus; and about the way Italy had handled Turkish requests to extradite the Kurdish leader Abdullah Öcalan. (When he was finally arrested and returned to Turkey, Öcalan was sentenced to death on 29 June 1999.) Then nature intervened. A devastating earthquake shook Turkey on 17 August, killing an estimated 14,000. Just a few weeks later, on 7 September, a smaller, but nonetheless powerful, tremor rocked Athens, causing 120 fatalities. In the face of the common suffering, Turkey and Greece put aside their differences to aid each other in locating victims, nursing the wounded and repairing damage, and, in a way that no one could have expected, they showed new willingness to cooperate in the last quarter of 1999. Turkish Prime Minister Bülent Ecevit made a significant concession to West European disapproval of Öcalan's death sentence, saying that Turkey would suspend it until his appeal was heard by the European Court of Human Rights. Meanwhile, Greece indicated its willingness to lift its veto on EU aid to Turkey and indeed its veto on Turkey's membership of the EU, under certain conditions (see pp. 144–46). As a result, at the Helsinki summit, the EU was able to reach agreement on the ticklish issue of Turkey's candidature.

Despite the improved political climate, the EU decision to 'promote' Turkey was still not an easy one (and what was perceived as heavy-handed US pressure for this development did not make matters simpler). At Greece's insistence, EU members decided to emphasise admittance terms which at first made Turkey uneasy. They called on the Turkish government, once again, to abolish the death penalty and to make sweeping political and economic reforms. They also made clear that Turkey would have to settle its Aegean Sea territorial dispute with Greece, a condition which particularly rankled with the Turkish leadership. Only after Solana personally flew to Istanbul during the summit to persuade Ecevit, did he declare himself willing to accept the EU's offer.

Moreover, while this move undeniably represented progress, it did not mean that Turkey, or any other applicant, could join the EU quickly. The biggest entry hurdle is the need to conform to the *acquis communitaire*, the EU's vast catalogue of laws. There are also internal hurdles. Before enlargement, the EU clearly needs to adapt its own institutions so that they can still function effectively with more than a dozen additional members. On 14 February 2000, the EU opened its inter-governmental conference (IGC), to discuss the issues. The two main questions the IGC faced were:

- whether to expand the role of majority voting (to avoid the deadlocks that might arise in an expanded EU through the need for unanimous decisions); and

- how to allocate power between larger and smaller states, in terms of either the number of commissioners per country, or the weight of votes in the Council of Ministers, or both.

The IGC is expected to consider these questions for the next 16 months. So, for yet another year, the EU's enlargement policy remained a mixture of real progress and vague promise.

Steps Towards a Security Identity?

The tension between real progress and vague promise also manifested itself in the ongoing debates over how best to develop the European Security and Defence Identity (ESDI). It was in this regard that the military action in Kosovo had its greatest impact on West European politics in 1999. The deficiencies in European defence capability were sadly exposed by the fighting; Lord Robertson went so far as to say that the Kosovo action had shown Europe to be a 'paper tiger.' The EU could not contradict the comment by US Secretary of Defense William Cohen that, although its combined defence spending approached 60% of that of the US, Kosovo showed that Europe could only deploy forces equal to approximately 10% of what the US could manage.

Moreover, European NATO members' forces were largely still geared towards territorial defence against an attack from the Soviet bloc, rather than towards rapid deployment to crisis regions. Although European countries sent only 2% of their combined armed forces to the Balkans, they did so slowly and with great difficulty. Military transport and other forms of deployment technologies were in extremely short supply. Several countries had no secure radio networks and had to use open airwaves that were monitored by the Serbs. Effective surveillance and intelligence gathering by the Europeans was negligible compared with American efforts; none of the French satellites, for example, could penetrate clouds, and their technology proved of little use during the Kosovo crisis. The second-generation French *Helios* II optic observation satellite now under development may address many of these difficulties.

Kosovo not only highlighted the inadequacies of the Europeans' fighting forces, it also generated a great deal of European irritation at American high-handedness. Criticism focused on US unwillingness to share information or to let European governments take part in decision-making.

This combination of sentiments – desire to follow-up on the December 1998 St Malo agreement, calling for increased European cooperation on security matters; painful awareness of EU defence deficiencies; and irritation with the US – served as a powerful impetus for the debate over how to give substance to ESDI. NATO acknowledged such a trend at its fiftieth anniversary summit in Washington on 24–26 April 1999. There, the Alliance announced that its overall goal would be to preserve peace and to reinforce security 'throughout the Euro-Atlantic region'. Europe could develop its own security 'identity' (Solana also used the term 'personality'), as long as the interests of non-EU members of NATO (read Turkey) were respected. Both the US and its European allies agreed to a 'defence capability initiative' (DCI), that required European nations to close the US–Europe technology gap in defence capability.

Shortly after the NATO meeting, the WEU voted for a gradual merger with the EU. Many questions remained open, not least what to do about the mismatch between WEU and EU membership, but at least the direction became clear. And new NATO Secretary-General Lord Robertson was one of the initiators of the St Malo agreement. Most importantly, at the Helsinki summit, the EU announced that it would develop its own rapid-reaction force. If the goals laid out in Helsinki are fulfilled, by the year 2003 the force will be able to field 50,000–60,000 troops, able to deploy within 60 days and sustainable in theatre for at least one year. It will initially report to an interim committee then to a standing political and security committee, and will be outfitted with self-sustaining command, control, and intelligence capabilities. Combat-support services and other logistical supports are also scheduled for development.

Such a force may be able to buy its new requirements in Europe: on 14 October, the head of Daimler Chrysler, Jürgen Schrempp, announced that the company's aerospace arm, DASA, would be merging with France's Lagardère Matra to form the European Aeronautic, Defence and Space Company (EADS). The new combine will become the third-largest defence firm in the world, after Boeing and Lockheed Martin. The merger caused much chagrin in the UK, since earlier talks between the Germans and British Aerospace had broken down.

However, if Europe is to upgrade its transport, surveillance, and other capabilities, it will need to increase spending on defence, research and development, and procurement. Whether it is willing to do so remained an open question during 1999. Many EU member-states, most notably Germany, were planning to cut defence spending in 1999. Cohen sharply criticised the planned German cuts on 1 December in a speech to top Bundeswehr leaders in Hamburg, pointing out the contradiction between budget-cutting and developing a greater security identity. At the end of 1999, Germany was spending a mere 1.5% of GDP on defence, only half the amount of a decade earlier. In this regard, it lagged behind other major European countries: the comparable figure was 2.6% in the UK and 2.8% in France, while in the US it was 3.2%. Schröder and Eichel proposed a defence budget for 2000 which was $1bn less than the DM47bn ($23.5bn) of 1999, and cuts of roughly the same order are planned in each of the following three years.

Another issue that was still unresolved in early March 2000 was the nature of the relationship between the European rapid-reaction force and NATO. On the one hand, such a force is a potential source of tension. It might inspire European leaders to act without seeking consensus in the Alliance. The question of whether there would be consultation between the allies before the force's deployment remained open. On the other hand, the vision outlined at Helsinki could help NATO if translated into more effective defence output. A more efficient, coordinated and deployable European force might be able to check crises before they became large enough to require full NATO involvement.

European leaders – Robertson among them – complained of an annoying American ambivalence about the proposed force. While the US made clear that it wanted its allies to spend more on their own defence, European leaders sensed US reluctance to yield the authority to take initiatives in security matters to the Europeans. There was further grumbling about the assumption, which some American leaders expressed privately, that the Europeans would never be able agree on how to finance the force anyway. For their part, European leaders viewed with scepticism Washington's proposals to develop a limited missile-defence system designed to protect the US against 'rogue states'.

Sorting out EU–NATO relations are an essential precondition for ensuring that moves towards improved European defence do not harm the transatlantic link. So long as ESDI genuinely improves European defence capacity, the greater 'Europeanness' in European defence may be tolerable to the US. But such improvements depend on some countries increasing their defence expenditure and none reducing it. This remains a huge challenge in peacetime when electorates prefer otherwise. More generally, the EU will have to learn to deal with defence and security issues: questions quite foreign to an organisation with legislative and regulatory powers and instincts, but little reputation in the defence and security areas.

Challenge 2000

The debate over security was emblematic of the year in Europe as a whole: it represented a combination of substance and shadow. Real progress, in the form of the agreement to develop a rapid-reaction force, highlighted just how vague some key aspects were.What would that force's relationship to NATO be? Would it deploy outside Europe? Meanwhile, in the individual states, shadowy dealings vied with substantial accomplishments. Former prime ministers and party leaders, often Cold War heroes, proved to have acted less than heroically when out of the spotlight. To what extent did their more dubious activities invalidate their accomplishments in achieving European unification? Was the corruption that became evident in 1999 a source for concern, or for satisfaction that it was coming to light and to trial?

Answers to these questions were not immediately apparent in early 2000. Despite the lingering issues, however, Western Europe could still look back on numerous successes in 1999. With the swift appointment of Prodi, the EU overcame the crisis of the Commission's resignation in less time than anyone had thought possible. Prodi proved to be a capable leader and, under his leadership, the Commission made progress on a range of necessary internal reforms. The euro helped to deliver price stability in its first year. There was undeniable movement towards EU enlargement, as Greece and Turkey began a process of *rapprochement*. The Helsinki summit heralded the establishment of a European rapid-reaction force. These successes will help the EU to meet the main challenge facing it now: creating stability in all of Europe, not just those countries flying the blue-and-gold flags of the Union.

Europe

Serbia Loses Another One

The war over Kosovo was inevitable from the moment Western governments decided that they would not tolerate another bout of slowly but steadily worsening violence as took place in Croatia or Bosnia-Herzegovina. All the many attempts to find a solution ultimately failed; the reality is that chances of a peaceful solution evaporated in the late 1980s. There were then moderate Kosovo Albanian leaders who were ready to settle for various compromises; and there were also some moderate leaders in Belgrade. But Serbian President Slobodan Milosevic's intransigence ultimately eliminated the former and marginalised the latter. Milosevic was fully aware that the province's growing radicalisation would result in violence; he simply assumed that he would triumph in this confrontation.

The air attacks that were unleashed on Serbia between March and June 1999 followed a full year of Western warnings to Belgrade and two previous 'peace agreements', both broken by Milosevic. In retrospect, it is clear that the February 1999 Rambouillet peace conference, led by Britain and France, had no chance of success. Both Milosevic and the Kosovo Albanian leaders, like all the people of the Balkans, merely played with the concept of autonomy, which formed the backbone of the Rambouillet peace proposals; both sides knew that the various forms of self-administration advocated for Kosovo were unlikely to succeed. Autonomous units will only work in countries which respect law and order, and where the minority and the majority populations still feel they share some common ground; neither of these ingredients were present in the Kosovo dispute.

In a curious way, therefore, the protagonists at the peace conference agreed on the crucial point: both sides knew that the autonomy plan on the table could only be a prelude to full independence. The Kosovo Albanians were ultimately persuaded to accept the proposals, partly because they had most to lose from any dispute with Western governments, and partly because US Secretary of State Madeleine Albright promised them a referendum on the ultimate disposition of their territory: a pledge tantamount to accepting their independence claim.

By the time Milosevic agreed to send his delegation to Rambouillet, he already believed, according to various Yugoslav sources, that he faced a choice between just two unpalatable alternatives: either to lose the province peacefully as part of a negotiated settlement, or to risk losing it through violence. Predictably, he chose the latter, because:

- he was not sure that refusal to accept a deal would result in Western military action;

- he was not persuaded that any military action that were to be unleashed on him would be either successful or sustainable;

- he assumed that, even if he faced attack from NATO, he held the initiative and would be able to stop the fighting by offering a deal; and

- he believed that, in the worst case, the province could be split, with Yugoslavia still maintaining at least part of Kosovo.

Since loss of life never bothered Milosevic, the risk seemed worth taking. No amount of good treatment by the West at Rambouillet and no amount of paper concessions would have changed this equation. Western governments also had very few choices. They could have swallowed another diluted deal of the kind Richard Holbrooke, the US regional envoy, negotiated during autumn 1998, and see it broken soon after-wards. That was the strategy pursued in previous Yugoslav conflicts. This time, European governments – particularly in the UK – regarded the option with horror. The experience in Croatia and Bosnia was of humiliation followed by precisely the military involvement which Western governments desperately wished to avoid. If history were repeating itself – and all of the indications during 1998 pointed to this – then it was better to face facts squarely and early, by precipitating events, rather than merely reacting to a Milosevic-dictated agenda, as Western governments have done since Yugoslavia started disintegrating in 1991.

So Violence It Was

There was nothing about the situation in Kosovo during March 1999 that dictated urgent military action against Milosevic. It could still be argued that the observers from the Organisation for Security and Cooperation in Europe – introduced into the province as part of the Holbrooke deal in November–December 1998 – should be given more time to calm local feelings. It was also clear that elements within the Kosovo Liberation Army (KLA) were just as responsible as the Yugoslav military for the repeated cease-fire violations during February 1999. But where Western governments were concerned, this was only part of the story.

A military operation against Milosevic was planned during summer 1998, but at that time the US administration preferred to wait. Waiting again after the Rambouillet talks broke down would have discredited the entire threat. More importantly, the situation appeared to be a classic repeat of the Bosnian débâcle: the formation of Serb militias to perpetrate crimes without directly implicating Belgrade, countered by the creation of Albanian terrorist organisations, seeking to provoke the Yugoslav military and draw Western governments into the conflict. All the tricks already so familiar from previous Balkan wars – cease-fires broken within hours of their signature; theological disputes about the appropriate powers for international observers; periodic massacres and unprovable allegations of even greater atrocities – were already evident in Kosovo.

However, NATO's argument that it had to act in order to avert an urgent humanitarian disaster was specious in March 1999; the Alliance chose to act then because it considered that postponing action carried greater risks, particularly to its own members. This argument was formulated for use in the quite different debate over NATO's decision to use force without further or specific reference to the UN Security Council. Concerns raised by senior legal advisers about the operation's legality were swept aside by politicians claiming justification on the basis of humanitarianism and urgency.

A subsidiary argument – advanced by UK Prime Minister Tony Blair in the early stages of the war – was that intervention was necessary to prevent the violence in Kosovo spreading to the entire region, ultimately embroiling Greece and Turkey. But there was no chance of a war between Greece and Turkey over Kosovo, nor was there much chance that the conflict in Kosovo – at least at first – would have destroyed Macedonia. Indeed, in many respects, the threat to Macedonia's internal stability increased after the NATO operation. And nobody bothered to explain how an impending humanitarian disaster could be averted by dropping bombs – even smart ones – from 10,000 metres. Kosovo was a war of choice in March 1999, agreed upon in order to avoid a war on Milosevic's terms at a later stage.

It was also a badly prepared operation, which achieved its immediate objectives as much by luck as by design. It is not known whether military planners recommended competing alternatives in the weeks before the air campaign. What is certain is that the NATO governments initially envisaged a relatively limited operation, lasting no more than a few days before Milosevic sued for peace. This assessment was faulty from the start, and evidence available at the time should have made this obvious.

The idea that Milosevic was either bluffing or that he was not prepared for a confrontation lasting more than a few days was based on experience in Bosnia, where NATO air-strikes in autumn 1995 brought hostilities to a swift end with the Dayton Peace Accords. But the comparison was invalid. By the time NATO acted in Bosnia, Yugoslav troops were already facing defeat at the hands of rearmed Croats and Bosnian Muslims. NATO also maintained the fiction that it was striking only at Serb paramilitary formations in Bosnia; Milosevic was considered a potential ally in finding a solution to the conflict. The air-strikes actually helped Milosevic in 1995, for they allowed him to persuade the Bosnian Serb leaders to settle on terms acceptable to Belgrade.

None of these ingredients was present in Kosovo in March 1999. Milosevic still believed that he could retain his control over the province, and he knew that his survival in power was at stake. It was therefore obvious all along that the Yugoslav leader was planning a long period of attrition, accompanied by spurious peace efforts and attempts to shatter Alliance solidarity. His strategy was to hold on to the province as long as was necessary for NATO's resolve to crumble, or for a 'peace deal' to be negotiated. For his soldiers in Kosovo, this required little more than hiding, often in abandoned Albanian villages.

The Violent Phase

By opting for a limited air campaign, and by explicitly and publicly ruling out the use of ground troops from the outset, NATO reassured Milosevic that it would fight the kind of confrontation that every Yugoslav officer has planned for since 1948. The entire Yugoslav military strategy was built on wearing down an enemy which was otherwise too powerful to be defeated. The strategy involved a large element of deception, but also a long period of resistance. Many of the tanks, whose destruction was announced with such regularity at NATO's daily press briefings, turned out to have been made of cardboard; a great deal of Belgrade's military equipment was cleverly camouflaged, using skills in which every Yugoslav soldier is well versed. The Yugoslav state and military undoubtedly sustained serious damage, but the morale of Milosevic's troops was not broken as NATO had hoped. The Yugoslav high command was capable of carrying out a speedy, complete and orderly withdrawal from the province at the end of the war, without losing either equipment or soldiers.

It required no fewer than 78 days of bombardment before NATO, the most powerful military alliance in the world, could subdue – but still not defeat – an otherwise ramshackle, small and impoverished Balkan state, which had already suffered a decade of wars and economic sanctions. It was not, by any standards, a victory to be trumpeted in historical annals.

In one respect, however, NATO's underestimation of the task ahead turned out to be fortuitous. If the UK and US governments – the most 'hawkish' in the Alliance – had said from the start that the operation would require months of air-bombardment, possibly followed by an opposed ground offensive, NATO would have been unlikely to have achieved the necessary unity to carry the operation out. The German, Italian and Greek governments, among other Alliance countries harbouring doubts about NATO's tactics, would have objected to the entire project. Once it had started, however, the campaign could not be abandoned without massive humiliation and the risk that NATO itself could disintegrate.

The Alliance was also helped by Milosevic's appalling behaviour. The planning of the air offensive should have taken account of the possibility that it would result, at least initially, in worsening conditions for the ethnic Albanians. Nobody seriously believed that merely dropping bombs would stop massacres on the ground. There is evidence of Alliance planning to airlift food to the province, though these plans were ultimately shelved, but there is no sign that the ethnic Albanians' enforced exodus was anticipated.

It is clear that, even when the flight began, its implications were not thought through. The impact of hundreds of thousands of refugees on Macedonia's security was ignored for too long; discussions about dispersing the refugees temporarily to other European countries started a week after the situation in Macedonia was already intolerable. Alliance officials have subsequently suggested that they were unable to make public preparations for the exodus, as to do so would have been tantamount to encouraging Milosevic to precipitate it. This assertion carries all the hallmarks of a *post facto* justification, intended to explain why an entirely predictable event caught Western governments by surprise.

However, the waves of refugees subsequently became NATO's main justification for the air war. There was something comic about this: in effect, NATO argued that it was duty-bound to fight in order to reverse something which the Alliance had unintentionally added to. But the argument is not as foolish as it may seem, and Western governments may have justice on their side. Clearly, Milosevic was hoping to sow divisions in NATO by starting a humanitarian disaster. Yet it is outrageous to suggest – as some commentators have – that the Alliance was 'responsible'

Europe

for the mass expulsion. NATO's air-strikes merely accelerated a policy which Milosevic had planned all along, and began before the bombings. The successful return of the refugees is, without question, NATO's biggest victory.

How it Ended

What brought the victory? Air power caused a great deal of damage, but Alliance officials now admit that over two months of bombardment were not enough to make an opposed ground offensive feasible. NATO commanders calculated that this would take at least another two months. For those who still believe that Kosovo was the first example of the triumph of air-power, these are sobering facts.

The Yugoslav ruler ultimately backed down because he realised that the air campaign, although not particularly successful, was an action upon which all NATO agreed. Alliance governments remained divided over ground options, but the air campaign proved miraculously cheap in terms of Western life, and Western public opinion was surprisingly indifferent to the 'collateral-damage' mistakes. Theoretically, therefore, the bombardment could have continued indefinitely; it had done less damage than Milosevic had feared, but it could have lasted much longer than he originally calculated.

Much more important from Milosevic's perspective was the realisation that NATO was gearing up for an eventual land offensive. The steps were initially hesitant, and the confusion in many Western capitals – particularly in Washington – was often great. However, Western governments were being impelled towards this option by frustration with the war's indefinite duration, and the view that the risks of a ground offensive were less serious than those that would arise from NATO's discredit if it failed to prevail. Milosevic knew that he could inflict some damage on incoming ground troops, but he also knew that eventually Serbia would suffer more seriously from the invasion than from losing Kosovo.

The final ingredient in Milosevic's decision to give in was Russia's changed priorities. Belgrade's hopes of Moscow's help were always misplaced: the Kremlin was infuriated by NATO's behaviour, but, short of confrontation with the West, there was little it could do. The Alliance knew before the air campaign started that the Russians would object; member states nevertheless decided to start the war because they calculated that Russian objections, however strident, ultimately did not matter. And so it proved.

The moment the Kremlin understood that NATO's air campaign would continue and that a ground offensive would eventually be launched, it moved to broker a settlement in the hope of preserving at least some Russian influence in the Balkans. In summary, therefore, Milosevic was persuaded he had to accept Western terms by a combination of diplomatic moves that isolated his regime, and the threat of a ground offensive. The air campaign by itself did not win the war; its use in combination with preparations for a ground offensive and clever diplomatic work achieved this feat.

The Non-Peace

When the Kosovo war ended on 11 June 1999, NATO's triumph appeared complete. Not only was Yugoslavia obliged to withdraw its entire presence from the province, including all military equipment and the civilian administration, but the United Nations resolution governing international operations in Kosovo allowed the Alliance to do as it pleased. The Security Council framed the resolution under Chapter VII of the UN Charter, permitting 'enforcement measures' against any party to the conflict that refused to apply the peace accord.

Theoretically, therefore, NATO could resume hostilities against Milosevic without any further reference to the UN, and it could use force against threats within Kosovo. Unlike any previous military operation in the former Yugoslavia over the past decade, the Alliance was not shackled by any legal restrictions: no sophisticated (or frustrating) interpretations of 'peacekeeping' or 'peacemaking' applied. Furthermore, unlike the 1995 peace deal in respect of Bosnia, no milestones have to be passed on the way to administering Kosovo. The UN has not decreed a timetable for elections, and has given no direction on the civilian institutions that may be established in Kosovo. Apart from the promise that the province's 'future disposition' will be subject to negotiations with Belgrade, every other matter has been left vague.

This ambiguity was deliberate. The European members of the Alliance prevailed upon the US in their determination to avoid the mistakes made in Bosnia. There, hasty elections resulted in the triumph of extremist nationalist politicians, and a highly prescriptive allocation of responsibilities between numerous institutions – from NATO to the World Bank, the International Monetary Fund and the UN High Commissioner for Refugees (UNHCR) – created havoc with the republic's administration. NATO vowed that this time it would be the supreme arbiter of events: the only body to allocate responsibilities, on the basis of needs rather than political calculations, and according to its own leisurely timetable.

The initial military deployment, starting on 12 June 1999, was a huge operational success: 22,000 NATO soldiers with heavy equipment poured into Kosovo – the biggest war-time deployment in Europe since the Second World War – without accidents or casualties and with relatively little political friction. In many respects, the military operation continued to be successful for many months: by the end of 1999, the UNHCR recorded the return of the ethnic Albanian refugees as the biggest success in its entire history. The dangers that the refugees would refuse to return or could not be accommodated in Kosovo before the onset of winter (the two nightmares which NATO entertained at the start of the conflict) were avoided. Furthermore, the material damage on the ground was less than Western governments originally feared. Most of Kosovo's housing stock was still useable – unlike in Bosnia, where 60% was destroyed by the time the war ended in 1995, and the basic infrastructure – electricity, safe drinking water and passable roads – continued to work. But while these achievements were undeniably important, there were negative points on the score-sheet. The Alliance failed to protect ethnic Serbs. The number of them who left the province is hotly contested, but it is clear that the Serb population has basically evaporated from the province, and is unlikely to return. A particularly profound demographic change is that the rural Serb population has vanished entirely and a substantial ethnic minority presence only remains in some towns; Mitrovica, where violent Serb–Albanian clashes took place in February 2000, is one dispiriting example.

Kosovo's Romany (or Gypsy) population has fared even worse than the Serbs with whom they sided during the war. They have since been openly victimised by the Albanians, and up to 120,000 Romany people may ultimately be evicted. They have no future in the province, although this is not openly admitted. NATO tried hard to prevent the destruction of Kosovo's minority populations, but a year after the war began, it was obvious that the process had, at best, only been slowed down.

The Alliance was also slow in planning the disarmament of the KLA, the most extreme Albanian organisation, although this was one of the original war aims. Little was done to plan for it during the air offensive , and afterwards there was no attempt to prevent the organisation's fighters returning to the province immediately. Subsequent disarmament agreements with the KLA were sporadic; the organisation which every Western government wished to see dismantled is now the only serious decision maker in the area. Just as significantly, there was no planning to administer the province after the war.

Returning ethnic Albanian refugees have taken most of the property left by the Yugoslav administrators and ethnic Serbs, and self-appointed committees – often dominated by thugs - now run the villages. The key to restoring law and order was supposed to be the creation of a local police force, trained by international police detailed to the province. This was envisaged in the 10 June 1999 Security Council Resolution 1244, but almost a year later, less than half of the expected international police had arrived, and the training was proceeding at a snail's pace.

The tardy arrival of the police was symbolic of a wider problem. European governments, which are Kosovo's main financial donors, wasted the first three weeks after the hostilities ended in meaningless disputes about the nationality of the province's civil administrator. Their choice, Bernard Kouchner (from France) then set to work in Pristina, on a tight budget and without a clear list of priorities. His periodic efforts to convene discussions between ethnic Albanian political leaders have singularly failed.

The absence of a clear timetable for the political process in Kosovo was originally touted as a great achievement: NATO is not bound by any unrealistic promises. But this decision carried its own dangers. The moderate elements in Kosovo are not getting stronger, as NATO hoped when it decided to postpone the elections originally planned for spring 2000. Furthermore, negotiations about the province's final status can not be undertaken with Belgrade until Kosovo's representatives carry a democratic mandate from their own people.

There is also a marked reluctance to commit financial resources. The European Union has accepted responsibility for most of the reconstruction costs. However, much of the pledged funds have yet to arrive, while the international institutions tasked to administer the money have multiplied, as have the bureaucratic turf battles. At the end of February 2000, no fewer than 422 non-governmental organisations were registered as operating in Kosovo. Some were very effective, but others were only there because they felt that they should be. Many engage in overlapping or mutually contradictory projects, but few are either ready or able to help with what Kosovo needs most: a civil administration and the forces of law and order.

As always, the West was better at fighting a war than maintaining a peace; great promises of economic aid made in the heat of battle were quietly shelved. The violence which erupted in Mitrovica in February 2000 highlighted all the shortcomings of the province's administration. However, the situation, while serious, was probably not of long-term significance. Clearly, Milosevic had an interest in fomenting trouble, as did some of the more extreme elements in the ethnic Albanian community, but the clashes were most unlikely to lead to the partitioning of Kosovo as some commentators suggested. Milosevic was too weak and NATO's military presence too overwhelming to allow this. In Mitrovica, NATO was simply paying for errors committed more than a year earlier.

Kosovo's immediate future does not look particularly encouraging, but neither is it disastrous. Despite US pressures, the province's independence is unlikely to be officially recognised, if only because this would entail a new clash with Russia, as well as violating the UN Security Council resolution. Nevertheless, Kosovo will have *de facto* independence, and will also have its own government and parliament by the end of 2000. Pressure for unification with Albania is almost certain to be resisted, and events in

Europe

Kosovo are unlikely to influence the Albanians of Macedonia. But the province will remain poor, badly administered, largely dependent upon foreign aid and run by clans of politicians, all claiming to represent 'democracy', all pledging their 'European vocation' and demanding integration within the European Union, while planning how to liquidate each other. Kosovo is one country where ethnic cleansing was reversed, only to be followed by another wave of a similar crime.

Improvements in the Eternal Balkan Mess?

For the rest of the Balkans, the coming year is likely to be much better: stability is genuinely returning to the region. There are certainly many remaining problems: Milosevic still controls Serbia and its future remains obscure; Bosnia is still divided; Montenegro may secede from Yugoslavia, and Albania is as poor as ever. However, the West has finally stumbled on a policy that will ensure that whatever crises may arise will be contained. The worst wars of the Yugoslav succession would appear to be over.

Milosevic continues in power, but this can not be construed as a 'defeat' for NATO, which never sought to overthrow him. The Serbian leader is now cornered, and it is difficult to see how he could emerge from his current isolation. His cooperation is no longer needed to handle Balkan conflicts. For the first time since 1991, he is seen as part of the problem rather than of the solution. He is an indicted war criminal; not even his more sympathetic neighbours can be seen consorting with him.

Nor is there much doubt among ordinary Serbs that he has led them to their worst defeat in more than a century, and that he can only promise further misery. Some of the petty sanctions imposed on Yugoslavia, such as restrictions on flights and visas, have been relaxed, and may be lifted completely. But the main sanctions will stay in place, partly because they are a cheap and useful weapon and partly because the neighbouring states no longer find them too onerous. Milosevic has caused a great deal of mischief by blocking the clearance of war debris from the Danube, but his hope of breaking the sanctions with this ruse has been disappointed.

It is impossible to predict how long Milosevic's regime will last, although a wave of assassinations in Belgrade in the early months of 2000 was a clear indication that he feels vulnerable. While opposition unity against his regime is important, it is probably not essential to achieving his downfall; the key will be the emergence of a leader who can gain the loyalty of the security services, the real mainstays of the regime. Their loyalty is unlikely to waver until large numbers of Yugoslavs take to the streets to demonstrate against Milosevic. That may take years or just months to happen, but the outcome is likely to be similar to events in Romania in December 1989: a military coup wrapped up in a popular uprising. Milosevic will meet a similar fate to that of Nicolae Ceausescu,

Romania's communist dictator. There is little to fear from his successor. He is unlikely to be a democrat, and may not even be a moderate man. He may well start his rule by offering immunity to many war criminals wanted for trial in the outside world. However, no subsequent Yugoslav leader will enjoy Milosevic's complete control over the armed forces, security services, economy and his own party. Post-Milosevic Yugoslavia may not be to Western tastes, but it will be malleable and eager to draw a line under ten years of warfare.

Independence for Montenegro?

There remains one act of the Yugoslav drama still to be played out: that of Montenegro. Many of Milosevic's stratagems to retain power after the collapse of communism have been copied in the republic, which now constitutes Serbia's only remaining partner in the Yugoslav Federation. Milosevic officially shed his Communist past and adopted the less threatening-sounding label of 'socialism' in 1990; his Montenegrin counterpart Momir Bulatovic followed suit immediately. Milosevic toyed with nationalism; Bulatovic did the same by repatriating the remains of Montenegro's long-dead King Nikola. But this nationalist gesture was without substance; to all intents and purposes, Montenegro remained an integral part of Yugoslavia and the country's federal structure , which was supposed to allow Montenegro equal footing with Serbia, was never taken seriously.

But things have changed. Montenegrins have tired of fighting Milosevic's hopeless wars, while suffering international ostracism and economic collapse. The election of Milo Djukanovic as president on 5 October 1997 represented a clear break. Like many other politicians in the region, his democratic and moral credentials bear little scrutiny. However, there are signs that he wants to reform Montenegro's institutions and break out of the isolation imposed on Yugoslavia. He provided a safe haven for Serbian opposition elements during the Kosovo war, and in early 2000 was demanding a complete overhaul of Yugoslavia's federal structures if Montenegro were to remain a member of that entity.

Milosevic's response has been predictable. He has tried, but failed, to remove Djukanovic from power. In May 1998 he promoted Momir Bulatovic, Djukanovic's mortal enemy to the position of Yugoslav Federal Prime Minister, in an attempt both to outflank the Montenegrins and to ensure that organised opposition to Djukanovic continues. In turn, the Montenegrin president raised the stakes in July 1999 by suggesting he would adopt a Western European currency, or an entirely new one, in order to shield Montenegro from Yugoslavia's rampant inflation. He also presented Belgrade with a list of constitutional demands in August 1999,

Europe

with the threat that, if they were not met, he would hold a referendum on independence. These moves made a war with Serbia possible, but not inevitable.

Milosevic and Djukanovic are playing a game in which both sides know their limitations. Djukanovic is fully aware that, while his country wants change, there is no consensus for independence. Montenegro is home to many ethnic Serbs, including many retired officers and regular soldiers from the federal Yugoslav army. The Montenegrin nationalist parties, locally known as the 'Greens', have never mustered great support; Djukanovic himself was elected precisely because he finessed the question of independence, not because he offered the choice to his people. Additionally, the Montenegrin economy is entirely dependent on Yugoslavia. According to the latest economic statistics, the tiny state's industrial production has fallen by 60% in the last decade, and Djukanovic would be unlikely to persuade his people that they would fare better in the first few years of independence.

Essentially, most Montenegrins are not persuaded that independence is the best course, but they are determined not to be taken for granted by Belgrade. Milosevic, in turn, knows that trying to undermine Montenegro is a game laden with grave risks. He has failed to overthrow Djukanovic because the Montenegrin leader has complete control over the local police. Milosevic can unleash the full power of the Yugoslav military on the republic, but cannot be sure of the outcome. Unlike the Croats or the Muslims in Bosnia or Kosovo, Montenegrins are viewed by most Serbs as brothers. An operation designed to remove Djukanovic could turn into a civil war in Serbia.

Milosevic lacks the crucial knowledge of how the West would respond to such a crisis. The West, apart from Italy, has opposed Montenegrin independence and tended to view the issue as yet another problem they would prefer to avoid. That position has changed in subtle ways. Western leaders are now treating Djukanovic as an important interlocutor and during the Kosovo war, NATO explicitly warned Milosevic against any destabilisation of Montenegro.

Nothing was said about recognising Montenegrin independence if Milosevic tried using force, but with the lessons of Croatia, Bosnia and Kosovo so fresh in his mind, he cannot assume that the West would withhold that recognition. If Montenegro secedes, Serbia would be relegated to the status of land-locked small country, knocked back to the borders it had before the Ottoman Empire disappeared. Even Milosevic would think twice before assuming this risk.

This complex dance in the Balkans is, therefore, made up of the following steps:

- Djukanovic threatens secession without actually declaring

independence, in the hope of attracting maximum concessions from Belgrade.

- Milosevic threatens force in the hope of stalling Djukanovic and avoiding any serious constitutional reforms, but does not actually use violence; and

- Western policy continues to be deliberate lack of policy, and keeping both sides guessing about NATO's reaction to any crisis that might break out. It is not a comfortable situation, but one which can be maintained for at least another year.

Given the West's difficulty in the Balkans for almost a decade, in trying neither to encourage secession nor allow Milosevic to hold Yugoslavia together with terror, the current Montenegro policy is probably the best that can be devised. The Serbs will eventually realise that their only hope lies in removing the dictator in Belgrade, and he is unlikely to discover new stratagems in the next year.

Better News in Neighbouring Regions

Beyond the deadly triangle of Serbia, Kosovo and Montenegro, the outlook for Balkan countries is almost entirely promising. The death on 10 December 1999 of Franjo Tudjman, Croatia's unchallenged leader for over a decade, has not only improved his country's prospects, but is also guaranteed to have a beneficial effect on the hitherto divided Bosnia. Tudjman was the archetypal Balkan rabble-rouser, adept at mobilising his people with promises of a glorious future based on nothing more than reminiscences about a supposedly glorious, and often fabricated, past. He led Croatia to independence in 1991, but condemned the country to five subsequent years of war. He promised a Western-style government, but delivered the traditional Balkan mixture of geriatric rule, corruption and nepotism, wrapped in the trappings of democracy, but with none of its substance. His acolytes divided the economy between them and, whenever an opposition politician dared to become too popular, he was quickly dealt with by Croatia's secret police – commanded by the President's son.

Unlike Slobodan Milosevic, whom he much resembled, Tudjman knew how to make himself useful to the West and thus derive the maximum benefit from every twist of the Yugoslav tragedy. He initially supported the carve-up of Bosnia by supplying ethnic Croats in that republic with weapons, just as Milosevic did to his ethnic Serbs. But in 1994 he switched sides and subsequently, with the West's secret connivance, drove Yugoslav troops from Croat territory. Milosevic spoke about creating an ethnically pure Serbia, but never achieved it; Tudjman, on the other hand, paid lip-service to a multi-ethnic Croatia, but evicted most of the ethnic Serbs, who amounted to almost a fifth of the country's population before the war.

Although no country pressed Croatia hard to allow the Serbs' repatriation, the country and its leader did pay a price for Tudjman's behaviour. Useful though he may have been to them, Western governments were increasingly embarrassed about their association with such a regime. Croatia was never subjected to economic sanctions, but some of its military commanders were indicted as war criminals and the country's applications to become a member of both NATO and the European Union were ignored. More importantly, Tudjman's chief international sponsors, the US and Germany, increasingly disregarded him and starved him of investment and credit. The Croatian economy never recovered from the war. The operetta-style uniforms which Tudjman designed for his armed forces looked magnificent; the shop windows did not. Tudjman's death was among his better services to his country. Predictably, his entire political structure evaporated as soon as he was gone.

The new government and President Stipe Mesic, elected on 24 January 2000 promised to right all previous wrongs: rapid privatisation of the economy is in prospect; the press already has much more freedom; human rights will be protected. Even the possible return of the ethnic Serbs is being touted. As always in the Balkans, such promises can not be relied upon. The country's new leaders are not exactly new: Prime Minister Ivica Racan once ran the local Communist party, while Mesic was the former Yugoslavia's last head of state in 1991. Although both were sidelined by Tudjman for almost a decade, they were originally part of a political system which was far from being either democratic or tolerant.

They deserve the benefit of the doubt, but little more. It is uncertain whether the government will be able to deliver its indicted war criminals to the International Court in the Hague, or to eliminate corruption at home, and the return of ethnic Serbs in large numbers will probably remain a dream. Ethnic cleansing is usually irreversible, unless it is reversed immediately, as in Kosovo

Nevertheless, the changes in Croatia bode well for the region. The new government is unlikely to support separatist ethnic Croats in Bosnia; they are now encouraged to cooperate with the local Muslims and Serbs. For the first time since the fighting ended with the 1995 Dayton Peace Accords, Bosnia has a realistic chance of functioning as a state. Nor are Croatia's leaders likely to be tempted into any deals with Milosevic, thus reinforcing the isolation of Serbia's dictator. Even if many of their reforms fail, Croatia's leaders will succeed in dismantling Tudjman's machinery of internal control. That in itself will be an achievement, giving an indication to neighbouring nations that no dictatorship can last forever, and that democracy can take roots in even the most inauspicious parts of the Balkans.

The situation is even more promising elsewhere in the region. While Albania will remain the poorest European state for some time to come, Western troop presence in the country alongside financial assistance will ensure a modicum of stability; there is no serious danger of an Albanian civil war for the first time since 1997. NATO's action in Kosovo was highly unpopular in Romania, Bulgaria and Greece. Nevertheless, the conflict has had almost wholly beneficial effects in these countries. In Romania and Bulgaria, the overriding fear has been that they would be relegated to a Russian sphere of influence. For them the most important message from Kosovo was that NATO is prepared to impose its will in the Balkans, even at the risk of confronting Russia. Support for NATO membership has consequently increased in both countries, whose efforts to join the Alliance will continue unabated.

The Greek government has also crossed a watershed: by supporting NATO's action despite popular antagonism, it effectively buried a streak of anti-Western sentiment which had permeated the country's politics since the 1960s dictatorship. That a government of the Panhellenic Socialist Movement (PASOK) – hitherto the main exponent of anti-Western sentiments – made this break with the past was particularly remarkable. And the shift in attitudes allowed Athens to relax tensions with Turkey. For the first time in decades, it became fashionable in both countries to talk about cooperation and friendship. In January and February 2000, the two states signed the largest number of bilateral agreements since the 1930s. Although the key problems of the Aegean and of Cyprus remain unresolved, many of the petty disputes between the two neighbours have been swept aside.

The Kosovo war's final, if not fully intended, consequence was the realisation in all Europe's capitals that the only way of dealing with the Balkan problems is by including the region in the European Union. The process will be lengthy and difficult, but, at their December 1999 Helsinki summit, the EU's leaders pledged themselves to open accession negotiations with Romania, Bulgaria and Turkey. The fears of isolation which governed the actions of most Balkan governments have been removed at a stroke.

Regional Team-work

The formation of a Balkans peacekeeping brigade, The Multinational Peace Force for Southeastern Europe, in December 1999 is a small but highly potent indicator of this new spirit of confidence and regional cooperation. At present, membership is limited to Greece, Turkey, Albania, Bulgaria, Macedonia, Romania and Italy. A total of 3,000 troops and their equipment are committed, but there will be no standing force: assigned units will remain stationed in their home states. The force's headquarters will rotate between the participating countries, changing every four years. The first base is in Plovdiv, Bulgaria to be followed by bases in Romania, Turkey and Greece.

Each member country will command the force for a two-year term, starting with Turkey followed by Greece. Turkish Brigadier-General Hilmi Akin Zorlu is the current commander. The presidency and headquarters of the political and military committee established under the agreement will be held by each of the participating countries for a two-year term. Greece holds the first presidency, followed by Romania; Nikos Dhimadhis, a Greek diplomat, has already started work as president.

The deal is highly ingenious. By rotating the political and military commands as well as the headquarters location, the participating countries have ensured not only that each government can claim a victory, but also that no country will have complete control of the force. A level of cooperation is therefore mandated from the start. Furthermore, by not having a standing force, the partners have finessed the problem of the strong emotions that would have been aroused by the possibility of Turkish troops being based on Greek soil.

Italy's inclusion indicates that the arrangement is not simply a club for Europe's otherwise ignored and marginal states, but has wider European significance. Finally, the United States – acknowledged by all Balkan countries as the supreme arbiter in their affairs – has accepted 'observer' status. Bulgarian President Petar Stojanov, who opened the headquarters, suggested that Yugoslavia itself might eventually be invited to join, but this appears highly improbable at present. The participant states have also ducked the thorny matter of Bosnian, Croat or Montenegrin participation.

In some respects, despite all that has happened, little has changed in the Balkans. The former Yugoslav republics are still in suspended animation, while the force of 3,000 Balkan peacekeepers would be unlikely to change the security situation, even if it were assembled. Yet, governments throughout the region are now able to point out that they are doing something to provide for their own security, rather than simply waiting helplessly for the West to come to their rescue. The key problems that have bedevilled the Balkans for centuries – economic backwardness and segregation from the rest of Europe – are now being addressed. The mood of renewed confidence is unmistakable. There may be trouble ahead in Kosovo, and Yugoslavia's final status remains unresolved, but the foundations of a stable region are already evident, and most of the impending crises can be localised. It would have been better if the West had adopted the policies which have brought this improvement a few years earlier, but at least these policies are being applied at long last.

Russia: Towards Authoritarian Reform?

Boris Yeltsin's resignation as Russian president on New Year's Eve 1999 left his anointed successor, the prime minister and former security minister, Vladimir Putin, with excellent prospects of being elected president on 26 March 2000. Putin, as expected, romped home, winning 52% of the vote, as compared to his nearest challenger Gennady Zyugamov, who garnered only 29.4%. It also left him with a country in a terrible mess: an economy which had undergone savage economic decline; collapsing public services; weak and deeply corrupt bureaucracy, police and revenue services; a chaotic, criminalised and gravely hampered 'free market'; an entrenched and arrogant financial oligarchy; severely weakened and demoralised armed forces; and a war in Chechnya, which, although relatively successful, seemed bound to lead to a long-running guerrilla and terrorist campaign.

Yeltsin had also bequeathed a weak democracy and a cynical, politically apathetic population – though Putin may not see these last features as disadvantages if, as many believe, his goal is to establish a more authoritarian regime in Russia. If so, he will be given many tools by the constitution created by Yeltsin for himself after the crushing of armed parliamentary opposition in 1993. Under that constitution, the presidency has very extensive powers to appoint the government, overrule parliament, issue laws by decree, and control the Defence, Interior, Foreign and Security Ministries directly, without going through the premier. Yeltsin, however, was too sick and bored by administration to use these powers consistently. The thought of them in the hands of the 47-year-old Putin, a former KGB officer, has caused widespread alarm, though also hopes that he might use them to finally push through stalled economic reforms.

The New Regime

Russia had three prime ministers in 1999, and their differing fates were due above all to the calculations of the Yeltsin 'Family': Yeltsin himself, his close relatives and their leading financial associates and partners in corruption. First, Yevgeny Primakov was removed on 12 May. He had been appointed in September 1998, in the wake of the financial crash in the preceding month, when it seemed that the entire regime might collapse. His great virtue was his capacity to form alliances with the Communist and nationalist majority in the parliament. But precisely this ability led to his developing a dangerous independence from the Family, leading to fears that once in office as president he might turn against them.

With the economy stabilised and the parliament once again reduced to near-impotence, Yeltsin dismissed Primakov, and replaced him with Interior Minister Sergei Stepashin, a former KGB officer, who, as head of domestic intelligence, had played a key part in launching the disastrous Chechen War of 1994–96. Despite the cooperation that Primakov had forged with the Communist-led majority in the Duma, it failed to react strongly to his dismissal – re-emphasising both the Duma's weakness as an institution, and the extent to which many deputies have been thoroughly corrupted by government gifts and favours. On 15 May, a move to impeach Yeltsin failed, and Stepashin was confirmed by the Duma on 19 May.

Stepashin was far more dependent on the Family than Primakov, and he also came to be seen as too weak to be president, in part because of his inability to check the increasing Chechen attacks on Russian forces in the Russian North Caucasus. These encouraged increasingly hawkish attitudes on the part of certain senior military figures, notably the Chief of Staff General Anatoly Kvashnin, who were still smarting from their defeat by the Chechens in 1996. There were even suggestions that the Russian security services somehow caused the Chechen attacks in order to provide an excuse for dismissing Stepashin and mounting a new attack on Chechnya. This seems far-fetched, however, in view of what is known of the Chechen perpetrators and their bitter hared of Russia. On 9 August, Stepashin was sacked and Putin, who seemed to combine the necessary toughness with longstanding involvement in the dealings of the Kremlin and its allies, was appointed prime minister.

The Man of the Hour

At the time of his appointment, Putin was widely seen as just another grey *apparachik*, appointed to serve the interests of the Family and the oligarchs, and this may turn out to be the case in the end. However, there are other potentially key factors that point to a different scenario. One is the continuing underlying power of the security services, and another is the apparent steely determination and ruthlessness of Putin himself, qualities in which he exceeded any of his predecessors as prime minister under Yeltsin, and of which he has given numerous demonstrations since taking over the premiership.

Portrayals of Putin as a mere stooge also missed his capacity to garner great popularity and prestige for himself in a very short space of time. This was mainly due to the Russian military operation in Chechnya, which began on 23 September 1999, and in December turned into a bloody battle to capture the Chechen capital, Grozny. Russians had developed a strong hostility towards Chechens because of their continual attacks on Russia in

1997–99, and, unlike the failed military intervention of 1994–96, the latest war was broadly popular in Russia.

Putin's popularity went well beyond this cause. His image as a young, decisive figure promised a bright change after years of drift, decline and national humiliation under the ageing, ailing Yeltsin. Putin's record as a KGB officer does not worry most Russians – after all, his two predecessors as premier and presumptive presidential successor, Primakov and Stepashin, also had KGB backgrounds. But whereas Primakov is 70 years-old and looked worryingly like becoming another elderly, ineffective president, Putin seems to offer the mixture of youth, modernity and toughness which most Russians want in the holder of that office.

During the 1970s and early 1980s, Putin was based in Communist East Germany. He returned to Russia during the reforms of former President Mikhail Gorbachev, and, like Stepashin, was apparently inserted by the KGB into the ranks of the reformist movement – in his case, in his native Leningrad, now St Petersburg. During the period of the Soviet Union's collapse, his combination of ability and KGB links led to his becoming First Deputy Mayor of the city from 1994 to 1996.

In this capacity, Putin gained a reputation for efficiency, discretion and ruthlessness. A vital factor in his rise was that he worked well with Deputy Mayor Anatoly Chubais, who in 1992 became Russian privatisation minister and a key figure in the transfer of state property to the pro-Yeltsin magnates. Chubais has reportedly boasted of having 'privatised' Putin. In 1996, Putin was brought into Yeltsin's office as deputy head of the notorious Kremlin property department, which has been accused of being at the heart of Yeltsin Family corruption. In July 1998, Putin was appointed to head the FSB, domestic successor to the KGB, the job from which he moved to become prime minister just over a year later. The most widespread account of Putin's activities in Germany suggests that he was charged with spying on the West German economy, as part of the Soviet Union's increasingly desperate attempts to match the West in technology. This background is encouraging in one way, because Putin is the first ruler in Moscow since Lenin to speak a Western language fluently, and, unlike Yeltsin and most of the older generation, he may have some genuine understanding of how Western economies work.

Nevertheless, within a few months it became clear that a future Putin regime will be based to a considerable extent on the security services. After his appointment as prime minister, Putin reportedly told a gathering of senior officers of the domestic and foreign intelligence services that they now had 'their man' in the Kremlin. Putin has spoken of the need for a strong state, and, drawing on the lessons of state collapse and failed reform under Yeltsin, a growing number of Western scholars now recognise that a

Europe

fairly strong and effective state is necessary if a stable and regulated free market is to emerge rather than a disastrous free-for-all.

Given the weakness of the democratic institutions, of the judiciary and police, and of the media, it may well be that the only forces in Russia with any chance of combating corruption and organised crime and laying the basis for a successful market economy are indeed from the former KGB. The question is whether these forces will be intelligent, honest, patriotic and, indeed, strong enough to carry out a programme of authoritarian reform, or whether their increased power will simply lead to a corrupt and economically ineffective quasi-dictatorship headed by Putin and run by themselves.

The KGB which Putin entered as a young man was heavily marked by the rigorous orthodox Communism of its chief, Yuri Andropov, a determined enemy of the Soviet system's growing corruption during the Brezhnev years. Since then, the former KGB has itself become extremely corrupt, and many of its officers have left to go into the private security business, often working for the magnates or for criminal bosses.

Putin has tried to project an image of Andropov-like rigour. He is helped in this effort by his icy personal appearance. Even if sincere, however – and Putin has worked in some of the most corrupt state institutions in Russia – it is highly questionable how far even the leadership of a strong Russian president could prevail against entrenched private interests able to deploy enormous wealth to corrupt Russian state services, and thus to undermine their effectiveness.

Putin's general approach to government and Russia's destiny was set out in an essay published on the Russian government website two days before Yeltsin's resignation. In it, he denounced the effects of Communism, and pledged to uphold democracy and continue economic reforms. Yet, he also spoke of the historic role played in Russia by a strong state, both in crushing 'disorder' and crime, and developing effective programmes to encourage domestic and foreign investment in key sectors of the economy, especially technological development: 'Russians see [a strong state] as a source and guarantor of order, and the initiator and main driving force of any change.' He stressed the need for a strong but sober patriotism, lacking a chauvinist or imperialist dimension. He emphasised his desire for good relations with the West, but also emphasised that the West must respect Russia's interests and great-power status. Putin aimed above all to convey the impression of a dedicated modernising state servant.

Various media figures and thinkers close to the new regime advanced the figure of Tsar Alexander III as a guiding image for the Russia of the future. If this has any meaning beyond empty historicising rhetoric, then the reference to that stern autocrat's period in power augers very badly for Russian democracy; fairly well for honesty, discipline and patriotism in state service; and very well for the Russian economy, especially the encouragement of foreign investment – assuming that Putin's parliamentary alliance with the Communists is purely tactical and does not reflect his long-term plans.

The Duma Elections and After

In the December 1999 parliamentary elections, the government's 'Unity' electoral bloc, which Putin had quickly thrown together in time to qualify for the elections in October, came second with 23% of the vote. The 'Fatherland–All Russia' bloc of former Prime Minister Primakov and Moscow Mayor Yury Luzhkov, which in mid-1999 was tipped to win the succession to Yeltsin, was beaten into third place with 13%, and subsequently split.

This reflected not only the relentless pressure of government propaganda in the media, but also second thoughts on the part of several regional governors who had previously backed Primakov, but now apparently saw Putin's winning the presidential election as virtually inevitable, and wished to be on the winning side. As for the Communists, they have repeatedly proved incapable of attracting support from a majority of Russians, and their constituency is elderly and shrinking.

Putin's first act on becoming president on 1 January 2000 was to declare Yeltsin immune from prosecution for actions while in office. This was undoubtedly an absolute condition set by Yeltsin and the Family. It was their last act of political importance, however, as Putin demonstrated on 3 January 2000 when he removed Yeltsin's daughter Tatyana Dyachenko from her position on the presidential staff.

The important question for the future is the nature of Putin's relationship with the big business magnates who acquired their largely illegal wealth under Yeltsin's presidency. No one doubts that Putin's success depends on the magnates' general approval, but this does not necessarily mean that he is their puppet. His uneasy relationship with the magnates was illustrated by the way the media (overwhelmingly magnate-controlled) reacted to the war in Chechnya.

At the start, in the wake of the bombing of several Moscow buildings, the media overwhelmingly supported the Russian campaign, and cooperated with the regime in giving space to Russian official propaganda, excluding Chechen voices, and above all playing down Russian casualties. In early January 2000, however, critical voices began to be heard from the media controlled by Vladimir Gusinsky, Luzhkov and others (but not from those controlled by Boris Berezovsky). One reason for this was a series of localised defeats, and mounting evidence that the Russian army was bogged down in Grozny. However, it has also been widely suggested that the journalists concerned, most of whom must now bow to their proprietors' wishes, would not have expressed themselves so forthrightly if they had not had permission from Gusinsky.

Gusinsky may well have become alarmed that, unlike Yeltsin in the 1996 elections, Putin had become so popular that he could win the presidential election without help from any of the tycoons or the support of their media, and therefore would not be beholden to them when in office. The growing media criticism of the war would therefore have been partly to remind Putin that the magnates were still very powerful and could do him much harm.

Putin's strategy in the new Duma seemed designed to show how little he needed allies. It had been assumed that his Unity bloc would dominate parliament in alliance with the business-oriented 'Union of Rightist Forces', which had received 8% of the vote, and in pragmatic cooperation with Fatherland–All Russia and the liberal *Yabloko* party, which had won 6%. There were strong suggestions that Putin might allow Primakov to become Speaker of the parliament in return for his withdrawing from the presidential race.

Instead, Putin taught the other centrist parties a contemptuous lesson, allying with the Communists (who had achieved 24% of the vote) to return the former Communist Speaker, Gennady Seleznyov, and to exclude the liberals and centrists from the chairs of almost all the key parliamentary committees. As a result, these fell under control of the Communists and Nationalists. While this action might have meant that Putin leaned toward a relatively statist economic policy, it above all suggested a considerable capacity for ruthless single-mindedness in dealing with anyone he perceived as his chief rival of the moment.

Fears of such an attitude's results began to grow in the Russian liberal media. One indicative case was the treatment of the Russian reporter Andrei Babitsky, who worked for the American-run Russian-language radio station 'Radio Liberty.' Babitsky, whose critical coverage of Russian conduct of the war in Chechnya met with official displeasure, was detained on 16 January 2000 and handed over to Chechens on 3 February in a supposed 'voluntary' exchange for Russian prisoners of war. Babitsky resurfaced in Makhachkala, the capital of Dagestan, at the end of February after weeks of speculation about whether he was still alive. He said in a statement to Amnesty International that during his detention he had been held both by Chechens and by Russians. The latter kept him in a so-called 'filtration camp', where he had been beaten with truncheons, forced to share a cell with 15 others, and continually heard other prisoners screaming under torture. Babitsky was allowed to return home to Moscow after sustained pressure upon acting President Putin by both world media and political leaders. In the second episode, Alexander Khinshtein, a sharp-tongued presenter and critic of Putin at a TV station controlled by Yuri Luzhkov, was threatened with psychiatric examination at a distant clinic in connection with what appeared to be a trumped-up motoring offence – a threat grimly reminiscent of Soviet behaviour towards dissidents. These events showed that while Putin had little regard for the free press he was at least susceptible to foreign pressure on high-profile human rights issues, as long as he could respond after a face-saving delay.

Yet Another Chechen War

The treatment of Babitsky, at least, appears linked to the Chechen War rather than a general desire to suppress dissent. On the other hand, Putin had portrayed himself as personally in charge of the war, and his first act on becoming president was to visit Russian troops in Chechnya. This meant that it would have been difficult for him to evade responsibility if things went badly wrong, and therefore that he was strongly interested in preventing criticism of the war.

The roots of the latest Chechen war lie in Chechen history and culture, but above all in the previous Russian military intervention of 1994–96, and the destruction, brutalisation and radicalisation it caused in Chechnya. That war was generally unpopular in Russia, and this mood helped to undermine Russian military morale. After Russia had suffered a number of defeats by the Chechen rebels, the country's growing war weariness helped to lead first to cease-fires and finally to a complete Russian withdrawal in autumn 1996.

The Russian assumption was that the Chechen Chief of Staff, General Aslan Maskhadov (a former Soviet artillery officer and known moderate) would be able to create a stable state in Chechnya, which would seek pragmatic relations with Russia. The independence question was to be shelved for five years under the Khasavyurt Agreements that ended the war.

Maskhadov was indeed elected Chechen president in January 1997, but proved incapable of establishing a stable state. The economy was ruined, unemployment was general, and the country was flooded with military warlords and their followers. The result was an explosion of criminality, and especially kidnappings, which claimed more than 1,300 Russian victims in surrounding regions (including two senior officials) and several foreigners.

This was also accompanied by the growth of radical Islamist groups, the so-called 'Wahabis', in both Chechnya and the neighbouring Russian republic of Dagestan. The most powerful of these, a Saudi Arabian called Habibullah Khattab, had previously fought with the *mujaheddin* in Afghanistan, allegedly alongside the well-known terrorist leader Osama bin Laden, author of the bomb attacks on US Embassies in Kenya and Tanzania in August 1998. His group includes many international Muslim volunteers from the Middle East and Afghanistan.

In April 1998, Khattab joined forces with a Dagestani Islamist leader, Hajji Bahauddin, the famous Chechen commander, Shamil Basayev, and other Chechen leaders to form a 'Congress of Chechen and Dagestani Peoples' dedicated to driving the Russians from Dagestan and uniting the region with Chechnya in one Islamic Republic. After a series of bomb attacks and ambushes directed against Russian forces in neighbouring regions, the forces of Basayev, Khattab and Bahauddin in August 1999 launched a major armed incursion into the Botlikh region of the Dagestani mountains.

Russian troops drove them out at the cost of heavy casualties, and then moved to suppress another Islamist centre further north. While fighting there was underway, a series of massive terrorist bombs beginning on 31 August claimed more than 300 lives in Moscow and other Russian cities. An unknown group, the Dagestan Liberation Army claimed responsibility, but there are widespread suspicions that the Russian security services may have planted the bombs in order to justify a new invasion of Chechnya. On the other hand, Basayev himself initially blamed Dagestani Islamists, and certainly the group around Khattab has both the expertise and the ruthlessness for this kind of attack.

The attack in Dagestan and the bombings gave the frustrated Russian generals their long-awaited opportunity to revenge their 1996 failure. This time they relied on heavy bombardment by artillery and rockets and from the air against civilian as well as military targets, to crush the Chechen rebels. After weeks in which the campaign went well, the Russian troops had to struggle to capture the Chechen capital, Grozny. There was remarkably slow progress for months, and the Chechens even managed to stage successful local counter-attacks in early January, briefly recapturing the centres of Shelli and Argun.

As a result, on 7 January 2000, Putin replaced two commanders of the Russian forces in Chechnya, Generals Gennady Troshev and Vladimir Shamanov. At the end of March 2000, the latest casualty figures were 2,036 soldiers killed and 6,076 wounded. On 18 January, Russian Major-General Mikhail Malofeyev was killed in an ambush and his body was not recovered until ten days later.

The continued ferocious Russian bombardment took its toll, however, and in early February the main Chechen forces withdrew from Grozny, suffering very heavy casualties when one column ran into a Russian minefield and was then cut to pieces by artillery. Three leading commanders were killed and Shamil Basayev himself was badly wounded. In the meantime, the Russians had also made significant progress in the mountains, gradually reducing the areas where the Chechen fighters could find refuge.

If the Russians are prepared to keep the present level of troops in Chechnya (estimated at around 100,000) and continue fighting for years if necessary, then they will probably be able to conquer the whole of Chechnya and break up any major guerrilla groups. For though the Chechens are superb fighters, the Russians have overwhelming superiority in both numbers and firepower. Moreover, with barely 2,300 square kilometres of territory (less than half of it mountainous), Chechnya is not in the same category as Vietnam, Algeria, or other huge areas where partisan wars have defeated large armies in the past. There is not much room to hide.

Even if Russia does 'win' the war in Chechnya, this will by no means end the violence there. The first danger could be large Chechen groups retreating over the mountains into Georgia, which the weak Georgian forces would probably be unable to prevent. If the Russians then pursued the Chechen fighters into Georgia, or if the Chechens began launching raids across the border, the result could be a major international crisis. Even more likely is that, if the Chechens can no longer fight the Russians openly, they will turn to terrorism. The corrupt and shambolic Russian security services would find it very hard to deal with a really determined terrorist movement; and not merely could such a movement cause serious casualties, but it could contribute to undermining Russian democracy and creating a new 'security state'.

A Strong Whiff of Nationalism

During the first months of Putin's presidency, relations with the West were overshadowed by strong Western criticism of the Chechen War, and particularly of Russia's bombardment of civilian targets. This tension prolonged the serious cooling of relations caused by NATO's military intervention against Yugoslavia earlier in 1999.

Russia, through its mediator Viktor Chernomyrdin, had played an important part in bringing President Slobodan Milosevic of Yugoslavia to accede on 3 June 1999 to what were in effect NATO terms. However, immediately afterwards, 200 paratroopers from the Russian peacekeeping force in Bosnia were rushed to Pristina airport in Kosovo, ahead of NATO's deployment to the province, in an effort to secure an independent role for Russia on the ground. If Russia had been able to reinforce this unit, and if the NATO command had over-reacted, a very serious situation might have resulted. Fortunately, Romania and Bulgaria, over which Russian forces would have had to fly in order to reach Kosovo, both refused to give permission, graphically illustrating the rise of Western influence in this region and the decline of Russian hegemony. The British commander of the NATO forces on the ground, General Sir Michael Jackson, also refused to obey an order from the NATO commander-in-chief, US General Wesley Clark, to re-take the airport.

Completely isolated, the Russian forces were helpless, and in a few days Moscow was forced to give up its hopes of an independent zone in Kosovo, which would probably have remained effectively under Serbian control. NATO's subsequent failure to protect many Serbian civilians in Kosovo from Albanian reprisals left Russians feeling that their stance against the NATO campaign had been morally justified. Bitterness towards the West among many Russians was increased by Western criticism of Russia's operation in Chechnya, which Russians tended to see as hypocritical.

However, Western criticism did not lead to specific action against Russia. In the new year, a series of Western representatives visited Moscow – including US Secretary of State Madeleine Albright, NATO Secretary-General Lord Robertson, and UK Foreign Secretary Robin Cook – signalling the desire of leading Western states to forge pragmatic relations with the new regime. The overwhelming probability that Putin would win the presidential elections left the West with little choice; US President Bill Clinton made this clear in mid-February, by declaring that Putin was 'a man with whom we can do business'.

To judge by his own public statements, Putin is not anxious for increased tension with the West, and would also prefer to pursue good working relations. While he is evidently patriotic and anxious to boost Russian power and influence, his career and personality also suggest that he is probably no fanatical firebrand, but rather a cautious bureaucratic pragmatist.

However, there is a strong potential on both sides to make stable relations very difficult. Putin's regime may make stronger efforts to assert Russian influence in the southern Caucasus. Georgia, in particular, could be gravely endangered if Chechen rebels retreat over its poorly guarded border and attempt to set up bases in the Georgian mountains. If the Russians pursued these forces onto Georgian territory, the stage could be set for a major showdown with the US, which in recent years has increasingly stressed its geopolitical and economic interest in Georgia as lying on the main route for oil and gas exports from the Caspian region.

There are also two Western moves that would almost certainly provoke a strong Russian response. The first is the likelihood that – if a test in April 2000 goes well – President Clinton will announce moves in June to introduce a US National Missile Defence system (NMD). Even if he does not, the bipartisan support for NMD in the US makes a decision in its favour almost inevitable, whatever the Russian position. This would be in breach of the 1972 Anti-Ballistic Missile Treaty and, unless Moscow agrees to amend it – which it has so far refused to consider – the US would be forced to abrogate the treaty.

The second aggravating step would be NATO enlargement to the Baltic States, which Russia has repeatedly said it would regard as gravely hostile. At present, there is strong opposition among European NATO members and many in Washington to any early move in this direction. However, if the Balts meet the membership criteria, it may be very difficult for NATO to refuse them entry, especially if the Alliance has in the meantime moved towards admitting less-qualified candidates in the Balkans. Although direct Russian retaliation against the Balts would be unlikely given their stability and Russia's military weakness, a NATO move to the Baltic would probably increase Russian attempts to damage US interests elsewhere.

Still a Problem Economy

In the second half of 1999 and the first months of 2000, the Putin regime benefited from a colossal unearned windfall – the steep rise in oil prices, which by the end of February 2000 had reached $30.00 per barrel, up from a mere $10.00 a barrel a year earlier. This contributed to a primary budgetary surplus of 2.2% of Russian gross domestic product (GDP). The latter rose BY 3.2% in 1999, according to Russian figures, although Western sources believe the increase was less. Russian exports were also helped by the low value of the Russian rouble after the financial crash of August 1998. The Russian stock market also saw a considerable recovery, although the sums involved are extremely small by Western or Far Eastern standards. The liquid capitalisation of all Russian stocks put together amounts to less than 5% of the market value of computer software company, Microsoft.

However, suggestions that the Russian economy has started to pick up appear highly premature. Oil prices could well fall again. Russia's economic fundamentals remain extremely weak. At a mere $4.3 billion, direct foreign investment in the country is very low by international standards, and it did not rise significantly in 1999. Unless Russia can either attract international investors, or bring back the tens of billions of dollars moved to the West by Russian businessmen and officials, there can be little prospect of major economic regeneration. Indeed, within a few years the Russian economy is bound to start declining again, as increasing amounts of Soviet-era infrastructure wears out

Russia, however, remains an acutely unfavourable environment for international investment. The economy is highly criminalised, and a mixture of bureaucratic corruption and dues extorted by a variety of 'Mafia' forces up prices throughout the system. Protection of shareholders' rights is extremely poor, as a number of major Western investors have found to their cost. Most of the really profitable assets formerly owned by the state – oil, minerals and aluminium – were illegally sold to the magnates for a fraction of their true value under the Yeltsin regime. The greatest remaining assets are United Energy System (UES), the energy monopoly now headed by Anatoly Chubais, and *Gazprom*, the world's largest gas exporter. However, in the course of his election campaign, Putin categorically ruled out splitting either of these up, which would appear to rule out the sale of any part of them to western investors.

Perhaps most importantly, the Russian banking sector is rotten and completely opaque. Most of the large Russian banks are probably bankrupt and incapable of channelling productive investment. It has so far been impossible for the state to regulate this sector effectively because of the financial magnates' political influence, their ability to extract a variety of open or hidden state subsidies, and their ability to hide their real assets in a maze of paper companies, which incompetent and corrupt Russian regulators are unable or unwilling to penetrate. The scale of the corruption, illegality and capital flight was exemplified in 1999 by a scandal involving the Bank of New York, whose senior Russian officials were apparently involved in laundering hundreds of millions of dollars.

Even if he wishes to, it seems very unlikely that Putin will be able to do much to clean up this mess, and he certainly will not be able to do so quickly. Even if he were prepared to launch an all-out war against the financial oligarchs – which could well endanger both his regime and his life – experience elsewhere in Eastern Europe underlines the difficulty of creating an effective modern banking sector with purely local resources. International banks need to have a major presence in Russia, just as industry needs a considerable amount of skilled management from overseas.

But Eastern European experience also suggests that, even when governments are strongly committed in principle to encouraging Western participation in the economy – which is by no means certain in Putin's case – they often find it very difficult in practice to surrender control over important economic sectors to foreigners, because of either political resistance or their own nationalist instincts. Statements already made by Putin about preserving key economic sectors from foreign control are not encouraging

Russia's Future

Putin's platform combines:

- professed respect for democracy;
- fostering a strong state;
- improving the free market while protecting the interests of the nation and the poor; and

- cultivating good relations with the West while defending
  Russian national pride, interests and great-power status.

This is a very appealing mixture to Russian voters; and most of it –
although perhaps not the commitment to democracy – is probably fairly
sincere in intention, since it represents the broad consensus among most
educated younger Russians. But the programme is extremely short on
details, and much of it may well be impossible given the decline of the
Russian state and economy over the past decade.

The questions are therefore both how Putin will set about
strengthening the state, and whether he will succeed. Having sided with
the Communists to defeat the 'liberals' in parliament, he may find that he
has unleashed an uncontrollable monster, which will act to block free
market legislation, especially where this involves foreign ownership, as has
happened so often in the past.

Moreover, parliamentary opposition to reform was only ever one part
of the problem. More important has been the new oligarchy's grip on the
economy, and the entire Russian state system's extreme corruption and
weakness. Putin will undoubtedly improve things to some extent, probably
beginning with the tax-collection authorities. However, in circumstances
where an honest and dedicated tax official stands a strong chance of either
being killed by the Mafia or framed for corruption by his own corrupt
colleagues, even this will be a truly Augean task.

Furthermore, over the past decade the local bosses and oligarchies
that govern Russia's regions have gained great power at the centre's
expense. Putin will probably have some success in redressing the balance
in favour of the central government, but given Russia's size and
complexity, any Russian regime will have to work in collaboration with
most of the regions, not against them. Russia may see a more authoritarian
regime at the centre, sharing power with semi-authoritarian regimes in the
provinces. This might be a recipe for political stability, but not for
economic reform.

How far Putin moves against the business magnates will depend on
his personal honesty, courage and determination, and on how far he can
rely on a corrupted bureaucracy and police. Putin's administration will
certainly strengthen the role of the security services, using the argument
that this is necessary to combat terrorism, corruption and organised crime.
If, as seems highly probable, the Chechen fighters turn to terrorism, this
will strengthen still further moves to create a Russian 'security state', in
which the military and security forces will have a stronger supervisory
role.

Putin has already moved to give the FSB a stronger role keeping check
on other ministries, and above all on the highly corrupt and incompetent
Interior Ministry. The success of Putin's economic strategy will also

depend on whether he really understands what reforms are needed to attract international investment, and whether he is prepared to allow foreign businesses to supplant failing Russian competitors.

With regard to democracy and media and other freedoms, early hints of Putin's outlook suggest that Russia may head towards a type of 'guided' democracy exemplified in some former Soviet Republics. In an international democratic league, Russia may come to lie somewhere on a spectrum between Turkey (at best) and Egypt (at worst). In such states, elements of democracy, pluralism and free media exist, but there are severe (though flexible) limits on how far they can go in challenging either the ultimate rulers or the system as a whole. Journalists or politicians who overstep these boundaries can suffer badly, but these states are far from being 'totalitarian'.

Putin's approach to foreign policy during his first three months of provisional office was pragmatic. He was at pains to demonstrate his desire for good relations with the West, despite tensions over Kosovo and Chechnya. In particular, he appears personally to have overruled senior officials in the Defence and Foreign Ministries who opposed NATO Secretary General Lord Robertson's visit to Moscow in early March 2000. It may well be that Putin thinks that by cultivating such links, he may be able to reduce the likelihood of US steps – over NATO enlargement and NMD – which would be against Russia's interests and which would force Putin to respond aggressively.

Putin seems likely to continue existing policies towards other parts of the world. It is very unlikely that Russia will swing towards the Anglo-American position on Iraq, or agree to end sales of nuclear technology to Iran, unless the US makes significant concessions in other fields. There is, however, nothing Russia can do to challenge US dominance in the Middle East.

Important sales of Russian military technology to China are likely to continue. They are a way of demonstrating Russia's capacity to harm US interests if Moscow is seriously alienated by American policies. Even more importantly, China is vital as the largest single market for the struggling Russian arms industry. A measure of Russian–Chinese international cooperation is also inevitable in view of both countries' resentment of US 'hegemonism'. However, unless both countries' relations with Washington deteriorate drastically, it is very unlikely that their relationship will develop into a full-scale anti-American alliance. Even if they joined forces, they would be far too weak to confront the US directly, and they both have far more to lose than to gain from a rift with Washington.

Overall therefore, while the prospects for Russian democracy and relations with the West under Putin are worrying, and those for the economy are uncertain, Russia has too strong a state tradition to slide remorselessly down to third-world status, as was occurring under Boris

Yeltsin. Sooner or later, there was bound to be a backlash, and Putin is a more acceptable face of this than some of the alternatives. For the West, any worry about Putin's intentions will be tempered by his evident pragmatism and Russia's obvious economic and military weakness; an army that had such enormous difficulty capturing Grozny is unlikely to be used to threaten Warsaw or Kiev.

Turkey: Into a New Era?

In the late summer of 1999, the Turkish political system appeared on the verge of collapse. The economy was mired in recession. The heavy death toll in the 17 August earthquake had demonstrated the high human cost of decades of corruption and nepotism. The government's dilatory and inefficient response to the disaster seemed to have eroded the last vestiges of public respect for their leaders. At 75 years-old, Prime Minister Bülent Ecevit was visibly ailing: unable to stand unaided for long and subject to frequent short-term memory loss. Yet there appeared little prospect of any successor being able either to hold together the disparate members of the four-month old tripartite coalition government, or to form an alternative administration without including the Islamist Virtue Party (FP). That inclusion would, it seemed certain, trigger intervention by the rigorously secular Turkish military. Even the one indisputable triumph of the year, the capture, trial and sentencing to death of Kurdistan Workers' Party (PKK) leader Abdullah Öcalan, seemed set to backfire, as Turkey's European allies repeatedly warned that executing Öcalan could irreparably damage Ankara's relations with Brussels.

But by mid-January 2000, the public mood in Turkey was buoyant, almost euphoric. The transformation was triggered by Turkey's inclusion in the official list of candidates for EU accession drawn up at the 10 December summit of EU leaders in Helsinki. After initial hesitation at the EU's linkage of accession to an improvement in Turkish relations with Greece, the doubts fell away. Suddenly, all of the country's problems appeared solvable. Within weeks, an anti-inflation programme backed by the International Monetary Fund (IMF) had sent interest rates tumbling and stock prices soaring. On 12 January 2000, the government announced that it would shelve Öcalan's execution pending a ruling by the European Court of Human Rights (ECHR). Even Ecevit appeared rejuvenated, walking briskly to his office in the Prime Ministry, delivering speeches without notes and even displaying flashes of the oratory that had once made him the best public speaker in the country.

Such was the change in the public mood that there was barely a ripple of protest as Ecevit vigorously lobbied for an extended term of office for President Suleyman Demirel, who had been publicly vilified just months earlier as an architect of the political culture so damningly exposed by the August earthquake. Nor were there many murmurs of dissent when Ecevit confidently predicted that Turkey could meet all of the criteria for EU membership by 2002, two years before the next review of the candidates' eligibility is due.

Yet in reality, EU membership remained a distant prospect. More dangerously, the allure of future accession had distracted Turkish public opinion from the failure to resolve the underlying causes of the collapse in national morale just four months earlier. Beneath the new found optimism, there was little sign of substantive improvement. If anything, the problems had merely become more complex and the stakes even higher.

The Grey Wolves Return to the Fold

The rapid growth in electoral support for the Islamist Welfare Party (RP) during the 1990s had alarmed both Turkey's Western allies and the Turkish establishment, particularly the military which sees itself as the guardian of the secular state bequeathed by Kemal Atatürk, the republic's founder. Yet the Islamists' electoral success had not been based on religion alone but on a combination of Islam and nationalism, and an explicit nostalgia for the Ottoman Empire. Its appeal was strongest amongst the peasantry, whether in the villages of Anatolia or in the sprawling shanty towns of rural migrants that now surround Turkey's major cities. By touting what was effectively an Ottoman definition of nationalism, based on religion rather than ethnicity, the Islamists were also able to appeal to devout ethnic Kurds, who could plausibly claim the same Ottoman heritage as their ethnic-Turkish counterparts.

Nevertheless, when the Turkish Constitutional Court shut down the RP on 16 January 1998, as the result of intense, behind-the-scenes pressure from the Turkish military, the Islamist movement was thrown into confusion. Its leaders were banned from active politics for five years, and its successor, the FP, faced the choice between resuming where the RP had left off, in which case it also risked closure, or making a clean break with its predecessor, in which case it risked losing RP supporters. By the beginning of 1999, the FP had done neither and appeared an enigma both to itself and to its opponents.

While the party was still searching for its identity, then Prime Minister Mesut Yilmaz of the centre-right Motherland Party (ANAP) lost a parliamentary vote of censure on 25 November 1998. ANAP's minority tripartite coalition had governed Turkey since June 1997, when military pressure had forced the resignation of an Islamist-led coalition. The censure vote was triggered by allegations of collusion between ANAP and the local Mafia in the privatisation of state-owned bank, Türkbank. Prime Minister Ecevit, the leader of the second-largest party in the coalition, the nationalist-left Democratic Left Party (DSP), took over as head of a caretaker government to take the country through to elections in April 1999.

A former social democrat, Ecevit had become increasingly nationalistic during the 1990s, combining fierce anti-Western rhetoric with populist economic policies and a reputation for personal honesty. Even though Ecevit was not directly responsible, the capture in Kenya on 15 February 1999 of PKK leader Öcalan gave a further boost to his nationalist credentials, merely because he happened to be prime minister at the time.

Öcalan's capture also proved an electoral godsend to the ultra-nationalist National Action Party (MHP). The party remained anathema to most middle-aged Turks, who remembered the excesses of its paramilitary wing, the Grey Wolves (named after the mythical grey she-wolf said to have led the Turks out of their ancestral home in Central Asia), during bloody street battles with leftist militias in the 1970s. But its ideological vigour, which synthesised Islam and an assertive ethnic nationalism, had proved increasingly popular amongst Turkey's rapidly expanding younger generation, which does not remember the 1970s and is impatient with the manifest failure of the mainstream parties' elderly leaders to provide either jobs or a basis for national pride.

Öcalan had been resident in Damascus, from where he had directed the PKK since its foundation. Syria found it prudent to push him out of the country in October 1998 when Turkish patience snapped and it threatened military strikes against Syria if it did not expel him. To many Turks his expulsion and subsequent capture in Kenya were not only a national triumph but also a vindication of the hard-line anti-PKK policies advocated by the MHP. Italy's refusal to extradite Öcalan to Turkey in autumn 1998 and his subsequent three-week sojourn in the Greek embassy in Nairobi appeared to confirm the party's allegations that Western countries were providing the PKK with moral and material support. With Öcalan securely behind bars on the prison island of Imrali, the MHP's election campaign rode on the overwhelming public clamour for his immediate execution, promising to hang him if it came to power.

In the April 1999 general election, the MHP won 18% of the national vote, up from 8.2% in the December 1995 poll. Most of its votes came from the young rural and urban poor, many of them ethnic Turks who had formerly supported the RP. Ecevit's DSP also increased its share of the vote from 14.6 % to 22.2%, making it the largest party in parliament, though still well short of an overall majority. The FP could only manage 15.4 %, compared with 21.4 % for the RP just over three years earlier. The biggest losers were the two parties of the centre-right, ANAP, whose vote fell from

19.7% to 13.2%, and the True Path Party (DYP) of former Prime Minister Tansu Çiller, whose vote dropped from 19.2% to 12%. The social democrats failed to cross the 10% barrier for representation, leaving the Turkish parliament without a genuine left-of-centre party for the first time in its history.

It took two months of tricky negotiations before a coalition between the DSP, MHP and ANAP, under Ecevit as prime minister, finally received a vote of confidence on 9 June 1999. Despite the ideological differences, there have been few signs of discord. MHP Chairman Devlet Bahçeli, a meticulous, 50-year-old life-long party bureaucrat, has concentrated on maintaining governmental and party discipline rather than pressuring his coalition partners into adopting a more assertively nationalist agenda. In January 2000, Bahçeli even succeeded in persuading MHP deputies to postpone bringing Öcalan's death sentence before parliament for ratification pending the result of his appeal to the ECHR, which may not be known until early 2001. At that point, if the appeal is lost, Bahçeli will probably be unable to resist pressure for the execution from the MHP grassroots.

Relative harmony and a healthy majority of 351 in the 550-seat unicameral parliament has enabled the coalition to push through a swathe of reforms, covering everything from banking to social security, privatisation and taxation. Yet in early 2000 it was still too early to assess their practical impact in what remained a very fluid legislative environment with poor rates of enforcement.

Perhaps more importantly, there was still no sign of a change in the political culture. In early 2000, applications were pending for the lifting of parliamentary immunity from more than 20 members of parliament charged with offences ranging from corruption to involvement with narcotics, smuggling and murder. Few expect the applications to succeed. In the April 1999 elections, two candidates used their local influence and successfully stood for parliament as independents purely to avoid prosecution. Friends and relatives of high-ranking politicians have continued to enrich themselves through lucrative state contracts and soft loans from state banks.

Yet, despite widespread public disillusion with politics and politicians, there remains little concerted pressure for change and, after an initial furore when a fresh scandal breaks in the press, the anger, if not the deed, is soon forgotten. Public cynicism has nevertheless meant that, unless they have a radical agenda, few young Turks now seriously consider a career in politics.

In early 2000, despite the undoubted improvement in Ecevit's health, there remained doubts about how complete or long-lasting his recovery would prove; nor does he have an obvious successor. More alarmingly, the absence of a serious alternative to Demirel, another 75-year-old veteran, had raised the possibility of an amendment to the Turkish constitution to allow him to continue as president when his current term expires in April 2000. With the possible exception of the Islamist movement, it was difficult to see where the next generation of political leaders would come from.

Political Islam Vacillates

The Turkish Islamist movement appeared to have lost direction during 1999. The FP's defeat in the April elections was followed on 2 May 1999 by a débâcle when one of its female deputies, Merve Kavakci, tried to attend the swearing-in ceremony in parliament wearing her Islamic headscarf. Secularist deputies created such an uproar that she was eventually forced to leave without taking the oath.

The incident was a gift to the FP's opponents. They were able to question the sincerity of the party's oft-repeated pledges to work within the system; while its inability to force the issue demonstrated its weakness to opponents and supporters alike. The FP's humiliation was completed two weeks later when Kavakci was stripped of her Turkish citizenship. It had emerged that, while studying in the US, she had successfully applied for American citizenship, but had failed to fulfil the procedural requirement of notifying the Turkish authorities.

The Kavakci incident raised questions about the political acumen of the FP Chairman Recai Kutan, a 73-year-old close associate of former RP Chairman Necmettin Erbakan. It also increased the tension between the party's old guard and the younger generation of Islamists under the leadership of the charismatic, 45-year-old former Istanbul mayor, Tayyip Erdogan. In 1998, Erdogan had been forced to resign as mayor after being convicted of inciting religious hatred by reciting a poem mixing military and religious imagery. Under Turkish law, Erdogan, as a convicted felon, is currently banned from active politics. But, since his release from prison on 24 July 1999, he has been discretely building a national political power base ready for the time, which even his enemies believe will eventually come, when his ban is lifted.

Moreover, despite the FP's poor performance in the 1999 elections, there is little to suggest that the Islamist movement is in decline, as opposed to divided. If Erdogan returns to the political arena, the FP is likely both to win back much of the support that had shifted to the MHP in April 1999, and to make inroads into the conservative wings of support for ANAP and the DYP.

Nor is there any evidence that the younger Islamists are more moderate than the old guard. They are just more pragmatic. During the late 1990s, as they came under greater pressure from the secular establishment, Turkish Islamists repeatedly stressed their commitment to greater democratisation, freedom of speech and even Turkey's eventual

Europe

accession to the EU, which they believe will safeguard their political rights. But they have remained silent in the face of the suppression of opinions, such as those of Kurdish nationalists, different to their own.

During 1999 there was also increasing evidence of rising support for the violent fringes of the Islamist movement. On 21 October, Ahmet Taner Kislali, a prominent secularist intellectual, was assassinated by a car bomb, which Turkish security officials attributed to members of an Islamist terrorist organisation, the Islamic Raiders of the Greater Eastern Front (IBDA–C).

In late 1999, another Islamist terrorist organisation, the Turkish *Hizbollah*, which had previously confined its activities to the pre-dominantly Kurdish south-east of the country, began to move into the cities of western Turkey. On 17 January 2000, the police raided a *Hizbollah* safe house in Istanbul, killed one of the organisation's leaders, Huseyin Velioglu, and uncovered enough documents in the building to warrant the arrest of more than 50 militants nation-wide. In early 2000, it was still too early to determine the extent of the damage to the organisation's operational capabilities. The Turkish security forces estimated that Turkish *Hizbollah* still had over 4,000 militants under arms and another 25,000 active sympathisers, mostly in the south-east of the country, where it was reportedly recruiting heavily amongst former members of the PKK.

Exit the PKK, Enter the Kurdish Problem

The PKK had already been in retreat militarily when Öcalan was expelled from Syria. His subsequent failure to find refuge in Europe dealt a severe blow to his plans to shift the struggle onto a political platform and his capture by Turkish special forces in Kenya on 15 February 1999 delivered the *coup de grâce*. It not only severely weakened the PKK's prestige and operational capabilities, but also triggered a potentially fatal power struggle within the organisation.

Öcalan's transfer to Turkey and his subsequent arraignment on charges of treason and mass murder heralded an outburst of nationalist celebration. For most Turks, Öcalan is personally responsible for the more than 35,000 deaths in the PKK's 15-year insurgency. His highly publicised trial on the prison island of Imrali in June 1999 often threatened to turn into a macabre carnival, as relatives of soldiers slain in the conflict converged on the nearby port of Mudanya, where they held daily, noisy demon-strations demanding his immediate execution. In court, during a rambling and often barely coherent defence, Öcalan unexpectedly renounced the armed struggle in what appeared to be a desperate attempt to avoid the gallows. Nevertheless, on 29 June 1999, he was convicted and sentenced to hang.

On 2 August 1999, as he waited for his case to go to appeal, Öcalan declared an open-ended cease-fire and called on all PKK militants to withdraw from Turkish territory, but his conviction was upheld. On 30 December 1999, his death sentence was forwarded to the Prime Ministry, from where, under Turkish law, it must be presented to parliament for ratification before it can be implemented. Öcalan's lawyers had already appealed to the ECHR. On 12 January 2000, the Turkish government, anxious to avoid antagonising the EU only a month after being named as a candidate for accession, announced that it would postpone presenting the death sentence to parliament until after the ECHR's ruling.

The Turkish authorities undoubtedly had other sound practical reasons for keeping the PKK leader alive, at least in the short-term. After his capture in Kenya, day-to-day control of the PKK passed to its Presidential Council, which was dominated by three veteran regional commanders, Cemil Bayik, Murat Karayilan and Öcalan's younger brother Osman. Both Bayik and Karayilan were reluctant to abandon the armed struggle, although the Presidential Council ordered PKK militants to obey Öcalan's call for a cease-fire and withdrawal to camps in the mountains along Turkey's borders with Iraq and Iran. Osman Öcalan argued that the PKK had to transfer its campaign onto a political platform.

On 20 November 1999, Karayilan arrived in the Netherlands, where he applied for political asylum, and by early 2000, Bayik and Osman Öcalan appeared locked in a power struggle, which threatened to weaken the PKK still further. Nor was it clear that, even if Osman Öcalan emerged victorious, as appeared likely, he would be able to coordinate a successful political campaign.

Even without such a campaign, an end to PKK violence could have far-reaching consequences, and, ironically, might accelerate the process through which Turkey's Kurds are granted greater political and cultural rights. The Turkish government would no longer be able to equate any expression of Kurdish identity with terrorism, and an end to the PKK's policy of infiltrating, or violently suppressing rival Kurdish organisations would help non-violent political movements to emerge. This would not only present a diversified, more subtle challenge to Ankara's current concept of a culturally and ethnically homogenised unitary state, but could increase international pressure on Turkey by attracting the support of her Western allies.

Psycho-economics or the Emperor's New Clothes

In January 2000, Turkey's new-found optimism was most palpable, and potentially most vulnerable, in the economy. On 9 December 1999, Central Bank Governor Gazi Ercel announced an ambitious anti-inflationary monetary programme, which sought to reduce annual retail inflation, running at 64.5% at end-November, to 25% by year-end 2001. In what, in retrospect, appears a master stroke, the announcement came the day before Turkey was named as a candidate for EU membership. Any initial doubts the markets may have had were submerged in the general euphoria at the prospect of accession, and banished entirely by the 22 December 1999 signing of a $4 billion stand-by agreement with the IMF.

The central plank of the Central Bank's programme was to abandon the retrospective linkage between Turkish-lira depreciation and the inflation rate. From January 2000, the Central Bank would allow the lira to depreciate in line with targeted, not realised, rates of inflation. To demonstrate its seriousness, the bank published a table of daily exchange rates through 2000 which it insisted it would apply, regardless of the inflation rate at the time. Privately, Central Bank officials admitted that the programme's primary aim was to reduce inflation by breaking what they termed an 'inflationist psychology'.

The result was instant and dramatic. Annual interest rates on bank deposits and purchases and repurchases of government paper fell from over 100% at the beginning of December 1999 to 35% by the end of the month. With nowhere better to go, money flooded into the stock market. By mid-January 2000, stock prices had more than doubled in US dollar terms in a little over a month. Turkish government officials were quick to note that the fall in interest rates would improve the country's chronic budget deficit, currently running at an estimated 12% of gross national product (GNP). In 1999, two-thirds of total budgetary revenue was consumed by debt servicing, most of it at real interest rates in excess of 30% per annum.

But there was a danger that an abrupt decline in returns on government paper could actually stifle economic recovery. In 1999, Turkish GNP is estimated to have shrunk by 4.5–5%. Since the early 1990s, Turkish banks have become heavily reliant on the high returns on their purchases of government paper, while commercial companies have become equally dependent on similarly high returns on repurchases of the same paper from the banks. If the source suddenly dries up, there are likely to be widespread bankruptcies.

Moreover, although the Central Bank's programme may have been well-timed psychologically, it has yet to be backed by government measures to tackle the economy's structural problems, which have fuelled high inflation. Bewilderingly, the programme was announced at a time when the rate of inflation was rapidly climbing. By the end of December 1999, annual retail inflation had risen to 68.8%, while wholesale monthly price increases of 4.1% and 6.6% in November and December respectively appeared to rule out an imminent decline. Yet unless there is a rapid fall in inflation during the first quarter of 2000, the markets are likely to lose confidence in the Central Bank programme. Banks will then refuse to buy government paper at what they believe will be a loss, interest rates will rise, thus further fuelling inflationary expectations; and the Central Bank will be faced with the choice between a humiliating climb-down and pricing Turkey's two main sources of foreign exchange, exports and the tourism industry, out of their respective markets.

Earthquakes: a Nation in Trauma

For most Turks, 1999 will simply be remembered as the year of the earthquakes. A massive tremor, measuring 7.4 on the Richter scale, struck the industrial city of Izmit, 100km east of Istanbul, in the early hours of 17 August, causing death and destruction on a scale unprecedented in recent Turkish history. For religious or health reasons, many of the victims were buried before they could be counted by officials, ensuring that the total death toll was certainly much higher than the official figure of 17,400, and perhaps as high as 25,000 or even 30,000. Another 49,000 were seriously injured and over 500,000 made homeless. The economic cost has been estimated at $6–10bn, approximately 3–5% of annual GNP, including the loss of some 140,000 jobs. On 12 November, another huge earthquake, this time measuring 7.2 on the Richter scale, struck the mountainous and more thinly populated province of Bolu, 150km east of Izmit, killing 832 people and seriously injuring another 5,000.

In the immediate aftermath of the Izmit earthquake, it briefly appeared as if the tremor would also transform the political culture, particularly the mixture of reverence and fear with which most Turks regard the state. In the first few hours after the quake, Ecevit, perhaps fearing that he would be seen as abdicating responsibility, rejected a proposal by Turkish Chief of Staff General Huseyin Kivrikoglu that he declare a state of emergency, which would have allowed the army to take overall control of the rescue operation. Yet the civilian authorities appeared paralysed. Although international aid and rescue teams began arriving in Turkey within hours, it took several days for the Turkish government to coordinate its own relief effort, by which time many of the injured trapped in the rubble had already died.

It also rapidly became clear that the biggest killer had not been the earthquake itself but the poor quality of housing, as contractors had either bribed local officials or relied on influential personal connections to ignore Turkey's theoretically stringent building regulations. The normally deferential Turkish press launched a series of unprecedentedly outspoken attacks on politicians for inculcating and perpetuating a bureaucratic culture of corruption and nepotism. The most scathing criticism was directed at President Demirel, whose 35-year political career has been dogged by allegations of bribery and links with members of the Turkish underworld. By mid-September, however, public bitterness appeared spent. It was further ameliorated by the speed and efficiency with which the government responded to the Bolu earthquake. By January 2000, some of the newspapers which had denounced Demirel just four months earlier were calling for his re-election as president.

The trauma of the earthquakes did have one positive outcome. An atavistic distrust of foreigners, which had become increasingly pronounced during the late 1990s, was swept away by the speed and generosity of the international aid effort. Nowhere was the transformation more dramatic than in attitudes towards Greece, which was one of the first countries to send aid and rescue workers to Turkey in the wake of the Izmit earthquake. On 8 September 1999, sympathy turned to empathy as Athens too was struck by a major earthquake, and it became Turkey's turn to send its own rescue teams to Greece.

Neighbours in Need, Friends Indeed?

The three weeks that PKK leader Öcalan spent hiding in the Greek embassy in Nairobi before his capture brought Turco-Greek relations to their lowest point since disputed possession of islets in the Aegean brought the two countries to the brink of war in January 1996. Yet ironically, the Öcalan incident also laid the foundations for the rapid improvement in relations later in the year.

His complicity in arranging for Öcalan to be flown to Kenya led to the sacking of the hawkish Greek Foreign Minister Theodore Pangalos. He was replaced by Georges Papandreou, who had long favoured better ties with Ankara. The earthquake diplomacy of August and September provided an opportunity that was quickly seized. Not only did Athens not use its veto over Turkey's inclusion as a candidate for EU accession, but Papandreou then made the first official visit to Ankara by a Greek foreign minister for 38 years on 20–22 January 2000.

While the warmer atmosphere has undoubtedly reduced tensions, it has failed to yield any substantive improvement in relations. In January 2000, Papandreou and his Turkish counterpart Ismail Cem signed four cooperation agreements, covering money-laundering, terrorism, illegal immigration and tourism. But Turkish suggestions of military cooperation were politely rejected by Athens. Nor was there any suggestion of movement on the countries' respective positions in any of their long-standing disputes.

In late 1999, the UN, taking advantage of improved relations between Turkey and Greece, renewed efforts to resolve the Cyprus issue by initiating proximity talks. During the talks in December and January 2000, Turkish Cypriot leader Rauf Denktash and Greek Cypriot President Glafkos Clerides met separately with UN Secretary-General Kofi Annan and his Special Adviser on Cyprus Alvaro de Soto, in an attempt to lay the ground for face-to-face negotiations.

The first two rounds of talks were held in New York on 3–14 December 1999, and in Geneva between 31 January and 8 February 2000, with a third round scheduled to begin in New York on 23 May 2000. Although UN officials remained optimistic that the two leaders would agree to face to face talks in late 2000, there was no indication of any movement in their mutually incompatible positions. Beyond that, in early 2000 both the Turkish and Greek governments were vehemently dismissing speculation that their apparent rapprochement would produce any change in their respective support for the Turkish and Greek Cypriot positions. Nor, given the strong public opinion in each country, where the Cyprus problem continues to be seen as a matter of national honour, did they appear to have much room for manoeuvre.

The Greek Cypriots maintain that a solution must be based on a unitary state, albeit with special minority rights and an international peacekeeping force to allay Turkish Cypriot fears of a repeat of the inter-communal bloodshed that preceded the 1974 Turkish invasion of the island. The Turkish Cypriots are equally adamant that any reunification of Cyprus must be based on a loose federation between two sovereign states, with the predominantly Turkish Cypriot north of the island retaining not only Turkish military protection, but also strict limits on Greek Cypriot movement and settlement.

Despite UN optimism, time appears to be running out for any solution which includes an imminent reunification of the island. The EU stated at the Helsinki Summit that settlement of the Cyprus problem was not a prerequisite for the accession of the Greek Cypriot south in the name of the whole island. Even though several EU member-states remain opposed to granting accession before a solution, the statement has by itself encouraged Turkish Cypriot hardliners, who have consistently warned that granting EU membership will trigger the north's integration into mainland Turkey. In practice, that process is already well advanced. The Turkish Cypriots and the mainland government have already signed agreements to harmonise the education, health, social-security and financial systems, while Turkish Cypriot farmers and businessmen are eligible for many of the same Turkish government investment incentives as their mainland counterparts. In early 2000, an estimated one-third to one-half of the 180,000 population of northern Cyprus consisted of first- or second-generation immigrants from the mainland, many of whom had married Turkish Cypriots.

Nor is there any indication that the younger generation of either Turkish or Greek Cypriot politicians is likely to be more conciliatory. Both Denktash and Clerides are in their mid-seventies. Clerides is already under intense pressure from younger Greek Cypriot politicians not to make any concessions in the proximity talks. Denktash is expected to win re-election as president of the self-proclaimed Turkish Republic of Northern Cyprus (TRNC) in May 2000. But the current TRNC prime minister, Dervis Eroglu, who is Denktash's main rival and generally assumed to be his eventual successor, is even more hardline. In February 2000, Eroglu bluntly declared that the status quo on the island was the solution to the Cypriot problem and promised that, unlike Denktash, he would not even cede territory to the south in return for a settlement.

Privately, Turkish officials also admit that Ankara is reluctant to relinquish control over its strategic foothold on the island. During 1999, Turkish Cypriot newspapers published confidential government documents that indicated a concerted policy in Ankara to ensure that all departments in the Turkish Cypriot administration included at least one native Turk. Privately, Turkish military officials assert that, although Turkey could reduce its troops in the north from the current level of around 30,000, the island's proximity to the Turkish mainland means that they could never be withdrawn completely, nor could Ankara countenance the presence of a potentially hostile government Cyprus.

In January 2000, Greece and Turkey had still to agree over the nature of their differences in the Aegean, much less to discuss possible solutions. Greece claims that the only problem is the definition of the territorial shelf, which should be decided by the International Court of Justice (ICJ) at The Hague, while Turkey maintains that there are also a number of other issues, which should be solved bilaterally. These range from mineral exploration rights and the ownership of a number of islets to Athens' plans to extend its territorial waters to 19.3km, which Ankara asserts would amount to a virtual blockade of its Aegean coast and would draw a military response.

Yet, under the conditions attached to the Helsinki offer of candidacy, Ankara undertook to resolve all of its disputes with Greece bilaterally by 2004, or to allow them to be settled by the ICJ. Ecevit has dismissed suggestions that the agreement marks a change in policy, merely describing it as an indication of Turkey's confidence that the two countries can resolve all of their differences amicably without recourse to the ICJ. But this is not how it is seen in Athens, which now has only to wait for Ankara to be forced to choose between accepting the Greek position and jeopardising its membership prospects.

EU: Betrothal at Last, but the Dowry is High

For most Turks, EU membership has always been as much about how they perceive themselves as the benefits and responsibilities of joining an economic or political grouping. For them, accession represents not only the culmination of the century-old Turkish dream of becoming part of Europe, but also recognition that the Turks should belong to what they perceive as an élite club of nations. On a psychological level, simply being named as an EU candidate at Helsinki was almost an end in itself. After initial hesitation at the special requirements, such as a settlement of its disputes with Greece, that Turkey must fulfil in addition to the Copenhagen criteria applicable to all candidates, the practical implications of membership were soon submerged in a flood of national well-being.

In January 2000, most Turks appeared unaware that there was an immense distance to be covered before accession could be achieved and that it therefore still remained a distant prospect. Although several macro indicators in Turkey, such as the rate of inflation and the public-sector borrowing requirement are still very wide of the economic criteria for membership, Turkish economic legislation is already broadly in line with EU norms. However, there are major legislative and conceptual discrepancies between the Copenhagen political criteria and Turkish laws and practices.

In early 2000, the Turkish authorities showed no signs of being prepared to ease restrictions on freedom of expression. On 18 January 2000, over a month after Helsinki, three Islamist journalists were sentenced to one year in jail for alleged anti-secular propaganda; while on 26 January, Turkish courts banned a translation of a history of Kurdish nationalism by an American professor. The Turkish government remains adamant that it will not countenance broadcasting or education in Kurdish. On 2 December, Kanal 21, a television channel in the predominantly Kurdish city of Diyarbakir was closed for a year for playing a Kurdish popular song.

The Copenhagen criteria also call for the military to be brought under civilian control. It has been suggested that the Turkish military be subordinated to the Ministry of Defence, rather than reporting directly to the president, as it does now. Yet even if this were done, in practice little would change. During the late 1990s, the Turkish military exercised power through informal means, primarily through a combination of public deference and an awareness of the army's historically proven willingness to intervene directly if necessary. Its mere expression of opinion was inevitably sufficient to ensure compliance, without any need for recourse to legally enshrined authority. The military's image of itself as the guardian of secularism is shared by most Turkish secularists, who, despite the rise of the Islamist movement, are still the majority. The recent upsurge in Islamist violence is likely to ensure that the Turkish military is unwilling to leave the political arena; and, as long as there is a fear of a possible Islamist take-over, and while there is so little confidence in the country's politicians, few secularist Turks will exert pressure for a change.

In January 2000, Turks remained generally unaware that EU membership required the *de facto* ceding of a measure of sovereignty to Brussels. As it becomes clear that accession is neither automatic nor imminent, there is a strong possibility that Turkey's initial euphoria over candidacy will give way to fear that meeting the membership criteria will make the country more vulnerable, not only to greater foreign political and cultural influence, but also to domestic challenges to the *status quo*, particularly from the Islamist and Kurdish movements. Unless such fears are offset by concrete benefits, such as substantial EU aid and a clear timetable for accession, there is a danger of a nationalist backlash and a growing suspicion that membership may not be worth the price.

Into a New Era, Again?

In the early 1990s, the late Turkish President Turgut Ozal was fond of promising his countrymen that the twenty-first century would be the century of the Turk, with a belt of Turkish influence stretching from the Aegean to China. At the end of the decade, the geographical focus had shifted to Europe, but in many ways the dreams were the same. Each promised a new era of opportunity, prosperity and above all, influence and prestige; each had a solid grounding in reality; with both, it was the image, not the practical details of how it could be achieved, that caught the public imagination.

The euphoria that followed the announcement of Turkey's candidacy for the EU may prove more dangerous than the despair of four months earlier. In the aftermath of the 17 August earthquake, there was a tangible sense amongst the Turkish public that things had to change and, perhaps for the first time, a realisation that it was up to individuals, not to the state, to change them. But as 2000 began, most Turks had reverted to relying on others to deliver their aspirations, whether it was the military, the state or the EU. There was a tendency to see opportunities, such as candidacy or the disarray in the Kurdish and Islamist movements, almost as solutions in themselves. Yet, without directly confronting both the country's existing economic, social and political problems or the new, and more subtle, challenges of EU candidacy, the Turkish public could yet be left ruing another frustrated dream.

Dimming Prospects in Northern Ireland

Although the five-and-a-half-year Northern Irish peace process has been agonising, it has also been partially successful. Annual deaths due to political violence have dropped by over 80% since the cease-fires declared in autumn 1994 by the Irish Republican Army (IRA) and the pro-British loyalist paramilitary groups. For the first time since the ill-fated 1974 Sunningdale government – brought down after five months by a loyalist general strike – there was, for ten weeks, self-rule in Northern Ireland and an agreement between the two sides to share power on an institutional basis. Because the IRA refused to disarm, however, the new Northern Ireland Assembly was suspended on 11 February 2000 and London resumed direct rule over Northern Ireland. Over the next month, efforts were made to reinvigorate the peace process, but it remained stalled.

Getting from There to Here

1999 was a crucial year for the Northern Ireland peace process. Near its end, the extraordinary Good Friday Agreement, which had provided the best-ever promise of resolving the long impasse in Northern Ireland, appeared often on the verge of political death, but it had tenuously survived. On 29 November, the executive cabinet was officially formed. Assembly members Martin McGuinness and Bairbre De Bruin of *Sinn Feín*, the IRA's political wing, were appointed minister of education and minister of health, social services and public safety, respectively. At midnight on 1 December 1999, power officially devolved from Westminster to the new Northern Ireland Assembly, ending a ten-month delay in implementing the Agreement. Within two weeks, the North–South Ministerial Council was set up, giving Dublin limited input into Northern Ireland's governance.

IRA disarmament (euphemistically called 'decommissioning') was the sticking-point that all along had threatened to scuttle the Agreement. Devolution had been scheduled for February 1999, but this had depended on the prior formation of an executive cabinet including *Sinn Feín*. The Ulster Unionist Party (UUP) – the largest political group representing the mainly Protestant provincial majority who want Northern Ireland to remain under British rule – had insisted that the IRA, which for over 25 years had waged a violent campaign to unite Ireland, begin disarming before the executive cabinet could be formed.

Breaking the impasse took months of agonising negotiations under the adroit chairmanship of former US Senator George Mitchell, who had returned to try to rescue the agreement he had done so much to create. Mitchell reasoned that unless the UUP tried power-sharing, nobody would

Europe

know whether IRA decommissioning was possible. On the other hand, unionists balked at the prospect of forming an executive on which two *Sinn Feín* members – especially McGuinness, who is widely believed to have been a leading IRA terrorist – would also serve.

Difficult though it was, a compromise was finally worked out. On 27 November 1999, after the IRA agreed to appoint a representative to the Independent International Commission on Decommissioning to discuss disarmament, the Ulster Unionist Council (UUC), the UUP's governing body, voted 480–349 to drop its demand that the IRA must first disarm before it could join the government. To win this consensus, however, UUP leader and assembly First Minister David Trimble promised to resign if the UUC were to decide on 12 February that there was by then insufficient progress on decommissioning for the UUP to stay in government.

In January 2000, General John de Chastelain, the chairman of the disarmament commission, held several discussions with Brian Keenan, the designated IRA liaison. De Chastelain submitted his scheduled progress report just inside his deadline of 31 January. It indicated that the IRA had not committed to disarmament. Perceiving that Trimble's position as UUP leader had to be preserved to keep the Agreement alive, UK Secretary of State for Northern Ireland Peter Mandelson rushed legislation through the UK parliament empowering him to suspend the Northern Ireland Assembly. He did so on 11 February – one day before the scheduled UUC vote.

Almost simultaneously, General de Chastelain tendered a second report stating that the IRA representative had, in discussions on 11 February, 'indicated … the context in which the IRA will initiate a comprehensive process to put arms beyond use, in a manner as to ensure maximum public confidence'. The British and Irish governments judged this to be promising but – without a specified date and technical metho- dology, or a clear definition of the 'context' of disarmament – inadequate to forestall or reverse the assembly's suspension. On 15 February, the IRA pulled out of disarmament discussions with de Chastelain and withdrew all proposals. A tentative timetable for discussions aimed at resolving the impasse was established by the British and Irish prime ministers on 1 March 2000. Although the assembly was still out of commission, both the IRA and the loyalist cease-fires appeared to be intact.

Decommissioning: Text and Context

The terms of the Good Friday Agreement do not require IRA decommissioning. They merely establish decommissioning as an objective of the peace process as a whole. The operative clause states:

> All participants … reaffirm their commitment to the total disarma- ment of all paramilitary organisations. They also confirm their intention to continue to work constructively and in good faith with

the Independent [International] Commission [on Decommissioning], and to use any influence they may have, to achieve the decommissioning of all paramilitary arms within two years following the endorsement in referendums North and South of the Agreement and in the context of the implementation of the overall settlement.

Although no date for decommissioning appears in the text of the Agreement, the referendums were held on 22 May 1998, and thus establish 22 May 2000 as the target date. On the basis of this provision, *Sinn Feín* argues that:

- the Good Friday Agreement does not require decommissioning, only that the parties use their influence to attain it;

- with the establishment of devolution and its attendant institutions delayed by the decommissioning impasse, republicans have not had enough time to establish the 'trust' in such institutions that the Agreement's original timetable would have allowed; and

- in any case, the UUP's interposing the earlier date of 12 February 2000 impermissibly changes the Agreement's 22 May 2000 deadline.

This is a defensible interpretation of the Agreement's text. However, it neglects the wider context. During the run-up to the Good Friday Agreement, it transpired that Trimble could not persuade the UUP to accept the Agreement without a UK government commitment that *Sinn Feín* would not be permitted to participate in government by holding seats in the Northern Ireland Assembly's executive cabinet unless the IRA had substantially disarmed beforehand. On 10 April 1998, the day before the Agreement was signed, Trimble received a letter from UK Prime Minister Tony Blair stating in the relevant part:

I understand your problems with paragraph 25 of Strand 1 [providing for the removal of any executive member who does not use exclusively peaceful means] in that it requires decisions on those who should be excluded or removed from office in the Northern Ireland executive to be taken on a cross-community basis. This letter is to let you know that if, during the course of the first six months of the shadow Assembly or the Assembly itself, these provisions have been shown to be ineffective, we will support changes to those provisions to enable them to be made properly effective in preventing such people from holding office.

Furthermore, I confirm that in our view the effect of the decommissioning section of the agreement, with decommissioning

Europe

schemes coming into effect in June [1998], is that the process of decommissioning should begin straight away.

While this letter skilfully fudges the timing issue, its clear intent is to reassure Trimble that his wish that *Sinn Féin* not be admitted to the executive prior to decommissioning will be honoured. Unionists argue that, insofar as such assurance was an integral part of the quid pro quo, it is effectively part of the Agreement. Thus they contend that the UUC, by allowing *Sinn Féin* into government prior to IRA disarmament, signified the renegotiation of the 'no guns, no government' condition, and justified the imposition of a shorter deadline. This is a reasonable interpretation of the spirit of the Agreement.

Sinn Féin notes, however, that the Agreement also specifies that decommissioning must begin only 'in the context of ... overall implementation'. To republicans, this context necessarily embraces comprehensive demilitarisation. That, in turn, is a four-way, rather than a two-way, street. It requires, in exchange for IRA decommissioning, not only loyalist disarmament, but also the reform of Northern Ireland's 92% Protestant-manned police force, the Royal Ulster Constabulary (RUC), and the withdrawal of British troops from the province. This reading of the clause, which calls only for 'decommissioning of all *paramilitary* arms' [emphasis added], appears unduly broad.

To expand the context of the Agreement further still, it should be noted that prior to entering multiparty negotiations in September 1997, *Sinn Féin* signed up to the so-called 'Mitchell Principles', which Senator Mitchell had established as a baseline good-faith requirement for all participants in the peace process. The core principles embody a commitment to democratic and exclusively peaceful means of resolving political issues, and a commitment to the total disarmament of all paramilitary organisations, verifiable to the satisfaction of an independent commission. Unionists tend to suspect that circumspect IRA representations, such as that reported by de Chastelain on 11 February, are, in substance and intent, mere endorsements of these commitments in theory alone, and do not seriously contemplate what unionists call 'actual' decommissioning in the near-term. Such endorsements may constitute a slight advance in IRA thinking, but they do not, as unionists see it, bring disarmament palpably closer.

Stripped of legal nicety, the republican position is that the substantial integrity of the IRA cease-fire since July 1997, and its willingness to consult with de Chastelain on an ongoing basis were sufficient demonstrations of good faith to allow *Sinn Féin* to take seats on the executive. Similarly laid bare, the UUP position is that no elected party can be allowed to participate on the executive level of democratic government with an intact private army at its disposal. Both sides are constrained from further compromise by extreme elements – republicans by hard-liners, who believe that handing over any weapons would be an unacceptable act of surrender; the UUP by the strong anti-Agreement sentiment of members of its own party and of the Reverend Ian Paisley's Democratic Unionist Party (DUP) and smaller unionist groups.

Salvaging the Good Friday Agreement

Trimble would face much dissent in a reinstated assembly, as he did in the original one. Of the 64 unionist seats, the UUP holds 28 while anti-Agreement members of the DUP and smaller parties hold 25. These politicians regained popular strength during the summer of 1999, when paramilitary punishment attacks (intra-communal shootings and beatings intended to deter 'anti-social behaviour', and not to advance a political cause) increased, and an IRA attempt to smuggle weapons from the United States was uncovered by the Federal Bureau of Investigation. Although UUP deputy leader John Taylor's last-minute change of heart may have won the 27 November vote for Trimble, five of the party's ten members of the Westminster parliament still considered the IRA's stance on disarmament an inadequate foundation for *Sinn Féin's* participation in government. Furthermore, Trimble's pro-Agreement position was weakened by the failure of the historically non-violent Social Democratic and Labour Party (SDLP) – the province's largest Catholic nationalist group – to agree to govern with unionists in the event of the IRA defaulting on its demilitarisation representations and *Sinn Féin* being expelled from the executive. Had the SDLP given this agreement, the assembly's suspension might well have been avoided.

Consigning decommissioning to an international commission has failed to de-politicise the issue. On the other hand, pro-Agreement unionists have relaxed their original position perceptibly. Early in the peace process, they insisted on total decommissioning before *Sinn Féin* entered even political negotiations, much less government. Now they require, at least initially, only a material gesture – though they have not quantified it. The degree to which the IRA will move towards decommissioning, however, is a function not merely of technical and logistical matters that can be disposed of hermetically, but also of political issues that attract fierce cross-community debate.

The most volatile of these issues is police reform. The release of the Patten Commission Report on 15 September 1999 illustrated just how far apart unionists and republicans were on this issue, and also demonstrated the centrality of collective memory and historical grudges in the long-standing conflict. The report, drafted by a commission chaired by former Hong Kong governor and current European Commissioner for External Affairs Chris Patten, went some way towards meeting IRA and *Sinn Féin*

Europe

demands. It recommended that the RUC's name and badge be changed and that a two-tier community-policing scheme be instituted. The report further prescribed that the existing oversight body, the Police Authority, be replaced by a police board, over half of which would be composed of political representatives, including at least two *Sinn Feín* members. On 20 January 2000, Secretary of State Mandelson announced that nearly all of the proposed changes would be implemented.

Unionists were outraged. They considered the name and insignia overhaul an insult to the 302 police officers killed, and the around 10,000 injured during the troubles, and they regarded the structural overhaul as giving the IRA an opportunity to infiltrate the police. The IRA and *Sinn Feín* were equally dissatisfied. They applauded the cosmetic changes, but because they see the RUC as a bastion of anti-Catholic unionist oppression, they did not feel these reforms went nearly far enough. They really want a total uprooting of the RUC, for which, of course, the report does not provide.

The IRA is equally unlikely to get its way with regard to the British presence. When power was devolved on 1 December 1999, troop strength in Northern Ireland stood at 15,000 – its lowest level in 30 years. Additional reductions may be considered, but a wholesale withdrawal is unlikely given the large quantity of arms held by the IRA and by loyalist paramilitaries, and the growing strength of anti-Agreement terrorist splinter groups. The latter include the 'Continuity IRA' and the 'Real IRA', which some intelligence sources believe number about 100 members between them, and the loyalist Red Hand Defenders. The security forces estimate the IRA's arsenal at close to 100 tonnes of weapons, including: 600 AK-47 assault rifles; a dozen 7.62mm medium machine guns; 20 heavy machine guns; two flame-throwers; at least two SAM-7 anti-aircraft missiles; 40 rocket-propelled grenade launchers; 40 Webley .455 revolvers; and 600 assorted detonators, as well as three tonnes of the plastic explosive Semtex.

The fundamental difficulty is that while the IRA sees arms as necessary insurance for as long as the RUC is Protestant-dominated and British troops are still deployed, unionists see the security status quo as necessary for as long as the IRA has weapons. Prior to the suspension of the assembly, the operative belief was that the impasse could only be resolved through a series of small steps of faith (leaps being implausible in Northern Irish politics) taken alternately by the two sides. The first examples of these were the unionists' grudging entry into government with *Sinn Feín* when the IRA had not yet begun decommissioning, and, to a lesser extent, the IRA's appointment of a decommissioning delegate to the international commission. While it sounds very reasonable, this concept does not work if the IRA does not intend to give up its weapons. So far, the small-steps-of-faith approach has simply enabled the republicans to outmanoeuvre unionists with rhetoric, even though they have issued no statement strictly committing them to IRA disarmament. The suspension of the assembly, insofar as it avoided Trimble's resignation, was a politically unavoidable step to the side.

In failing to begin any tangible disarmament during the 72 days between the executive's inception and its suspension, the IRA clearly let pass the optimal moment for the political breakthrough required to consolidate the settlement. With the IRA disengaged from the international commission, its partial disarmament is less likely. *Sinn Feín* President Gerry Adams has always claimed that he could not deliver an IRA weapons surrender for tactical reasons, but now he is probably telling the truth. Now that most republican (and loyalist) prisoners have been released pursuant to the Agreement, IRA hard-liners no longer feel that they have to indulge Adams' preference for politics to the extent that they did previously.

The only chance of decommissioning taking place is if IRA members sympathetic to Adams defy the hard-liners and give up some of their arms. Historically, such splits have sapped republican will, and the movement abhors disunity. Yet republican leaders were unable to prevent an incipient split in late 1997, when several dozen republicans, concerned with what they saw as Adams' tilt towards temporary compromise on a united Ireland when he signed up to the Mitchell Principles, started the '32-County Sovereignty Committee'. Elements of that group later organised the Real IRA, which was responsible for the August 1998 Omagh bomb that killed 29 and injured hundreds. A 1986 split produced 'Republican *Sinn Feín*', based in the Irish Republic and linked to an anti-Agreement group known as the 'Continuity IRA' that arose in 1995. The Continuity IRA has recently pledged to wreck the peace process. It was responsible for bombing a hotel in Irvinestown, County Fermanagh, on 6 February 2000 and a British Army barracks in Ballykelly, County Londonderry, on 25 February 2000.

While an IRA split followed by decommissioning would allow the assembly's suspension to be lifted and permit *Sinn Feín* to rejoin the new devolved government, it would also probably mean a resurgence of anti-Agreement terrorist activity carried out by republicans and potentially by loyalists in reaction. But the overwhelming support for the Good Friday Agreement among Northern Irish nationalists suggests that anti-Agreement republican terrorists would have even less popular support than the Provisionals had. With the most politically powerful republicans (notably, Adams and McGuinness) on the side of peace, dissidents would be denied any of the synergy with *Sinn Feín*, which, since the 1981 hunger strikes, provided the IRA with a strong public image. Anti-Agreement republicans would also get less operational support from their communities, and, following the historical pattern, pro-Agreement Republicans would move to restrain rival groups coercively. But because splits have compromised republicanism in the past, even the more politically inclined republicans may prefer to forsake the peace process rather than risk another fracture.

Even in a political vacuum, with the Good Friday Agreement rendered unworkable, the peace process has produced significant changes at both political extremes that make the reduced level of violence sustainable. First, the IRA's vaunted 'international dimension' has shrunk. Although *Sinn Féin* has often drawn on official and popular sympathy in the US, the Clinton administration and virtually every major US newspaper laid the blame for the collapse of the peace process squarely on the IRA's failure to move on decommissioning in January 2000. Perhaps as a result, Adams' public statements after the assembly's suspension indicated that he intended to continue seeking a political solution.

Second, while the foot-soldiers of the loyalist paramilitaries have been diverted into drug-dealing, racketeering, and internecine feuding, the loyalist leadership – long dismissed as thugs by mainstream unionists, who see terrorism as tainting their cause – has unexpectedly developed a high level of discipline, a small electoral base, and some political sophistication by virtue of participating in the peace process. Although there have been some serious sporadic breaches of the loyalist cease-fire, it has been generally intact for over five years. The Ulster Volunteer Force's political wing, the Progressive Unionist Party, won seats in the new assembly; the Ulster Freedom Fighters' political wing, the Ulster Democratic Party, sits in local councils.

The current impasse – or indeed, a resumption of IRA terrorism – would give the newly respectable loyalist movement an opportunity to consolidate its position on the moral high ground. By staying quiescent, they would deprive their republican counterparts of the tit-for-tat dynamic that sustained the conflict's critical momentum for 25 years. In keeping with their traditional stance that they are a 'reactive' force, however, the two main loyalist paramilitary groups have declined to hand over weapons until the IRA does so. There is a small chance that a disarmament gesture on their part would prompt a similar move by the IRA.

Where Is Here?

The agreed framework for cross-community self-rule in the province contained in the Good Friday Agreement provides both nationalists and unionists with a strong motivation to make it work, as any future process is unlikely to produce anything better. Three relationships, or 'strands', have been created by the Agreement:

- between unionists and nationalists within Northern Ireland;

- between the new Northern Ireland Assembly and the Republic of Ireland; and

- between the Republic of Ireland and the United Kingdom.

Only the first two of these are substantively critical; the third merely establishes British-Irish consultative institutions.

Under the first strand, the UK retains sovereignty over Northern Ireland unless a Northern Irish majority votes otherwise; Westminster devolves power to a Northern Ireland assembly (elected by proportional representation); and key acts and decisions of the assembly require cross-community consensus, either by parallel majority consent of both unionists and nationalists or by a 60% supermajority.

Under the second strand, the Republic of Ireland has repealed from its constitution the territorial claim on Northern Ireland. A North–South Ministerial Council was formed, including members of Northern Ireland's assembly and of the Republic of Ireland's parliament. This council's actions, including delegation of powers to six cross-border 'implementation bodies' (covering distinct areas such as food safety, aquabusiness, and inland waterways), must be approved by the assembly and the parliament, to which the cross-border bodies are also accountable.

Even if the assembly is resurrected, governing pursuant to these awkward arrangements will be slow and difficult. That is perhaps inevitable, however, when two main groups seeking opposite sovereign ends must rule together. The overridingly important feature of the Good Friday Agreement is the sub-sovereign separation it accomplishes between Northern Ireland and its 'mother countries' – the UK and the Republic of Ireland – that is satisfactory to both sides.

The IRA's refusal to comply with the evolved conditions for *Sinn Féin's* participation in government, however, has caused both unionists and republicans to harden their positions on decommissioning. It appears likely that the Northern Irish players will have to renegotiate those conditions. Workable devolution is therefore farther away than it was a year ago, and will probably require another battery of arduous negotiations to be brought appreciably closer.

Given the renewed enmities caused by the assembly's suspension, such negotiations may fail. But written agreements and final settlements, while the ultimate objectives of peace processes, are not their only positive achievements. The Northern Irish peace process has yielded a diminished IRA, more self-restrained loyalism, and a level of terrorist violence lower than that prevailing before the August 1994 IRA cease-fire that began the peace process. Moreover, even if the Agreement is not fully implemented, the UK government is likely to retain a number of its elements, such as

Europe

police reform, some formalised cooperation between Northern Ireland and the Irish Republic, the human-rights commission, and perhaps some of the recommendations in the upcoming review of the justice system. Given London's strong motivation to try to preserve the IRA cease-fire, it is no coincidence that most of these measures are aimed at pacifying republicans.

The Middle East

T HE EFFORT TO NEGOTIATE a comprehensive peace between Israel, the Palestinians, Syria and Lebanon inched slowly forward in 1999 and early 2000 through a series of starts and stops that created alternating moods of optimism and pessimism. When Ehud Barak won the presidential election in Israel in mid-May 1999, and unveiled a highly ambitious programme for further talks with Yasser Arafat, coupled with a new schedule of withdrawals of Israeli troops from parts of the West Bank, a palpable sense of relief arose. It appeared that the two leaders would lift the negotiations out of the semi-comatose state in which former president, Binyamin Netanyahu had left them. The optimism that accompanied the first talks between the two soon settled into a watchful waiting, as both sides jockeyed for position. The talks are set to continue, however, and Barak continues to insist that the date he has set to complete the process, 13 September 2000, will be met.

The talks with the Syrians have been stymied. Despite strong encouragement from the US, including a meeting between President Bill Clinton and President Hafez al-Assad in late March 2000, it has not been possible to bridge the presentational gap that is delaying a settlement. There is every indication that most substantive issues were resolved in a series of meetings in Washington at the end of 1999 and later through the mediation efforts of Clinton and Egyptian President Hosni Mubarak. Both sides, however, must keep their domestic opposition in the forefront of their considerations and neither side seems willing to make the breakthrough that is essential if success is to be achieved. In the interim, Israel has made it clear that it will unilaterally withdraw from southern Lebanon without a prior agreement with Syria, a move that is certain to raise the temperature in that border area.

As a result of the landslide victory that the reforming parties won in the 18 February 2000 Iranian parliamentary elections, temperatures at home, in the region and in US–Iranian relations have dropped. Although there is still a strong current of conservative theological feeling in the country, the outcome of the elections has made it clear that the government is moving inexorably towards democracy. The US has made a number of good-will gestures, hoping to be able to renew a positive relationship with Iran, but they have yet to be reciprocated. It will clearly take some time before those who retain nostalgia for the heady days of the Iranian revolution can be pushed out of positions of power.

Map 3 The Middle East

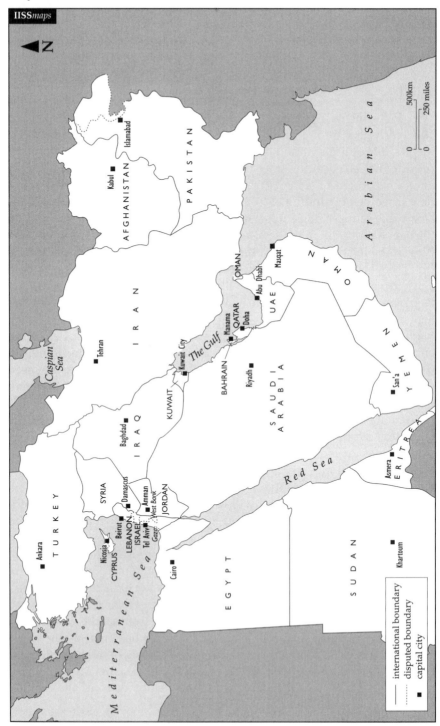

There was also good news from the Maghreb in North Africa. A surprisingly smooth succession from King Hassan II of Morocco, who died in July 1999 after 38 years on the throne, to his relatively unknown son Mohammed VI heartened that country's citizens and neighbouring countries. And King Mohammed's unusually liberal initiatives have also been encouraging. There was less violence in Algeria and Tunisia's economy continued to improve. Even Libya's Colonel Moamer Gadaffi moved far enough towards verbal liberalisation to warrant the US taking a somewhat softer line on its 'rogue' status. Yet these developments are only a thin veneer on the political and economic problems facing the region. The major challenge facing the leaderships in each country is to manage their efforts at top-down liberalisation while keeping them from spinning out of control.

Resurrecting Middle East Peace Prospects

Ehud Barak's stunning victory in the May 1999 Israeli elections clearly reflected the sentiments of a large proportion of the Israeli public, their disillusion with incumbent Prime Minister Binyamin Netanyahu and their yearning for a revival of the peace process. The international community quietly heaved a collective sigh of relief. Barak had presented himself as carrying the mantle of Netanyahu's predecessor, Yitzhak Rabin, and from the outset of his government, the peace process was his first priority. His moves appeared to be aimed at forging a new sense of common purpose between Israel and its Arab partners and regaining their trust. Barak set an ambitious programme to bring about a comprehensive peace in the region within his first 15 months in government. Although much of the campaign was based on domestic issues, Barak's election represented a mandate from the Israeli public to move the peace process forward. In 1996 Israelis had felt that Shimon Peres was moving too fast; this time they punished Netanyahu for stalling.

While Barak spoke of giving equal priority to all aspects of the peace process, his actions and words revealed a higher priority to a treaty with Syria. Syrian President Hafez al-Assad's deteriorating health added to the sense of urgency. Barak had also pledged in his election campaign that he would withdraw Israeli troops from Lebanon within one year of taking office, which, under the best of circumstances, would require a resumption of talks between Israel and Syria to avoid continued hostilities on the Lebanese border. Even though talks between the two countries were

The Middle East

stalled at the time, the Israeli Knesset voted in March 2000 to support a unilateral withdrawal of Israeli troops, a solution that would undoubtedly lead to an escalation in violence on the Lebanese front. Furthermore, Israeli bombing raids on Lebanese infrastructure in June 1999 and February 2000 drew vehement condemnation from the Arab states, and compounded Syria's fears that it may be forced to capitulate to Israeli demands on the Golan Heights issue.

Efforts to get Syrian–Israeli peace talks back on track remained blocked until direct intervention by President Bill Clinton brought the two sides to resume negotiations in December in Washington from 'the point where they had left off'. Positive language from both sides awoke speculation that a deal had already been sewn up and that the two sides were close to signing a peace treaty. That hope did not last. It soon became clear that the countries' expectations differed concerning the substantive issues in discussion. The negotiations quickly became paralysed and were finally suspended by the Syrians until they received assurances that Israel would be willing to commit itself to a withdrawal from all of the Golan Heights, back to the 4 June 1967 line. Clinton made a further effort at the end of March 2000 to bring the two sides back to the negotiating table when he met with Assad in Geneva for three hours of talks. There was no immediate indication, however, that this effort was successful.

Barak's immediate inheritance on the Palestinian front was the Wye Memorandum of 1998, unilaterally suspended by Netanyahu after the first of three designated withdrawals. To differentiate his approach from that of Netanyahu, Barak held his own discussions with the Palestinian leaders and agreed a modified version of Wye at the beginning of September. It appeared that relations between the two sides had turned a new corner. But, after a promising start, negotiations fell back into their familiar pattern of foot-dragging and mistrust, and in January, the Palestinians suspended all contacts with Israel. Memories of the optimism engendered by Barak's election were fading, and talk of the possibility of comprehensive peace in the region grew more sober. In early March 2000, US mediators arranged renewed negotiations, and showed that the dash of realism that super-seded the unwarranted high hopes of early 1999 might yet accomplish solid progress.

On the Palestinian side, Yasser Arafat was under domestic pressure to achieve gains without making further concessions to the Israelis. Despite Arafat's still-considerable personal stature as the symbol of Palestinian nationalism, he has steadily been losing his grip on the Palestinian people. In November 1999, unprecedented dissent culminated in the signing of a document by 20 leading Palestinian figures decrying Palestinian Authority (PA) corruption and mishandling of the peace process. Arafat's refusal to delegate even to his negotiating team meant that he took the blame for failure to achieve progress on Jerusalem, the Israeli settlements and the return of the Palestinian refugees. This autocratic tendency has increased Arafat's workload and exacerbated his ailing health, intensifying the urgency of his desire to establish a Palestinian state sooner rather than later. Such conflicting pressures have left Arafat with little room for manoeuvre.

This inclination to monopolise is also reflected in the Palestinian Authority's management of the economy. Despite limited moves towards reform, which were welcomed by the International Monetary Fund (IMF), PA corruption and mismanagement have led donors to default on their pledged funds. The floundering Palestinian economy depends heavily on these donations, and the resulting crisis has forced the PA to raise food prices and to cut public and welfare spending, precisely the wrong measures to take. In February–March 2000, teachers protested against the absence of a public-sector pay rise since the Palestinian Authority was established in 1994. Such economic pressures have heightened Arafat's need to make tangible gains in the peace process.

A Seismic Shift in Israel

On 17 May 1999, Barak defeated incumbent Prime Minister Netanyahu in the Israeli elections, by a margin of almost 400,000, gaining slightly over 56% of all votes cast. Whilst polls in the days immediately prior to the election had signalled Netanyahu's defeat, no one had anticipated such a decisive victory. After three turbulent years of *Likud* government, Barak's election slogan: 'Israel wants a change' clearly reflected the sentiments of a large proportion of the Israeli public and their disillusion with Netanyahu.

Barak's victory was as dramatic as it was surprising. During the initial months of 1999, it was still widely expected that Netanyahu would win the election. This analysis was based on two assumptions: firstly, it was generally believed that Netanyahu retained the confidence and loyalty of the voters. This was despite criticism of his style of leadership by his coalition partners and even by some former members of his own party who had left the *Likud* to work towards his downfall. Secondly, as leader of the opposition, Barak had failed to capture the imagination of the Israeli public and was thought to be a less skilled election campaigner than Netanyahu. Pessimism about Barak's chances led to Yitzhak Mordechai's candidacy for premiership. Highly popular as Netanyahu's defence minister, he was seen as the only person who could gain the crucial support of disaffected Sephardi voters, and bring about a change of government at a time when growing divisions between Israel's various ethnic and religious groups increasingly threatened domestic instability.

In contrast with the 1996 election, domestic issues – with an unemployment rate of 9% the economy was pushed high up on the agenda – and the broader questions of personal character and leadership qualities

The Middle East

were central features of the campaign, with the peace process playing a lesser role. Yet, although it did not feature prominently, it was ever present as a backdrop. In 1996, Netanyahu won the election by playing on the public's fears and insecurities about the peace process with the Palestinians, famously promising 'peace with security'. He exploited Israelis' lack of trust in Shimon Peres, who, Netanyahu claimed, would re-divide Jerusalem and was incapable of providing security. Barak was not such a soft target. His military credentials as a former chief of staff and Israel's most decorated soldier were his strong point, and he exploited them to meet Netanyahu head-on over the issue of security. Barak further enhanced his security credentials by gaining the support of Matan Vilna'i, a former deputy chief of staff, and Yossi Peled, a former head of the Northern Command, both of whom Netanyahu had courted to be his defence ministers. Furthermore, Mordechai, whose election campaign had lost momentum, withdrew his candidacy and lent his support to Barak.

Following in Netanyahu's footsteps, Barak stressed that he would provide peace with security. While he was vague about the specific policies he intended to adopt, Barak was uncompromising concerning his criteria for future negotiations with the Palestinians: no concessions on Israeli sovereignty over Jerusalem; no return to the 1967 border; no 'foreign army' west of the Jordan river; and no evacuation of major settlement blocs. A major surprise in the campaign was Barak's announcement that he would put any final status agreement with the Palestinians to the Israeli public in a referendum. This successfully neutralised a sensitive election issue, but risked holding the Palestinian track hostage to the vicissitudes of Israeli domestic opinion. Meanwhile, without specifying terms or conditions, Barak promised to revive negotiations with the Syrians, and re-affirmed Rabin's pledge that a peace treaty with Syria would be put to a referendum. He also pledged that he would withdraw Israeli troops from Lebanon within a year of taking office.

Netanyahu had met Arafat; had pulled the majority of Israeli troops out of the troublesome West Bank town of Hebron; and, in the Wye River Memorandum, had agreed to the further transfer of territory to the Palestinians. Israelis did not, in fact, believe that Netanyahu was fully committed to the peace process, and they did not perceive the election of Barak as jeopardising their security. Although Barak himself won a clear-cut vote of support from the Israeli electorate, in the elections for the Knesset, the One Israel List (an alignment of the Labour Party, the Gesher movement headed by David Levy, and Meimad, a moderate religious movement), which he headed, faired significantly worse. It secured only 26 Knesset seats and 663,000 votes, barely a quarter of all votes cast.

This was the second Israeli election under the new electoral system in which Israelis cast two votes: one for the direct election of the prime minister; and the other for the party of their choice in the Knesset, the 120-

seat parliament. This allows Israelis to vote for their preferred candidate to lead the country while simultaneously choosing the party that best reflects their specific domestic concerns. As in 1996, the Israeli public continued to desert the two main parties and to vote for smaller parties representing particular interests. Netanyahu's overwhelming defeat, which led to his immediate resignation from political life, was mirrored by the dramatic collapse in the *Likud* vote, which fell from 32 to 19 seats, with most of its previous support going to *Shas*, a Sephardi religious party.

The new electoral system has led to a fragmented political system, with some 15 factions represented in the current Knesset. Barak's freedom of manoeuvre hinged on his choice of coalition partners and demanded great political dexterity. For the first time in the history of Israel, a secular-based coalition excluding the religious parties was an option. Bringing in the *Likud* – with former foreign minister, Ariel Sharon as caretaker leader – would have given Barak a working majority, and enabled him to deal with civic issues and the question of religion and state. Such a coalition would, however, have limited his freedom of manoeuvre on the peace process, since *Likud* would have demanded a significant decision-making role as their price for joining forces with Barak.

The coalition Barak finally chose and presented on 6 July 1999 included the religious parties and *Meretz* (a party that promotes civil and secular issues), thus allowing him greater scope to deal with his number-one priority, the peace process. Seven parties and 73 members of the Knesset made up the coalition: One Israel, *Meretz*, the Centre Party, *Yisrael B'Aliyah* (a Russian immigrant party) and the three religious parties: *Shas*, National Religious Party (NRP), and United Torah Judaism. Although Barak has promised a government of change, four of his coalition partners and seven of his ministers served under Netanyahu.

This is an uneasy *mélange*, brought together only by the distribution of Knesset seats but with no unanimity on how to achieve peace. Nevertheless, Barak's choice of coalition partners allowed him greater freedom to attend to the peace process and, when he presented his government to the Knesset, he made it clear that was not only his government's priority, it was his. He showed that he intended to take sole charge of the peace process by keeping the Defence Ministry for himself.

The Israeli–Palestinian Track

Barak's inheritance on the Palestinian front was the Wye River Memorandum, which had been unilaterally suspended by Israel on 16 December 1998 after the first of three designated redeployments of Israeli troops in the West Bank. The dissolution of the Israeli Knesset pending the election effectively put the Israeli–Palestinian track on hold for the first part of 1999; there was little prospect of its renewal until a new government was in office. Netanyahu had tried to show commitment to Wye by proposing in February the partial implementation of the Memorandum, with the opening of a safe-passage route and the release of further Palestinian prisoners. But his offer was rejected by the Palestinians, who insisted that any implementation of Wye must include further redeployments.

Most diplomatic activity in early 1999 centred on preventing a unilateral declaration of Palestinian statehood when the five-year Oslo interim period ended on 4 May 1998. As the deadline drew near, Arafat came under increasing international pressure to desist from taking such a course of action, for fear of its potentially disruptive consequences, the uncertainty of the Israeli response and its possible negative impact on the Israeli elections – namely strengthening Netanyahu and the right wing.

In response to this pressure, Arafat concentrated his efforts on both trying to extract promises of future recognition of Palestinian statehood in exchange for refraining from a unilateral declaration, and on obtaining guarantees that, once negotiations were resumed, a new deadline would be set so that they would not drag on indefinitely. The US and the EU worked to provide Arafat with enough assurances and incentives to prevent him from declaring independence. The EU Council of Ministers in Berlin on 24–25 March issued a statement, loosely coordinated with the US, which laid out its most explicit declaration to date in support of Palestinian statehood, much to Israel's chagrin. It reaffirmed the 'continuing and unqualified Palestinian right to self-determination including the option of a state'. The Berlin Declaration also called for an early resumption of final status negotiations 'on an accelerated basis', and stated that negotiations should be concluded 'within a target period of one year'.

Clinton then sent a letter to Arafat on 26 April, the day before the PLO Central Council was set to debate the statehood question. It called upon Israel and the PA to resume negotiations swiftly after the Israeli elections and to accept a one-year timetable for the conclusion of a final settlement. The letter expressed support for the Palestinian right to self-determination, stated its preparedness to accept a state resulting from negotiations and criticised Israeli expansion of settlements. To appease the Israelis, the American proposal did not contain any explicit date for a final agreement.

These strong international diplomatic efforts to stave off a unilateral declaration paid off. The 4 May date passed quietly. When Barak's victory came, it was cautiously welcomed by most Palestinians. Barak had been a reluctant champion of the Oslo process and, unlike his Labour party colleagues, had kept his distance from Arafat, rarely meeting with him. Although minister of the interior in Rabin's cabinet, he had abstained in the Knesset vote on the Oslo II accords. He was particularly concerned with what he perceived as the lax security provisions of Oslo, and had been a vocal proponent of extending the timetable for the redeployments stipulated in the accords.

During his first six weeks in office, all Barak's energies were concentrated on forming a new government. Then he turned his full attention to the peace process. In quick succession, he held short meetings with Egyptian President Hosni Mubarak, Arafat and King Abdullah of Jordan, and then boarded an aircraft to consult with Clinton in Washington.

Barak did not want his first act as prime minister to be interpreted as simply carrying out the agreements signed by his predecessor. Instead he sought to put his own stamp on future negotiations with the Palestinians. In his conversations with Arab leaders, Barak promised that he would move quickly to implement the Wye Memorandum, but indicated that he would prefer to delay the third stage of the second redeployment outlined in Wye, and to combine it with a final-status agreement. In Washington, Barak laid out an ambitious timetable for the coming year, hoping to achieve a 'comprehensive framework for Middle East peace', including peace agreements with Syria and Lebanon within 15 months – a time frame chosen with the forthcoming US presidential elections in mind. At the same time, he sought to reduce the US role in the negotiations. He felt that at Wye, the US had become both mediator and judge, and he wanted to restore its previous role as facilitator between the two sides. The Palestinian side, however, felt that US and international mediation was necessary to resolve a conflict where the military and economic balance weighed so heavily in Israel's favour.

In his second meeting with Arafat at the Erez checkpoint (Gaza) on 27 July, Barak reiterated that he was willing to carry out the Wye redeployments as signed if the Palestinians so demanded, but that he would prefer to delay further redeployments until a final agreement was close to completion. Arafat replied that he sought the quick and full implementation of Wye, but was willing to have an Israeli–Palestinian committee examine Barak's ideas.

This set the tone for the tortuous path of negotiations over the next few months. A joint committee headed by Palestinian Saeb Erekat and Barak's chief negotiator, Gilad Sher, met at the beginning of August but broke up almost immediately over Israeli requests for an extended timeframe for the further redeployments. The proposed completion date of February 2000 was considerably beyond the twelve weeks stipulated in the Wye agreement. The Palestinians were also surprised by Israel's proposal for the drawing up of a 'declaration of principles' on the final-status agreement, an idea that Barak had previously aired but not formally presented to them. Negotiations continued through the month, often acrimoniously, with Arafat accusing Barak of a breach of trust and Barak accusing the Palestinians of inflexibility, and both sides turning to the Americans and Egyptians to help mediate and support their positions.

At the end of the month, US Secretary of State Madeleine Albright went to the Middle East to help bridge the gap between the two sides. On 4 September 1999, at the Egyptian resort of Sharm-el-Sheikh, Arafat and Barak put their signatures to a new memorandum charting the way for a final settlement between Israel and the Palestinians by September 2000.

Under the terms of the agreement, Israel agreed immediately to redeploy its forces from 7% of the West Bank (some 400 square kilometres), transferring it from full Israeli control ('Area C') to areas under Palestinian civilian jurisdiction ('Area B'). Two further withdrawals were scheduled to take place:

- on 15 November, a 2% transfer from Area B to Area A (under full Palestinian control) and 3% from Area C to Area B;

- on 20 January 2000, a 1% transfer from Area C to Area A, and a 6.1% transfer from Area B to Area A.

As with the Wye Memorandum, the Sharm-el-Sheikh agreement did not include maps detailing the specific areas to be transferred to the Palestinians but left them to be determined. However, Israel failed to consult the Palestinians, or even the maps they submitted, concerning the areas of withdrawal, and ultimately withdrew from sparsely populated pockets with little strategic importance. The agreement did not deal with the third and final redeployment set out in the Oslo II Accords, assigning a joint Israel–Palestine Committee to negotiate it at a future date.

The agreement also drew up a timetable for the implementation of a number of outstanding issues from the Oslo II and Wye Accords:

- 10–13 September 1999: Release of 200 Palestinian prisoners.

- 1 October: Construction of Gaza port to begin.

- 1 October: Opening of southern safe-passage route between Gaza and the West Bank.

- 5 October: Delineation of the northern safe-passage route between Gaza and the West Bank.

- 8 October: A second group of 150 Palestinian prisoners to be released.

- 30 October: The reopening of Shuhada Road in Hebron to Palestinian traffic.

The Sharm el-Sheikh agreement was more than a modified version of the Wye Memorandum. It broke new ground by calling for the immediate resumption of final-status talks – on borders, settlements, refugees, water and Jerusalem – and also by setting 13 September 2000 as the target date for a final-status deal. A further innovation was the decision that, by mid-February 2000, the two sides should draw up a 'Framework Agreement on Permanent Status' setting out the parameters of these negotiations.

The Sharm el-Sheikh agreement was heralded as a great success. It put Israeli–Palestinian negotiations onto a more positive footing and lent a renewed sense of urgency to proceedings. On 5 September the Israeli cabinet approved the agreement by 21 votes to two, and three days later the Knesset comfortably endorsed the agreement. Israel immediately began to withdraw its troops and release Palestinian prisoners. On 13 September, in a ceremony held at the Erez checkpoint, final-status talks once again resumed, and at the beginning of October the first safe-passage route was opened, enabling Palestinians to travel between the West Bank and Gaza.

The optimism engendered by all this activity quickly ebbed. Negotiations between Israel and the Palestinians soon resumed their familiar pattern of foot-dragging, recrimination and suspicion. Having established an ambitious timetable at Sharm el-Sheikh for the completion of the negotiations and for drawing up a framework agreement, Barak spent the next six weeks procrastinating over who should head the Israeli delegation before appointing Israeli ambassador to Jordan Oded Eran. His choice was unpopular among the Palestinian side, which felt that Eran's position did not reflect the importance of the negotiations. Discussions on the framework agreement did not begin until 8 November.

More critically, the date for the second withdrawal (originally scheduled for 15 November) passed with the two sides failing to agree on the areas of land to be transferred to the Palestinians. This impasse was finally broken in the first week of January 2000, but by then the Palestinians had been sidelined by the resumed Syrian negotiations, and little progress was made in drafting the framework agreement. Relations between the two sides continued to deteriorate during January, with Palestinian confidence in Barak waning and public statements becoming increasingly acrimonious. The third redeployment, set for 20 January, was postponed. The Palestinians had rejected outright the areas Israel was proposing to hand over to their full control (Area A) and were especially incensed that the Israeli maps contained areas around Jenin, Hebron and Tulkarm but did not include any of the areas neighbouring Jerusalem. In particular, they had been led to believe that Abu Dis would be part of the agreement.

With the 13 February 2000 deadline looming, there was considerable apprehension that no agreement was in sight. In an attempt to break the impasse, Arafat and Barak held a meeting at Erez on 3 February, but this only magnified their differences and the meeting quickly broke up. Three days later the PA announced that it was suspending all negotiations with Israel until the dispute over the third withdrawal was resolved. It took a month of intense mediation by the United States, with Egypt working closely in the background, for a compromise to be hammered out. Barak and Arafat met twice in Ramallah in long sessions and then travelled to Sharm el-Sheikh on 9 March to show their appreciation for Mubarak's mediation efforts and to announce the details of the new package.

Barak's original desire had been to lessen the American role in the Palestinian track. The compromise deal, however, was the result of a return to more direct engagement by the US in the negotiation process. Without that engagement, the negotiations would have remained stymied. In addition to the compromises that both sides made, they agreed to meet in Washington on 20 March to resume negotiations over the Framework Agreement, which they now aimed to complete by May.

In return for the Israelis accepting a renewed US role, the Palestinians agreed to accept that the 6.1% of the West Bank that was due to be handed to them under the earlier Sharm el-Sheikh agreement would not include areas neighbouring Jerusalem. The land was finally handed over on 21 March. In return, they extracted agreement from Barak that discussions over the scope and timing of third and final Oslo II redeployment would be determined by the two sides and carried out by the end of June. Barak had originally hoped to delay this third withdrawal and merge it into the final-status agreement. The parties emerged out of the Sharm el-Sheikh summit with a sense of optimism that mirrored that of the signing ceremony six months earlier. This could be seen in the fact that the date for completion was kept at 13 September, making it an enterprise even more ambitious, and difficult to complete, than it had originally seemed.

The Israeli–Syrian Track

Barak's victory also led to expectations of a resumption of negotiations with Syria, which had lain fallow for the duration of Netanyahu's period in office. Barak had promised during his election campaign to withdraw Israeli troops from Lebanon within the context of an agreement with Syria by the summer of 2000, a pledge he repeated on taking office. For Israel to extract itself from its Lebanon imbroglio, a renewal of talks with Damascus would be essential.

Meanwhile, reports of Assad's deteriorating health gave rise to speculation that the ageing president was keen to capitalise on Barak's election to resolve the Golan Heights issue and smooth the way for his son and predicted heir, Bashar al-Assad. Bashar's succession seems increasingly likely, but, because he is allegedly opposed by the Syrian military, how long he will manage to keep his grip on the leadership is in question.

Mutual messages of goodwill between the Israeli and Syrian leaders were relayed through British journalist and Assad confidant, Patrick Seale.

Syrian willingness to cooperate with Israel was further highlighted by its uncharacteristic restraint in the face of the June 1999 Israeli attacks on civilian power plants and bridges in Lebanon, where Syria is the real power broker. Syria's dire economic situation – characterised by high population growth and soaring unemployment – is undoubtedly encouraging Damascus to be more lenient with Israel. The aid, trade opportunities and increased foreign investment that could arise from a peace deal are desperately needed and are the subject of growing appeals from a Syrian business community grown tired of Damascus' insular and highly centralised economy and vast bureaucracy.

The portents for peace, therefore, looked promising. The Israeli public was increasingly weary of the toll on lives that the war in Lebanon had been taking, and Israelis recognised the close link between a change in Lebanon and negotiations with Syria. During the election campaign, Barak had said he would follow the path trod by Rabin, an unambiguous message that he was prepared to make a territorial compromise on the Golan to reach a deal with Damascus. Moreover, the future of the Golan had not been a critical element during the campaign. This was in sharp contrast to the 1996 election, when the Third Way Party had won four seats on a platform focusing exclusively on the issue of Israel's retention of the Golan. This time the party failed to win a single seat. Equally telling, a majority of settlers on the Golan had voted for Barak.

Shortly after the election, leaks to the Israeli press revealed that in the middle of 1997 Netanyahu, through the intercession of US businessman Ron Lauder, had sought to revive talks with Syria and had been prepared to make territorial concessions on the Golan. Netanyahu confirmed that these reports were true, while claiming that Syrian insistence on a return to the 4 June 1967 border had led to the failure of his efforts.

Optimism that compromises were finally within reach was fuelled in June by the unprecedented exchange of public gestures and compliments between the two leaders. This was further encouraged by reports that Syrian Vice-President Abdel Halim Khaddam had, in mid-July, met with four rejectionist Palestinian groups based in Damascus: the Popular Front for the Liberation of Palestine (PFLP); the Popular Front for the Liberation of Palestine-General Command (PFLP-GC); the Fatah Revolutionary Council; and Al Saiqa. He allegedly called on the groups to cease the armed struggle and switch their focus to the political realm. The Israeli army also reported in July that attacks by Hizbollah on Israeli and SLA troops in Lebanon had fallen to their lowest level in years, a sign, many thought, that Syria was reining in Hizbollah in preparation for the renewal of talks with Israel.

However, hopes of an imminent resumption of negotiations soon receded. Syria insisted that any future talks be resumed at the point at which they were broken off in March 1996, and that Israel publicly commit itself *a priori* to withdraw to the June 1967 border – a condition Barak was not willing to accept. Diplomatic activity then concentrated almost exclusively on the Palestinian track. The US, however, was working behind the scenes with Clinton intervening personally with a series of telephone calls to Assad and Barak. On 8 December, Clinton was able proudly to announce that talks between Barak and Syrian Foreign Minister Farouk al-Sharaa would pick up the following week in Washington 'at the point where they left off'. The formula was sufficiently vague to allow both sides to return to the table without publicly conceding their starting points.

The fact that the negotiations were to resume at such a high level excited speculation that differences between the two sides had already been ironed out and that a peace treaty might be signed as early as spring 2000. Optimism rapidly transformed into political realism, however, during the two days of meetings between Barak and al Sharaa in Washington. The atmosphere was decidedly frosty, especially after al-Sharaa, catching both Barak and Clinton off-guard, delivered a terse, uncompromising statement at the opening ceremony. He also side-stepped clear encouragement by Clinton to offer a symbolic handshake at the start of the talks.

The meeting turned out to be more procedural than substantive in nature. Although the issues and parameters of the Syrian track are more distinct than those of their Palestinian counterpart, bridging the gap between the two sides was clearly not going to be an easy task. Since the Madrid Conference in October 1991, negotiations between Israel and Syria have addressed four key issues, the 'four legs of the table' as late Israeli Prime Minister Yitzhak Rabin referred to them: Israeli withdrawal from the Golan Heights, security arrangements, normalisation of relations and the timetable of fulfilment. For Syria, the central issue is a complete Israeli withdrawal from the Golan Heights to the lines of 4 June 1967 allegedly agreed by Peres in 1996. For Israel, security arrangements and the nature of the peace are critical if they are to withdraw from the Golan. With Barak reiterating Rabin's pledge that any peace treaty would be put to a referendum, persuading the Israeli public that withdrawal from the Golan would enhance, rather than weaken security, was crucial.

At the conclusion of the two-day summit in Washington, the two leaders agreed to journey to Shepherdstown, West Virginia, on 3 January for extensive talks. The setting and structure of the Shepherdstown talks resembled the increasingly familiar pattern of Israeli–Arab negotiations: the parties met in an isolated town away from the glare of the media and audiences at home to work out their differences. Although the two parties were involved in face-to-face talks, the Americans were careful to remain present throughout the negotiations, mediating and drafting proposals.

The principal task facing the US was to develop a framework for the discussions and to reach consensus on the point of departure. Israel was loathe to begin discussions on demarcating the future border without prior and substantive progress on future security arrangements and normalisation of relations. The compromise reached was that four committees – addressing the demarcation of borders, security, normalisation and water resources – would meet simultaneously. The discussion of water resources, with its implications for borders and security arrangements, was an addition to the agenda that had not previously been discussed by the two countries.

The Shepherdstown meeting broke up after eight days, having achieved little. During the meeting it appeared that the parties were talking as much to audiences at home as they were to each other. American hopes of preventing leaks were shattered when international Arab newspaper *Al Hayat* and Israeli paper *Ha'aretz* published differing versions of a draft peace treaty that had been drawn up by the Americans. The *Al-Hayat* version contained a number of inaccuracies; Israel confirmed the authenticity of the *Ha'aretz* version. The draft suggested Syrian willingness to engage in normalisation with Israel and to meet a number of Israel's security concerns. In particular, although Syria would not accept Israeli troops manning an early-warning station on Mount Hermon, Syria was prepared to accept US and French personnel at such an outpost. Syria was embarrassed by the leak of the American draft and responded by publicising its own set of demands not included in the draft document. These included an insistence that any early-warning station on Mount Hermon should be limited to a period of five years, with Syrian officers also stationed there, and that future security measures had to incorporate a just solution to the Palestinian refugee problem.

The parties were scheduled to return to the United States for a third round of talks on 20 January, but they left Shepherdstown further apart than at the start of the meeting. The Syrians were angry with Israel for what they saw as deliberate foot-dragging over demarcation of the border. They announced that they would not return to the negotiating table unless they received written guarantees that discussions over demarcating the border would resume in earnest, and that the new border would be based on the 4 June 1967 line.

Disentangling From Lebanon

Developments on the Syrian track cannot be separated from a general shift in attitude towards Israeli policy in South Lebanon. Following a series of Israeli battle casualties in early March 1999, Israel's continued presence in

Lebanon became an election issue, with the prime-ministerial candidates all promising to bring about a quick and orderly withdrawal of troops. None, however, spoke of a unilateral withdrawal without an agreement.

In relative terms, 1999 was a 'good year' for Israel in that fatalities were down to 13. At the end of December, with a resumption of negotiations with Syria in mind, Israel released five Hizbollah prisoners held in administrative detention. This followed an unprecedented two-day cease-fire brokered by the International Red Cross that allowed Hizbollah to remove the bodies of members killed in clashes with Israel and the Southern Lebanon Army.

The collapse of the Syrian talks in early 2000, however, coincided with a rise in tension on the border. At the beginning of January fighting escalated and seven Israeli soldiers were killed. Israel responded by bombing power stations in Lebanon in February. The attack had been preceded in June 1999 by an even larger-scale attack on civilian power plants and bridges, and both bombardments drew sharp condemnation from the Arab states and internationally. Popular outrage was further fuelled by US attempts to defend Israel's highly damaging show of strength, and by Israel's threat to withdraw from a committee set up to enforce the April 1996 Understanding agreement not to strike civilian targets, which the bombardments clearly flouted.

Mounting tension intensified the debate in Israel over its continued presence in Southern Lebanon, with many politicians calling for an immediate withdrawal of Israeli forces and an end to the twenty-year fiasco. On 5 March, after two marathon sessions, the Israeli cabinet unanimously decided to withdraw the Israel Defence Forces out of Lebanon and back to the international border by July, with or without an agreement. The decision is immensely popular in Israel and could help swing a referendum Barak's way if an agreement could be reached with Syria by then.

The withdrawal also affects Lebanon and Syria. Israel's bombardments are widely perceived in the Arab world as a warning to Damascus that it will not be able to use Hizbollah to oppose a unilateral withdrawal – or to stage cross-border attacks in the event of such a withdrawal – without attracting massive reprisals against Lebanese infrastructure. This would guarantee an end to the current Syrian–Israeli negotiations. The threat of a unilateral withdrawal has also inspired panic among the South Lebanon Army (SLA) Israel's 2,500-strong proxy militia in the southern Lebanese occupied zone. Although Israel will probably provide asylum to around 200 senior commanders, the rank and file, as well as locals who benefited economically from the occupation, will have to fend for themselves in a country where the government and majority of the population view them as collaborators and traitors.

Again in the Balance

Barak's election in the summer of 1999 injected new life into the moribund peace process. He promised to pursue negotiations on all fronts with equal vigour; to conclude peace treaties with Syria and the Palestinians within 15 months; and to withdraw Israeli troops from Lebanon by the following summer. By the end of 1999, Barak's vision seemed to be on course. The Sharm el-Sheikh agreement had re-started negotiations with the Palestinians, and Syria and Israel were set to embark on an intensive round of talks. Yet within weeks of the new year, both tracks had ground to a halt with the prospects of achieving a comprehensive peace in the region by autumn becoming increasingly illusory.

Barak's increasing problems at home in maintaining the cohesion of his coalition mirrored the stalling of the negotiations. Opposition to his policies and management of the peace process became more vocal. Ministers within his own party began to voice concerns over what they saw as his neglect of the Palestinian track and a disproportionate emphasis on trying to secure a deal with Syria. These difficulties were exploited by the opposition. *Likud* sponsored a bill that would require a majority of all eligible voters – not just those who chose to vote – to pass the referendum on any peace negotiated with the Syrians. In effect, this would push up the majority from 50% to 65%, a so-called 'supermajority'. In Israel there is no provision for absentee voting, and at any given time at least 15% of eligible voters are away from a polling place. The first reading of the bill was supported by three parties in Barak's coalition– *Shas*, Yisrael B'Aliyah and the National Religious Party – handing the government a humiliating defeat.

Even if the bill is not ratified, in late March 2000 the prospects for any substantive progress towards peace had become captive to an increasingly unrealistic timetable. All parties were aware that the US presidential elections in November would soon reduce the amount of time and attention the incumbent administration would be able to devote to its essential mediating role, particularly on the Syrian track. In addition, the Israeli cabinet's decision to withdraw from South Lebanon by July, if necessary unilaterally, will make the need to revive negotiations between Israel and Syria imperative.

Both countries have much to lose should the withdrawal occur without any agreement about future security arrangements. At the beginning of March, Barak told the Israeli cabinet that four previous prime ministers – Shamir, Rabin, Peres and Netanyahu – had all entered into negotiations with Syria knowing that this would entail a withdrawal on the Golan Heights to the 4 June 1967 line. His statement led to speculation that a new formula was being devised to enable both parties to return to the table without losing face. If negotiations are not resumed by May, however, the prospects for their revival until after a new American administration is installed are minimal.

Arafat's government is faced with not just the prospect of a diminishing American role over the course of the year, but serious growing unrest amongst Palestinians over the lack of substantive progress. During 1999, Barak continually spoke of devoting his efforts equally to all tracks of the peace process, but hopes of progress with the Syrians were gained at the expense of negotiations with the Palestinians. In 2000, however, this situation will not be sustainable. The Palestinian track cannot again be put on the backburner. Arafat postponed declaring statehood on 4 May 1999, but it is unlikely that the 13 September deadline can pass peacefully without significant progress in resolving final-status issues between Israel and the Palestinians.

Iran: Crisis and Consensus

Parliamentary elections on 18 February 2000 resulted in a landslide victory for those eager to reform Iran's government, under the leadership of President Mohammed Khatami. Not only were the conservatives defeated, but the proponents of a 'third way', headed by former President Hashemi Rafsanjani, also fell by the wayside. For the first time, the rural areas and provincial towns voted along the same lines as the capital, Tehran. The lowest number of clerics since the revolution in 1979 (44 out of 225 elected MPs) were successful in the first round. Leading clerics remained silent during the election campaign, while references to Islamic ideology, or even to Islam, were scarce. Although hard-line conservatives waged a rearguard action – with, for example, the attempted assassination of prominent Khatami supporter Saeed Hajjarian on 12 March – the elections have entrenched democracy, and even initiated a process of secularisation. There is still, however, a question-mark over the size of the rift between 'conservatives' and 'liberals', and over its impact on domestic and foreign policy. Behind the current conflict, there is in fact a deeper continuity.

The System: Struggle and Continuity

The conflict between 'liberals' and 'conservatives' is more than a mere struggle for power: it relates to the democratisation and management of the revolutionary inheritance itself. Today, that inheritance has essentially been reduced to a rigid moral order (the compulsory veil, the second-class status of women and strict control of social behaviour, including leisure activities).

'Liberals' believe that reforms of substance are impossible without democratisation, aimed at creating a popular consensus in favour of change. They fear that halting reforms will provoke unrest, in particular from young people born and educated under the Islamic regime, but detached from it and aspiring to a consumer and leisure society. The young are an important section of Iranian society: 64% of the population was under 25 years of age in 1999. The 'conservatives' do not deny the need for structural reform, including of the economy, but fear that uncontrolled democratisation would rapidly destroy the regime, as *perestroika* did in the Soviet Union. They advocate an approach akin to China's: maintaining the regime's authoritarian and ideological integrity, while at the same time liberalising the economy. Where the 'liberals' want free elections, as provided for in the constitution, 'conservatives' use all available brakes – quite a few of which are also in the constitution – to slow the dynamics of popular expression. These brakes include:

- the 'Guide' of the revolution, Ayatollah Seyed Ali Khamenei, who can remove the president from office and dissolve parliament;

- the Council of Guardians, the supreme decision-making body, which can block election candidates whom it deems 'non-Islamic'; and

- the judiciary, whose head is appointed by the Guide, and who can initiate prosecutions on political and ideological grounds. Targets include newspapers, intellectuals and even ministers.

These differences notwithstanding, there is no clear-cut division between 'conservatives' and 'liberals'. All of the protagonists belong to the same inner core of those who mounted the revolution, and all have assumed high positions within the regime. Khatami, for example, was Minister of Culture from 1989 to 1992; former Tehran Mayor Gholam-Hossein Karbaschi was first appointed by the regime as mayor of Isfahan in the late 1980s; and Ayatollah Hossein Ali Montazeri, one of Khamenei's most virulent critics, was the late Ayatollah Ruhollah Khomeini's designated heir until early 1989. There are radicals among Khatami's supporters. Ayatollah Youssouf Sane'y, the president of the '15 Khordad Foundation', instigated the *fatwah* against British author Salman Rushdie, while Ayatollah Sadegh Khalkhali was, as Prosecutor-General, responsible for the bloody repression which followed the revolution. Abbas Abdi, the chief hostage-taker at the American Embassy in 1979, is now a liberal.

Moreover, the factions are far from homogeneous within themselves. Some conservatives, like Ali Khamushi, the president of Tehran's Chamber of Commerce and a leading member of one of the conservative factions, the *motafele*, are in favour of privatisation and economic liberalisation. Others, among them the leaders of the powerful and largely unaccountable foundations, are statists. These foundations, notably the Foundation for the Oppressed and the Foundation for the Martyrs, are in effect monopoly companies, which manage the huge assets confiscated from the Pahlevi family and close affiliates of the Shah's regime. The 'tax-free zones' of the Gulf islands, like Keshm, were set up by Rafsanjani.

The liberal coalition includes long-serving technocrats like Karbaschi, who believe that serious reforms imply democratisation and popular consensus. They also argue that the conflict with the US, which they deem purely ideological and not a function of Iran's interests, needs settling. Former revolutionaries like Khatami and the philosopher Abdol Karim Soroush have concluded that setting up a genuine Islamic society is impossible, and do not believe in the primacy of ideology. Finally, a coalition between young reformist clerics such as Mohsen Kadivar and old conservative ayatollahs like Mohammad Fazel-Lankarani and Ahmad Azari-Qomi judge that the revolution, far from empowering the clergy, has in fact compromised it by engaging it in the exercise of power.

The latter consideration is important. Within the Islamic revolution, the state defines the position of religion, not the reverse. The Council of Guardians is a purely political and elected body. The Guide is not the highest-ranking mullah, nor is he appointed by the religious leadership, but by the Council of Experts, itself an elected body. His function is more political than religious. Virtually all of the clergy's economic resources are now under state control, while the imams of large mosques are appointed by the Guide. Many have become civil servants.

The constitutional system rests on three pillars: the Guide, the president and parliament. Conservatives aim to prevent liberals from securing a majority in parliament by censoring reformist candidates and bringing the most influential to trial. However, the most radical conservatives would like Khamenei to remove Khatami from office, as Khomeini did Abol Hassan Bani-Sadr in 1981. To mount a real coup, they need Khamenei's explicit consent – which they are unlikely to get. Although deep down a conservative, Khamenei lacks Khomeini's prestige or legitimacy. His interest is to appear as an arbiter above the factions.

Khamenei's response to the series of crises that faced the regime in 1998–99 showed that he did not endorse the conservatives' efforts to discredit the liberals' position. In July 1998, a court convicted Karbaschi of embezzlement, sentenced him to five years in prison and ordered him to pay a fine of around $500,000. Karbaschi is popular with Iran's educated youth, and his trial had to be postponed twice following mass student protests. In December, some intellectuals were murdered by agents of the secret services. In July 1999, the regime faced its most serious challenge since the revolution, when student-led riots broke out in Tehran and other cities in response to parliament's passage of a restrictive press law. The police and Revolutionary Guards stormed student dormitories, leaving at least one student dead and dozens injured; several hundred were arrested. In June 1999, Interior Minister and Khatami ally Abdollah Nouri was impeached by parliament; he was sentenced to jail the following October. In December 1999, the Council of Guardians forbade many candidates from participating in the forthcoming elections, citing their 'incompetence' or lack of 'Islamic credentials'.

In the wake of each of these incidents, Khamenei acted as arbiter, not as the head of the conservative faction. He called for the arrest and punishment of the intellectuals' murderers; he endorsed the dismissal of Tehran's police chief, who ordered the attack on the students in July 1999; and in January 2000 he pardoned Karbaschi. Many of those barred from the February elections were ultimately allowed to run.

The final consensus is reached within the powerful Expediency Council, which moderates disputes between the government, parliament and the Council of Guardians. Since all factions within the Expediency Council wish at all costs to avoid popular unrest, the current conflict-prone equilibrium is all the more likely to last. Many conservatives are aware that a popular explosion is likely without reforms. They wish to slow down and control the pace of change, rather than return to the revolutionary era. This is welcome news to Khatami, who does not have a clear economic-reform programme in mind, and can blame his tardiness in implementing change on the conservatives.

Continuity in Foreign Policy

To what extent does the factional struggle influence Iran's foreign policy? Is it conceivable, in the event of a conservative backlash, that Tehran will once again attempt to export its revolution? The short answer is no. Since Khomeini's death in 1989, major foreign-policy decisions have been taken by consensus, and have been based on Iranian national interests, rather than Islamic militancy. Nonetheless, the power struggle can cut initiatives short, such as the aborted *rapprochement* with the US in 1998, or slow them down, as in the case of relations with Europe. But it plays no part in Iranian regional policy, which has been marked by improved relations with conservative Arab regimes, the consolidation of strong ties with Russia and Armenia, a mixture of hostility and caution towards the *Taleban* in Afghanistan, efforts to maintain the status quo with and within Iraq and condemnation of the Arab–Israeli peace process.

The main principles of Iran's foreign policy since the death of Ayatollah Khomeini in 1989 are a function of its self-assertion as a regional power. As a result of failure as much as pragmatism, exporting the revolution has been abandoned as a policy goal. In the 1980s, revolutionary Iran used *Shi'a* minorities abroad to destabilise the conservative Arab regimes which supported Iraq, then abandoned them to severe repression.

178 The Middle East

This fate befell *Shi'a* in Iraq in 1988 and 1991, when their most holy city, Najaf, was bombed by Saddam Hussein; in Bahrain, which saw *Shi'a* uprisings in the 1990s; and in Afghanistan, where Mazar-i-Sharif fell to the *Taleban* in August 1998. The anti-*Shi'a* sentiment that has accompanied the radicalisation of conservative Sunni Islam – murders of *Shi'a* and Iranians in Pakistan and the *Taleban*'s anti-*Shi'a* policy, for example – has both surprised and worried Iran. Nonetheless, Tehran has always sided with Christian Armenia against *Shi'a*-dominated Azerbaijan.

When he became president on 23 May 1997, Khatami had no qualms about endorsing the main strategic objectives adopted by his predecessor, Rafsanjani:

- efforts to improve relations with conservative Arab regimes, including Saudi Arabia, which culminated in the Organisation of the Islamic Conference (OIC) summit in Tehran in November 1997;

- approval of *Hizbollah*'s integration into Lebanese party politics; and

- achieving a *rapprochement* with Russia against a possible US encroachment in the Caucasus and Central Asia.

The Gulf and the Wider Middle East

The Middle East, and in particular the Gulf, is Iran's strategic priority. In the 1980s, Tehran tried to advance its interests by destabilising the oil monarchies (supporting uprisings in Mecca in 1987), and through indirect confrontation with the US. As a result, the US military presence in the Gulf reached unprecedented levels, forcing Iran to change tack in the early 1990s and try to improve relations with conservative Arab regimes, notably Saudi Arabia. In early 1998, Foreign Minister Kamal Kharrazi, Rafsanjani and the conservative chairman of parliament, Ali Akbar Nategh-Nouri, toured the Gulf, and reassured its monarchs that there was a consensus in Tehran behind this new policy. Iran ended its support for the *Shi'a* opposition in Bahrain and restored diplomatic ties with the Bahrain government in December 1998, and has kept the spiritual leader of the *Shi'a* opposition, Ayatollah Mohammed Shirazi, under house arrest in Qom. Relations are good with Oman, and have been normalised with Qatar and Kuwait. The last bone of contention remains the dispute with the UAE over the Gulf islands of Tunb and Abu Musa, which Iran has occupied since 1971. Tehran's case for ownership of the islands rests on a secret agreement between the Shah and the UAE signed in 1971, highlighting the degree of continuity that characterises Iranian foreign policy.

In Iraq, Iran supports the status quo: a weakened but still-united country. Here again, there is continuity with the foreign policy of pre-revolutionary Iran. The Islamic Republic's position rests on the Algiers Agreement of 1975, which defined the border between the two countries, and which was endorsed by Iraq in 1990. Tehran remained quiet during the inspection crisis which led the US and UK to resume air strikes on Iraq in 1998. The UN Special Commission (UNSCOM) has received qualified Iranian support – unsurprisingly, since Iran, along with Iraq's Kurds, has been the only victim of Iraq's chemical weapons.

Despite Khatami's relative moderateness, in his 'Dialogue of Civilisations' speech in 1997 he singled out the Israeli 'Zionist regime' as the only state Iran would not recognise. Iran publicly opposes the Middle East peace process, and is thought to have increased arms shipments to *Hizbollah* in southern Lebanon in January and February 2000, after the Shepherdstown peace talks between Israel and Syria, to fuel military clashes with the Israelis and sabotage further negotiations. Syria has strategic interests in making peace with Israel – for example, weakening Israel's alliance with Turkey, which threatened to invade Syria in 1999 in response to Syrian support for Kurdish rebels. Furthermore, Syrian President Hafez al-Assad, whose health is failing, is believed to want a deal in order to relieve his successor (probably his son Bashar) of the burden of war. Nevertheless, a deal would undoubtedly strain relations between Iran and Syria relations.

Iran and Syria have had a strategic alliance since the Iran–Iraq war, in which Syria supported Iran. Although Iran furnished Syria with low-cost oil in the early 1980s, for the past decade the two countries' relationship has been essentially political, based on intelligence co-operation and shared animosity toward Israel. Iran is the principal sponsor of *Hizbollah*'s guerrilla campaign against Israel in south Lebanon, and has routed supplies for *Hizbollah* through Syria. An accord between Israel and Syria would require Syria to disarm *Hizbollah* and expel Iran from Lebanon.

That Iran would resist withdrawing its support for *Hizbollah* is a realistic possibility, particularly in the absence of a final status agreement between Israel and the Palestinian Authority. In October 1999, when Hassan Nasrallah, head of *Hizbollah*, visited Teheran, Iranian officials are believed to have discussed with him how to maintain support for *Hizbollah* both by bypassing Syria and by enhancing cooperation with radical Palestinian groups. In June 1999, Iran Air resumed direct flights to Beirut after nearly 30 years. According to a December 1999 *Washington Post* article, US intelligence reports indicate that Iran has supplied *Hizbollah* with long-range Katyusha rockets capable of hitting Haifa, and that Iran's material support to *Hamas* increased in 1999 after several years of reductions.

Some Israeli Defense Force (IDF) intelligence officers also fear that Iran might successfully pressure Assad's successor to abrogate any peace

The Middle East

agreement. While Israeli President Ehud Barak considers this an unrealistic calculation, given that Syria would lose Western aid, the IDF's position does indicate the depth of Israeli hard-liners' scepticism about the possibility of a sustainable agreement with Syria and their convictions about the degree of influence Teheran enjoys in Damascus. In any case, concern and uncertainty about Iran's reaction to an Israel–Syria peace agreement has produced significant divisions among Israeli ministers as to how to approach Syria in negotiations.

The Caucasus, Central Asia and Afghanistan

Iran's single objective in the Caucasus and Central Asia is to secure a stake in pipelines transporting the area's oil and natural gas to markets in the West. Tehran fears being sidelined by US policies, such as its support for the route between Baku in Azerbaijan and the Turkish port of Ceyhan. As a result, Iran would like to see a strong Russian presence in the region as a counter-weight to the US, and has established only lukewarm relations with the newly independent states. It encouraged Tajikistan's Islamic opposition to sign the Moscow agreements in June 1997, and has not supported the Muslim rebels fighting Russian rule in Chechnya. The rebels are constantly referred to as separatists in the Iranian press.

Iran has no strategic designs on Afghanistan, which it views less as an opportunity than as a liability. Tehran would prefer to avoid having to deal with the problem Afghanistan poses: massive immigration, drug-trafficking, arms smuggling and the destabilisation of Pakistan's mostly Sunni province of Baluchistan. The rise of the *Taleban* took Iran by surprise, and Tehran is not pleased about its staunchly anti-*Shi'a* policies and support from Pakistan. Tensions came to a head in August 1998, with the *Taleban*'s massacre of Iranian diplomats in Mazar-i-Sharif.

For purely tactical reasons, Iran supports the anti-*Taleban* Northern Alliance led by Ahmad Shah Masood. Tehran's ultimate objective is to see the 'Afghan question' solved via the advent of a *Pushtun*-dominated government in Kabul that would respect the border and the rights of the *Shi'a*. In October 1999, Iran resumed its dialogue with the *Taleban*, and reopened its frontier with Afghanistan – just as the UN Security Council approved sanctions against the *Taleban* for its support for terrorist suspect Ösama bin Laden.

Normalisation with the West

Iran's relations with the European Union have vastly improved following Khatami's pledge in October 1998 that Iran would not carry out the *fatwah* against Salman Rushdie. However, Khatami's statement differed little from then Foreign Minister Ali Akbar Velayati's 1996 commitment to the same effect, highlighting again the extent of the foreign-policy consensus in Tehran. Velayati is now an adviser to Khamenei.

Relations with the US have also improved, albeit by not much, and not very fast. Washington's tone has become more conciliatory, as has Tehran's, but the relationship remains tense. The most important of the sanctions imposed by the US in July 1996 remain in place; US pipeline policy in Central Asia and the Caucasus is at least partly aimed at sidelining Iran; and Tehran remains accused in the US of supporting international terrorism and seeking to develop its own weapons of mass destruction. The discreet dialogue begun after Khatami's visit to New York in October 1998 quickly petered out.

Iran's attitude towards the Middle East peace process remains a key stumbling-block to better relations. Washington believes that some kind of dialogue should be opened between Iranians and Israelis, or, at the least, that Iran ceases its strident denunciation of the peace process. For Tehran, this would amount to its exclusion from the Middle East. The chances of a rapid improvement in US–Iranian relations are, therefore, remote. The difficulties were underlined in March 2000 when, in a speech to the American–Iranian Council, Secretary of State Madeleine Albright announced a number of moves designed to facilitate official talks between the two countries. According to Albright, the US would lift its ban on imports of Iranian luxury goods and, in line with long-standing Iranian demands, would seek a legal settlement that could free Iranian assets in the US frozen since the revolution. She also, in effect, apologised for past US policy towards Iran, including the Central Intelligence Agency (CIA)-backed coup in 1953. Albright's announcement was an unabashed effort to encourage Khatami's allies after their extraordinary success in the February parliamentary elections.

Iran's official response came almost immediately. A Foreign Ministry spokesman welcomed the speech as a positive advance, and stated that Iran would reciprocate by opening its borders to US foodstuffs and medicine. But Iran's Ambassador to the UN rejected Albright's offer to open talks, saying that they could only be useful if carried out 'under a normalised situation, devoid of pressure, allegations, and grandstanding'. More conservative groups went much further: both the Supreme National Security Council and the Revolutionary Guard's spokesman accused the US of attempting to meddle in Iran's domestic affairs.

Several celebrated judicial cases have not helped relations with the West. The judicial system has become a coveted prize in the struggle between reforming and conservative forces. While the government has replaced the conservative Ayatollah Mohammad Yazdi as chief justice with a moderate, Mahmoud Hashemi, Iranian justice still hinders *rapprochement*. In January 1997, two Iranian Jews were hanged for spying.

The Middle East

In January 1998, German citizen Helmut Hofer was sentenced to death for having an affair with a Muslim woman, although he was later released. In March 1999, 13 Iranian Jews were arrested in Shiraz for alleged espionage, for which they face the death penalty. The charges may be religiously motivated fabrications; sources inside Iran have suggested that the accused were merely producing and selling illegal alcohol.

Elements of the powerful Jewish lobby in the US have insisted that the cases must be dismissed and the prisoners released before any of the concessions under consideration by President Bill Clinton, such as lifting sanctions on non-oil imports, are put into effect. In October 1999, 28 US Senators protested against the State Department's designation of the democratic opposition group People's *Mujahadeen* as a terrorist organisation, and cited the espionage cases as evidence of 'little perceptible change' in Iran. Although three of the 13 suspects were released on bail in February, the trial of the rest, which will be held before the conservative Revolutionary Court, was scheduled to go ahead on 13 April. The conviction or, worse, execution of any of the suspects would constitute a serious setback for US–Iranian relations.

The changes in Iranian society and government since the mid-1990s have had a clear effect on the country's conduct of foreign policy. Policy is now overwhelmingly framed in classical terms of regional-power assertiveness, rather than by ideology. Unfortunately, however, it will take some time for the image of a militant Islamic Iran to be erased from most memories, including of those in Iran who retain a deep nostalgia for the revolution.

The Maghreb: Regional, Global or Marginalised Players?

For once, North Africa featured in the news in 1999 as much for encouraging reasons as for the violence that attracted so much attention to Algeria throughout the 1990s. A number of dangers were averted, not least a much feared succession crisis in Morocco following the death of King Hassan II in July 1999, after 38 years on the throne. His relatively unknown son and successor, Mohammed VI, in fact delighted Morocco, launching initiatives in the second half of 1999 that included women's education, the development of Morocco's neglected northern regions and a more nuanced approach towards resolving the future of the Western Sahara.

In Algeria, President Abdelaziz Bouteflika became the new head of state in April. The violence abated temporarily with a renewed, if politically inconclusive, cease-fire declaration in June 1999 by the Islamic Salvation Army (AIS). Once in office, Bouteflika launched his main initiative – a new referendum – in September. The results of the referendum, which were to test the people's feeling about the so-called *concorde civile*, were never in doubt since the question asked was a simple one: 'Are you for or against peace?' Unsurprisingly, nearly 85% of the electorate voted for peace, but a conclusive and lasting end to violence continues to elude Algeria.

In Tunisia, President Zine el-Abidine Ben Ali swept the polls with a 99.4% reconfirmation vote in October for his third and constitutionally final term in office. Only the most sceptical of observers dared question whether such a result was a good or bad portent for the future of pluralism in a state still afflicted by human-rights difficulties. Meanwhile, Colonel Moamar Gadaffi of Libya returned to the scene, as far as Europeans were concerned, when he finally agreed in April 1999 to surrender to Scottish justice two Libyan intelligence agents suspected of involvement in the 1988 bombing of Pan Am flight 103 over Lockerbie, Scotland. Under an unusual but effective compromise, a special court operating under Scottish rules and with Scottish judges was set up in the Netherlands for their trial, due to start in earnest in May 2000. UN sanctions in place since 1992 were provisionally lifted in April 1999, and business in the lucrative hydrocarbon sector, assisted by renewed air-links with Europe, looked set to create a mini-boom in the Libyan economy over the next few years. Only the US – if not American business interests – remained aloof from these new opportunities, pending clearer signs that Gadaffi has definitively renounced support for international terrorism.

Despite the optimism they engendered, these developments constitute only the thinnest veneer over the political and economic problems facing North Africa's leaders. One challenge will be to make the Maghreb function economically as a region, rather than each state forging its separate links to the European markets with which the region is increasingly tied. Another related hurdle is that of finding common ground amongst the widely differing styles of governance that separate North African states. At a time when they can ill-afford inter-regional competition, the Maghreb's common economic goals of liberalisation, privatisation and globalisation seem ineluctably to pit one state against another in the struggle for international attention and foreign direct investment. Few investors, domestic or international, are responding speedily other than in the energy sectors of Algeria, Libya and Tunisia.

Liberalisation also has its pitfalls and repercussions on domestic political spheres, especially where the spectre of rapidly increasing youth unemployment confronts the whole Maghreb. Over 50% of the Maghreb's population is aged under 18, a statistic which provokes European fears of uncontrolled migration as much as it induces anxiety among the region's

The Middle East

economic planners and internal-security forces. The days of direct Islamist threats to regime survival in North Africa may now appear to be past, but as Algeria demonstrates, subduing the last vestiges of violent opposition requires more comprehensive political solutions than have been thus far offered.

In the wake of the March–June 1999 Kosovo campaign, the Maghreb's political establishments are preoccupied with protecting the privileges of state sovereignty from possible external incursions. The trade-off between fostering economic openness and safeguarding the security of entrenched regimes is at the heart of the choices they face. Most have opted to direct their energies inwards, towards political control, and outwards, beyond the immediate region, towards sources of economic support. The possible exceptions, such as Morocco, may yet prove to be the more successful, if risky, balancing acts.

Creating a New Atmosphere in Morocco

The variegated political landscape of the Maghreb often makes the region resemble an experiment in applied political theory, and 1999 was no exception. After averting a succession crisis in the summer, Morocco was able to push ahead with its transition to a constitutional monarchy, discrediting predictions of an untimely hiatus in the process after Hassan II's death. It was to the latter's posthumous credit that, in practice, the institutional underpinnings of Morocco's nascent pluralism were barely shaken by the departure of its main architect. A key figure to survive the changeover, with the full support of the new King, was Prime Minister Abderrahman Youssifi, who had been carefully chosen by Hassan II in early 1998 to lead a government of *'alternance'* drawn largely from erstwhile opposition parties.

Less certain was the future of the long-standing and unpopular Minister of the Interior, Driss Basri. As the chief of Morocco's internal security forces for more than 25 years, and head of an elaborate network of regional and local governorships, Basri earned the sobriquet 'the unmoveable minister' in an otherwise shifting cabinet. Under the constitutional reforms that preceded the general elections of 1997, four key ministries (justice, religious affairs, foreign affairs and the interior) remained in the King's direct gift. Having proved his loyalty in one of two serious attempts on Hassan II's life in the 1970s, Basri was Hassan II's man *par excellence*, accountable only to the palace as the hard man of a system whose punitive side is only thinly veiled.

It was thus with surprise – and ill-concealed joy in some quarters – that the majority of Moroccans greeted Mohammed VI's decision to sack Basri in early November 1999, barely three months after succeeding to the throne. Basri's departure marked a clear break by the new King with his father's heritage and repressive tendencies in government. Less distant from the populace, and more prepared to engage directly with develop-ment issues, the 36-year-old monarch nonetheless faces considerable obstacles to fulfilling the hopes he has created. Dismantling a whole system of surveillance and control is less simple than dispensing with the services of its chief henchman, especially where economic and political vested interests, are well entrenched and inter-linked.

The easiest, if most symbolic, achievements were realised early on. These included the return in October 1999 from exile in France of Morocco's longest-standing political prisoner, Abraham Serfaty, as well as, in November, that of the family of Mehdi Ben Barka. In the mid-1960s, Ben Barka – an ideological opponent of Hassan II – was killed in Paris in mysterious circumstances only recently exposed by the French press. Through these acts, and by confirming Youssifi, himself a human-rights activist, at the head of government, Mohamed VI has clearly signalled his intention to move away from Morocco's reputation for human-rights abuse. A commission of enquiry is to investigate the 'disappearance' of innumerable Moroccans over the years. Intentions, however, may change more readily than their objects. The imprisonment in February 2000 of an air-force officer, Mustapha Adib, for revealing military corruption, aroused considerable local and international protest amongst human-rights groups, but was greeted with silence by the still unrepresentative political parties and mainstream establishments.

The harder questions, moreover, are structural and firmly linked to the economy. The combined burden of Morocco's top-heavy beaurocracy and its foreign debts absorb 85% of the state budget. This leaves only 15% of revenues to tackle other problems including an illiteracy rate that even official figures set at 64%, rising to 90% amongst rural women. The widening urban–rural divide constitutes perhaps the most striking development problem. The affluent pockets of Casablanca, Rabat and Salé on the east coast contrast with the agrarian interior, where 50% of Moroccans still live in villages without running water, electricity or proper roads.

Plans to redress this situation are not helped by Morocco's economic dependence on the harvest, which can be heavily affected by unreliable rainfall. Droughts have caused growth in gross domestic product (GDP) to fluctuate widely, with 6.3% growth in 1998 falling to almost nil in 1999, even though Morocco continues to win cautious plaudits from inter-national agencies monitoring its liberalisation efforts and privatisation programmes.

The biggest boost for Morocco in 1999 came from the unlikely quarter of the public tender issued for a new mobile-phone network. Under intense international competition, the new licence was awarded in summer 1999 to a bid led by Spanish telecommunications group Telefonica, bringing in a

The Middle East

record $1.076 billion in foreign exchange. Continued liberalisation in the telecommunications sector, as well as the sale of other state-owned industries, new tourist complexes and the gradual privatisation of the national airline are planned, but these only indirectly support social-development projects, such as those envisaged for women. Restructuring enterprises accustomed to employing too many over-qualified staff is bound to cause problems for the already saturated labour market. In Morocco, as elsewhere in the region, there are limits to what can be achieved in the short run without jeopardising a social fabric that, despite intense poverty, still holds its diverse components together.

That Morocco's Islamists have not sought to exploit this situation beyond the universities and poorer urban quarters in cities such as Casablanca and Fez is also a credit to Hassan II's clever manipulation of the rival strands of the movement. The legalised wing, folded into the Party of Justice and Development, holds ten seats in the national parliament and, as its name, Unity and Reform, suggests, is committed to reform rather than to a radical paths to gaining a political platform. It is less clear whether the same is true of the more populist movement, *Al Adl wa-Ihsane* (Justice and Charity) whose leader, Sheikh Abdessalam Yassine, has been a long-standing critic of the monarchy. He notably remained under house arrest when the new King liberated other political prisoners.

As a descendant of the Prophet, Mohammed VI is as aware as his father was of the need to maintain the monarchy's traditional and religious authority. He has quickly distanced himself from the jet-setting image of his youth in favour of a more religious public role. It is an open question, however, whether the King could consistently mobilise the large numbers of people, that Yassine's group rallied for peaceable meetings on the beaches of Casablanca in summer 1999 and for street protests against the lifting of restrictions on women in March 2000. By early 2000, Mohammed VI appeared to be winning the competition for hearts and minds in Morocco. Nevertheless, his ability to produce results is far from being a foregone conclusion.

The Western Sahara: The Perennial Problem

The regional conflict over the Western Sahara, now some 25 years old, refuses to fade away. Yet another date was set at the beginning of 1999 for the long-delayed referendum to choose between incorporation into Morocco or self-determination. The year ended with the date being postponed again. This sequence is almost an annual event, since the names, location and exact numbers of eligible voters from amongst a largely nomadic population is constantly disputed. Less open to question is that a negotiated settlement will have to precede rather than succeed the eventual convening of the referendum. With only limited resistance to

Moroccan gains on the ground in recent years, hardly anyone believes that the international community, led by the UN, will countenance the creation of a new state that would almost certainly fall under Moroccan influence.

The Algerians have maintained fluctuating levels of support for the independence fighters of the rebel group, *Polisario*, and its political wing, the Saharan Arab Democratic Republic (SADR). Its overall aim is to prevent the sanctioning of Moroccan hegemony over the region's destiny. Algeria is particularly concerned about self-determination, partly because of its own history, but perhaps more because of the growing Moroccan *fait accompli*.

The advent of Mohammed VI appeared to alter the details, if not the substance, of the Moroccan position on the Western Sahara. The new king has replaced Basri's heavy-handed tactics, which had led to riots in the Saharan capital of El-Ayoun in September 1999, by reviving a tribal council for the region. Where tensions continued between Morocco and Algeria, whose common border has been closed since 1994, it was more over allegations of Moroccan support for fleeing Algerian Islamists than over the Sahara. The requisite face-saving on both sides still needs to be engineered by the precariously funded UN Mission for the Referendum in Western Sahara (MINURSO) which is monitoring the details of a final settlement. The story may continue for some time, but it is unlikely to bring either side to war when both have so many domestic diversions to occupy their energies.

Algeria: More of the Same, with Perhaps a Bit Less

In Algeria, the political scene changed slightly with the election of Abdelaziz Bouteflika as President in April 1999, even if this only thinly disguised his designation as heir apparent by the coterie of generals who really decide Algeria's fate. Few Algerians have faith in the generals' strategic vision for engineering peace in Algeria (if that is indeed what they seek), but their tactical strengths have yet to be challenged. Even when sweeping changes to the military hierarchy were announced in early 2000, it was clearly just an exercise in removing the former President Liamine Zeroual's friends, to help to consolidate the existing military high command under General Mohammed Lamari.

The extent to which Algeria's presidents are able to exercise their own authority has never been entirely clear. It nevertheless becomes apparent – usually with hindsight – when they have been reined in. For example, the appointment of Bouteflika's government was delayed for eight months by behind-the-scenes rows over the interior and defence ministries. Bouteflika won only a partial victory in the multiparty line-up announced in December. The fact that Algeria could survive so long with only a caretaker government spoke volumes about the real centre of power.

Bouteflika has some strengths, however. He has been able to combine a willingness to talk – to the foreign media as much as to Algerians through the local television and press – with the fact that he was absent from Algerian politics for twenty years. During the worst years of Algerian violence during the 1990s, Bouteflika was working in a private capacity in the Gulf. This hiatus followed his earlier career in the 1960s and 1970s as foreign minister under the legendary President Houari Boumedienne. It has surprised few, therefore, to hear him describe the 'golden era' of the 1970s as a template for what Algeria might again become.

What this rhetoric overlooks, however, is that the importance of military backing for the regime in power has barely changed over the years. Explicit demands for the military to leave the political arena have continued to be marginalised and relegated to a second order of priority in an otherwise relatively open political debate. The first priority remains, at least officially, to subdue military violence to politically acceptable levels, with only nominal concessions to pluralism.

Bouteflika's election was also marred by the withdrawal at the last minute of the other six candidates, who alleged that the results had been fixed in advance in Bouteflika's favour. Standing alone, he gained 73% of a vote in which there was a 60% turnout, but this gave him little popular legitimacy. Only by summer 1999, when he appeared to have brokered a new deal with the AIS – the military wing of the banned Islamic Salvation Front (FIS) – did his star begin to rise. Popular backing for his *concorde civile* – or call for peace and civil harmony – in the September referendum confirmed Bouteflika's new status. The problem, as excluded political parties continued to point out, was that a military deal did not constitute a political settlement. The group of erstwhile presidential candidates, including another former foreign minister, Taleb Ibrahimi, and Hocine Ait Ahmed, leader of the Front of Socialist Forces (FFS), signed a 'manifesto of liberties' in May 1999, calling for the pursuit of genuine democracy in Algeria. This appeal, like the similar 1995 'Rome platform', went largely unanswered.

With the endorsement of major elements in the FIS leadership – including Abbasi Madani, who has been under house arrest in Algiers since 1997 – Bouteflika encouraged smaller Islamist armed groups to join the AIS in laying down their weapons. The details of the AIS deal – and whether Bouteflika played as great a role as the generals in its negotiation – were never made public. Thus, the extent to which the situation had changed remained uncertain, since the AIS had been adhering to a unilateral truce since October 1997.

Ironically, however, the FIS did not appear to have been consulted, and the FIS leaders were far from united in their support for the AIS deal or the follow-up *concorde civile*. This was notably true of Abdelkader Hachani, the most prominent FIS moderate. When Hachani was killed in central Algiers in November 1999, it was evident that he had become dangerously exposed to opposition, not only from within his own ranks, although they are increasingly divided, but also from elements within the main Algerian political establishment. As ever in a country where political assassinations give rise to multiple conspiracy theories, the hardline Islamists of the Armed Islamic Groups (GIA), who are opposed to any accommodation with the authorities, took the blame.

With the AIS all but neutralised, the main objective of the *concorde civile* was to pave the way for an amnesty under certain conditions for the remaining armed groups. The effort was to include group members who had only been engaged in support activities, while excluding all those who had been actively engaged in the killing or rape of civilians. By the deadline of 13 January 2000, 80% of armed groups, according to official reports, had surrendered. Elements within the AIS, however, seemed to disagree with the call of their leader, Madani Mezrag, for overall integration with the Algerian armed forces, while the elusive GIA was now split between rival factions intent on pursuing some form of violent resistance at all cost. The result has been a continuation of low-level attacks.

Throughout autumn 1999 and early 2000, a constant trickle of violence – such as killings in the rural Mitidja area and the apparently random slayings of civilians at false roadblocks – claimed the lives of up to 1,000 people. The overall death toll since 1992 – officially recognised by Bouteflika – is 100,000 victims, so there has been a considerable drop in the level of violence, but it hardly amounts to full normalisation. Following the January expiry of the amnesty, the Algerian authorities declared that they would pursue all residual 'terrorists' with renewed force. They have done little to disarm the militias and guards armed during the 1990s to defend villages against Islamist attack. Even though these groups – numbering up to 80,000 men – are now supposed to come under the control of the police, they are capable of provoking considerable violence, even if only at a local level.

On Algeria's economic front, however, it is business as usual. Although Bouteflika accused both Morocco and Tunisia of having jumped the regional gun in signing association accords with the European Union, it is not clear what Algeria would gain by pursuing negotiations towards the same end. Hydrocarbons represent 95% of Algeria's export earnings, with an increasingly lucrative emphasis on supplying southern Europe with gas through an extensive series of pipelines and the renovated gas-liquefying plant at Arzew on the north coast. Although the drop in oil prices in the first half of 1999 adversely affected Algerian revenues, foreign reserves remained high, and confidence in joint ventures with international firms to locate and exploit new reserves remained buoyant.

Only unemployment – running at an official 30% – presents a worrying indicator of future instability. Little of Algeria's gas and oil wealth finds its way into the pockets of the mass of the people. Despite the weariness caused by war and economic deprivations over the last decade, popular quiescence cannot be taken for granted.

Little Change in Tunisia But More in Libya

In Tunisia, President Ben Ali continued to play a shrewd game, deflecting international criticism of his human-rights record by periodically releasing political opponents from prison and house arrest with the same arbitrariness with which he subsequently rearrested the same or related opponents. The international human-rights community targeted Tunisia during 1999, when the French authors of an earlier publication directed at Hassan II and entitled *'Notre Ami Le Roi'* (Our Friend the King) repeated the exercise against Ben Ali under the title of 'Our Friend the President'. Published just before the October presidential elections, the book's detailed appraisal of Ben Ali's autocratic control over Tunisia caused an inevitable furore, but Tunisia's main European partners did not pursue its key accusations with much zeal.

This is partly because, of all its regional neighbours, Tunisia is a model pupil of the International Monetary Fund. Low inflation, high growth rates (at an annual average of 5%), budget surpluses and a manageable foreign debt have placed Tunisia in a regional class of its own. Since violence broke out in Algeria in 1992, Ben Ali has successfully argued to his international partners that liberalisation in Tunisia cannot take place on all fronts at once. The potential rewards to be reaped from successfully upgrading and grooming the Tunisian economy for exposure to free trade are too high to allow the exercise to fall victim to Algerian-style Islamist violence. Virtually all opponents in Tunisia are deemed to be Islamist, or, since many of them are lawyers, are held to be Islamist sympathisers and defenders seeking to 'disturb public order' through 'defamation and the spreading of false information', as most of their charge sheets read.

Ben Ali's record has some merits. Well-publicised cases of human-rights activists being silenced and detained have overshadowed gains in other social and economic areas. The status of women in Tunisia, for example, has been held up as a model in a region where women have frequently and continuously borne the brunt of violence and official neglect. The political problem is that, beyond the presidency and the umbrella party, the *Rassemblement Constitutionnel Démocratique* (RCD), which currently holds 80% of parliamentary seats, there are few poles around which to organise debate. Small, officially vetted parties exist, but their secretaries-general were allowed to stand in the 1999 presidential elections only if they had been in their positions for at least five years. This new constitutional measure was widely seen as a move to prevent the *Mouvement des Democrates Socialistes* (MDS) – the only measurably

independent party – from fielding its own candidate, given that his predecessor had been arrested within the previous five years. Unless this
provision is changed within the next five years, it may well cause problems
for Ben Ali's successor, since Ben Ali only resigned as RCD secretary-
general following his October 1999 re-election.

If economic reform continues at the same pace, however, a gradual
opening-up of the political system may eventually become possible, but
here time is not necessarily on Ben Ali's side. In early 2000, the first signs of
rumblings at street level – symbolised by a taxi drivers' strike in February
2000, and more worryingly, week-long riots in the heavily unemployed
south – began to trouble the calm so long taken for granted in Tunisia.

Whether the 'political reforms' announced at around the same time by
Colonel Gadaffi in neighbouring Libya will have a palliative effect on the
population is a less safe assumption. Renewed interest after years of
international neglect has led to much speculation about the potential
domestic opposition to Gadaffi, and whether it would be tribal, Islamist or
both. Speculation has also been rife over the social and economic impact on
his co-citizens (Libya being a 'People's Republic') of sanctions imposed by
the US since 1986 and, to a more limited extent, by the UN and the EU
since the early 1990s. One such account has held widespread drug abuse
by a young and disenchanted population to be a major source of internal
instability.

Whether this assumption is accurate or not, evidence suggests that
Gadaffi is still at the helm of the state he has led through various mood
changes since 1969, despite his effective abolition of half of Libya's central
government in March 2000. As a result, local 'Basic People's Congresses'
and 'Popular Committees' are apparently to enjoy devolved administrative
powers in all but foreign affairs, finance, justice, information, public order
and African Affairs. Few believe that much substance underlies Gadaffi's
further intention of appointing a formal head of state (where the colonel
himself is merely the 'Guide of the Revolution'). The significance of the
African Affairs portfolio remaining with the 'central' authorities, however,
lies in Gadaffi's latest international vision for Libya: namely, a closer
alliance with its African, rather than with its European and, even less, with
its Arab neighbours. Yet, financial and technical backing for Gadaffi's
renewed infrastructural projects is unlikely to come from the south, and
there are signs that he is open to European investment, so long as it is not
of the speculative kind that laid waste to the Asian Tiger economies in
1998.

By the second half of 1999, it seemed that Libya's main European
partners – above all Italy and Germany – were prepared to cooperate. The
Italian hydrocarbon giant, Eni S.p.A., entered into a new pipeline and
offshore exploration agreement worth $5.5bn. With the White House and
Congress refusing to mitigate their enmity toward Gadaffi, it may be left to

The Middle East

commercial pressures in the US to push forward the debate on his continuing 'rogue' status.

Regional Blues

Despite the European Union's attempts to encourage greater regional cohesion, the Maghreb remains a resolutely individualistic set of political and economic entities. A regional dimension does exist in the form of the Arab Maghreb Union (UMA) which has enjoyed intermittent existence since its formation in 1987. However, since Libya (alongside Morocco, Algeria, Tunisia and Mauritania) is part of this grouping, the US, if not most of Europe, has had at best minimal enthusiasm for its further development. As far as Brussels is concerned, Libya has now come in from the cold, and the EU was swift to issue an invitation to Gadaffi to join the largest club in the Mediterranean – the Euro-Mediterranean Partnership (EMP) initiative – as soon as UN sanctions were suspended in April 1999.

Two philosophies dominated the debate in 1999. The first was that regionalism is increasingly seen as a prerequisite for this region's entry into, and participation in, a more globalised world. This applies as much to the demands of economies of scale to attract investors to the region's markets as it does to the cooperative security initiatives now on offer – still bilaterally – from both the EU and NATO in the Mediterranean region. The second strand of thinking was that if free trade were the goal, why should the Maghreb stop at the Mediterranean Free Trade Zone (excluding agriculture) which is all that the EMP seems to propose?

The American approach to the Maghreb, often cited as the 'Eizenstat initiative' after the now retired Under-Secretary of State for Economy, has been to encourage its own idea for regional economic partnership, encompassing Morocco, Algeria and Tunisia, but expressly not Libya, nor the all-but-Sub-Saharan Mauritania. The general 'Eizenstat message' has been that if these states want to attract private-sector investment, they must attempt to break down the internal barriers between them. If not, US businesses engaged in the region will continue to locate themselves in Europe, where the whole region, not just one market at a time, can be reached.

This approach implies a hint of criticism of the EMP, the bilateral association accords of which may have increased, rather than diminished, regional competition over external trade and investment. In a speech in March 1999, Eizenstat pointed to the EMP as having been instrumental in solidifying the north–south dimensions of regional trade at the implied expense of east–west, or horizontal, linkages between the Maghreb's economies. The reality, however, is that no one wants to fund the infrastructural costs of building the road and transport links needed to uncouple the Maghreb from its centrifugal dependence on Europe.

Maghreb leaderships have been swift to cite 'Eizenstat' as an alternative to European dominance, even though neither Eizenstat nor his successors have pledged any funds towards promoting the initiative. This, as ever, is left to the private sector, whose main interest remains that of ensuring the smooth delivery of energy resources northwards into Europe. The diversification of gas supplies has mitigated fears of Europe's strategic dependence on Algerian and Libyan energy. New Norwegian supplies have come on-line, supported by costly but efficient means of ensuring that a gas pipeline cut off, for example, by terrorist activity is operating again within twenty-four hours.

Future Imperfect

As ever, the major challenge facing all the leaderships of the region is to manage the human dimensions of change at a time when they have a less than comfortable domination of the instruments needed to keep the region at peace. The tried-and-tested combinations of co-option, coercion and corruption have come under increasing local and international scrutiny. On the one hand, as elsewhere, local organisations have become adept at using new technologies to systematise and advertise their protests against human-rights violations, injustice and deprivation. On the other, the ramifications of international trade have made inroads into sectors and regions hitherto shielded from global influence.

The irony is that the strategies adopted to move each state into the twenty-first century are those – like economic liberalisation – most conducive to encouraging questioning from a better informed and less centrally influenced citizenry. If Europe's headache is to keep the more mobile of these peoples from drifting northwards in a disorganised and illegal fashion, it is the Maghreb's headache merely to keep them organised. As well as concessions, the calculations of the region's proponents of 'top-down' liberalisation will have to concede more to the peoples of the region if their various political experiments are not to spin out of control. If they do not, as the new century advances, the Maghreb may be thrust from the margins to the centre of Europe's security concerns in a shorter time than observers on either shore of the Mediterranean may have imagined or would like to contemplate.

Asia

T HE FEELING OF HELPLESSNESS that had swept over East Asia with the financial and economic crash of 1997 turned into a mood of renewed optimism as a steady recovery got under way in late 1998, and held firm in 1999. With the exception of Japan, where gains in early 1999 were reversed in the second half of the year, all of Asia's economies improved. There is still far to go before the recovery is complete, and the region's leaders recognise that there is even the danger of another financial crisis, but the speed of the recovery has been universally encouraging. Yet that speed has brought its own risk, for it has left a widespread feeling that the financial-system reforms that were undertaken in the wake of the collapse need not be completed.

Reform of the region's political systems is still more important; here the news is more encouraging. When Asian economies were booming, and all the talk was of the coming 'Asian Century', many Asians agreed that this had only happened because many countries were under authoritarian rule. It soon became clear, however, that those countries with democratic governments generally weathered the storm with least damage. Thailand and the Philippines have newly elected leaders; South Korea has begun to prosper again under a leader who has spent most of his life in opposition. In Indonesia, the pressures for change were so great that they toppled first Suharto and then the interim president, Bacharuddin Jusuf Habibe, who was forced to call an election in mid-1999.

The new president, Abdurrahman Wahid, leads an unwieldy coalition government, formed during arduous rounds of bargaining after the June 1999 election. He has subsequently spent much of his time on visits abroad, seeking help with the economy, and on adroit manoeuvres to bring the military under civilian control. While Wahid has had considerable success in this key task, the country is still threatened by violence from independence movements in outlying provinces. Indonesia's outlook is fragile, but if this huge state can stay intact, and nurture its weak democracy, the outlook for the region as a whole will be vastly improved.

In other parts of Asia, ideological conflicts have sharpened, causing tensions to rise. China and Taiwan are locked in struggle over unification, which Beijing insists upon, and the US is trying to calm the uneasy atmosphere. In South-east Asia, optimism engendered by the February 1999 Lahore Agreement has long since dissipated. India and Pakistan engaged in skirmishes near the Line of Control in Kashmir during summer 1999, and since then the temperature of their propaganda attacks has

Map 4 Asia

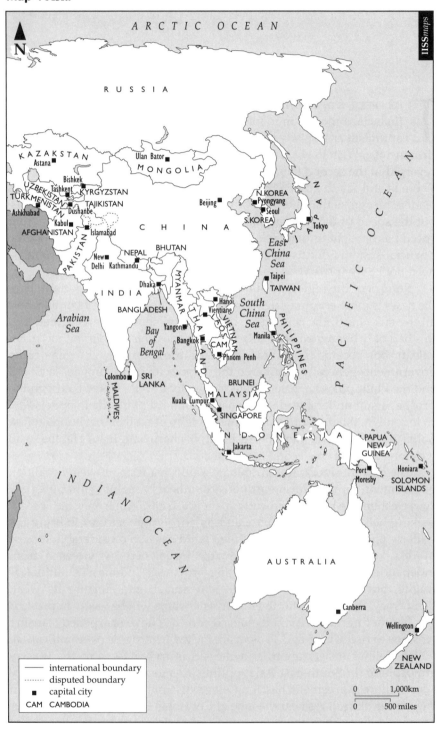

soared. Now that both nations have nuclear arms, calming the situation is vital. Here too the US has been very active through a visit to the area in March 2000 by President Bill Clinton. The need for statesmanship has never been greater, for in both the Taiwan Straits and South Asia, the balance between conflict and peace can easily tip either way.

China: Problems on All Fronts

Chinese President Jiang Zemin encountered a series of disparate and perhaps unpredictable political problems during 1999. Although individually none was enough to challenge the regime's capacity to rule, each illustrated China's deep and continuing weaknesses and, collectively, they suggested a regime that was uneasy with the outside world and with its own society. Thus the ramifications of NATO's March–June war over Kosovo and the bombing of China's Belgrade embassy in May cast a pall over Sino-American relations. Even though this began to be addressed towards the end of 1999, the episode has left a deep mark on China's foreign-policy outlook.

Domestically, the main challenge to the regime arising from the continuing reform process, at least as seen by Jiang Zemin himself, was the April 1999 demonstration by an ostensibly quietist Buddhist sect composed largely of the middle-aged – the *Falun Gong*. Condemned as a cult and prosecuted with the full coercive force of the regime, these most unlikely alleged subversives refused to withdraw from sight. Despite continual harassment and the arrests of thousands of their colleagues, members of the sect continued to register their quiet protests in open public view well into 2000.

Asia

The Beijing leadership claimed victory in February 2000 over both these challenges, and also claimed victory in resisting Taiwan leader Lee Teng-hui's call in July that China–Taiwan relations should be treated as 'special state to state relations'. But here too it was not evident that Beijing's military bluster in the 1996 crisis had proved effective. That episode had exposed China's inability to solve the Taiwan problem militarily, even though its missiles could inflict much damage on the island.

In early March, Beijing raised the temperature by issuing a lengthy document on the Taiwan issue, which threatened to use force if Taipei refused to negotiate on unification indefinitely. This was probably a bid to influence the upcoming Taiwanese presidential election, but it failed to deter the Taiwanese from electing the very candidate the Chinese most opposed. Nevertheless, the bellicose language caused considerable concern in Taipei and Washington.

Meanwhile, China's sluggish economy continued to cause concern. At the end of 1999, agreement was reached with the US administration on Chinese entry into the World Trade Organisation (WTO), but confirmation by the US Congress was thrown into doubt by Beijing's aggressive posturing on Taiwan. If China still manages to achieve WTO membership it would be seen by the outside world as a welcome augury of positive change. But it would also raise uncertainties about how the country's largely uncompetitive economy would cope.

The Impact of Kosovo

Two aspects of NATO's bombardment of Serbia particularly exercised China's leaders. First, they opposed the doctrine of humanitarian intervention if it meant an unprovoked attack on a sovereign country because of alleged atrocities committed by its government against its own citizens. Second, they opposed the use of force without prior authorisation from the UN Security Council. China's leaders saw both these aspects of NATO's action as setting ominous precedents that might be used against the People's Republic. They condemned the episode as a further illustration of the US's dangerous hegemonist tendencies.

The Chinese reacted in this way in the context of a steady deterioration in Sino-American relations since the high point during US President Bill Clinton's visit to China in 1998, when the countries announced their agreement to work towards a 'strategic partnership'. By early 1999, a Congressional Report had accused the Chinese of systematic spying on American nuclear and missile secrets and the atmosphere had been further clouded by accusations of illegal contributions to American election campaigns by the Chinese authorities. Matters were not improved when the fence-mending visit to the US by Premier Zhu Rongji in April 1999 was set off-course by Clinton's rejection of Zhu's compromise offer on terms for joining the WTO. Clinton recognised his mistake and attempted to reopen the matter before Zhu's return to Beijing, but it was too late. The early mistake was compounded by the details of the Chinese offer being published on the Internet. This not only added to Zhu's embarrassment, but it also exposed him to his domestic critics and placed him in political difficulties.

Not surprisingly, the Chinese opposed from the outset any Western attempt to force Yugoslavia to halt its oppression of the Kosovo Albanians. Indeed, NATO decided to use force without UN authority because it seemed highly probable that China and Russia would veto any resolution to confer authorisation in the Security Council. To ensure that the Chinese got the 'authorised' message about the injustice of the Western attack, official Chinese reporting entirely ignored Serbian atrocities in Kosovo. This reporting was regarded as so biased even in China that academicians in Beijing petitioned the authorities, warning that it might endanger relations with Muslim countries.

Such misgivings were almost immediately cast aside when five cruise missiles struck the Chinese embassy in Belgrade on 8 May (Beijing time). The news stimulated a visceral xenophobia that had not been seen in China since the Cultural Revolution. Violent demonstrations were immediately unleashed against Western embassies and consulates. The US was particularly targeted; one consulate building was entirely burnt down and others were severely damaged. The American Embassy in Beijing was the focal point for stone throwing, but the British and other Europeans (including even the Albanians) were attacked in the same way.

The demonstrations seemed to be spontaneous, but once under way they were marshalled by the Chinese authorities who ended them after a few days. The remarkable thing was that the main demonstrators were largely students from prestigious universities, who had a fuller picture of Balkan developments from access to the Internet and to Western broadcasts. They, like virtually all ethnic Chinese both within the People's Republic and outside – with the possible exception of the Taiwanese – unhesitatingly believed that the bombing was a deliberate attempt to punish and humiliate China. By contrast, most Westerners believed that the bombing was a result of all-too-familiar administrative mishaps.

The Chinese government demanded not only an apology and full recompense, but also a full report of the decision-making that led to the bombing and the punishment of those responsible. It took until the end of 1999 for an agreement to be reached. In it the Americans agreed to pay $4.5m in compensation to the families of the three Chinese killed and to the 17 who were injured, and a further $28m in recompense for the destroyed building. The Chinese agreed to pay $2.87m in respect of the damage to US official buildings in China.

This formal settlement did not reconcile the Chinese to US explanations of the incident, and the episode continued to provide opportunities for hard-liners among the leadership to try to rally support for their antipathy towards the United States. Examples were Li Peng, head of the National People's Congress and ranking second in the Communist Party, and Chi Haotian, the influential Minister of Defence. At the height of the clamour in May, they both made separate public pronouncements that the Chinese people were 'united in the hatred of the common enemy'. Interestingly, General Xiong Guangkai, who headed the first Chinese military visit to the US since the bombing in January 2000, made a point of saying publicly that friendly China–US relations could not be fully restored until there was a proper account of the episode.

The bombing, and the entire conduct of the Kosovo campaign, have impressed upon China's leaders the enormous margin between US power and that of any other aspirant to great-power status. One result has been

China's continuing search for diplomatic partners to counter alleged American hegemony. This was clearly evident during Jiang Zemin's visits to Britain and France in October 1999 and in China's dealings with other Asian governments. Since May, the Chinese have been more insistent than ever in emphasising that the UN Security Council (where they have the right of veto) is the only body whose authorisation can legitimise international intervention by force, or by any other means, in the domestic jurisdiction of sovereign states. At the same time, however, China's dependence on the United States continues to be a central feature of its foreign relations. It remains China's largest market, safeguards security in the region, and is the ultimate source of an international economic regulatory system that has served China well. Much as Chinese may query aspects of US security arrangements with Japan, or complain that American policies in the region amount to the containment of China, they also recognise that the alternative to American 'hegemony' may be even worse, at least in the short- and medium-term. China's return to isolation or halting its reform process can no longer be contemplated without risking economic and social misery which would undermine the regime's hold on power. The meeting between Presidents Jiang and Clinton in the course of the Asia-Pacific Economic Cooperation (APEC) forum in September helped to improve the atmosphere between their two countries, and to pave the way for the subsequent agreements on compensation and, ultimately, on the terms of Chinese entry to the WTO.

Coping with a 'Provocative' Taiwan

There is little that has more clearly illustrated China's predicament in its dealings with the United States than the way it handled what it regarded as yet another provocation by Taiwan's President Lee Teng-hui in 1999. This was Lee's declaration, in an interview with a German broadcaster on 9 July, that relations across the Taiwan Strait should be treated as 'special state-to-state relations'. Beijing interpreted this as a rejection of its 'one China' formula. It reacted with a barrage of verbal hostility and threats that were augmented by inspired reports in the Hong Kong press of threatening military manoeuvres, few of which were independently verified.

Since the US holds the key to the military balance across the Taiwan Straits, both sides could be said to be competing for Washington's attention. Washington itself was taken by surprise by Lee's statement and it made clear its displeasure about having its delicate relations with China suddenly disturbed in this way. The timing and substance of Lee's statement may well have been influenced by the approaching Taiwanese presidential elections on 18 March 2000, but it was probably also a reaction to what Taipei viewed as a shift in the balance of US favour towards China.

Beijing's problem is that, according to polls, less than 2% of Taiwanese find anything attractive in the formula of 'one country two systems' that served as the basis for negotiating the return to Chinese sovereignty of Hong Kong in 1997 and Macao in December 1999. Beijing's only alternative, the threat of military force, lacks credibility given Washington's continued determination to sell Taiwan enough arms to defend itself, and US insistence that Taiwan must not be forced under Chinese sovereignty.

Beijing's main weapon is therefore using diplomatic means to isolate Taiwan as a sovereign entity. Beijing clearly hopes to use its growing international weight to increase the pressure on Washington to reduce support for Taiwan and, correspondingly, to induce Taiwanese leaders to accept Beijing's terms of reference. Both sides thought that China had progressed in that direction when President Clinton, during a visit to China from 25 June to 3 July 1999 publicly affirmed his commitment to the so-called 'three noes'. In other words, the US would not support:

- Taiwanese independence;

- two Chinas, or one Taiwan–one China; nor

- Taiwan's entry into organisations where sovereignty is a membership condition.

In Taipei it was argued that Clinton's statement occasioned Lee's controversial remarks

The immediate crisis ended with the violent earthquakes that hit Taiwan in September. Although Taipei complained that Beijing used the sovereignty issue to score points over the administration of international aid to earthquake victims, Beijing stopped its harsh propaganda and no more was heard of its military exercises in the Strait.

Beijing appears to have learned from its experience in the March 1996 Taiwanese presidential elections that trying to intimidate the electorate by firing missiles offshore is counter-productive. When it came to the March 2000 elections it appeared satisfied with firing a 'White Paper' instead. This was notable for reminding the Taiwanese of former President Deng Xiaoping's threat 16 years previously that undue Taiwanese procrastination over negotiating terms for reunification could in itself lead to military action. This threat probably does not extend to attempting a direct attack on the island. Most military analysts agree that China will not have the necessary air control, or sufficient troop-transport landing craft to ensure an amphibious landing until 2005 or 2006 at the earliest. It could, however, weaken Taiwan's resolve through cruise-missile attacks designed to disrupt its economy. China has been increasing the number of cruise missiles deployed opposite Taiwan by some 50 per year since 1998. There are now 200 in place and they could become a threat in the near future.

Despite the accompanying fierce rhetoric, the overall purpose of the exercise seemed to be to prepare the ground for resuming negotiations once a new President has been elected in Taiwan. Nevertheless, in its own crude way, Beijing tried to prevent the election of Chen Shui-bian, the candidate of the Democratic Progressive Party (DPP), because of his past support for independence, despite his 'honeyed words' to the contrary. As was the case in 1996, when China tried to prevent the election of Lee Teng-hui, the Taiwanese electorate on 18 March once again demonstrated their commitment to democracy by ignoring Beijing's thunder. Now that China has failed again to see its preferred candidate elected, it can be expected to test him early on by insisting that negotiations open soon.

Washington also came in for severe criticism for continuing to supply arms to Taiwan. All of this played into the hands of Beijing's opponents in Congress and increased President Clinton's difficulties in harnessing sufficient Congressional support for his bill to grant China permanent normal trading status. Given the bill's importance for stabilising China's access to its largest market and prospects for entering the WTO, US leaders openly speculated about possible divisions in the Chinese leadership that might explain the country's apparently counterproductive behaviour.

The Challenge Within: The *Falun Gong*

It is a curious reflection of the contradictory and unpredictable effects of modernisation and globalisation upon China that its leader saw the most potent social challenge to Communist Party rule in 1999 to come not from the educated young pressing for greater democracy, but from a sect of middle-aged people practising the most traditional kind of meditation. One day in April 1999, the citizens of Beijing and their supreme Party Leader, Jiang Zemin, were taken by surprise as 10,000 quite ordinary people suddenly appeared, sitting in silent meditation before the Communist Party headquarters.

They were registering a protest against the denunciation of their movement in a provincial journal. This might not have seemed too serious to Western onlookers, but there were a number of things about their sudden appearance that shocked the Chinese leadership. Not only had the security agencies, that are normally so adept at monitoring independent organisations or associations, failed to appraise Jiang of this unexpected challenge, but it appeared that some senior officials, including generals who had survived the Long March, were devotees of the sect, known as the *Falun Gong*. It further transpired that *Falun Gong's* leader, Li Hongzhi, had taken the precaution of moving to the United States a few years earlier, and communicated with his followers through the Internet.

Falun Gong practitioners claimed that through meditation they could be in touch with what they claimed was 'the wheel of the law' within them, and thus become better and healthier human beings. Such sects and practices have been active in China since ancient times. Indeed, some modern nationalists have praised them as Chinese contributions to world health. Experts in *Qigong* (a similar exercise in Buddhist-type meditative exercises) treated Deng Xiaoping himself in his dotage. However, doubtless recalling that Chinese history is replete with examples of such sects rising in rebellion and even toppling dynasties, Jiang Zemin declared the *Falun Gong* to be a pernicious and dangerous cult that reeked of superstition and was a menace to its practitioners' health and even to social order.

A new law was hurriedly passed through the National People's Congress condemning *Falun Gong* as a cult. It suffered a massive campaign of vilification and persecution with devotees arrested and incarcerated in thousands. Undaunted, practitioners continued to present themselves in silent protest in major public places, including even Tiananmen Square. Bound by their beliefs and common practices, they did not need tight organisation and were in constant touch with each other. Most of the *Falun Gong* practitioners came from cities in the interior. They were drawn from all levels of society, including students, office workers, civil servants and even members of the Communist Party and the security services.

The issue acquired an international dimension when China demanded the extradition of the movement's founder and the United States refused. Human-rights organisations in Hong Kong as well as in the West collected damning evidence of persecution. Western governments were quick to protest at the arbitrary treatment of these apparently non-violent devout people. Beijing did not help matters by insisting that all religious organisations must register with the appropriate authorities. This was seen as further evidence of the regime's religious intolerance and persecution. Rather than succumbing to Beijing's pressure, *Falun Gong* members continued their silent and public protest throughout China. The sect's success at spreading its message at home and abroad, and the nervous and ham-fisted response by the regime, including Jiang Zemin personally, showed how far the Communist Party's capacity to control Chinese society had been diluted.

The Impending Challenge of the WTO

On 15 November 1999, Chinese and American negotiators finally agreed terms on which the US government would support China's entry into the WTO. The terms were not officially published in China, but the US has indicated that they will eventually open considerable sectors of the Chinese economy to foreign investment and competition, as well as to increasing trade. These sectors will include banking, telecommunications and other key modern business areas. Imports of wheat and other agricultural commodities can also be expected to increase because of tariff reductions.

204 Asia

Clearly the agreement gave a boost to the reformers within the party leadership and the consequences of entry will be profound. While it would be naïve to think that China's leaders would sit back and allow foreign competition to cut swathes through Chinese industry and agriculture, and deepen their already difficult unemployment problem, there can be no doubt that China faces a great challenge. Hitherto sheltered sectors of the economy, particularly the state-owned enterprises, will in principle be subject to crippling competition. According to a recent survey by the State Council only 26% of the country's industrial stock is up to international standards. The retooling and the restructuring that would be required to address these and other problems would take decades rather than the few years normally envisaged in WTO entry agreements. Given the difficulties that foreign companies and governments have experienced in nailing-down agreements with the Chinese and then in getting them implemented, China's entry to the WTO will clearly not be the complete answer for those anxious to increase their access to the legendary market of 1.2 billion customers.

From a Chinese perspective, a giant step has been taken which is bound to have enormous repercussions within the country. The government has been deeply divided over the issue. The key factor that apparently tipped the balance in favour of joining the WTO at this time was the state of the economy. Growth, which peaked at 14.2% in 1992, slowed down for the subsequent seven years. Although it is officially claimed that growth was 7.8% in 1998 and 7.1% in 1999, observers generally think these figures are too high. They point to the static level of private consumption to back their view that the true state of the economy is relatively sluggish.

Indeed, for the past three years the benchmark retail price index has been falling, and economic growth has been sustained largely through government investment in fixed assets. Foreign investment has also declined, especially since the onset of the Asian financial crisis in summer 1997. According to the State Statistical Bureau, reporting at the end of February 2000, foreign investment fell by a further 11.4% to $40.4bn in 1999. It was the threat to continued economic growth that triggered China's agreement to seek WTO entry at this point. Ultimately the regime's capacity to manage China's manifold problems and to maintain itself in power turns on its ability to deliver sufficient economic growth and development. Chinese spokesmen have made clear that they expect membership of the WTO will in itself boost the economy by encouraging a significant increase in foreign investment and a new surge in exports.

Interestingly, China has not shown any great urgency to settle terms of WTO entry with the European Union. Rather than pursuing key negotiations rapidly in the wake of the agreement with the United States, the Chinese have held back. The delay has coincided with suggestions that the economy began to show signs of recovery at the end of 1999 and in early 2000. Foreign investment has begun to increase once again and exports have begun to pick-up, largely as a consequence of recovery in other East Asian economies. Whatever the reason, by March 2000, China had yet to reach agreements with the 32 other countries (including the EU) that will be necessary before it can be considered for formal entry.

Problems Postponed

This would suggest that the consensus within China over entry into the WTO is fragile, as many of the potential losers in both the industrial and agricultural sectors still have significant political influence. Hence, even if terms of entry were to be agreed in time with the all of the outstanding WTO members, and China were to become a full member, it would be naïve to expect that easy compliance with WTO rules would soon follow. While the Chinese could expect greater ease of access to Western markets, entry to the Chinese market will continue to be fraught with delays, obstructions and the manifold difficulties that are all too familiar to Western companies doing business in China.

As China enters the year of the 'Golden Dragon', the regime faces difficult decisions on the WTO. Membership will stimulate forces in society that threaten to further erode the leadership's grasp on power. At the same time, Beijing will have to face continued challenges from Taiwan. These will be postponed until after the election there makes clear which tendency concerning its relations with Beijing takes the helm, but the newly elected president, Chen Shui-bian, indicated in his first speeches that he would maintain the present course, but with great care. Much will depend on US views, which will not be altogether clear until after its own election. China's leaders will not find it easy to agree on these matters, for they will be preoccupied with their own tussle for power, as Jiang Zemin tries to ensure that he will retain power after changes in leading positions at the March 2002 meeting of the National People's Congress.

Japan Still Floundering

Japan entered the new century hoping for better things, after the country's worst decade since its 'economic miracle' took off in the second half of the 1950s. The economy averaged barely 1% annual growth during the 1990s, and, although rising interest in high-technology stocks fuelled a stock-market boom, in late 1999, the market still ended the decade at only around half the level of ten years earlier. 'Japan Inc' had not unravelled completely, but it was certainly not as all-powerful and all-conquering as it had seemed in the late 1980s.

The economy did slightly better in 1999 than in the previous two years and at least managed to achieve a modicum of positive growth. Notwithstanding extravagant claims by supporters of Prime Minister Keizo Obuchi for 'Obuchinomics', whatever recovery the economy had achieved seemed to have been despite, rather than because of, government policies. The new initiatives hardly differed from the traditional pump-priming exercises which were tried – and which invariably failed – during most of the 1990s; the tenth stimulus package of the decade was announced in November 1999. As Obuchi apparently reverted to a 'go slow' on reform in the second half of the year, however, Japan's corporate leaders appeared to give up hope of the stimulus packages succeeding and began their own restructuring.

In the early stages of the 1997–98 Asian financial crisis, many of Japan's neighbours – along with the US and Europe – had expected Japan to help restore economic health to the region. Tokyo certainly contributed significantly to financial salvage packages, but could not meet the expectations that a revived Japanese economy would be the locomotive of broader regional recovery. Instead, the nascent revitalisation during 1999 of some of the other regional economies, led by the star performer South Korea, provided some consolation and impetus to the flagging Japanese economy.

Obuchi might have found some consolation in his political achievements. He had successfully massaged his coalition relationship with the prickly leader of the Liberal Party (LP), Ichiro Ozawa, and he even managed to bring the resuscitated New *Komeito* Party into the coalition before the year-end. Time-consuming bargaining ensured that his position within his Liberal Democratic Party (LDP) remained firm, but his rivals began gathering to take advantage of any slip-up *en route* to or during the elections due by October 2000. The LDP ended the 1990s as it had begun the decade, as the dominant political party, but the legacies of its 1993 fall from grace, most notably a series of mutating new political parties, had made retaining that eminence far harder work.

Obuchi's preoccupations with economic recovery programmes and party-political manoeuvring meant that, if anything, Japan played an even lower-key role in international affairs than in the previous few years. Hopes that Japan might take a higher profile in the 'brave new world' promised in the aftermath of the 1991 Gulf War and the collapse of the Soviet Union were not fulfilled during the 1990s, although Tokyo made a large financial contribution to the humanitarian effort in Kosovo. Yet, as 1999 ended, Japan was responding to the humanitarian crisis in East Timor through the same 'yen not men' mechanism it had employed nearly a decade earlier in the Gulf War.

Come into the Coalition

Reviving the economy remained the top priority of Japan's coalition government in 1999. Although the signals were mixed, the economy gave the general impression of being slowly on the mend. By the end of the year, the cabinet spokesman felt able to declare that the economy was 'still in a severe state but past the worst time'. Obuchi was unlikely to repeat the mistake of 1996, when an apparent economic revival was sent into reverse by the badly timed introduction of a consumption tax. However, three interrelated problems continued to trouble his government's economic policies. First was the stubbornly high – at least by Japanese standards – unemployment rate. Second was the slow pace at which the business sector was restructuring. Financial companies had been forced to bear the brunt of corporate restructuring in the previous year or two, but in 1999 the manufacturing and service sectors also took action. The third dilemma was ballooning government debt, accentuated by the government's tendency to try to solve problems by throwing money at them. Even Finance Minister Kiichi Miyazawa was concerned enough to argue, when unveiling his draft budget in December 1999, that while heavy spending was still necessary for the coming year, this would be the last expansionary budget. His prospects of weaning Japan away from its reliance on public borrowing, however, were by no means certain, not least because that would mean turning off the taps on government spending and, worse from a vote-gathering perspective, even raising taxes.

It was against this background of economic uncertainties and opposition-party criticism of his failure to resolve them speedily, that Obuchi sought to sustain his political fortunes. He had achieved something of a political coup by coming to a deal with Ozawa in January 1999, but both their personal and inter-party relationships remained difficult throughout the year. A series of political issues, ranging from electoral reform to nursing-care schemes, helped to keep the two niggling at each other and provoked several dramatic, but ultimately abortive, threats that Ozawa would walk out of the coalition. These added spice to the debate, which intensified towards the end of 1999, over whether the LP would take the final step and merge with the LDP, from which most of its members had defected in 1993.

Although Obuchi's popularity slowly improved after the deal with Ozawa, the LP did not control sufficient votes to give the coalition an overall majority in the two houses of the *Diet*. This problem led Obuchi to cast out feelers to the opposition New *Komeito* party, a revamped version of the *Komeito* party which had briefly been in power in the mid-1990s anti-LDP coalition governments and had strong links with an influential Buddhist sect. Not all within the LDP shared Obuchi's coalition-building enthusiasm; some resented Ozawa's re-engagement, blaming him for having ruptured the LDP back in 1993, while others remained suspicious of the religious overtones behind the *Komeito*. The old *Komeito* had indeed tried to cultivate a dovish image, but its successor party, driven by ambition to be in power, began to edge closer during 1998–99 to the LDP's conservative thinking on a number of issues, in particular those relating to security and nationalist identity. Informal understandings turned into formal cooperation – and a cabinet seat for New *Komeito* – in October.

Obuchi's desire to pull in the New *Komeito* had been strengthened by the fiasco of the Tokyo gubernatorial election in April 1999, when the LDP's official candidate lost out badly to Shintaro Ishihara, the maverick ex-LDP politician. Ishihara, who had gained international notoriety a decade earlier as the co-author of an anti-American nationalist tract entitled 'Japan that can say no', was elected with the help of extravagant electioneering about closing down a US air base in Yokota and supporting Taiwan rather than mainland China. While his ability to implement his pledges was restricted by his inability to secure a majority within the Tokyo metropolitan assembly, his ventures into foreign affairs, including a controversial visit to Taiwan in November 1999, continued to irritate and embarrass the Obuchi government.

The LDP–LP–*Komeito* coalition had a dominant position in the two houses of the *Diet*, particularly as the only significant opposition, the Democratic Party (DP), a hotchpotch of refugees from earlier political parties across the political spectrum, seemed unable to mount a serious challenge, even after a change of leadership. However, tensions between the three coalition partners were by no means eliminated and working out a cooperative electoral strategy for the three parties looks fraught with difficulties.

Along Nationalist Guidelines?

Obuchi's political deal-making with the LP and the New *Komeito* gave him the opportunity to push through the *Diet* several pieces of legislation which were inherently controversial, not least because cumulatively they were taken to suggest that a more nationalistic approach was emerging from Japan.

The most important legislation derived from the September 1997 Japan–US agreement on defence guidelines, a revision of joint guidelines originally drawn up in 1978. The revised guidelines called for enhanced coordination, within existing constitutional constraints, in peacetime as well as in time of war. US and Japanese officials had been meeting regularly to map out the military and political implementation of the new guidelines, but progress was slow until North Korean activity effectively forced Japan to increase the pace. The August 1998 launch of a North Korean missile over Japan was a tremendous shock to the Japanese government and people, and acted as a catalyst in switching public opinion in favour of the guideline legislation. Concerns about North Korea received renewed impetus in March 1999, while the bills were under consideration by the *Diet*. Two North Korean ships, supposedly fishing boats but almost certainly armed spy ships, entered Japanese territorial waters and were fired at and chased by coastguard and Maritime Self-Defense Forces (SDF) ships. The guidelines legislation was successively passed by the two houses of the *Diet* in April and May 1999, but the original 1997 guidelines were modified in order to secure the New *Komeito* support needed to ensure passage through the Upper House. The net effect of these revisions was to water down their effectiveness:

- by removing the ability to make ship inspections;

- by adding a new provision requiring *Diet* approval before SDF support operations in non-combat zones could be carried out; and

- by narrowing the definition for action from 'situations in areas surrounding Japan' to 'situations in which the peace and safety of Japan are gravely threatened'.

Japanese opposition parties and some neighbouring countries, notably the two Koreas and China, criticised this new legislation, but for Japanese defence officials, the measures simply met the need to change the alliance with the US into something normal and workable. Public opinion polls showed general Japanese support for steps to improve national security. Although the North Korean actions certainly helped to speed up the passage of the contentious legislation, the guidelines were not a simple knee-jerk reaction; rather they reflected a cautious and typically incremental Japanese response to persistent US prodding over many years for Japan to take a more pro-active role within the alliance. The new legislation was still hemmed in by sufficient restrictions and ambiguities to ensure that Japan would play a far more limited role than the US.

While Obuchi and the LDP were able to keep public opinion broadly with them over the defence guidelines, they laid themselves open to greater criticism with two other steps that had nationalist overtones. The first was granting legal status to the *hinomaru* (national flag) and *kimigayo* (national anthem), whose use at school and official ceremonies has been slowly increasing in recent years, even though the post-war reforms aimed at destroying Japanese militarism revoked their legal recognition. Few Japanese have a problem with the national flag, but public opinion is decidedly more mixed on the national anthem, which exalts the Emperor and is closely associated with pre-war nationalism.

The second and politically more dangerous step was the coordinated action of the LDP with the LP, New *Komeito* and even the DP in securing *Diet* agreement in July 1999 for constitutional 'research panels', to be set

Asia

up during the year 2000. These would act as forums for discussing, in particular, possible constitutional revision, including Article IX, which prohibits Japan from using force to settle international disputes and even from maintaining armed forces. However, the issue of constitutional revision, which has been raised intermittently over the past four decades, is difficult to resolve. The stringent constitutional requirements for voting support for any amendments, both within the *Diet* and through a public referendum, have made the LDP, even at the height of its powers, reluctant to risk marching down this road. Although the political fortunes of the left-wing parties, the self-styled defenders of the 1947 'peace constitution', are currently at a low ebb, the general public are likely to prefer the status quo and constitutional revision will occur later rather than sooner.

Further controversy was provoked in mid-October by Shingo Nishimura, an LP politician serving as the vice-minister of the Defence Agency, who suggested in an interview with the magazine *Weekly* that there ought to be parliamentary debate about whether 'Japan had better be armed with nuclear weapons'. Obuchi had no option but to sack Nishimura. Deep popular sensitivities on nuclear issues in Japan extend even to the peaceful development of nuclear power – underscored by an accident at the Tokaimura nuclear fuel processing plant in late September in which one negligent worker died.

Although mainstream LDP politicians favour bolstering Japan's defence capabilities, even they were unwilling to support Nishimura's extreme proposals. The Defence Agency was allowed, in late 1999, to put forward its first request in three years for an increased allocation in the forthcoming 2000–01 budget. However, the key elements in its submission were new tanker aircraft to allow mid-air refuelling, and improving capabilities to respond to guerrilla attacks by infiltrators and rogue ships. These were implicitly related to heightened concerns about North Korea. The North Korean factor, together with the Tokaimura accident, also stimulated the Obuchi government to consider new legislation in late 1999, which would enable Japan to respond more effectively to emergencies of all types, and which would also 'prepare the necessary framework to counter possible attacks' on Japan.

Does all this add up to a resurgent and ultimately dangerous nationalism in Japan? National pride is a protean concept, that, in Japan as elsewhere, can flourish after successful recovery from a national disaster or act as a solace or even diversion in times of trouble. Many Japanese are unhappy that patriotic symbols or actions that would be considered quite normal in other countries, are criticised as aberrations in Japan. However, there is little evidence of any deep hankering for a return to the expansionist and imperialist nationalism of the pre-war era, other than amongst a few inconsequential fringe groups and right-wing politicians.

Present-day Japanese sentiments may best be described as 'soft nationalism': the Japanese have invested a great deal of time and energy in a socio-political system and an external posture from which they have drawn considerable advantage by, essentially, keeping their heads down. Popular sentiment and systemic inertia exercise a strong restraint on assertive nationalism even today.

Looking to Asia Again

Signs of Japanese willingness to do more in the security area nevertheless helped to keep Japan–US relations on an even keel. The Americans were disappointed, but not surprised, by the lack of strong rhetorical Japanese support for the NATO war over Kosovo. They welcomed the defence guideline legislation, however, and were also pleased when the new Governor of Okinawa Keiichi Inamine agreed to push ahead with building a new joint-use military-civilian airport to replace the Futenma air base, which is due to close. The large Japanese trade surplus with the US continued to be a talking point. US negotiators and Congressmen periodically lost patience with Japan over specific disputed issues, in particular opening-up the Japanese insurance market, but overall, the bilateral relationship remained comparatively calm during the year, even if it often gave the impression of marking time.

Japan's relations with its two largest neighbours also lacked momentum. Obuchi visited China in July 1999, but with China and Japan each wary of perceived signs of growing nationalism in the other, the bilateral relationship remained generally cool. The dream of a peace treaty with Russia became increasingly faint. Japan did, however, pay more attention to other Asian neighbours, partly because of the perceived need to reassure them that the revised defence guidelines did not herald revived militarism. Another reason was the lingering economic, social and political effects of the Asian financial crisis.

Japan's warmer rapport with South Korea was in contrast to its tense relationship with the unpredictable North. Despite the rhetoric of Japan–US–South Korean solidarity over policy towards Pyongyang, the Japanese approach had for much of 1998–99 been tougher than that of South Korea, which was busy practising its 'sunshine policy'. Towards the end of 1999, however, Tokyo began testing the water for better relations with North Korea. The breakthrough came in December 1999, when former Prime Minister Tomiichi Murayama led a multi-party visit to Pyongyang. This led to talks about talks, aimed at reopening negotiations on establishing diplomatic relations, which had been suspended since 1992. The Obuchi government lifted most of the sanctions it had imposed after the 1998 missile launch, but subsequent preliminary diplomatic talks, and the North Korean seizure of a retired Japanese journalist on grounds of spying, suggested that the journey to normalisation was certain to be slow and tortuous.

The other important regional foreign-policy issue was the turmoil in Indonesia and, in particular, the crisis in East Timor. After its humiliating failure to contribute other than financially to the Gulf War, Japan passed the 1992 International Peace Cooperation Law. This allowed the SDF to participate in UN peacekeeping operations (PKO), such as in Cambodia in 1992–93. East Timor appeared to offer a second opportunity for Japan to contribute constructively in an Asian context, but the five principles of the PKO law constrained the SDF from being used in circumstances which called for peace-making rather than peace-keeping. Japan was also reluctant to use its economic clout to encourage more positive Indonesian action to end the carnage in East Timor, and rejected an Australian request to reconsider its massive aid commitments to Indonesia. Since it could not use the SDF, Japan sent only three civilian policemen to join the UN operations in East Timor. Once again it was forced to fall back on money as its contribution. It offered humanitarian aid to refugees as well as $100 million to cover roughly half of the expected costs of the multinational forces.

While the international community did not pressurise Japan on troop contributions to the same extent as during the Gulf War and the Cambodian settlement, Tokyo's inability to send more than money to East Timor provoked new debate within Japan. This highlighted the significant differences within the newly formed coalition government over whether the PKO law should be amended to allow, in time, Japan's full participation in UN peacekeeping operations. Japan wants to gain a UN Security Council seat and, although the major barrier to this probably remains the international disputes over the optimal number of Council members and whether the veto should be extended to new ones, Japan's failure to tackle the PKO question is another handicap. Unable, or unwilling, to take up an active role in East Timor, Japan will continue to find it difficult to press its claims for permanent membership effectively when it appears so reluctant to accept the moral imperative of participating in the riskier aspect of UN operations.

Japan was clearly more comfortable when dealing with regional economic-policy issues. In October 1998, Japan launched the Miyazawa Initiative giving aid to the five countries worst affected by the Asian financial crisis – Indonesia, Malaysia, Philippines, Singapore, South Korea and Thailand. In November 1999, Obuchi took advantage of being at the unprecedented 'East Asian summit' in Manila, with the leaders of the ten members of ASEAN (the Association of Southeast Asian Nations), China and South Korea, to announce a new broader aid package. Dubbed the 'Obuchi Plan', it promised $500m to set up a comprehensive programme promoting regional cooperation through human-resource networks.

Whereas the Miyazawa Initiative had been designed to provide short-term funds to help specific Asian states recover from the currency crisis, the Obuchi Plan was targeted at more countries over the medium- and long-term.

The East Asian summit and Obuchi's January 2000 tour of mainland South-east Asia were used to sound out other Asian nations on what issues should be discussed when Japan hosts the summit of the Group of Eight (G-8) in Okinawa in July 2000. Japanese officials even talked about presenting a unified 'Asian perspective' at the meeting. For Japan and for Obuchi, who is likely to try to postpone Lower House elections until after the summit, the Okinawa G-8 will mark a significant test of Japan's leadership and of its ability to start the new millennium in a more positive internationalist mode than it ended the last.

The Korean Peninsula: Picking Up the Pieces

Perhaps surprisingly, 1999 was a quiet year of recovery on the Korean Peninsula. South Korea emerged from its economic crisis somewhat faster and in better shape than had seemed possible in 1998. Not all problems were resolved – what to do with the *chaebol*, the big conglomerates, remained a major problem, with the government sending mixed signals about how far it was committed to reform. Politically too, South Korea met with considerable turbulence, but despite criticism, President Kim Dae Jung stuck with his domestic and North Korean policies. While his approach continued to enjoy a high reputation internationally, at home his popularity fell and, as his presidency progressed, there were signs of growing domestic dissatisfaction with politics and politicians, together with demands for a new beginning.

Asia

For North Korea too, things have begun to look up, even if to outsiders the economy and the daily lives of most people still appear bleak. The worst of the food shortages may be over and there are signs that agriculture is returning to normal, although some flood-damaged areas, especially where salt water covered the fields, will take years to recover. Apart from fertiliser production and a small amount of light manufacturing, industry remains in a parlous state.

North–South relations changed little formally. Despite a naval clash off the west coast in summer 1999, which appeared threatening until the North Koreans backed down, Kim Dae Jung stuck to his 'sunshine policy'. One result was that North–South economic links grew. The North continued its campaign for bilateral links with the United States, though remaining highly suspicious of US motives, and began to cast around for increased contacts with other Western countries. This effort was slow to develop, although North Korea did manage to reach agreement with Italy on diplomatic relations.

South Korea: Economic Advances, Political Stagnation

In strict economic terms, South Korea seems to have successfully weathered the worst of the storm that struck in 1997. Growth in gross domestic product (GDP) in the last quarter of 1999 was estimated at around 10%, following on from 4.6%, 9.8% and 12.3% in the three previous quarters. This represented a remarkable turnaround since the end of 1998, when South Koreans looked back on a year in which the economy had contracted by 5.8%. Inflation in 1999, at 0.8%, was the lowest since 1965, the early days of the Park Chung Hee regime. Other economic indicators were bright, and even the unemployment figures showed a downward tend. The won, which plummeted in 1997 to just below 2,000 to the US dollar, had climbed back to 1,150 to the dollar by the end of 1999.

Perhaps inevitably, the improved figures led to some slackening in the impetus for fundamental reform of the economic system. Although the Daewoo conglomerate was near bankruptcy, South Korea's government was reluctant to face the issue and allow it to go under. Reform of the financial sector, regarded by many outsiders as the litmus test of the overall commitment to fundamental change, slowed down. The government, despite its brave words in 1997–98, was reluctant to push too hard, as it was not prepared to see Korean industries suffer too much. Capacity in most key industries remained too high, and fundamental reform of the *chaebol* seemed as far off as ever. Evidence of continued close links between the government and the *chaebol* was demonstrated by the Hyundai group's involvement with North Korea – nothing so sensitive could exist without a strong measure of government backing. There is still a siege mentality at work: South Korea needs these industries to survive. Changes in the external environment, such as increased oil prices and economic downturns elsewhere in the world, however, could cause problems for South Korea in 2000.

Politically, it was a less successful year. Although the economic turnaround is clearly linked to President Kim Dae Jung's term of office – he came to power just as the crisis broke and, after a hesitant start, seemed to grasp the need for drastic measures – his popularity, always greater outside the country than inside, has steadily declined since 1997. Although he is still seen as personally upright and honest, and has carried on with some elements of his domestic-reform programme, to most South Koreans, the government appears much as it always has. There has been a series of scandals involving ministers' families, and allegations of corruption accumulated throughout the year. Lee Jong Chan, the former head of the National Intelligence Service and one of those seen as a possible successor to Kim, was embroiled in a dispute over allegations that he had taken compromising papers with him on departure from office. This not only damaged his presidential hopes, but eventually brought down his successor as well.

The National Assembly, where Kim Dae Jung's coalition does not have a majority, spent much of the year in deadlock. Kim's effort to forge a new and broader party to replace his present minority coalition in the April 2000 elections met with little success. In office, Kim has already shown some of the characteristically authoritarian tendencies of his predecessors – he comes from the same tradition, after all – and he has shuffled his ministers with a similar frequency. If he fails to create a new party, he may decide it is necessary to use more heavy-handed methods to get business done in the second half of his presidency.

Disillusionment with the government is also reflected in its loss of two December by-elections in Kyonggi province, and the appearance of citizens' groups whose main purpose is to compile lists of politicians that they believe to be so tainted that they should not be allowed to stand again. Among those so identified was Kim Dae Jung's coalition partner and long-term political rival, Kim Jong Pil, whose political career stretches back to his role in the 1961 military coup that brought Park Chung Hee to power.

When the criticisms unfolded in January 2000, Kim Jong Pil had just resigned as prime minister in order to lead his party into the next general election. Kim and other leading politicians professed outrage at the attacks on their integrity, and demanded action on the (technically illegal) lists. But here was a sign that ordinary people are becoming tired of the highly personalised and faction-ridden political process that has been such a feature of South Korea since its independence. In a move that clearly disconcerted some of his former coalition colleagues, Kim Dae Jung welcomed their activities as a sign of a 'big move towards participatory democracy'.

Asia

In some ways, Kim Dae Jung maintained his reputation as a reforming president. There were large amnesties for prisoners, including the release of the last of the long held North Korean 'spies', although most of those freed were ordinary criminals rather than political prisoners. Trade-union rights were further strengthened with the legalisation of the Korean Confederation of Trades' Unions in November. Kim's attempt to reform the so-called National Security Law (actually a series of laws, some dating back to the 1950s) failed because of parliamentary problems.

Internationally, Kim has undertaken a number of forward-looking initiatives. He has been active in trying to find a solution to the problem of Burma. His decision to send South Korean troops to the peacekeeping operations in East Timor was welcomed internationally, even though at home it led to widespread concern that the Korean business community in

Indonesia might become targets. That this did not happen did not lessen the criticism. There were fewer critiques of another significant move: the meeting between Kim, Japanese Prime Minister Keizo Obuchi and the Chinese premier Zhu Rongji in November 1999. While it would be a mistake to read too much into this meeting as a guide to future cooperation between the three countries, there was no doubt that it represented a significant change.

Predictably, policy towards North Korea also caused problems for Kim Dae Jung. His insistence that the 'sunshine policy' should remain firmly in place, even in the face of what was seen as North Korean provocation in the West Sea during the summer, won acclaim outside Korea, but there was sniping at home. Kim's refusal to be provoked was taken as evidence by some that he is soft on communism. However, South Korea's fierce naval response sank one North Korean gunboat and sent the others back across the Northern Limit Line, temporarily silencing such criticism. But in February 2000, when Kim stated that, from what he had seen, the North's Kim Jong Il both was capable of running the country and was, in fact, doing so, there was further outrage.

North Korea: Slow Progress

There were no dramatic developments on North Korea's domestic front; rather, a slow – some might say crawling – process of change could be discerned. Although there were still food shortages and for most people life appears to be bleak, the food supply was improving and other things did not get worse. Visitors reported that there was less electricity available for domestic use in the cities, and there was evidence of lack of heating during the winter. Paradoxically, this was seen by some as a good sign – the electricity not available for household lights was being diverted to industrial use.

The 1999 harvest showed a modest improvement of about 5% on the previous year to 4.16 million tonnes (according to South Korean estimates – the North Koreans reported 4.34m tonnes to the UN Food and Agriculture Organization). This was the first rise above the 4m tonne mark since 1994. Although inadequate to feed the population, let alone to provide a surplus for manufacturing and other purposes, this was at least a move in the right direction. According to the North Koreans and aid agencies, international food aid is still required, and it continues to flow in. Reluctance to allow full monitoring of aid distribution in some parts of the country has continued to cause problems with some non-governmental organisations, but the problems seem generally to have had local causes, rather than to be part of a general policy. There is still much concern at the long-term effects of food shortages on the more vulnerable sections of the population, including children and nursing mothers.

North Korea's international trade remained in the doldrums; manufacturing facilities are few and, even when working, operate at a mere fraction of their capacity. Intra-Korean trade, however, seems to be climbing: in January 2000, the South Korean Ministry of National Unification reported that it had reached $333.44m in 1999, an increase of over 50% on 1998. Some 581 firms participated in this cross-border trade. The Hyundai-organised tourist trips to the Diamond Mountains (Kumgang-san) remain an important component of the trade, and look set to increase despite the occasional complication. In 2000, the organisers hope to include foreigners in the groups, although they have said that, to avoid complications, they will exclude Japanese and Americans.

One new development was that Kim Jong Il became more active in economic matters, an area in which he had hitherto shown little interest. He has been reported as visiting farms and factories and, like his father, issuing guidance. He was also closely associated with new campaigns encouraging the use of scientific methods, and demanding that people work harder. The specific guidance may be less important than the general encouragement to do something about the problems. Certainly, there have been reports of more local initiatives on economic matters, with new crops being introduced, and much land re-zoning and double cropping.

Kim Jong Il's interest in economic matters was not the only sign of change. For the first time since the death of Kim Il Sung in 1994, local elections were held, and a budget was put before the Supreme People's Assembly. Although it painted a gloomy picture of economic decline, North Korean officials were at pains to say that the worst was over. More significant than the specific details, always scarce in such North Korean documents, was the fact that a budget had been published at all, perhaps another sign that the long hiatus in state, government and party activities, so evident since 1994, is now coming to an end.

There was still no evidence by early 2000 of any formal opposition to Kim Jong Il's rule, nor of the collapse of state authority long predicted by commentators outside North Korea. Nevertheless, the state's inability to feed the population has had a clear effect on the tight controls hitherto in place. Visitors who have travelled outside Pyongyang report much movement of people in search of food. Controls still function effectively around the capital, and towards the Demilitarized Zone between the two Koreas, but elsewhere they seem to be in abeyance. The centre's failures, it is claimed, have allowed a certain degree of initiative to flow to local village and community leaders, who now find themselves faced with the responsibility of feeding those in their charge. It will not be easy for Pyongyang to re-establish full control even when, and if, the crisis has completely abated.

Internationally, North Korea is more active. Although it has continued to close diplomatic posts in Third World countries, it has opened a consulate in the Hong Kong Special Autonomous Region, and is making efforts to open links with a variety of countries, including the European Union and several of its member states. So far only Italy has responded, establishing diplomatic relations on 5 January 2000. Talks are under way regarding diplomatic relations with the Philippines, and the North Koreans have also put out feelers to Canada and Australia.

After years of deadlock in negotiations with the Japanese, contacts have now been resumed. As there are several contentious issues involved, nobody expects a swift breakthrough, but the fact that North Korea was willing to begin talks at all was another sign of a more active foreign policy. And, after years of procrastination, North Korea and Russia finally signed a treaty of friendship in February 2000, replacing the 1961 treaty that the Russians had described as no longer appropriate. While the earlier treaty, like a similar one with China signed the same year, had provided for military assistance in case of conflict, the new one avoids any such commitment.

Most effort, however, has focused on building a relationship with the US. Since 1994, when concern over North Korea's nuclear ambitions brought the US into direct negotiations with North Korea, leading to the Agreed Framework on freezing the nuclear programme, the relationship has steadily grown deeper and more complex. That this is so is not always evident from the rhetoric on both sides, which still has strong Cold War echoes. The reality, however, is that the North Koreans and the Americans are talking and negotiating on a wide range of issues, and North Korea has become the main recipient of US aid in Asia, whether in the form of heavy fuel oil as a substitute for the abandoned nuclear power, or of humanitarian aid.

The US annually supplies North Korea with some 500,000 tonnes of heavy fuel oil, worth nearly $60m. Under the Agreed Framework, it is committed to continue to do so until the completion of the first of the three light-water reactors being built by the Korean Energy Development Organisation (KEDO). Site-preparation work for the reactors was nearly completed at the end of 1999, and main construction work has begun. The project is far behind schedule, however. The original planned completion year of 2003 cannot realistically be met, and the target date has now been revised to 2007 or 2008. Despite the long delay, support for the project among the main countries involved (South Korea, the US and Japan) is firm, even though the original cost estimate of $4.6bn will obviously be exceeded. The North Koreans are unhappy about the length of time involved, but they seem to understand that the change of date is inevitable. In the meantime, they are using the delay as a bargaining card to garner concessions in other areas and to trawl for more cash.

The US position continues to be driven by concern over North Korea's potential as a source of insecurity in the Asia-Pacific region, and as a proliferator of missiles and other weapons of mass destruction. US worries in 1998 regarding a large hole being dug at the village of Kumchang-ni were eased only when a US team inspected the site and found that a hole was all it was. (But the US paid for the privilege of visiting.) Then, in 1999, US apprehension focused on the possibility of a further rocket launch. The North Koreans denied any such ambitions and agreed to talk – also agreeing not to test rockets while talks continued. The talks have continued, and the North has not tested its rockets, although it may still be selling missiles, maintaining that it has a sovereign right to do so and that it needs the money.

Although there are those in the US who criticise this policy of engagement, it was endorsed in an October 1999 report on North Korean policy by former Secretary of Defense William Perry. Commissioned in 1998 and compiled with wide consultation, the report argues that the United States should cease paying North Korea for behaving properly, and recommends that relations with Pyongyang should be put on a more normal footing. The North Koreans, suspicious as always, have nevertheless responded and the talking continues.

There is no one explanation for this burst of North Korean activity in the outside world. Like the modest signs of a return to more normal practices on the domestic scene, it may simply reflect a machine that is slowly beginning to function again. The need for food and other aid is certainly an important consideration, both in withdrawing from poor Third World countries such as Mongolia and trying to build up contacts with the richer West. It is, after all, from the West that most aid has come in the last five years. Having previously been dependent on the former Soviet Union and China, the North Koreans seem content to move towards dependency on the West. They preserve spiritual independence, however, by remaining critical of those who feed the country. Their desire to have direct contacts with the US may be a long-standing one, but they are still very suspicious of the ultimate end of US policy; they may believe that broader links with the West may help to provide some security against overdependence on the US.

Stagnation in North–South Relations

North Korea's new-found willingness to deal with the outside world was not reflected in relations with South Korea. The North views Kim Dae Jung's sunshine policy with deep suspicion, and has refused direct dealings with the South Korean government. Pyongyang remains willing to take South Korean money, however, provided it can curb the risks of contamination; tourism to the isolated Diamond Mountains is one thing, but South Koreans on the streets of Pyongyang are another matter entirely. That the relationship was still tense was demonstrated by naval clashes in the West Sea in March 1999, where North Korean fishing boats and their naval escorts came south of the 'Northern Limit Line'. The UN Command had unilaterally introduced this line, which is not a recognised boundary, at the time of the Korean Armistice, to prevent clashes between North and South. This has been a lost cause. Over the years, there have been periodic clashes as North Korean boats ventured into the lucrative crab-fishing waters. In 1999, South Korean naval forces reacted with heavy fire to what was deemed North Korean provocation. The North retreated (and Kim Dae Jung was able to argue that the sunshine policy was not just appeasement), but the potential for further confrontations remains high, and the North may be more prepared the next time.

Otherwise, the steady trickle of defectors from the North has continued, but the expected flood failed to materialise, and there are still a few who go the other way. The growing number of North Korean economic refugees in China – and to a lesser extent, Russia – is of concern to the South. The problem was highlighted when the Chinese returned one such group to North Korea, despite protests by South Korea and others. A solution will be difficult, especially since South Korea has no wish to absorb a flood of poorly qualified North Koreans who would find it difficult to adjust.

Outlook

Although major problems continue to bedevil the Korean Peninsula, some progress was made during 1999. In many ways, North Korea has become less threatening to its neighbours. It has also weathered the economic difficulties of the past five years. The problems have not been solved, however, and are probably not solvable without major economic restructuring, but the North survives for the present. Closer engagement with the US may help to reduce further its potential for aggression, although its fiery rhetoric will probably continue to exasperate those on the receiving end.

The North may only have a limited time to exploit the favourable climate that now surrounds it. Kim Dae Jung's sunshine policy is not popular with large segments of the South Korean electorate, and he may find it harder to promote it after the April 2000 general elections. Further clashes in the West Sea, for example, could well cause problems. Kim Dae Jung has a further three years as president in front of him, however, and temporary setbacks may be overcome. The North's window of opportunity with the US may not persist: there is no guarantee that the next US president will follow the Clinton administration's policies, and North Koreans may have to face a more hostile and less responsive US in coming years. North Korea may well revert to a more aggressive stance. For the present, however, the policy of gradually drawing North Korea into dialogue seems to be working.

Turbulence and Conflict in South Asia

The exchange of nuclear tests by India and Pakistan dominated relations between them in 1998, raising tensions to dangerous levels. Yet, events during 1999 proved even more turbulent. Hopes for a *rapprochement* between these two long-standing antagonists, raised by Indian Prime Minister Atal Behari Vajpayee's February meeting in Lahore with his Pakistani counterpart Nawaz Sharif, were dashed three months later by an 11-week conflict in Kashmir costing over a 1,000 lives. Political upheavals added to the tensions. The Indian government fell on 17 April 1999, after a mere 13 months in office. On 12 October, the day after Vajpayee was eventually called upon to form a new government, Sharif was toppled by his Chief of Army Staff, General Pervaiz Musharraf, and charged with offences which could carry the death penalty.

After the coup, Pakistan's priorities were to restore domestic stability, rebuild discredited institutions and invigorate a chronically weak economy. India also sought to consolidate its economy by resuming its halting liberalisation programme. New Delhi's strategists were meanwhile moving towards a maximalist interpretation of 'minimum deterrence', which might ultimately consist of a triad of land, sea and airborne nuclear-delivery systems, underpinned by increased conventional forces. General Musharraf's evident support for the summer's military operations in Kashmir, and his presumed involvement in its planning, offered little prospect of new moves towards *détente*. Following the hijack of an Indian Airlines aircraft by Kashmiri militants on 24 December, forcing the release one week later of three prisoners detained in India, the new century began with renewed concern for the stability of the region, as well as for the political and economic viability of Pakistan itself.

Indo-Pakistani Relations: Perfidy and Tragedy

At the start of 1999, relations between India and Pakistan raised hopes of a new beginning. In February, Vajpayee became the first Indian Prime Minister ever to make a land crossing to Pakistan, when he travelled from Amritsar to Lahore on a newly inaugurated bus service. The symbolism of this journey, and of India's acceptance of partition, was underlined by Vajpayee's visit to the Minar-i-Pakistan, a national monument marking the site of the first formal appeal for the creation of a separate homeland for the Muslims of British India. The Lahore Declaration issued by the two prime ministers on 21 February, and its accompanying Memorandum of Understanding, raised expectations of a new spirit of flexibility and realism. It stated that there should be no interference by either country in the other's internal affairs, and called for further discussions covering security, nuclear-related issues and, crucially, Kashmir. The following month, after a meeting of the South Asian Association for Regional Cooperation (SAARC), the two foreign ministers agreed a timetable for implementation. But the Lahore Declaration was unpopular in Pakistan, and there was wider scepticism about the prospects for genuine progress.

Hopes indeed proved both short-lived and ill-founded. In April, India test-fired the intermediate-range *Agni* 2 ballistic missile. Claiming that the 'Lahore spirit' had been breached, Pakistan swiftly countered with the launch of the *Ghauri* 2. On 9 May, the Indian Army came across an unusually large number of armed intruders on the Indian side of the Line of Control in Kashmir, near the small towns of Kargil and Dras. The Line of Control, which divided the pre-independence state of Jammu and Kashmir, had been set out in the 1972 Simla Agreement following India's military defeat of Pakistan, and represented minor changes to the cease-fire line after the 1947–48 conflict. Violations had become commonplace since the renewal of tension in 1989, with frequent exchanges of artillery fire. This time, however, the location was unusual and the numbers of intruders and the ensuing conflict were on a scale not seen since the 1971 Indo-Pakistani war. Some 2,000 militants, described by Islamabad as *mujaheddin* or 'freedom fighters', occupied key ridges up to a height of 4,500 metres. From there, they threatened the only road between the towns of Srinagar and Leh – the Indian supply route to the Siachen Glacier, where Indian and Pakistani forces have been locked in a stand-off for 15 years.

New Delhi was caught unawares. Indian security forces normally patrolled this inhospitable area only in the warmer months. It was not clear how long the intruders had been there or whether, as many in India claimed, Sharif was aware of the operation when he met Vajpayee three months earlier. New Delhi swiftly sent large numbers of additional troops to the scene, and denounced Pakistan's presumed involvement. On 26 May, India launched air-strikes against the intruders – the first in Kashmir since 1971. Within days, the Indian Air Force had lost two MiG fighters and a helicopter gunship.

Vajpayee described the infiltration as a 'violation of the Lahore Declaration and of the Simla Agreement'. Indian Home Minister Lal Krishna Advani accused Pakistan of waging an undeclared war against India and, on 23 June, characteristically stated that 'it would be prudent on the part of India to prepare for war'. Despite bitter fighting, Indian forces refrained from crossing to the Pakistani side of the Line of Control. Casualties mounted during the following weeks and Indian forces succeeded in wresting back some terrain. But by the end of June, New Delhi was expressing increased concern about Indian casualties and the difficulty of dislodging the intruders without cutting off their supply routes on the other side of the Line. Facing an election, the Indian caretaker government, which was certain that the Pakistani Army units were actively engaged, could not allow Pakistan to retain its gains. Pakistani Foreign Minister Sartaj Aziz, meanwhile, declared that 'we will not hesitate to use any weapon in our arsenal to defend our territorial integrity' – a clear reference to nuclear weapons. The risk that the conflict would escalate seemed very real. International concern mounted, as did pressure on Islamabad to restrain the intruders and to cease its support for them.

Washington's early condemnation of Pakistan, and a statement issued by the Group of Eight (G-8) industrialised countries on 20 June, left no doubt that the US and the West regarded Pakistan as the initiator of the conflict. Nor did Pakistan receive any support from its erstwhile ally, China. Chinese statements after Sharif's visit to Beijing in the final week of June remained strictly neutral, and echoed Western calls for the Line of Control to be respected. Losing both the military and political battles, Pakistan's position had become unsustainable. In an unscheduled visit to Washington, Sharif publicly agreed with President Bill Clinton on 4 July that 'concrete steps would be taken for the restoration of the Line of Control in accordance with the Simla Agreement'. Two days later, Musharraf stated that between 1,500 and 2,000 'Kashmiri freedom fighters' would be asked to leave their positions. He subsequently acknowledged that Pakistani armed forces had engaged in 'occasional and aggressive patrolling' on the Indian side of the Line of Control. Although falling short of an admission of active military involvement, as New Delhi had alleged, these and other statements publicly confirmed Pakistan's official support for, and influence over, the *'mujaheddin's'* operations. The main fighting had ended by 24 July, although encounters continued long afterwards, leaving over 1,000 dead and many more injured.

The Kargil conflict raised disconcerting questions about Pakistani motives, the nature of Pakistani governance and the balance between the political and military establishments. There was no official Pakistani explanation beyond the barely credible line that the freedom fighters had acted on their own initiative. But was Sharif aware of the plans beforehand and did he enter the Lahore meeting in bad faith? If he was consulted in brief or misleading terms, or if he was not aware of the operation until after it had actually started, this would suggest that the military leadership had launched an initiative with far-reaching political and strategic implications which lacked democratically based analysis or political control.

Whatever Sharif's involvement beforehand, he publicly supported the offensive when it was under way and, at least initially, showed no signs of attempting to overrule military opinion or of trying to quell popular support. The involvement of Musharraf is more certain. In an extraordinarily frank interview given to the Indian newspaper *The Hindu* in January 2000, Musharraf claimed that Sharif had consulted him before the Lahore Declaration, but that he had objected to the pact because of its 'lack of emphasis on Kashmir'. He maintained that Sharif knew about the

Asia

Kargil operation – 'everyone was on board'. As Chief of Army Staff, Musharraf would have been a key figure in the approval and planning process.

Several factors could have led to the Pakistani attempt to secure a toe-hold in Indian-held Kashmir. After a period of relative quiet, anti-Indian sentiment in the Kashmir Valley had risen again over the previous year or two; international opinion seemed sympathetic towards Pakistan after India's initiation of the nuclear tests in May 1998; and India was on the point of further strengthening its armed forces. The nuclear capabilities of both sides, and India's repeated emphasis on the inconceivability of a nuclear exchange, suggested that low-intensity opportunism in Kashmir would not lead to a militarily damaging escalation. A new international focus on the Kashmir issue, with a re-emphasis of Pakistan's determination to force India to the negotiating table, might ultimately secure an outcome favourable to Pakistan. The action might be justified internationally as redressing the balance, following India's 1984 occupation of what Islamabad claimed was a Pakistani part of the ambiguously delineated Siachen Glacier area: territorial gains in Kargil could be used as bargaining chips. Transcripts of alleged conversations between Musharraf and Indian Chief of General Staff Lieutenant-General Mohammed Aziz at the end of May 1999 (dismissed by Pakistan as fabrications, but seemingly authentic) are consistent with this hypothesis.

However, Pakistan had seriously miscalculated the risks. The intruders' early success dangerously emboldened them. They occupied larger areas of territory, and penetrated deeper across the Line of Control than they had anticipated and, once installed, did not want to relinquish their gains. An attention-seeking ploy turned into a grave military and political threat to which the Indian caretaker government, in the throes of an extended election campaign, was compelled to respond. New Delhi was determined to throw the intruders back, using whatever resources were necessary.

Internationally, the Pakistani action was regarded as a clear violation of an arrangement which, despite each country's formal territorial claims, had existed for 27 years and had been re-emphasised in the Lahore Declaration just three months previously. Any attempts to take and hold territory by force would be dangerous. Both countries' possession of nuclear weapons could lead to disproportionate consequences. The Western and Chinese refusal to countenance the Pakistani operation, while attaching no 'balancing' blame to India for its response, was both a surprise and a disappointment to Islamabad.

New Delhi's ability to anticipate crises and defuse them through early political action was put into question by its failure to detect the intruders until they were well established. Consequently, large numbers of army reinforcements had to be deployed and vast stocks of ammunition expended. However, New Delhi's judicious restraint in not extending operations across the Line of Control, or engaging in hot pursuit, served India well internationally. And it no doubt suited India's strategic interests to arouse concern that such forebearance might not last indefinitely.

The implications of the Kargil crisis, however, went much further, demonstrating that the possession of nuclear weapons and the absence of full-scale war since 1971 were no guarantee of continued peace. Nuclear deterrence would not prevent low-intensity conflict. Far from reducing defence expenditure, as many Indian apologists had argued before the nuclear tests, conventional capabilities would need to be enhanced to keep the nuclear threshold at a high level. This was borne out in the budget announced on 29 February 2000, which boosted defence spending by 28.2%, the largest ever single-year increase. The supposed nuclear balance, and the resulting constraints upon India's freedom of military action, had apparently fostered a belief in Islamabad that Pakistan could advance its interests over Kashmir with impunity. In September, there were credible reports that five rounds of 'unofficial' talks between an Indian journalist, R. K. Mishra, and former Pakistani Foreign Secretary Niaz Naik had come close to reaching agreement on a settlement to the Kashmir issue. If this was true, the Kargil conflict may also have poisoned the seeds of a lasting peace (although Track 2 diplomacy had hitherto achieved few tangible results).

Nor did Kargil prove to be the South Asian equivalent of the Cuban missile crisis, when both countries involved realised that they had been to the brink and resolved not to run such risks again. Serious incidents around the Line of Control persisted, and the two leaderships continued to exchange bitter rhetoric. Vajpayee referred to Pakistan as an 'enemy country'. In January 2000, Indian Defence Minister George Fernandes expressed Indian readiness 'to fight and win a limited war, at a time and place chosen by the aggressor', while Musharraf declared that Pakistan 'would teach India a lesson' if it violated the Line of Control.

Pakistan: Strains Beyond the Limit

Islamabad sought to portray the Kargil episode as a moral victory which, according to Naik, had succeeded in drawing international attention to the Kashmir conflict. But Sharif's agreement with Clinton and the withdrawal from the Kargil area was widely regarded in Pakistan as a humiliation, particularly for the army. Blame for the Kargil débâcle focused on Sharif personally.

Dissatisfaction with Sharif had, however, been building up well before the Kargil conflict. Pakistan had long risked destruction by internal forces, a situation exacerbated by a history of government mismanagement. Sharif had alienated wide sections of the population: the army; the judiciary; and the three smaller provinces by concentrating power among Punjabis. He even antagonised businessmen by imposing a sales tax. The budget of 12 June 1999 emphasised the shortcomings of an economy where corruption – always rife in Pakistan – appeared to have reached unprecedented levels. Sharif's efforts to enshrine the supreme position of *Sharia* (Islamic law) were blocked by the Senate, and were widely seen in Pakistan as an attempt to boost his own authority. Under the proposed constitutional amendment, the government would be the ultimate arbiter of what was 'right' and what was 'wrong'. Strife between the Sunni Muslim majority and the Shi'a minority continued unabated, with a major outbreak of violence in late September. Najam Sethi, the influential editor of the *Friday Times*, was arrested without charge in May and detained for a month. Non-governmental organisations were banned. In June, Sharif replaced the Governor of Sindh province with a supporter, further enraging the *Mohajir* community in Karachi. Using his party's two-thirds majority in parliament and the wide new powers accumulated since his election in 1997, Sharif was seeking to neutralise all opposition. Qazi Hussain Ahmad, leader of the *Jamaat-e-Islami* party, accused him of betrayal. Retired generals joined in the criticism. In mid-September the opposition formed a 19-party alliance to force his resignation, amid international speculation that his leadership might not be sustainable.

In an atmosphere heavy with rumour, and following visits to Washington by Pakistani dissenters (and subsequently by Sharif's brother, Shahbaz Sharif on 20 September), US government officials stated that the US would 'strongly oppose' any attempt to change the government by 'extra-constitutional means'. Sharif, concerned that the Army might supplant him, welcomed this curious development, but Pakistani public opinion was not impressed.

The situation came to a head on 12 October, when Musharraf was on an official visit to Sri Lanka. Sharif, ignoring his recent pledge that Musharraf would remain in office until 2001, announced that the Chief of Army Staff would retire early. He was to be replaced by General Kahwaja Zia-ud-Din, then head of Inter-Services Intelligence. The plane carrying Musharraf back to Pakistan was informed that it could not land at Karachi airport. Evidently following a pre-arranged contingency plan, Pakistani Army units immediately took control of key installations and the public media, arrested Sharif, Zia-ud-Din and others, and took steps to ensure that Musharraf's plane would indeed land.

That night, Musharraf made a brief address to the nation, declaring that the armed forces had moved in 'as a last resort, to prevent any further destabilisation'. Three days later, a state of emergency was declared, the constitution and legislature were suspended and Musharraf was named the country's 'Chief Executive'. On 17 October, Musharraf declared that Pakistan's economy had crumbled, its credibility had been lost, its public institutions destroyed and the federation severely damaged. He noted that the constitution was being 'temporarily held in abeyance'; unlike in previous military take-overs, martial law was not being imposed, and a true democratic system would be instituted in the shortest possible time. He added that President Rafiq Tarar would stay in office and the country's prime governing institution would be a National Security Council, headed by himself, and comprising the other two service chiefs and specialists in legal, financial and foreign policy, and internal affairs. He maintained that there would be no change in foreign policy, and referred in conciliatory tones to the United States and India. An uncompromising restatement of policy on Kashmir was softened by an announcement that more forces would withdraw from the international border with India – which excluded the Line of Control. This move was described in the Indian press as 'sugar-coated bullets'. These events were widely welcomed in Pakistan, as criticism was heaped on Sharif and his predecessor, Benazir Bhutto, for their alleged corruption.

International reaction to the coup was mixed and complex. The violation of the democratic process was widely condemned. The Commonwealth suspended the new regime from its councils, following procedures established after the 1991 Harare Declaration, which requires members to observe basic standards of democracy and human rights. Of more immediate concern to Islamabad was a statement by a senior International Monetary Fund official on 18 October that the IMF would wait to see what happened before resuming funding – at that time foreign-exchange reserves would only cover four months' imports. Clinton wrote to a US Congressman in December that 'we cannot have business as usual with Pakistan until it returns to a democratically elected government'.

But business with Pakistan has seldom been usual, and the precise international consequences of the coup, like those of the nuclear tests the previous year, remained unclear. Calls for the restoration of democracy were tempered by sympathy for Pakistan's situation. The flaws in Sharif's governance were widely recognised. Mindful of Pakistan's turbulent history, even the Commonwealth fell short of expelling the country, thereby allowing technical assistance to continue. Official statements made no demands for Sharif's administration to be restored. Foreign observers drew attention to the shortcomings of successive supposedly democratic regimes, and advocated making use of the opportunity to establish stability and promote a serious Indo-Pakistani dialogue. Musharraf quickly toured Islamic countries to seek understanding for his action and financial support. Meanwhile, he declined to say just when democracy might be restored.

In February 2000, responsibility for policy formulation and control over strategic nuclear forces and strategic organisation was given to a National Command Authority (NCA) chaired by Musharraf. A strategic-plans division, headed by a senior army officer, would draw up a reliable command, control, communications, computers and intelligence (C⁴I) network. Thus, the three key nuclear advisory and decision-making functions – head of government, head of the NCA and chief of the Army – were vested in the single person of Musharraf. No details were released about the nature or direction of Pakistan's nuclear doctrine.

India: A Year of Challenges

In India, the *Bharatiya Janata* Party (BJP) was beset by internal political problems almost from the day it took office in March 1998. By early 1999, a collapse was inevitable. Vajpayee faced constant dissent and difficulties from within the 18-party coalition he had cobbled together. And his own BJP ranks were restless about the policy compromises made to forge a consensus around the 1998 National Agenda for Governance. The May 1998 nuclear tests helped to appease sections of his party and were generally popular, but proved insufficient to improve the party's electoral chances.

Controversy about economic liberalisation, corruption, internal dissent and the unruliness of some of the BJP's coalition partners all contributed to an impression of weakness and lack of control, reinforced by defeats for the BJP in state-legislature elections in late 1998. But pressure from its most mercurial coalition partner, former Chief Minister of Tamil Nadu Jayalalitha Jayaram, proved the final straw. Partly because she was thwarted in her attempts to secure key cabinet posts for members of her All India *Anna Dravida Munnetra Kazhagam* (AIADMK) party, and partly as a means of neutralising the threat of corruption charges against her, she withdrew her support for the government on 14 April 1999. Three days later, the government fell when it lost a confidence motion by one vote.

The ensuing general election – the third in three years and the thirteenth since independence – was the fourth in a row to return an uncertain verdict. The BJP secured 182 of the 543 seats – the same as it had in 1998 – but with 1.8% less of the vote. Its main opponent, Sonia Gandhi's Congress(I) Party, gained 2.7% of the vote, but lost 27 seats. Unlike Congress, however, the BJP had assiduously cultivated potential partners and was in a better position to form a government. The ensuing National Democratic Alliance government, a coalition of 24 parties, commanded 297 seats, against 134 held by Congress and its small number of allies. Vajpayee thus became the first sitting prime minister for 28 years to be reinstated after an election. With only 112 seats, Congress(I)'s electoral performance was its worst ever.

Not surprisingly in an electorate of over 620 million people in 537 constituencies, with a 60% poll, it was impossible to discern the exact causes of the result. These elections, however, were more 'presidential' than usual. Vajpayee was portrayed on BJP posters as 'the man of India's destiny', a measured, moderate and reassuring leader who had proved his mettle during the Kargil crisis. To keep its disparate collection of allies on side, the BJP downplayed the contentious aspects of its *Hindutva* programme, which (in contrast to the secularism espoused by most other parties) calls for a renaissance in Hindu culture and values.

Congress(I) had pinned its hopes on Sonia Ghandi's appeal as custodian of the Nehru–Gandhi dynasty, a proposition that the BJP sought to undermine by emphasising her Italian birth. The campaign's impact was further weakened by Sharad Pawar's breakaway Nationalist Congress Party (NCP) faction, which took a similar line, and by uncertainty as to whether Gandhi or former Finance Minister Manmohan Singh would be prime minister in the event of a Congress victory. By refusing pre-poll alliances, described by one of its senior leaders as a 'recipe for Balkanisation', Congress was left emphasising a national platform which had little distinctive content or appeal (not least because its BJP-led opponents had commandeered many of its policies). Its potential allies, with whom it might have swung the vote, and the electorate more generally were, however, more interested in regional and local issues.

The September/October elections were a victory for alliance politics. The resulting government stood for a programme markedly similar to that of the government under the same leadership that had fallen six months previously. The Nehru-Gandhi trademark proved insufficient to overcome Congress's weak organisation, its lack of a platform with appeal across the whole country, and concerns about the party leader's lack of experience.

Thinking Strategically

Some weeks before voting began, the caretaker government released a six-page draft proposal for India's nuclear doctrine, prepared by the National Security Advisory Board (NSAB) established in November 1998. This document set out a justification of India's nuclear tests, and argued that the country should pursue a doctrine of credible minimum deterrence within a policy of 'retaliation only'. The size and nature of nuclear forces would depend on the prevailing strategic environment, but it would be based on a triad of aircraft, land-based missiles and sea-based assets. These forces would need to survive a surprise attack, a first strike and 'repetitive attrition attempts', while retaining 'adequate retaliatory capabilities'. The document also recommended that effective conventional military capabilities should be maintained, and that space-based assets should be established for early warning, communications and damage assessment.

The government stressed that the document was still in draft form and that no decisions on implementation had been taken. But the decision to publish just two months after the document's completion (a decision which dismayed its authors) suggests that the government believed it would gain electoral advantage as a result. Despite the many internal inconsistencies, reflecting the difficulties in securing a consensus, the NSAB draft pointed to capabilities well in excess of prevailing levels, which would require considerable, though unspecified, expenditure. Outside India, it aroused concerns that Indian thinking was developing towards a maximal interpretation of the concept of minimum deterrence. These concerns were enhanced by the Indian Foreign Minister Jaswant Singh's public conclusion that the Kargil conflict showed that more resources were needed for India's defence forces.

With a solid renewed mandate and reasonable economic performance, the mood in India at the end of the year was confident and defiant. The December BJP conference at Chennai chose as its motto *'Ikkeesvin Shatabdi, Bharat ki Shatabdi'* – the next century belongs to India.

Hijackers and Hostages Go Free

But the old century in South Asia declined to go peacefully. On 24 December, five men hijacked Indian Airlines flight IC814 to New Delhi soon after it left Kathmandu. It landed at Amritsar, leading to much subsequent criticism that the authorities then allowed it to fly on out of Indian airspace. After diversions to Lahore and Dubai, the plane settled in Kandahar airport in Afghanistan. The hijackers' initial demands were for the release of 35 detainees in Indian jails – supporters of the Kashmir separatist movement – and $200m. They killed one passenger and threatened to blow up the plane with its 154 passengers and crew.

The *Taleban* authorities which control Kandahar, and whose sympathies lie with the Kashmiri separatist movement, cooperated with Indian authorities and publicly condemned the hijack. But they refused to allow any foreign military intervention to resolve the situation, suggesting that they would intervene themselves if the hijackers resorted to further violence. The incident ended on New Year's Eve. Following the intervention of the Indian Foreign Minister Singh, who was on the spot in Afghanistan, New Delhi released three detainees on the hijackers' list to the Taleban authorities, although India, in common with all but three countries, does not recognise their government. The five hijackers were given safe passage from the airport, and the hostages walked free.

The incident was accompanied by fierce partisan commentary in India and Pakistan. Vajpayee claimed that the hijack was 'an integral part of a Pakistan-backed campaign of terrorism', while Islamabad maintained that India was capitalising on it by denigrating Pakistan. It was widely seen in India as being of a piece with the Kargil conflict six months previously. US spokesmen suggested that the hijackers and the three released detainees were members of *Harkat ul-Mujahideen*, the same group which, under the name of *Harkat ul-Ansar*, had kidnapped and murdered five Western tourists in 1995. Maulana Masood Azhar, the most prominent of the detainees who swiftly emerged in Pakistan, called for a Holy War against India in front of huge assemblies.

All this highlighted many concerns about terrorism-related issues in the region:

- *Taleban* control of Kabul and seven-eighths of Afghanistan;

- support and recruitment for the Sunni/Pushtun *Taleban* from within Pakistan;

- the use of Afghanistan and Pakistan as terrorist refuges and training grounds, and as heroin-production centres;

- the murky issue of possible active support for militant groups by Pakistani official authorities; and

- hitherto unfulfilled US demands for the extradition of Osama bin Laden, the businessman-turned-terrorist linked to the 1998 bombings of US embassies in Kenya and Tanzania.

Although probably less sympathetic to the *Taleban* and to Islamic militancy than many previous Pakistani leaders, Musharraf has shown little sign of coming to grips with any of these issues.

More of the Same?

The deficiencies of the previous democratic regimes in Pakistan allowed the military leadership to appeal to public understanding in their attempts to resolve problems which earlier administrations had been unable to tackle. The absence of democratic checks gave them a freer rein, and the country had another chance to avoid ungovernability. Yet the arrival of a military regime did not in itself eliminate any of the long-standing difficulties, and Musharraf and his advisers face hard decisions about priorities regarding the economy, sectarian violence, over-centralisation, institutional weaknesses, feudalism, the harbouring of terrorists, security and general corruption.

As in the past, it will be much harder to achieve real reform than to oust the sitting government. Musharraf has already faced growing criticism within Pakistan for lack of progress, particularly in relation to the economy, where he has no previous experience. But attempts to do too much too soon would risk preventing the establishment of the national consensus necessary to carry out reforms. The military leaders need to recognise that when, as they have declared, they hand over to a more democratically based administration, much will remain to be done.

International opinion expects that the transitional period should not be protracted. But Musharraf's own emphasis on the prior need to secure economic progress, and to examine new political structures before returning to 'civil rule with some modification', does not suggest an early outcome. Nor does the assassination of Sharif's chief defence lawyer in March 2000 suggest any early return to political stability.

As always, India faces domestic and social challenges arising from the size and diversity of its massive and increasing population. Its brand of democracy has proved to be of fundamental value in facing these challenges in the half-century since independence. Despite the inevitable conundrums inherent in coalition politics, India's new government appears more stable than any recent predecessor and economic growth has proved relatively healthy.

But the government has yet to transform electoral success into social and security results. Its continuing problems impinge directly upon its relationship with Pakistan. Following the anti-Pakistan rhetoric of senior Indian ministers in 1998, which arguably contributed to the instability in 1999, the BJP leadership has kept the party's more extreme supporters largely in check, but they remain restless.

Even so, relations between India and Pakistan markedly deteriorated during 1999, and in early 2000 were at their lowest point since the 1971 war. In February, India conducted a major military exercise involving 2,000 troops near the border with Pakistan. In mid-March, Pakistani Foreign Minister Abdul Sattar accused India of hostile acts across the Line of Control and warned that this could lead to a limited war. At about the same time, George Fernandes predicted an increase in Pakistani military activity along the Line of Control and a 'hot' summer for India's security forces. In the face of these rising tensions, there seemed scant prospect of direct talks between the two neighbours. Islamabad insisted that the Kashmir issue should take centre stage, while New Delhi declined to have any such discussions while Pakistan pursued its objectives by force.

India's foreign relations elsewhere were developing with unprecedented intensity. China's fury in 1998 at being named by India as its greatest potential threat dissipated sufficiently to allow talks to resume. US–India engagement had never been closer. A dialogue between Jaswant Singh and US Deputy Secretary of State Strobe Talbot, started after the 1998 nuclear tests and stalled after eight rounds by the Indian government's fall a year later, resumed in late 1999. Part of the discussions led to the decision by President Clinton to visit India on 25 March 2000, the first US president to do so since Jimmy Carter in 1978.

There was no chance that Clinton's visit could be isolated from the tensions of the sub-continent, and Washington decided that the President should also make a brief stopover in Pakistan on 25 March. This was fiercely opposed by India, which maintained that Clinton should not confer any respectability on the military regime. Pakistan, meanwhile, pressed for US intervention over Kashmir – anathema to India.

While Clinton's visit might fulfil his longstanding personal wish to visit the subcontinent, and might further US commercial interests in India, the prospects for advancing other US and international objectives look bleak. But now, with both India and Pakistan possessing nuclear weapons, the consequences of misjudgement by either are more dangerous than ever. Both governments claim that others exaggerate the risks, but their actions belie this. There should therefore be no relaxation of efforts that could reduce the dangerous tensions that threaten these two countries. Any enhancement of internal and external confidence, particularly where Pakistan is concerned, would do much to promote stability in the region and hence economic and social advance.

Indonesia: Agonising Progress

It should have been a decisive year for Indonesia's political future in 1999. Former President Suharto's 32-year dictatorship, which ended in May 1998, had obscured two critical and related issues. By 1999, they could no longer be ignored, or contained by the repressive government machinery. Could the country allow its natural pluralism freer rein without tearing itself apart? And could the country's territorial boundaries remain intact, despite the pressures for independence building up in some of its constituent regions?

The general elections held in June 1999 and the indirect presidential poll in October suggested an optimistic answer to the first question. The voting was flawed in numerous respects, but it produced a leadership that many outside observers – as well as Indonesian voters – regarded as far closer to the ideal than had seemed imaginable beforehand. However, the disaster in East Timor, culminating in its transition to independence, appeared to many as the start of a process of disintegration, or, to use a fashionable analogy, of Balkanisation. The very concept of Indonesia – a relatively recent construct, formed in the 1940s from the Dutch East Indies – seemed at risk.

Yet, while the future and durability of Indonesian democracy is less assured than the election results seemed to promise, the country's integrity is less imperilled than some pessimists believe. The events of 1999 were not, after all, decisive, and Indonesia's future remains unpredictable. At best, it could still become a vibrant pluralist country with far more power devolved from the centre in Java. At worst, it could fall apart into mutually hostile nation states, destabilising the entire region; or, to prevent that

Asia

outcome, the army might reassert the dictatorship it seemed to have relinquished so recently. It would then be forced into conflict with the large numbers of Indonesians who would resist such a retrograde lurch.

Habibie: a Transitional Figure

Suharto's successor, President Bacharuddin Jusuf Habibie, charmed many foreigners – especially Westerners – with his engaging air of openness, candour and liberalism. Many Indonesians, however, remained deeply suspicious. There are two distinct reasons why Habibie found it hard to establish himself as a popular figure. The first, and most obvious, is that he was so closely associated with the disgraced Suharto regime. He was a lifelong protégé of the former president, and succeeded him by dint of having been Suharto's nominee as vice-president. That Suharto appeared to have appointed Habibie because he was simply not of presidential calibre, and had implied as much on national television just before his resignation, hardly helped to override objections that the new president was little more than a crony.

The one way in which Habibie might have refuted these accusations would have been to ensure vigorous efforts were made to investigate the Suharto family's wealth and to prosecute its members for corruption. He signally failed to do this, and was much damaged in February 1999 when the magazine *Pandji Masyarakht* published an apparently factual transcript of a telephone conversation he had held with the Attorney-General, Andi M Ghalib, in which the two men seemed to play down the seriousness of the Suharto investigations. One Suharto son – Hutomo Mandala Putra, known as Tommy – was charged with a relatively minor offence. But the government never acted upon the wide belief that the Suharto family held misappropriated funds worth billions of dollars in offshore accounts. This was ascribed either to government members' loyalty to the old regime, in which many had served, or to motives of self-interest. Suharto's lawyers had threatened to name other names and to produce evidence against Habibie himself if the probe into their clients' affairs became too intrusive.

The other commonly cited reason for mistrusting Habibie was his perceived penchant for politicising religion. Like nearly 90% of Indonesia's 210 million people, he is a professed Muslim. However, some critics accused him of links with believers who wanted Islam to play a stronger role in politics – an issue that has been debated since the origins of Indonesia as a modern state. The constitution is based on *Pancasila*, the principle that all must profess a belief in God, but are free to follow their own faith. Habibie's former chairmanship of the Association of Islamic Scholars (ICMI) and his links with reputed fundamentalists meant that it was hard for him to win the backing of influential sectors of society, notably the ethnic Chinese businessmen who dominate the economy.

The Contending Forces

Despite the common accusation that Habibie and his regime were merely interested in a sham transition to democracy, the *Dewan Perwakilan Rakyat* (DPR), or parliament, elected in 1997 under the old regime's manipulated system, voted through reforms in January 1998 that paved the way for the country's first free elections since 1955. They took place on 7 June. Among the most important reforms were:

- Political parties were legalised. Under Suharto they had been limited to an institutionalised 'functional group', *Golkar* (whose function was to win elections) and two 'opposition' parties;

- DPR seats allocated automatically to the armed forces were cut from 100 in 1992 and 75 in 1997 to 38;

- An electoral system based on proportional representation by province was introduced. Under the old arrangements, *Golkar* was guaranteed around 70% of the votes, so the niceties of seat allocation were almost irrelevant.

Parties led by three opposition politicians had already emerged as the main challengers to *Golkar*, which was split between a Habibie faction and one more loyal to his state secretary, Akbar Tandjung, the party chairman. In November 1998 the new parties entered an uneasy alliance: their leaders were:

- Megawati Sukarnoputri, the daughter of Indonesia's founding president, Sukarno, who inherited the vestiges of his nationalist party. She enjoys great prestige in much of the country because of her lineage, and was also seen as a symbol of resistance to Suharto, whose henchmen had engineered her exclusion from national politics in 1996. But she had disappointed many opposition supporters with her passive role in the dying days of the Suharto regime. Indeed, all through 1999, Megawati often appeared to believe that power should come to her by right, without her having to fight for it.

- Abdurrahman Wahid, known by most Indonesians as 'Gus Dur', who also owed his position to dynastic succession. He was the head of *Nahdlatul Ulama* (The Awakening of the Scholars) a 30m-strong, Islamic social and educational group, which both his father and his grandfather had also led. The popular following this gave him also allowed him a certain latitude as a public figure. He was the chairman of a 'democracy forum' set up in 1990, and a staunch critic of ICMI and what he saw as attempts to politicise Islam. That he was also a shrewd, if bewildering,

Asia

politician had emerged in the 1997 election campaign, when he appeared on platforms with one of Suharto's daughters, despite his close relationship with Megawati.

- Amien Rais, former leader of the other mass Muslim organisation, the 20m-strong *Muhammadiyah*, resigned from a leading position in ICMI and became in 1997–98 the disparate opposition's most vocal, prominent and persistent anti-Suharto campaigner. He subsequently also resigned his *Muhammadiyah* post to head the National Mandate Party (PAN). This had an avowedly secular stance, but it hoped to appeal both to the Muslim grass roots and to the urban youth and others who had cheered Suharto's downfall.

Almost as soon as Suharto was forced to stand down, there were calls from influential parts of society for a 'government of national unity', or *praesidium* to govern the country in the run-up to elections. The Habibie government was simply not trusted to oversee the process. Megawati, Gus Dur and Amien Rais were invariably seen as key members of such a body. However, their inability to agree with one another was a major obstacle, and the proposal, which would have implied ditching the constitution, at least for an interim period, never came to anything. What is remarkable, however, is that the electoral process, overseen by the Habibie administration, ended up producing an outcome rather similar to this ideal.

The Surprising Smoothness of Politics

The election campaign, although marred by some violence, was relatively peaceful, even compared with the 1997 election whose outcome was certain. Nor did the result seem to be outrageously unfair, despite thousands of reports of minor violations and millions of invalid votes. On the contrary, the poll was a triumph for those who had trusted in the moderation and common sense of ordinary Indonesians.

Of the 48 parties that competed, the most successful, as expected, was Megawati's Democratic Party for Struggle (PDI-P), which won 35m votes, 34% of the total. *Golkar* was decisively beaten into second place with 22% of the poll. These then became the two largest 'fractions' in the 700-member People's Consultative Assembly (MPR), which convened in October to elect a president and vice-president. PDI-P had 154 seats and *Golkar* 120. The third largest group, with 58 seats, was the PPP, a Muslim-based party which had been one of the three permitted parties during the Suharto era. Next were the National Awakening Party (PKB), representing *Nahdlatul Ulama*, and hence Abdurrahman Wahid, with 51 seats and Amien Rais's National Mandate Party (PAN), with 41.

To the consternation of many Indonesians, particularly the PDI-P voters, the period between the 7 June general election and the presidential vote on 20 October was marked by back-room political horse-trading reminiscent of the Suharto regime. The outcome was an 'anyone-but-Megawati' alliance, capitalising on Muslim prejudices against both her gender and her perceived weakness on religious issues (although a Muslim, she enjoys considerable support from Balinese Hindus, from Christians and from those wanting politics to remain secular). Megawati herself continued to stand aside from the political fray, apparently failing to understand that the rules of the game had changed so thoroughly that Suharto-style aloofness, far from being a necessity, was now a handicap.

Habibie, unable to unite even *Golkar* behind him, and certain to provoke outrage if he won at Megawati's expense, was never a likely alternative. He was also fatally wounded by the scandal at Bank Bali, where, in the process of the subsequently aborted acquisition by UK bank Standard Chartered, auditors discovered that large sums of money had apparently been siphoned off to fund *Golkar's* election campaign. On 19 October 1999, Habibie was humiliated by a narrow MPR vote to reject his 'accountability' speech – which the constitution requires the president to make to the assembly – and he withdrew from the presidential contest early the next day.

That left the way open for Gus Dur, whose appeal was wide enough to attract a winning coalition. He persuaded Megawati to run for election the next day as his deputy, thus appeasing her supporters. Amien Rais had already been elected to the important post of speaker of the MPR, while *Golkar's* Akbar Tandjung had been made speaker of the lower house, the DPR. A remarkable 'rainbow alliance' of the most powerful competing forces in Indonesian politics had found a way to coalesce. This was reflected in the new president's cabinet, which included figures from the old regime (most importantly from the army) as well as prominent opponents of Suharto.

It was a shrewdly balanced line-up, but even many of Gus Dur's most fervent admirers question whether he will be a successful president. This is partly because of health problems – he is nearly blind and has suffered two strokes – but also because, despite his democratic credentials, he has, rather like Megawati, often appeared too willing to rely on the almost feudal loyalties inspired by his *Nahdlatul Ulama* post to secure his political objectives. He is further sometimes seen as too enamoured of intricate political manoeuvres, which have led him into some confusing political about-turns. To his fans, like one senior Indonesian journalist, he resembles a river; he may meander through sharp bends, but his ultimate destination, the sea of democracy, is never in doubt. But such flexibility is easier to admire in an independent religious figure than in a president expected to provide strong and consistent leadership. In particular, Wahid's early vacillations on issues of national integrity, notably in Aceh, raised the spectre that the army might lose patience with him.

The Trashing of East Timor

By the time Gus Dur was elected, the secession of Indonesia's most recent accretion, East Timor, was inevitable. Indonesia had invaded the territory in 1975, after the colonial power, Portugal, withdrew, and had formally annexed the territory in the following year. The local population never accepted the occupation, partly because of the terror and destruction with which it was enforced. A long-running guerrilla resistance campaign ensued in support of a relatively moderate demand: the promise of a referendum on East Timor's status after a transitional period of roughly ten years.

On 27 January 1999, on the eve of the latest round of unproductive talks at the United Nations between Indonesia and Portugal, which the UN still regarded as the administering power, Indonesia suddenly announced that it was acceding to the referendum demand. Crucially, however, Habibie ignored the resistance movement's suggestion of a transitional period, and spoke of wanting the question solved by the end of the year. There were several suggested motives behind this surprise move:

- concern about the election and the reaction of a future MPR;

- pique prompted by Australia, the only Western power to recognise Indonesia's annexation, deciding to support a referendum;

- a complicated plot to thwart East Timorese independence – believed by many in the territory;

- concern about the extravagance of deploying a garrison of 20,000 troops in one recalcitrant and poor territory at a time of tension across the nation; or

- belief in the government's own propaganda that pro-independence sentiment was confined to a vocal minority.

Whatever the reason, it turned out to be a disastrous and irresponsible policy failure.

As a gesture of good faith, East Timor's independence leader, Xanana Gusmao was freed from prison in February 1999, but he remained under house arrest in Jakarta. Under an agreement finally reached in New York in May – and reluctantly approved by Xanana – a referendum was held in August, asking voters whether they wanted to stay within Indonesia, under new arrangements giving the territory a greater degree of autonomy. If they rejected the proposition, East Timor would be offered independence. The referendum campaign, held under UN auspices, was marred by violence – mainly intimidation of independence supporters by 'integrationist' militias, which were clearly formed, armed and trained by the Indonesian army. Despite their efforts to terrorise the populace, there was a near 100% turn-out for the vote, and 78% chose independence.

In response, the militias and the Indonesian army ravaged the territory, burning buildings, ripping out the telephone system, killing some opponents and driving more than a third of the population into exile. The UN mission was besieged and finally forced to withdraw, to be replaced in September by an Australian-led peacekeeping force. This subsequently made way for a UN transitional authority, which set about rebuilding East Timor from scratch.

Quite what made the Indonesian army behave with such apparently motiveless malignity will be debated for a long time. The claim that rogue local elements were to blame can not be sustained. The outrage was planned. Indeed, the UN was aware of preparations before the vote for receiving up to 250,000 East Timorese in refugee camps in Indonesian West Timor. Ironically, the UN viewed this positively as a sign that Jakarta expected to lose the vote, and, believing some of its own propaganda about large-scale support for continued integration, was getting ready for a flood of voluntary exiles.

Another theory is that the orgy of destruction was organised in the spirit of a neighbourhood bully warning others 'don't mess with me'. It may indeed have been intended to scare secessionist groups elsewhere. If so, it was a remarkably stupid idea. Such thuggery could only heighten anti-Jakarta sentiment. And, although the army has long held that concessions in East Timor would start the unravelling of the whole nation, the territory is in a class apart because of its history, legal status, and the level of international guilt about its unhappy fate.

Who's Next?

The most immediate threats of further secession come from two territories at opposite ends of the archipelago, in both of which small-scale guerrilla wars have been fought for years. In Aceh, in northern Sumatra, the army seems to be making many of the same mistakes as in East Timor. During a period of apparent openness under Habibie, the brutality of some past repressive measures in the territory was admitted, but there was no attempt to exact redress from the perpetrators. Meanwhile, here too, unrest appeared to be fomented by groups recruited by the army. The regime lost the opportunity to court a disaffected territory by marking its distance from the old dictatorship. By the time Gus Dur came to power, it seemed that a referendum in Aceh would massively endorse separation from Indonesia. It did not help that the new president appeared to offer a referendum on separation, only to amend the question later to one on whether Islamic *sharia* law should be introduced in the region.

In Irian Jaya, Indonesia's easternmost territory, Wahid at least had the chance to start a campaign for continued integration. In December, he apologised for the army's past behaviour, and conceded one anti-Indonesian demand: that the territory be renamed 'West Papua'. That will not be enough to satisfy the guerrillas of the Free Papua Movement (OPM), but there may still be time for a moderate Indonesian government to win some support.

The same is true in some other areas where Indonesia faces disaffection, if not insurrection. This tends to be true of the richest parts of the country – such as the oil-rich Riau archipelago between Sumatra and Singapore – which chafe at the proportion of the revenue generated by their natural resources, such as oil, that ends up in Jakarta. In these places, as in Aceh and Irian Jaya, another powerful reason to believe that independence is unlikely is the lack of any international support for such a move. While East Timor was never regarded as part of Indonesia under international law, no country formally recognises any other separatist claim in the archipelago. The OPM may receive some support from Papua, New Guinea and the South Pacific states, and Islamic groups in the Middle East may back Aceh's independence movement; but that hardly amounts to diplomatic pressure on Jakarta. Indeed, the possibility of Indonesia's disintegration makes its neighbours – notably Singapore and Malaysia – extremely nervous, seeing it as a prescription for regional instability, maritime lawlessness, and large-scale movements of refugees.

The Danger Within

The most immediate threats to Indonesian civil order in early 2000 did not come from secessionist threats but from outbreaks of communal violence in the Molucca islands. Sparked in January 1999 by a fight between a Muslim migrant and a local Christian minibus driver, the violence had, a year later, claimed more than 1,000 lives, and had provoked the imposition of what amounted to martial law and a naval blockade. Large-scale demonstrations in Jakarta called for a *jihad*, or holy war, to protect Muslim interests. They also demanded the sacking of Megawati, whom Gus Dur had deftly made responsible for restoring calm in a worsening situation.

Equally horrific bloodshed in 1999 resulted from fighting which erupted in Kalimantan between indigenous Dayaks and Muslim immigrants from Madura, an island off Java. In parts of Java itself, riots, murder and mayhem occasionally scar communal relations. In many places, as in the Moluccas, as well as East Timor and Aceh, *agents provocateurs* appear to be involved. Why should anyone have an interest in instability with such dreadful consequences? Some suspect Suharto loyalists; some accuse parts of the army. One legacy of the opaque politics of the Suharto years is that few Indonesians are ever ready to take events at face value. Conspiracies are seen behind every horror.

Whether or not they are true, the rumours keep alive the fear that the army might move to reassert its political role. It still clings to the doctrine of *dwifungsi* (dual function) which guarantees it a voice in politics. General Wiranto, once Suharto's bodyguard, and the last army chief of his regime, survived into Gus Dur's cabinet as 'coordinating minister for political and security affairs'. At the end of January 2000, however, his continued hold on this position came into question. On 31 January, an Indonesian government commission of inquiry condemned the military for the mass killings, rape and deportation in East Timor, and it named General Wiranto along with five other top generals for possible criminal prosecution.

Gus Dur, who was on a visit to Europe trying to convince investors that Indonesia had turned a corner in its efforts to democratise and install a free-market economy, immediately requested Wiranto's resignation. Although Wiranto at first refused, and continued to oppose the president's wishes for another two weeks, Gus Dur returned to Indonesia in mid-February and suspended him pending further investigation. On 28 February, the president took another significant step in his campaign to consolidate civilian control over the military. As part of a shuffle of 47 senior officers, he appointed General Agus Wirahadikusumah to take command of the Strategic Reserves Command, the military's best trained and most formidable unit, which in the past has ensured a key role for the army in the nation's political affairs. Wirahadikusumah has often clashed with more conservative generals, including Wiranto, by publicly defending the concept of civilian supremacy over the armed forces and indicating that the army leadership should abjure politics and return to its major task of defending the nation.

That Wiranto held on to a senior post for so long is indicative of the greatest danger to Indonesia's precarious transition: that a humiliated, unpopular army, citing any one of a multitude of threats to civil order in the country, might have decided to impose its authority, as it did in 1965, bringing Suharto into power. The success that Wahid has achieved in his slow and careful campaign to put the military back in the barracks needs to be followed up before Indonesia can be certain that its transition to electoral democracy has been completed. But the future looks far more optimistic in the first year of the new millennium than it did in the last year of the previous one.

Africa

A FRICA PRESENTED TWO CONTRADICTORY FACES IN 1999. One was the ugly face that the world had come to expect: an unending litany of political upheaval, ethnic resentment, social breakdown, economic deprivation and warfare. The other was unexpected: in some parts of the huge continent there was a slow, struggling, sometimes painful, transition to democratisation and economic growth. It was in support of the latter that America's new ambassador to the United Nations Richard Holbrooke spoke when he called for an international effort to make January 2000 a month dedicated to Africa.

There were a number of smoothly run democratic elections that suggested change and renewal. International leaders went to Nigeria in May 1999 to hail the first democratically elected leader for 17 years. South Africa again showed the way with a spectacular, though inevitable, win by the African National Congress (ANC) candidate Thabo Mbeki, in the second post-apartheid election on 2 June. Malawi's second multi-party elections on 15 June were close-run and bad-tempered, as were the 19 September elections in the Central African Republic, but citizens of Botswana went to the polls quietly on 16 October. The military junta that seized power in Niger in April 1999 kept its pledge of returning the country to democracy by holding elections on 24 November, but they were won within the ranks by retired army colonel Mamadou Tandja. On 3–5 December, Mozambique held its second election since its civil war ended in 1992; Joaquim Chissano was re-elected president handily.

It appeared in several countries that the more positive future some hoped Africa would enter in the twenty-first century had arrived a year early. There are plenty of opportunities for the new millennium to shine, however. A referendum on multi-party politics in Uganda and elections in six other countries are due in 2000. Attention will focus on the electoral fate of two of Africa's remaining dinosaurs, Daniel arap Moi in Kenya and Robert Mugabe in Zimbabwe. There are those, perhaps whistling in the dark, who hope they will be brought to dance to the tune of democracy and credible elections.

But in Africa old habits die hard. The military in Côte d'Ivoire chose Christmas Eve to mount an unexpected coup, overthrowing President Henri Konan Bédié. Despite a long history of poor fiscal management and debt, a small political élite has held the country together since its independence from France 40 years ago. Since the death of its founding

Map 5 Africa

father Félix Houphouët-Boigny in 1993, however, the calm has been an uneasy one. Tensions rose higher in 1999, when Bédié's government was plagued by charges of embezzling European Union funds. This led to a suspension of EU and International Monetary Fund (IMF) aid in June.

Even more damning was military and public anger at Bédié's attacks on former deputy Managing Director of the IMF, Alassane Dramane Ouattara, who had become his rival for the presidency. Bédié tried to ban Ouattara from competing in elections scheduled for October 2000 by declaring him a foreigner. A warrant was issued for Ouattara's arrest, on the basis of Bédié's claims that he had forged his birth certificate. Bédié also ordered the political imprisonment of some of Ouattara's supporters, charging them with rioting. He followed this up by encouraging xeno-phobic violence against Ouattara's fellow Dioulla-speaking northerners, mainly Muslim people with kinship ties along the Sahel in Burkina Faso and Mali.

Ivorians rallied overwhelmingly behind the overthrow of Bédié by General Robert Guei, who was known to be pro-Ouattara. Guei made the usual pledges of fresh elections and a return to civilian rule, and because the coup was unexpected, many Ivorians believe that the army will fulfil its promise. If it does, it will be an unusual change for the continent. For the most part, events in Africa ran their usual dispiriting course; strong men playing games with talk of peace, while attempting to increase their power through violence and war.

Fragile Peace and Continuing War

The prospects for peace across the continent were being heavily touted at the annual summit of the Organisation of African Unity (OAU) held in Algeria on 12–16 July 1999. Peace agreements to end two of Africa's complex and brutal conflicts, those in Sierra Leone and the Democratic Republic of Congo (DROC), had just been reached. The warring factions which had devastated Sierra Leone over eight years of fighting, signed the Lóme peace agreement on 7 July, thus offering a glimmer of hope that change was on the horizon.

The peace that was thus achieved was a very fragile one, however, and Sierra Leoneans continue to wonder if President Ahmed Tejan Kabbah will survive in power until the elections scheduled for 2001. The gradual withdrawal of his main ally, Nigeria, from its peacekeeping and protection service, leaves him vulnerable both to attacks from the many armed groups in the country and even to a palace coup from hardliners dis-satisfied with his leadership.

The putative end of the civil war in Sierra Leone raised expectations that West Africa was gradually emerging out of a cycle of violence that had spread from Liberia to Guinea-Bissau throughout the 1990s. But the region remains volatile. Not only has it been affected by the coup in Côte d'Ivoire but Liberia, whose civil war ended three years ago, still suffers from numerous insurgencies and sporadic violence along the borders it shares with Sierra Leone and Guinea.

The problem lies with Liberia's warlord president Charles Taylor. President Taylor played the role of eminent statesman by ensuring that his rebel friends in Sierra Leone signed the peace deal. He then organised, on 26 July, Liberia's National Day, a grand ceremonial burning of weapons captured by the intervention force, the West African Cease-fire Monitoring Group (ECOMOG), from Liberia's seven-year civil war. But neither gesture hides the fact that Taylor presides over a state that is in total shambles and an economy that is in a disastrous shape, clear invitations to continued instability.

Further south, peace agreements continue to be made and torn up with startling regularity. Regional conflagration raged unabated in the DROC in central Africa despite a number of paper agreements. The DROC has been fighting an internal and regional war since July 1998, with little hope of freeing its territory of rebel forces from outside the country. It was no surprise, then, that President Laurent-Désiré Kabila was the first to sign the Lusaka cease-fire agreement on 10 July 1999, along with the five neighbouring states (Angola, Namibia, Rwanda, Uganda and Zimbabwe) which are deeply involved in the conflict. Three Congolese rebel groups did not sign until 1 and 31 August because of divisions among their leaders.

This hardly mattered, for Lusaka was a false dawn. The conflict has also taken its toll on neighbouring states, in particular Angola, where another long-standing civil war has been raging for 25 years between the *Movimento Popular de Libertação de Angola* (MPLA) government of José Eduardo dos Santos and *União Nacional para a Independencia Total de Angola* (UNITA) and its leader, Jonas Malheiro Savimbi. Another victim of the continuing fighting is the alliance between Rwanda and Uganda, which fell apart on the battlefields of the DROC when their policy diverged on how to conduct their military and political strategies.

Burundi, too, has been sucked in to a minor role in the DROC because of cross-border insurgency by its rebel groups. It has been unable to control ethnic killings, which have left this country in daily turmoil. The escalating violence by both government security forces and rebel groups against civilians means that the country is on the brink of a catastrophe. The cycle of violence in Burundi intensified between August and September 1999, with various reports of killings by the Hutu ethnic group and reprisal attacks against the rival Tutsis. In October, rebels also killed a number of UN officials involved in delivering aid.

The effort to find a solution to the war in Burundi in talks which have been held in Arusha, Tanzania, was dealt a blow with the death of the long-time mediator, the former president of Tanzania, Julius Nyerere, on 14 October 1999. The former South African president, Nelson Mandela, was appointed peace mediator in December, but he is accused by rebels of siding with the government. The rebels' attitude makes it doubtful that Mandela will succeed where Nyerere failed, in breaking the logjam in a conflict estimated to have cost 200,000 lives since 1993.

There was no shortage of international diplomacy on the continent; it simply was ineffective. In fact, there was something strange about the international response to African conflicts in 1999. The year started off with UN peacekeepers dramatically leaving Angola, and closed with their return, if only as military observers, to Sierra Leone and the DROC. More curious was the plea by UN Secretary-General Kofi Annan, for the organisation to re-deploy troops in Angola after the humiliating retreat earlier in the year. The UN spent part of 1999 on a mission to correct a catalogue of mistakes made by the international community in Africa. Annan began the effort when he openly challenged the double standards of Britain and the US over Kosovo, East Timor and Africa. But then, after an inquiry he had commissioned strongly criticised the UN for failing to prevent the 1994 Rwandan genocide, he was forced to express his bitter regret and apologise. The first session of the UN Security Council in the twenty-first century was dedicated to a discussion of African problems, with AIDS and the economy a top priority.

If there is to be a 'brave new world' on the continent, much will depend on the political and economic progress of Africa's two largest and strongest powers – Nigeria and South Africa. Both countries are held up as symbols of positive change in Africa. But in both countries their domestic problems tarnish the positive image their leaders wish to present. Nigeria's unpredictable and precarious internal politics remain a constant nightmare. President Olusegun Obasanjo made a brave start to remedy one obstacle through a programme to restructure and redefine the role of the Nigerian Army. He began by announcing a plan for reducing its bloated numbers, but there remains uncertainty about the size of the cut. Obasanjo's other reformist policies will give Nigeria's economy a chance to recover, if they can be carried out. Forecasts of an upturn in oil and gas prices in 2000 will not only ease economic decline, but will also help improve investor confidence in one of Africa's biggest markets.

The main challenges to Obasanjo's and to Nigeria's prospects remain its long-standing religious and ethnic divisions. The introduction of Islamic Law (*Sharia*) in the north-western state of Zamfara has exacerbated long-standing tensions between Muslims and Christians, the two main religious groups in the country. Since then a number of other states in the north-west have brought in *Sharia*. Christians condemned the law, which dictates the amputation of limbs and decapitation for certain offences. The first signs of tensions to appear after military rule ended in May 1999, came in mid-December, when Muslim militants attacked and vandalised 18 Christian churches in the central town of Ilorin.

More serious rioting broke out in the northern city of Kaduna at the end of February 2000, when at least 500 people were killed, whole neighbourhoods were destroyed and many Christians of the Ibo ethnic group fled the area. Obasanjo, who is himself a southern Christian, but whose election depended on Muslim votes in the north, had been reluctant to take a firm stance on the introduction of *Sharia*, suggesting instead that it was a passing problem that would 'fizzle out'. In the face of the rioting, however, the government on 29 February reached an agreement that none of the northern states would continue to introduce the full measure of *Sharia*.

Nigeria's religious divisions are intertwined with ethnic differences, and the two together ensure explosive relations among Nigeria's 108 million people. The highest tension is in the Niger Delta, the main oil-producing area, which contains 50 to 100 different linguistic and ethnic groups. A history of political tensions among federal, state and local government over the distribution of oil revenues has often resulted in violent eruptions. Competition for resources has become intense, and the feeling of marginalisation among the different ethnic groups has led to sporadic communal conflict.

The emergence of increasingly militant groups, or quasi-military youth organisations such as the Ijaw youth groups, has been a factor in the violence. At the end of May 1999, fighting broke out near the southern oil town of Warri, between Ijaws and Urhobos on the one hand, and Itsekiris on the other, over the relocation of a local council headquarters. The conflict caused nearly 200 deaths. A clash between Ijaws and Ilajes, an ethnic sub-group of the Yoruba, occurred in September 1999 in the Niger Delta state of Ondo over ownership of the Opuoma oil field. It resulted in some 15–20 casualties. The deadly mix of religious and ethnic enmity in Nigeria has brought the country close to the state it was in before the 1967–70 civil war. Without strong, and rapid, action by the Obasanjo regime, that terrible time is all too likely to recur.

Violence has also wracked South Africa, tarnishing that country's transition to democracy. There, however, the problem was neither religious nor ethnic; hopes that South Africa would emerge as a model for an African awakening were continually challenged throughout 1999 by a wave of violent crime. And the problem threatens to be worse in 2000. Without a total overhaul of the failing police system, whose brutality, incompetence and corrupt practices have been thoroughly and convincingly documented, the government will not be able to control the continued rise in crime. One of the major factors in the crime-wave is unemployment, which climbed as high as 40% in January.

The high unemployment rate continues to expose the juxtaposition of two distinct worlds in this vast country: a white community whose standard of living far outstrips that of a black population, whose serious poverty and lack of future prospects leaves it teetering on the brink of social alienation. One effect of violent crime that is becoming ever more serious is the denting of the confidence of foreign investors who might otherwise become involved in the South African economy. Still more serious is the threat of racial clashes, which will halt the political advances made by South Africa since 1994 if no way is found to halt social disintegration amongst blacks. Yet there is considerable confidence in South Africa that the economy will soon revive and that this threat can be averted. There are certainly better prospects here than in either Central Africa or in the Horn of Africa where efforts to achieve an end to warfare have been to no avail.

Central Africa's Interlocking Wars

The Lusaka cease-fire agreement, signed during summer 1999 by the warring factions in the Democratic Republic of Congo (DROC) and regional leaders, provided a framework for tying all the strands of this complex war together. The agreement has two aims: it addresses the DROC's internal political crises and it attempts to meet the regional security demands of Angola, Burundi, Rwanda and Uganda. The internal dimension, however, depends largely on DROC President Kabila's willingness to open an 'inter-Congolese dialogue' and to share power in a transitional government, but, since signing the agreement, he has made no move in this direction.

Instead he has wavered and defied calls for dialogue between him and the rebel groups. Kinshasa, the capital city, is still on a war footing, with governmental forces searching the streets for likely recruits. Government spending on weapons and military equipment is unrecorded, but it must be high in relation to the country's resources. Military helicopters continue to hover in the skies. Kabila's warmongering means that there is nothing on the horizon that could arouse optimism about the prospects for political order. One thing remains certain – if Kabila's key allies, Angola, Namibia and Zimbabwe, withdraw their support, the balance of forces will dramatically favour the rebels and ensure the president's downfall.

The Congo is now a fragmented state; different armed groups and centres of authority, including the armies of five foreign states, control various regions of this vast country. Civilians are forced to scrabble for a livelihood in an anarchic and divided terrain. Divisions among the rebel groups make it impossible to devise plans for national unity. The original rebel movement, the *Rassemblement Congolais pour la Démocratie* (RCD) split early in 1999: the 'Goma' faction, led by Emile Ilunga, is backed by Rwanda

Africa

and the 'Kisangani' faction, renamed RCD–*Mouvement de Liberation* (RCD–ML) and led by Ernest Wamba dia Wamba, is backed by Uganda. Uganda is also supporting a third rebel group from the north-west province of Equateur, the *Mouvement de Liberation Congolais* (MLC) led by business-man-turned-politician, Jean-Pierre Bemba. MLC and RCD–ML rebels renewed fighting in January 2000, with claims that government forces and allies were besieging the northern and eastern provinces.

South Kivu remains a highly volatile region where potential violence against the *Banyamulenge* (Congolese Tutsis) still threatens. How to forestall continuing violence in this region, which has been the starting point of conflicts between the DROC and Rwanda and Uganda since 1996, was not effectively dealt with in the peace agreement. The most it attempted was a request that parties to the conflict take all necessary measures to normalise the situation along the DROC's international borders. The eastern region of the DROC is in a desperate state and could explode at any time as the pro-government *Mai-Mai* militia increases its hostile propaganda against the Tutsis. The possibility that this will lead to new violence ensures that Rwanda remains engulfed in the tragic internal violence of the DROC.

It is largely because this war can still drag the entire central African region deeper into a quagmire that regional security is given prominence in the Lusaka agreement. The war was started from outside the DROC, by Rwanda and Uganda, and will be resolved only when their concerns are met. The *Interahamwé,* the militia which was behind the 1994 genocide in Rwanda, plus elements of the former Rwandan army, *Forces Armées de Rwanda* (ex-FAR) still lurk in eastern DROC and surrounding countries. They are estimated to be between 15,000–27,000 strong, and they have been fighting alongside other regional rebel forces, including the Burundian *Forces pour la Défense de la Démocratie* (FDD), the Ugandan Allied Democratic Force (ADF) and the Lord's Resistance Army (LRA). Their presence threatens the stability of Burundi, Rwanda and Uganda.

The Rwandans claim that Kabila, whom they helped to put in power in 1997, was encouraging the *Interahamwé* to attack Rwanda. So Kigali, with the assistance of Burundi and Uganda, decided to solve the problem by deposing the DROC president. Their attacks in July 1998 were thwarted by the intervention of Zimbabwe, Namibia and Angola, the latter spurred by reports that the Angolan rebel movement, UNITA, was exploiting instability in the DROC to reopen its 'guns-for-diamonds' trading route in the western part of the country. The Lusaka agreement's call for a mechanism for disarming militias and armed groups is a response to the security concerns of neighbouring states, as is the request for the *génocidaires* to be handed over to the International Criminal Tribunal for Rwanda.

But even if the Lusaka agreement delivers regional security, regional leaders will probably not roll back their heavy military presence in the

DROC. The leaders involved in the conflict have wider geo-strategic agendas , which cannot be met without interfering in the internal affairs of their neighbours. An equally important dilemma facing these leaders is that they have been challenged at home for their costly involvement in the war. They need a face-saving exit to maintain their grasp on power. The war, which began to remove or to save Kabila, has evolved into one which involves the future of several central and southern African leaders. Without a successful outcome, some leaders face the prospect of coups, insurgencies and mutinies.

Zimbabwe's President Robert Mugabe has already felt the consequence of meddling in regional wars. Throughout 1999, he had to face strong protests about the country's economic decline and high military spending. In February 2000, Zimbabweans voted down a referendum in which Mugabe had invested a great deal of his own prestige. The question was of a constitutional change that would have allowed Mugabe to run for yet another term as president. With its failure, his influence has been curbed and he will have to find another road to his goal.

Parliamentary elections have been scheduled for between April and June 2000. The elections will be a stringent test of Zimbabwe's wavering democracy. Although analysts predict Mugabe's ruling Zimbabwe African National Union-Patriotic Front (ZANU-PF) should win handsomely, it faces a stiff challenge from the new union-backed Movement for Democratic Change (MDC), which has focused on deteriorating living standards over two decades of virtual single-party rule. Opposition groups can cite economic indicators that show that the government is likely to preside over another year of economic decline in 2000, with growth in gross domestic product (GDP) of just 2%. More importantly, it will miss all of the fiscal and macro-economic targets agreed with the IMF. The deficit is forecast to remain above 5% with inflation averaging 40%. Given these estimates of further economic, and therefore political, deterioration at home, Mugabe desperately needs peace in the DROC, but there is little sign that he will see it soon.

Other regional leaders, such as President Yoweri Museveni of Uganda, have been tarnished with accusations that they are fighting a war for profit and are not aiming to find a peaceful solution. Foreign donors, particularly the World Bank, the UK and the US are growing impatient with Uganda's continued presence in the DROC and increased defence spending since the beginning of the conflict in July 1998. Museveni's claims that the Ugandan army was in the DROC to secure the country's borders from rebel raids was dealt a severe blow in March 1999 when the *Interahamwé* killed eight Western tourists in Uganda.

The international community has increasingly become a bystander in this regional war. The UN brought those engaged in the peace process to New York on 24–28 January for an open debate in the Security Council, but the dates for sending in a team of 500 observers has shifted so often that the prospect of also sending in the peacekeeping force suggested in the Lusaka agreement seems remote. The Joint Military Commission (JMC), set up until a UN peacekeeping mission is deployed, is still facing financial and logistical difficulties in pursuing its tasks of investigating cease-fire violations, developing a mechanism to identify and disarm militia groups and monitoring the withdrawal of foreign troops.

The viability of the Lusaka agreement will depend on how quickly a joint JMC–UN team gets military observers into the field. However, there is a limit to what the UN can do in the DROC. There is not much peace to keep. The prospects for disarming many militia groups look bleak as none of the countries have shown willingness to embark on this part of the Lusaka agreement. The war in the DROC continues to expose the volatile internal order and insecurity complex of several central and southern African states.

Cracks between Rwanda and Uganda

The war in the DROC has dented one of Africa's closest political–military alliances. Since 1994, Rwanda and Uganda, or rather the ethnic Tutsi leaderships of both countries, have collaborated to reshape political order in the region. Museveni's grandmother is a Tutsi, and his parents were victims of the 1959 Hutu revolt in Rwanda that resulted in the massacre of Tutsis and the flight of large numbers into exile in neighbouring Uganda. While in exile, Tutsis supported Museveni and his National Resistance Movement (NRM) in overthrowing the regime of Milton Obote in 1986. After his victory, Museveni placed many Tutsis in his army, including Colonel Paul Kagamé who became vice-president of Rwanda in 1994. In return for their support, Museveni helped exiled Rwandan Tutsis to create the *Front Patriotique Rwandais* (RPF) movement, which with the help of the Ugandan Army took power from the Hutus after the 1994 genocide in Rwanda.

Since the Tutsi victory in Rwanda and later in Burundi, Kagamé has tried to use the alliance with Uganda to maintain and consolidate Tutsi security in central and east Africa. Together, Rwanda and Uganda control just under half of the DROC, which contains great mineral wealth. The future security of both allies is directly tied to the outcome of the Lusaka peace agreement, but the Tutsi partnership is under strain over diverging strategic and diplomatic interests. Museveni does not share Kagamé's vision of Tutsi political and military dominance in the region. Indeed, Ugandan officials see the Tutsi plight as a destabilising factor. Museveni reiterated the resentment felt by many Ugandans towards the 'general arrogance of Rwanda' and the Tutsi desire to dominate the region when he reported on Uganda's role in the DROC in August 1999. The report clearly highlighted Museveni's exasperation with Rwanda when he asserted that its leadership needed to find a compromise strategy towards the conflict in the DROC.

Signs of Uganda's deteriorating relations with Rwanda could be seen when Museveni signed the Sirte agreement with Kabila in Libya on 19 April 1999, calling for a cease-fire, the withdrawal of foreign troops and the deployment of African peacekeepers. On the ground, divisions between Rwanda and Uganda are also reflected in their backing of different splinter groups from the original RCD rebel movement. The Rwandan and Ugandan armies clashed in Kisangani on 7 and 14 August 1999 because of their support of different armed groups. Heavy fighting broke out at the airport, with each side accusing the other of launching ambushes and raids.

However, there were no Rwandan or Ugandan rebel groups in Kisangani at that time, bearing out the criticism of both countries that their involvement in the DROC has shifted significantly from concerns about national security to battles for political influence in the DROC and for commercial control of diamonds, gold and coffee concessions. A delicate balance of power is taking shape in eastern Congo between Rwanda and Uganda, which could lead to further fragmentation and a *de facto* partition of this region.

It is reported that Museveni will be less concerned with overthrowing Kabila if he gains reassurances over border security. Kagamé, on the other hand, has maintained his objective of replacing Kabila with a sympathetic ally answerable to Rwanda. Militarily, Rwanda gained the upper hand in the battle in eastern Congo, but it has some way to go in consolidating political support from other African governments, which are increasingly concerned about Kigali's brutal counter-insurgency agenda in central Africa. Significantly, relations between Museveni and the pro-Kabila Mugabe have improved since the Lusaka agreement was concluded. There have been reports that the two leaders have agreed a plan that ensures that they maintain their influence over political and security matters in the regions they control. But Rwanda is determined to pursue its moral crusade against the *génocidaires*, whom they believe to be a mortal danger to the survival of the Tutsi regime.

The End of the Road for Jonas Savimbi?

Angola's long-running civil war became intertwined with the conflict in the DROC when the government of President José Eduardo Dos Santos noted links between UNITA and remnants of the government's old adversaries, former Congolese leader Joseph Mobutu's defeated *Forces Armées Zaïroises* (FAZ), plus Rwanda and Uganda. At the start of the conflict in the DROC, Angola had forces of at least 7,000 in the western region of the country. It kept them there mainly to repel UNITA forces which sought to use the Congo as a back door through which to mount new incursions into Angola. However, the resumption of internal war between the Angolan army, *Forças Armadas de Angola* (FAA) and UNITA since the start of 1999 has forced the government to scale-back its involvement in the DROC to just under 2,000 troops.

A renewal of full-scale fighting between the FAA and UNITA destroyed the Lusaka Protocol peace agreement, which ended the Angolan civil war in 1994. It cannot any longer be considered even as a framework for re-opening negotiations between the warring factions. The government has refused any future diplomatic engagement with UNITA and UNITA leader, Jonas Savimbi, now labelled a war criminal. It is instead prepared to fight a war on three fronts against UNITA: at home, including the oil-rich northern Angolan enclave of Cabinda, where there is a long-standing secessionist movement; in the DROC; and in Congo-Brazzaville, another country that serves as a rear-base for UNITA's 'guns-for-diamonds' trading routes. In fact, these routes earned Savimbi approximately $120m in 1999. Diamond sales for the whole of Africa were worth about $6.8 billion, of which some 3.75% came from conflict areas – Libya, Côte D'Ivoire, Sierra Leone, DROC and UNITA-held areas of Angola. This has brought the Angolan government into conflict with several of its neighbours, especially Zambia, which it suspects is supporting Savimbi. The extent of the FAA's military reach makes it clear that Angola is fast becoming a very potent regional military power, intent on destroying any force that sides with UNITA.

Events in Angola towards the end of 1999 took a dramatic turn in favour of the government. Dos Santos has been using the country's vast oil reserves (which in 1999 provided it with revenue of at least US$1bn) to buy new armaments and munitions. Its successful capture of key UNITA strategic locations, including its traditional field headquarters at Andulo, an important base for the rebel's military supplies, and Bailundo on 14 September, have gradually altered the balance of power in favour of the government. UNITA also lost the Malanje corridor in the north, a useful route for trafficking diamonds and weapons between Angola and neighbouring DROC. The FAA has deployed additional strength north into the DROC to set up a line of defence, but also to prevent UNITA forces from taking over the coveted DROC diamond centre of Mbuji-Mayi.

It is difficult to be certain whether even a weakened UNITA is facing defeat. Savimbi is intent on winning his battle for the leadership of Angola. He has decided that an Angola that is not governed by him will remain at war. Although UNITA forces have been withdrawing to the DROC, Namibia and Zambia, and hiding inside Angola, there are still questions as to how much damage has been inflicted on UNITA and what capacity it has to continue its war. UNITA still has a large store of weapons and a range of combat helicopters capable of attacking and damaging government-held territories. And after spending a year employing conventional tactics without much success, it began, early in January 2000, to restructure its military strategy by reverting to the traditional guerrilla methods that in the past have served it well.

In addition, UNITA still benefits from its network of allies within and outside the region. Savimbi has friends scattered throughout Africa; if he loses one (for example, Congo-Brazzaville) or is unable to rely on another (for example, Zambia), he is able to turn to yet others (for example, Burkina Faso and Togo) for help. It is this network which has so effectively undercut attempts by the UN Angola-sanctions committee, set up in June 1999 to curb the massive diamond-smuggling operations that have nourished Savimbi and his movement for over five years.

At the end of 1999, the war shifted to Angola's southern border with Namibia. Hit-and-run attacks reportedly conducted by UNITA took place in Namibia's remote north-east Caprivi Strip in January 2000. Namibia has been drawn into the Angolan conflict primarily because of UNITA's alleged association with separatists in the Caprivi. Through this action, UNITA was trying to ensure that Namibia would not support Luanda, but Savimbi's actions here have backfired. Heavy fighting in the area took place during the Christmas period, after Namibian President Sam Nujoma, citing their mutual defence pact, granted Angolan troops the use of his country as a base from which to attack UNITA forces' southern strongholds in Angola.

Nujoma's decision to involve Namibia in Angola's war came at a critical time for his government, which was also facing accusations of human-rights abuses in its handling of the separatist tensions in the Caprivi Strip. Namibia's involvement was a further sign of how a conflict in this region can ratchet up to yet another regional conflagration. In another indication of the same phenomenon, fresh Angolan troops were reported to have deployed along the border with Zambia in January in a bid to wipe out UNITA rebel positions in the eastern provinces of Moxico and Cuando Cubango.

The combination of the war in Angola and that in the DROC has set back the prospect of economic and political development in a region that should serve as a catalyst for economic growth on the African continent. The unending wars have put a further large dent in South African President Thabo Mbkei's claims that there is, or will be, an African renaissance, based on sustained political development and economic stability throughout the continent. Angola and the DROC both contain fabulous mineral riches, but the fighting in these countries puts them among the 15 poorest nations in the world. Instead of being used as a force to produce wealth, civilians in both countries are buffeted by the conflict, sometimes forced to leave their homes, in danger of losing their limbs from land mines, or are killed or die every day from hunger and ill health.

Sadly, the future development of Angola and the DROC has been mortgaged for more weapons and military hardware.

News of Luanda's successes against UNITA has not enhanced security, or made surviving in Africa's bloodiest country any easier. The Angolan government has a catalogue of economic problems, arising largely from the manner in which the economy is used to fund the war. Dos Santos' regime has done little to demonstrate its concern for the humanitarian, social and developmental catastrophe confronting its citizens. Indiscriminate violence against civilians and human-rights abuses by government forces have led many Angolans to conclude that even without Savimbi, Angola would not be at peace.

Militia Wars in Congo-Brazzaville

While the war rages on in the DROC, hardcore militiamen, backing various political leaders, continue to spread violence in the neighbouring state of Congo-Brazzaville. The cycle of violence in Congo-Brazzaville has been overshadowed by that afflicting its bigger neighbour. Yet, almost 500,000 people have been made homeless and forced to live deep in the jungle, while weapons continue to flow into a country that is fast becoming another graveyard on the continent. The government and the rebel militia groups have both committed an equal number of atrocities against a population that has quickly abandoned its villages.

This is hardly surprising, for those who now make up the government were previously rebels, and the former regime has become the rebels. The current leader, General Denis Sassou Nguesso, ousted an elected leader, President Pascal Lissouba in October 1997, with the military assistance of the Angolan government. Lissouba and his rebel militia are now fighting in the bush. The situation could change quickly again. Nguesso's power-base is very fragile and, like his counterpart in the DROC, his survival is largely dependent on the Angolan military.

In November 1999, government and rebel forces signed a peace agreement in the port of Point Noire, Congo-Brazzaville's second city and the base of the off-shore oil industry that funds the present government. In December, the government passed an amnesty bill in parliament for the rebel militias, the *Ninjas* and the *Zoulou*, but not for their political leaders, Lissouba and the former prime minister, Bernard Koelas, who was also ousted. Yet, the *Cobra* militia group, which supports Nguesso, continues to mount attacks against his political opponents. As in the DROC, implementing the peace is likely to be difficult as various armed groups continue to fight against what they describe as Nguesso's northern-based dictatorial regime. Anarchy reigns over the south where armed gangs have used the government's inability to control violence to terrify the population, causing yet more to flee further into the jungle.

Little Hope In Sight

Although most governments would benefit from an end to the fighting in this region, their control of the situation has eroded. Central power has declined in the different states, and the power of warlords and local barons has grown. A UN report on the problem in Congo-Brazzaville speaks of a whole generation of youth that has resorted to a life of plunder and extortion, and suggests a bleak outlook for that country. Much of what it says is applicable to the whole of the region. Whatever their original reason for picking up guns, these youths now live by them. Government leaders may try to make peace through signing pieces of paper; these vicious warriors have no interest in, nor expect any benefit from, peace. As always, in the ceaseless fighting in Africa, it is unarmed and peaceful civilians who are the victims.

Horn of Africa

War, anarchy and political instability remained the characteristic features of politics in the Horn of Africa in 1999. The conflict between Eritrea and Ethiopia, which erupted into war in May 1998, continued throughout the year, despite efforts by the US, Rwanda, the Organisation of African Unity (OAU) and several individual African leaders to find a resolution. In addition to the debilitating effects on the two warring nations, the conflict has had a destabilising effect on political alignments in the entire region. Despite a UN Security Council resolution early in the year banning the sale of arms to Eritrea and Ethiopia, the two countries found new sources of weapons and ammunition supplies, most of them from the former Eastern Bloc.

In Sudan, the fighting between the Muslim north and the predominantly Christian south continued, but by the end of the year the conflict was complicated by power struggles within the ruling National Congress Party. The 1999 showdown between the Islamic fundamentalist leader Hassan al-Turabi and President Omar Hassan al-Bashir, had been expected for some time. In Somalia, the anarchy that descended over the country in the early 1990s, was still clearly visible throughout 1999 and in early 2000. Some Somali factions, which were relatively dormant until 1998, found fresh supplies of weapons, thanks to the Eritrea–Ethiopia war.

These problems had serious implications not only for regional security, but also for the pace of development and the democratic process in Eritrea, Ethiopia, Somalia and Sudan. The wars and conflicts in these four countries also had deleterious humanitarian effects, which included the

Africa

planting of new landmines, population displacements and the increasingly widespread military recruitment of child soldiers. Indeed, as has been always the case in the Horn, security issues in 1999 were closely inter-twined with human rights, political and economic development, internally displaced persons and refugees.

Continuing an Insane War

The fighting between Ethiopia and Eritrea started over the Yirga Triangle, a piece of desert along the common border. It is often assumed that African boundaries were fixed by colonial authorities in the late nineteenth century and have remained intact, but that is not always the case. The Ethiopia–Eritrea war resulted from a colonial border that has shifted many times in the past 100 years. Italian colonial authorities drew the initial boundary in the 1890s, but Italy modified it in 1936, following the Italian occupation of Ethiopia in the previous year. When the British authorities assumed control of Eritrea following the defeat of Italy in the Second World War, they restored the original line, but it was again modified following Ethiopia's decision to control Eritrea as its own province in the 1960s. The border between Eritrea and Ethiopia is not as clear as the governments of the two states have claimed.

The conflict has been repeatedly described as a border war, but it is a border war to only a small extent. Since May 1998, the two countries have indeed been exchanging fire along their common boundary, but the conflict between them is much wider. It has been about regime legitimacy, state sovereignty, nation building, currencies and access to port facilities. Above all, it involves the personal pride of the two leaders – President Isaias Afwerki of Eritrea and Prime Minister Meles Zenawi of Ethiopia, who were allies against former Ethiopian dictator Mengistu Haile Mariam until the early 1990s. Because this war has many causes, it has been difficult to resolve.

In early February 1999, each country claimed that it had accepted mediation efforts by the OAU, backed up by UN Security Council Resolution 1226 of 29 January 1999, but this turned out to be more wishful thinking. Eritrea initially refused to accept the OAU's proposal that it withdraw from the disputed Badme area, which it occupied in May 1998, pending negotiations. Fighting continued and was concentrated around Badme and Zela Ambesa, in north-western Ethiopia. The hostilities seemed to subside in mid-February, but Ethiopian Foreign Minister Seyoum Mesfin ruled out a new cease-fire despite appeals from the OAU, the UN and foreign leaders, including US President Bill Clinton.

The UN Security Council passed Resolution 1227 on 10 February 1999, calling on both sides to end the fighting and resume diplomatic efforts, but it had little discernible effect. Ethiopia repossessed the Badme area on 28 February 1999, and shortly afterwards Eritrea announced that it had accepted the OAU proposal that it withdraw from the area pending negotiations. The fighting continued intermittently in the following three months, with both sides using infantry, tanks, artillery and aircraft. The UN, which kept revisiting the issue, called for another ceasefire on 23 June. The following day, Eritrea welcomed the ceasefire call, but Ethiopia launched a new offensive on 25 June. By mid-1999 the two countries had deployed some 500,000 troops on either side of the border, and in early 2000 they still maintained large forces in the area.

The people of the two countries, many of whom have been displaced from their homes, are unhappy about the war. Ordinary Ethiopians especially detest the fact that they have to make sacrifices for yet another useless conflict. The OAU, which established a Conflict Management Division, and the Intergovernmental Authority on Development (IGAD), an umbrella organisation for the Horn of Africa, have both tried and been unable to resolve the dispute. The UN appointed an envoy, Algerian diplomat Mohammed Sahnoun, to mediate, but despite several meetings with the leaders of both countries, he was unable to bring an end to the fighting.

If this conflict had been an ordinary border dispute, these efforts, and the US–Rwanda initiative in 1998, would probably have been enough to resolve it. But the involvement of a superpower merely played on the egos of the two leaders. Other parties, including the DROC, Egypt, Italy, Kenya, Libya, Tunisia and Uganda, have all been involved in trying to find a solution, but they have merely crowded the field without producing any new proposals. While Ethiopia has been opposed to the involvement of large numbers of negotiators, Eritrea seemed to enjoy the attention it was receiving from the international community.

Both the Ethiopian and Eritrean governments have described the war between them as 'insane', but neither of them appears to find enough sanity to withdraw from it. In 1998, Mesfin claimed that it was 'Eritrea that imposed this war on Ethiopia by committing aggression and occupying Ethiopian territory'. Indeed, Eritrea did occupy a rocky part of the border in May 1998, but it was Ethiopia that escalated the conflict into war. In the meantime, Asmera has claimed that it does 'not see any rationale to this conflict'. It seems that both countries are engaged in a costly war that they themselves despise.

The war, and especially the reason for fighting, has effectively undermined much of what Afwerki and Zenawi stood for. In Washington and other Western capitals, they were regarded as some of the 'renaissance' leaders in Africa, alongside Yoweri Museveni of Uganda, Thabo Mbeki of South Africa and Paul Kagame of Rwanda. One reason why the US government, and especially former National Security Advisor Anthony Lake, became involved in the mediation efforts might be that Washington oversold the credentials of these leaders. However, it has now become clear that nothing about them suggests either that they are democrats or that they have a vision for leading Africa out of its problems.

When Eritrea gained independence in 1993, it decided to use the Ethiopian currency, the birr, and the two countries agreed that Ethiopia would continue to have access to the Eritrean ports of Assab and Massawa. Eritrea has now introduced its own currency, and, as a result of the war, Ethiopia has no access to the ports. The war has had mixed effects in the region. To replace its access to Massawa and Assab, Ethiopia has chosen to rely on Djibouti, which has inevitably become a diplomatic and strategic ally of Addis Ababa. In the meantime, within Djibouti the war appears to have given confidence and some military momentum to a low-level rebellion dominated by the Afar, an ethnic group inhabiting Djibouti, Eritrea and Ethiopia. This is not surprising given that some of the disputed areas on the Ethiopia–Eritrea border are within Afar-populated territory. Suspicions that Eritrea supported the rebellion, and the perception that a diplomatic alliance had been established between Addis Ababa and Djibouti led to Eritrea and Djibouti breaking off diplomatic relations.

There have been further claims that Eritrea has cooperated with several Ethiopian rebel movements, particularly those associated with the Oromos, Ethiopia's largest ethnic group, and the Somalis. It has been claimed that Eritrea was behind efforts to unite different Oromo groups, several of which have linked up with the Oromo Liberation Front (OLF), with a view to putting more pressure on the Ethiopian government. While the Eritrean government has denied giving support to proxy forces or factions within Ethiopia, there have been persistent press reports that Ethiopian dissident groups based in Somalia have been obtaining their arms from Asmera.

In contrast with the OLF, other dissident groups in Ethiopia have rallied behind the government in the war effort. The conflict has therefore helped Addis Ababa to achieve a semblance of national unity. At the same time, it is widely believed that Ethiopia has been courting Eritrean dissidents, with a view to destabilising Eritrea. In 1999, the Ethiopian government press gave considerable coverage to a new Eritrean dissident group, the Alliance of the Eritrean National Forces. The Eritrea–Ethiopia war has been a boon to Sudan. So long as its two neighbours are fighting each other, they can not continue to support the anti-Khartoum rebels. In fact, the war led Ethiopia to explore acquiring access to the sea through Sudan. Both Eritrea and Ethiopia were quick to improve relations with Khartoum following the showdown between fundamentalist leader Turabi and President Bashir in December 1999.

Islam and Political Instability

The power struggle in Sudan between Bashir and Turabi appears to have ended on 12 December 1999, when Bashir sacked Turabi as Speaker of the National Assembly. The president also imposed a three-month state of emergency and dissolved parliament pending new elections. Turabi has staged political comebacks several times in the past, so whether his sacking as Speaker is sufficient to weaken his political power-base is hard to tell.

Bashir and Turabi had ruled Sudan jointly since the former staged a military coup in mid-1989. Prior to the coup, Turabi's political party, the National Islamic Front (NIF), was a junior partner in a government led by Sadiq al-Mahdi of the *Umma* Party. Bashir's coup was apparently an Islamist-engineered takeover, which subsequently enabled Turabi to assume vastly increased political powers. Some observers believe that without Turabi's scheming and support, Bashir's coup would not have taken place. Bashir is the president of the ruling National Congress Party, while Turabi is its secretary-general. In this post, Turabi still retains considerable political power and influence in the country. He continues to direct the party's intellectual and propaganda activities, as well as overseeing its administrative and financial affairs, which are strictly based on Islamic *Sharia* laws. Thus, Turabi's power has been little reduced by the loss of his formal position as Speaker.

The struggle between Bashir and Turabi has been portrayed partly as a clash over democratic reforms, but this would suggest that Turabi was in favour of democracy and Bashir was opposed to it, which is not necessarily the case. Turabi was not a democrat, and he presided over a parliament that merely rubber-stamped his, or Bashir's, decisions. Nonetheless, his sacking has raised fresh questions about the pace of democratic reform in Sudan. Bashir's dissolution of parliament came shortly before it was due to vote on Turabi-orchestrated reforms which would have reduced Bashir's powers and increased those of the speaker. In short, the struggle was largely about naked personal ambitions, rather than democratic reforms. Given the tyrannical tendencies displayed by both Bashir and Turabi, democratic reform seems unlikely to proceed very far as long as either remains in power.

With Turabi out of office, Bashir was able to pursue reconciliation with the traditional northern politicians, Sadiq al-Mahdi, leader of the *Umma* Party, and Muhammad Osman Mirghani, leader of the Democratic Unionist Party. Whether the northerners are going to achieve meaningful unity as a result of this re-arrangement of musical chairs is not easy to tell. Turabi's forced departure raised fears that it would be a prelude to political instability in northern Sudanese politics, or even another military coup, but neither occurred. Indeed, by early 2000, the ruling National

Congress party had organised several reconciliation meetings between Turabi, Bashir and their supporters. The power that Turabi continues to exercise through the party, and the speed with which reconciliation has taken place, raises the question of whether there has been any substantial change in Khartoum's power equation since 12 December 1999.

What has been interesting is that Turabi's sacking inspired hope in neighbouring states, which were also desperate to improve relations with Sudan. During the 1990s, Turabi had made Sudan an isolated, even pariah, state. Not only did he support Islamic militants in neighbouring countries, but also Sudanese government-supported agents were said to have been behind the 1995 attempt to assassinate Egyptian President Hosni Mubarak. Sudan is also said to have provided storage facilities for Iraq's weapons of mass destruction. The US government, which has imposed sanctions on Sudan, has claimed that Khartoum has been hosting and training Islamic terrorists. Several Arab countries have had reservations about Sudan's brand of Islam, and have been reluctant to give aid to the country.

After nearly a decade of isolation, Bashir started to make overtures to governments in the region in 1999, but his efforts were often undermined by Turabi and his supporters. Bashir's showdown with Turabi therefore had implications for regional stability and security. It may have been a signal to neighbouring states and the international community as a whole that Sudan had put aggressive Islamist policies behind and was trying to embrace international norms and live peacefully with its neighbours. Indeed, following Turabi's departure from power, Bashir visited or sent emissaries to several countries, including the DROC, Egypt, Eritrea, Libya, Oman and Qatar. He also tried to improve relations with Ethiopia, Kenya and Uganda. Egypt and Uganda, which had both previously accused Sudan of supporting their own rebel Islamic fundamentalist groups, promised in early 2000 to resume diplomatic relations with Sudan.

Indeed, Bashir's showdown with Turabi reversed a number of diplomatic relations in the region, but neighbouring states may have been too quick to celebrate Turabi's 'departure'. Eritrea and Ethiopia were key regional players in the US efforts to isolate Sudan. Following Bashir's confrontation with Turabi, Eritrea quickly resumed diplomatic relations with Sudan, re-opened their common border, and Afwerki made his first visit to Khartoum in February 2000. During Eritrea's struggle for independence from Ethiopia prior to the overthrow of the Mengistu regime in 1991, Afwerki often operated from Sudan. However, independent Eritrea severed diplomatic relations with Khartoum in 1994, after accusing it of trying to destabilise the regime in Asmera. Eritrea's rapid move to re-establish relations following Turabi's sacking was a result of its war with Ethiopia, which has increased its desire for more friends in the region. It may find, however, that the relationship with Sudan is a fair-weather friendship.

The struggle between Bashir and Turabi is a sideshow compared to the fighting in southern Sudan, which has been going on for 17 years. The war has made it difficult for Sudan to export oil, which is produced in the disputed south. The Canadian company that extracts Sudan's oil, Talisman Energy, has repeatedly been accused of financing the war against the south Sudanese. The main opposition grouping in the south, the Sudan Peoples Liberation Movement (SPLM), led by John Garang, was still active in 1999 despite the fact that some southerners, who broke away from the SPLM in 1991 because of ethnic, policy and personality differences, continued to undermine the movement by working with the Khartoum regime.

The SPLM is much weaker than it was prior to 1991 due to a number of factors: lack of support from Eritrea, Ethiopia and Uganda, which have been preoccupied with other concerns; disillusionment among its ranks; and continuous splits. A further indication of divisions among the southerners emerged in late January 2000 when a new rebel group, the South Sudan Liberation Movement (SSLM) was formed in Upper Nile. The SPLM immediately condemned the formation of the new group, but the split has meant a further weakening of the anti-Khartoum forces. While the southerners are divided along ethnic and ideological lines, the majority of them do not want to settle for anything less than independence.

In 1999, as in previous years, Sudanese government representatives and liberation fighters held peace talks on a number of occasions, with the usual lack of results. The gap between the two sides has not narrowed despite many years of negotiations. The southerners, who are predominantly Christians, still resent political and economic domination by the Muslim, Arabic-speaking northerners. The IGAD, which has been negotiating peace in Sudan, has been weakened by the fighting between two of its members, Eritrea and Ethiopia. Kenya, which has hosted the peace negotiations, has not been keen to see the parties move ahead on to new grounds. The only new initiative that the IGAD could get all the parties to agree upon, was the idea of a referendum on the south's future, including the option of independence. Seeing the IGAD so weakened, Khartoum had no interest in negotiating in good faith. In early 2000, while the parties continued to say they were willing to talk to each other, a solution to the Sudanese conflict was still far off.

Deepening Anarchy

The Eritrea–Ethiopia war has had an even more debilitating effect on the situation in Somalia than it has had on the IGAD's ability to mediate in the problems in south Sudan. Throughout 1999, Somalia was particularly vulnerable to new influxes of arms and ammunition because of the anarchy that has ruled over its fragile political landscape since the state totally collapsed following the ousting of Siad Barre in 1991. Much of the country remained as anarchic as it has been since the UN forces departed five years ago. There is no government in Mogadishu apart from factional leaders interested in nothing but looting and extortion. Several parts of the country have broken away and declared themselves independent states, but the international community has refused to accord them recognition.

The north-western 'state' of Somaliland, which declared itself independent in 1991, appears to be a natural partner of Ethiopia, because of its strategic port of Berbera. In the north-east, the mini-state of Puntland, which declared its 'independence' more recently, is also thought to be allied with Ethiopia, which has sent a 'diplomat' to represent its interests in the Puntland capital, Bosasso. The Kismayu-based faction leader, General Mohammed Hirsi Morgan, a son-in-law of Siad Barre, also received weapons from Ethiopia. Other factions allegedly supported by Ethiopia in 1999 include the Somali National Front (SNF), a Marehan group led by Omar Hajj Masale, and the United Somali Congress–Patriotic Movement (USC-PF), led by Omar Hashi Adan of the Hawadle clan.

In southern Somalia, and especially the Mogadishu area, Eritrea has been allied with Mohammed Hussein Aideed, head of the Somali National Alliance (SNA) and son of the infamous Mohammed Farah Aideed, who gave the UN forces a hard time in the early 1990s. In June 1999, Aideed's forces, which had occupied the town of Baidoa the previous month, were driven out by the Rahanwein Resistance Army (RRA), backed by an Ethiopian force of up to 3,000 troops. Ethiopians reportedly used tanks and artillery in the attack, which was part of a strategy to prevent Eritrea from opening up a new front. Ethiopian forces effectively extended control over much of southwestern Somalia. For his part, Hussein Aideed acknowledged in 1999 that he received support from Eritrea and Uganda. Eritrea is reported to have armed Ethiopian rebels from the OLF, some of whom had entered Somalia to support the Aideed faction. Other Somali factions allied to Eritrea include an Ogadeni faction led by Omar Jess, and the Somali National Movement (SNM) led by Abdi Warsameh Isaq, from the Dir clan.

The alliances that Eritrea and Ethiopia have formed with Somali factions are not very deep and are of very limited benefit to either country. Indeed, political factions in Somalia are so unpredictable that any alliances can be expected to change several times within a short period of time.

The Way Ahead

The way ahead for the Eritrea–Ethiopia war is clear, but not easy to bring about. A peaceful resolution of this conflict remains elusive because the mediators have approached it as if it were an ordinary border dispute that would be amenable to a technical settlement. If the war was genuinely one of border demarcation, the mediators could easily assist, drawing on wide experience of disputed border issues in Africa that has accumulated over the years. In such a case, the OAU, the US–Rwanda team and other external mediators could prescribe bilateral or multilateral measures to be followed.

However, this is a border war that stems from many factors that have very little or nothing to do with the border. The unresolved problems between Eritrea and Ethiopia touch on personal pride, sovereignty, legitimacy and the nature of political institutions. They involve economic development, national currencies, trade and Ethiopia's lack of direct access to the sea. These are long-term problems that require careful and steady institution-building. Outsiders can help prescribe some institutions, but they cannot impose national and regional institutions that underpin authority in the wider social, political and economic contexts of legitimacy. The solution will have to come from within. Neither side has yet shown any sign that it is prepared to try to find that solution. The conflict is one that can be expected to run for some time yet.

Africa

Prospectives

O NE OF THE MORE DISTURBING DEVELOPMENTS as the new millennium dawned was the appearance of the US and Europe marching to different drummers. That they disagreed on a number of key issues was neither new nor unusual. There have always been strains in the Atlantic Alliance, as could be expected from a grouping of independent, democratic states. But those strains were made manageable by the willingness of both sides to operate on the basis of mutual trust, to communicate at the highest levels with candour, confident that each was pursuing a common objective. The danger for the coming years is that the bridge of communication seems to have broken down and, unless some way is found to reconstruct it, the loss of trust could have a profound impact on the Alliance's cohesion.

The US finds it difficult to grasp why its plans to construct a limited national missile defence (NMD) to protect itself from 'rogue' states is neither understood by European nations nor welcomed. Europe is irritated by the US reluctance to give a clear signal of approval for its plans to develop the European Security and Defence Identity (ESDI). The US feels Europe should be doing more to close the technological gap that has opened between US and other NATO forces. Many European members of NATO expressed their anger at what they saw as US arrogance and unilateralism with regard to war with Yugoslavia over Kosovo in 1999. Both sides accuse the other of not fulfilling commitments in the effort to glue the badly torn province back together.

If unchecked, these indications of eroding transatlantic solidarity could have profound consequences for the Alliance's ability to function as a structure of cooperation and international order. NATO governments must recognise the need to knit up the fabric of trust on which the Alliance rests. This will be particularly difficult in a US election year. Both presidential candidates, Al Gore and George Bush, will be playing to the public mood, which tends to be one of political provincialism, in hopes of gathering more votes. The loosening of the bonds that have made the Western Alliance so important to the search for security has not yet gone so far that it is irreversible; unless recognised and tended to, however, it could easily become driven beyond repair.

The NMD Chasm

The US has had little success in convincing its European critics that its plans for NMD deployment are needed, sensible or useful. They point out that NMD has yet to be proved technically feasible. None of the tests that has been held so far, even under the most ideal conditions, have been fully successful. Many Europeans do not believe the system will ever work as intended. And even if it did, the critics are convinced that rather than bringing stability the move will be destabilising.

There are few in Europe who believe that the so-called 'rogue' states are led by men so irrational that they would threaten the US with weapons of mass destruction carried on ballistic missiles – even if they were able to do so. The critics argue that the massive nuclear and conventional strike capacity maintained by the US would deter all potential adversaries, large or small, with nuclear capabilities which might threaten the continental US.

Unless Russia is prepared to amend the Anti-Ballistic Missile (ABM) Treaty to permit NMD – which it might do if given a large enough pay-off – the US has threatened to act unilaterally. Most European governments argue that this would further strain the US–Russia relationship, which is already under pressure. They also argue that China, which can not be convinced that the US would expend enormous sums to protect itself against a putative threat, will undoubtedly consider that NMD deployment is really directed against its small nuclear arsenal. It can therefore be expected to construct and stockpile many more nuclear weapons to ensure that it can circumvent US missile defences. Thus, rather than making the world more secure, NMD would risk the development of a greater threat.

For many years there was some question, even in the US, of whether NMD could be made sufficiently effective to warrant its construction. By 1999, however, the question was no longer whether it would be deployed, but when. The concept has gained overwhelming public support. The US finds it difficult to understand why Europeans can not recognise that Americans believe in the 'rogue' state theory and naturally wish to protect themselves. Washington is certain that Moscow, despite its protestations to the contrary, will be prepared to amend the ABM Treaty, and also believes that much of what the Chinese say about the matter is bluster; Beijing is pragmatic enough to recognise that NMD is a reaction to new threats abroad, not part of a strategy to contain China.

This is a wide gap to be bridged. What makes it more difficult is that the habit of high-level consultation and communication among the Allies has worn away. At the least, it is essential that both sides recognise the dangers inherent in the situation and resurrect the communication link that might bring better understanding. Even if that is unattainable, it should be possible for all to decide that there is too much at stake not to find compromises that will bolster mutual trust.

The NATO Gap and ESDI

The brief war in Kosovo during 1999 underscored the disparity between the US and its allies in the possession of, and ability to use, advanced technology and force in military operations. Unless remedial action is taken soon, this asymmetry will increase and begin to undermine the future effectiveness of NATO forces. The US believes that overcoming the disparity will require time, conviction and, especially, money. Washington points out that European defence budgets are already too low and many countries are planning to cut them further. Since the US defence budget is rising, the gap is certain to widen rather than contract. To prevent this, NATO launched the Defence Capabilities Initiative (DCI) in April 1999 to enhance allied capabilities in five key areas.

The European allies demonstrated their recognition of the problem by their agreement to the DCI. They drew a somewhat different conclusion to the US, however. Prodded by the UK and France, they felt that what was needed was to move ahead with the construction of a European rapid-reaction force, a force which had been talked of for many years without any action to establish it. In December 1999, the EU approved the formation of a corps of up to 60,000 troops by 2003.

The EU argues that the rapid-reaction corps would be separate from, but complementary to, NATO. It would be available for the EU to deal with humanitarian and peacekeeping crises in Europe without a need for US help. The Europeans forecast that the corps could be used in situations where NATO would be reluctant to act. They also emphasise that when plans for such a force have been discussed in the past the US has always expressed support.

In fact the US is deeply concerned by the prospect. Many Americans believe it will draw funds that are needed to support NATO; they feel it will unnecessarily duplicate NATO assets, and get in the way of the effort to modernise the Alliance. While making these arguments, however, many of these critics do not believe the force will ever come about. They condescendingly disparage the ability of the Europeans to get their act together, or to find the will to make the increases in defence spending that would be required. Even though some Europeans, like General Klaus Naumann, former chairman of NATO's Military Committee, do not think a rapid-response force can be created by 2003, sneering by Americans is not helpful, nor does it replace meaningful communication.

Other Irritants

Private industry in the US and UK leads the world in the accelerating bio-technological revolution. Wave upon wave of developments over the last decade will not only challenge established ethical and environmental standards, but will also raise questions affecting public safety and international security. As with information technology, the rapid developments in bio-technology are overtaking policy-makers' ability to react and the general public's ability to comprehend. While the US is dominant, there is strong transatlantic cooperation in the private business and academic sectors. In the interests of public health and security, close cooperation between Americans and Europeans is vital in this area. Unfortunately, in the arena of public debate, loudly expressed differences based on lack of understanding are helping to poison the transatlantic atmosphere.

One of these arguments revolves around genetically modified foods. Americans have been growing, and eating, modified soy beans and corn, among other crops, for many years without any ill effects. They do not see them causing any environmental damage, they do not think they are dangerous. On the contrary, they can see huge benefits, particularly for poor, developing countries, since these methods ensure a much larger harvest of enhanced foods. Americans cannot understand the European talk of 'Frankenstein' foods, or of the alleged dangers to the environment that scientists in the US tell them do not exist. Even those most sympathetic to the European viewpoint cannot see why experiments to prove the argument one way or the other should be banned.

Nor do Americans worry about hormone-fed beef, which they have been eating for many years without, at least thus far, ill effects. Here again they believe their scientists who tell them such meat is not dangerous, but healthy. From the US viewpoint, European objections are at best merely Luddite, a desire to do things the way they have always been done, which is how Americans think of the Old Country anyway. If not that, then a worse explanation pertains: Europeans are trying to secure their own market niche through the use of false premises. Clearly this is an area that requires open and honest discussion, not a slanging match.

The safety questions surrounding genetically modified foods and hormone-fed steer focus on only a fragment of the developing bio-technology revolution. Managing the galloping changes this science will bring, along with managing the information-technology revolution, will be a vital task for advanced nations. The US and Europe should be organising their approaches to the new technologies so that they will be able to shape their development without hindering it. Nations on both sides of the Atlantic must recognise that these revolutions can not be stopped, or even held back. If the US and Europe do not learn to pull together in finding the best way to handle the challenges, they will rapidly be pulled apart.

Both sides of the Atlantic have a role to play in managing the strategic implications of all the various technological revolutions with which the twenty-first century is opening. These revolutions, and the economic changes they bring with them, have important political consequences. The most obvious is the changing relationship between governments and governed. Economic globalisation is being accompanied by a stronger attachment to national identity, as people cling to the roots that a harmonised world economy strips away. At the same time, governments have a duty to promote the more open world trade system from which economies benefit, but which awaken their citizens' fears. Into this gap NGOs march, as they have done over genetically modified foods, and a host of other areas. Government leadership is still required to ensure that broad policy agendas are not submerged in parochial dispute. Governments have a greater responsibility to guarantee that their own national positions are discussed early and often with their counterparts so that crippling disputes are less frequent.

Quick, But Solid, Repairs Are Needed

The transatlantic Alliance has always been more than a traditional military pact along nineteenth-century lines. It began as a grouping of like-minded societies, with similar cultural, political and economic outlooks and goals. As such, it played a significant role in leading the international community towards a more humane and secure world. The disarray that has developed over a number of contentious issues should not be allowed to destroy this fundamental role. There is not much time to work on repairs, however. The looming presidential-election campaigning period in the US will prevent either of the two candidates from moving beyond a desire to mirror the public mood. What is needed, however, is statesmanlike action, which reaffirms the relevance and vitality of the Alliance. It remains the case that transatlantic solidarity can become a powerful force for good. Petty divisions leave the management of world politics, which is highly dependent on inventive policy-making, devoid of creative leadership. If an effort is not begun soon to stop the damage that is being done, the Alliance will lose its ability to act together, and the consequences, although not fully foreseeable, will be profound.

IISS*maps*
Strategic Geography 1999 / 2000

———	international boundaries	💥 ✨	attack(s)/incident(s) and skirmishes
—·—	province or state boundaries	*Dar El Beida* ⊕	international airport
----	disputed and other boundaries	*Al Kharj* ⊕	air base
══	roads		
▭▭▭	railways	*Tengiz* ▧	oilfield
SONORA	province or state		
🔺	built-up areas	━━ ━ ━	pipeline/proposed pipeline
▣	capital cities	⬤	oil refinery
●	cities/towns	∿	rivers
10 👤	number of deaths	⋯	seasonal or intermittent rivers
10 ✚	number of injuries	☁	lakes
10 ⬡	number of refugees	▲	mountain peaks (height in metres)

Europe *NATO's air campaign against Yugoslavia*

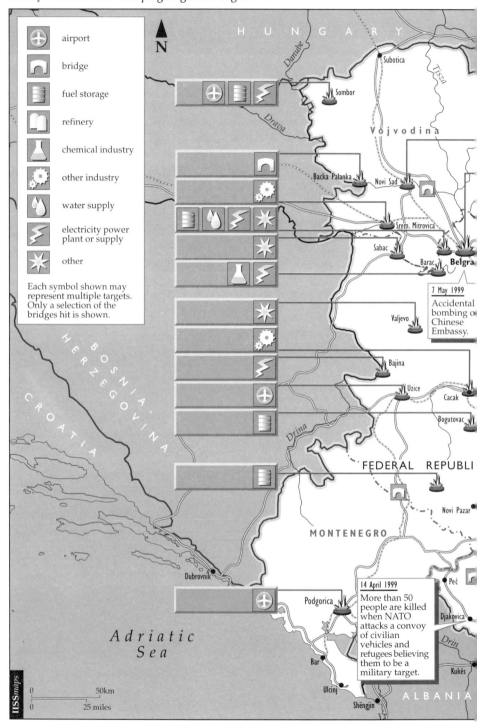

airport

bridge

fuel storage

refinery

chemical industry

other industry

water supply

electricity power plant or supply

other

Each symbol shown may represent multiple targets. Only a selection of the bridges hit is shown.

HUNGARY

Danube

Subotica

Tisza

Drava

Sombor

Vojvodina

Drava

Backa Palanka

Novi Sad

Srem. Mitrovica

Sabac

Barac

Belgra

7 May 1999
Accidental bombing o Chinese Embassy.

Valjevo

Bajina

Uzice

Cacak

Bogutovac

Drina

FEDERAL REPUBLI

Novi Pazar

MONTENEGRO

BOSNIA-HERZEGOVINA

CROATIA

Dubrovnik

Podgorica

Peć

14 April 1999
More than 50 people are killed when NATO attacks a convoy of civilian vehicles and refugees believing them to be a military target.

Djakovica

Adriatic Sea

Drin

Bar

Kukës

Ulcinj

Shëngjin

ALBANIA

0   50km
0   25 miles

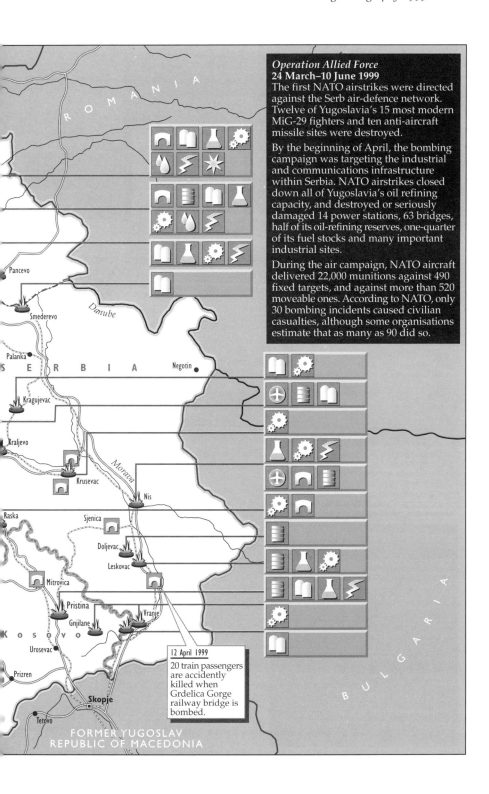

Operation Allied Force
24 March–10 June 1999
The first NATO airstrikes were directed against the Serb air-defence network. Twelve of Yugoslavia's 15 most modern MiG-29 fighters and ten anti-aircraft missile sites were destroyed.

By the beginning of April, the bombing campaign was targeting the industrial and communications infrastructure within Serbia. NATO airstrikes closed down all of Yugoslavia's oil refining capacity, and destroyed or seriously damaged 14 power stations, 63 bridges, half of its oil-refining reserves, one-quarter of its fuel stocks and many important industrial sites.

During the air campaign, NATO aircraft delivered 22,000 munitions against 490 fixed targets, and against more than 520 moveable ones. According to NATO, only 30 bombing incidents caused civilian casualties, although some organisations estimate that as many as 90 did so.

12 April 1999
20 train passengers are accidently killed when Grdelica Gorge railway bridge is bombed.

Europe *The Kosovo campaign*

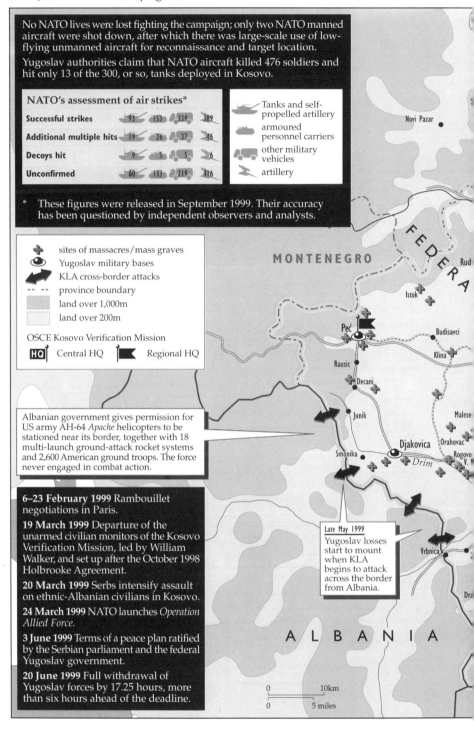

No NATO lives were lost fighting the campaign; only two NATO manned aircraft were shot down, after which there was large-scale use of low-flying unmanned aircraft for reconnaissance and target location.

Yugoslav authorities claim that NATO aircraft killed 476 soldiers and hit only 13 of the 300, or so, tanks deployed in Kosovo.

NATO's assessment of air strikes*

Successful strikes	93	153	339	389
Additional multiple hits	19	26	37	46
Decoys hit	9	5	5	6
Unconfirmed	60	133	219	416

Tanks and self-propelled artillery

armoured personnel carriers

other military vehicles

artillery

* These figures were released in September 1999. Their accuracy has been questioned by independent observers and analysts.

sites of massacres/mass graves
Yugoslav military bases
KLA cross-border attacks
province boundary
land over 1,000m
land over 200m

OSCE Kosovo Verification Mission
HQ Central HQ   Regional HQ

Albanian government gives permission for US army AH-64 *Apache* helicopters to be stationed near its border, together with 18 multi-launch ground-attack rocket systems and 2,600 American ground troops. The force never engaged in combat action.

6–23 February 1999 Rambouillet negotiations in Paris.

19 March 1999 Departure of the unarmed civilian monitors of the Kosovo Verification Mission, led by William Walker, and set up after the October 1998 Holbrooke Agreement.

20 March 1999 Serbs intensify assault on ethnic-Albanian civilians in Kosovo.

24 March 1999 NATO launches *Operation Allied Force*.

3 June 1999 Terms of a peace plan ratified by the Serbian parliament and the federal Yugoslav government.

20 June 1999 Full withdrawal of Yugoslav forces by 17.25 hours, more than six hours ahead of the deadline.

MONTENEGRO

F E D E R A

Novi Pazar

Rud

Istok

Peć

Budisavci

Klina

Rausic

Decani

Junik

Malese

Djakovica

Orahovac

Smonika

Rogovo

Drim

V.

Late May 1999
Yugoslav losses start to mount when KLA begins to attack across the border from Albania.

Vrbnica

Dra

A L B A N I A

0   10km
0   5 miles

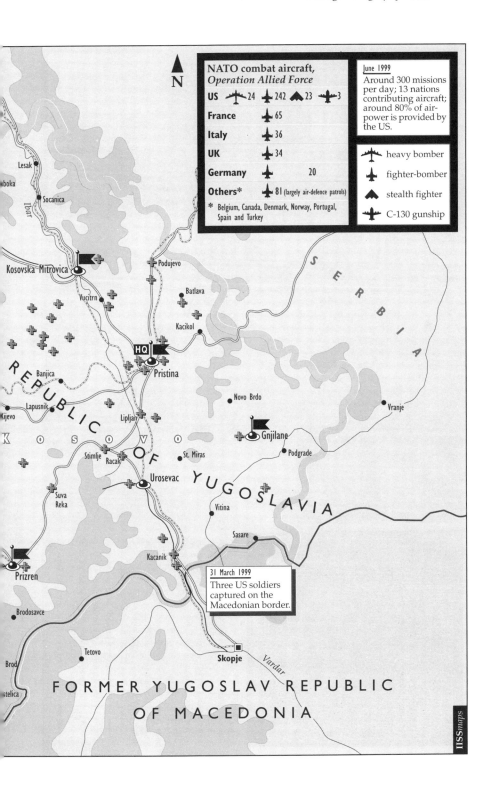

NATO combat aircraft,
Operation Allied Force

US	24 242 23 3	
France	65	
Italy	36	
UK	34	
Germany	20	
Others*	81 (largely air-defence patrols)	

* Belgium, Canada, Denmark, Norway, Portugal, Spain and Turkey

June 1999
Around 300 missions per day; 13 nations contributing aircraft; around 80% of air-power is provided by the US.

heavy bomber

fighter-bomber

stealth fighter

C-130 gunship

31 March 1999
Three US soldiers captured on the Macedonian border.

IISS*maps*

Europe *KFOR deployments in Kosovo*

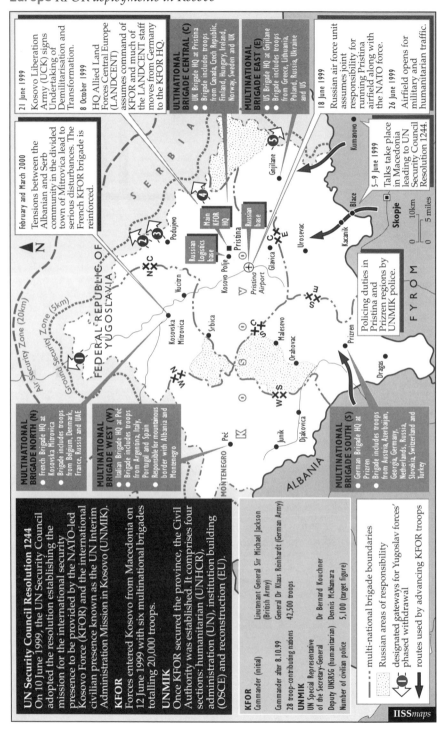

21 June 1999
Kosovo Liberation Army (UCK) signs Undertaking of Demilitarisation and Transformation.

8 October 1999
HQ Allied Land Forces Central Europe (LANDCENT) assumes command of KFOR and much of the LANDCENT staff moves from Germany to the KFOR HQ.

MULTINATIONAL BRIGADE CENTRAL (C)
● UK Brigade HQ at Pristina
● Brigade includes troops from Canada, Czech Republic, Finland, Hungary, Ireland, Norway, Sweden and UK

MULTINATIONAL BRIGADE EAST (E)
● US Brigade HQ at Gnjilane
● Brigade includes troops from Greece, Lithuania, Poland, Russia, Ukraine and US

18 June 1999
Russian air force unit assumes joint responsibility for running Pristina airfield along with the NATO force.

26 June 1999
Airfield opens for military and humanitarian traffic.

5–9 June 1999
Talks take place in Macedonia leading to UN Security Council Resolution 1244.

February and March 2000
Tensions between the Albanian and Serb community in the divided town of Mitrovica lead to serious disturbances. The French KFOR brigade is reinforced.

MULTINATIONAL BRIGADE NORTH (N)
● French Brigade HQ at Kosovska Mitrovica
● Brigade includes troops from Belgium, Denmark, France, Russia and UAE

MULTINATIONAL BRIGADE WEST (W)
● Italian Brigade HQ at Peć
● Brigade includes troops from Argentina, Italy, Portugal and Spain
● Responsible for mountainous border with Albania and Montenegro

MULTINATIONAL BRIGADE SOUTH (S)
● German Brigade HQ at Prizren
● Brigade includes troops from Austria, Azerbaijan, Georgia, Germany, Netherlands, Russia, Slovakia, Switzerland and Turkey

Policing duties in Pristina and Prizren regions by UNMIK police.

UN Security Council Resolution 1244
On 10 June 1999, the UN Security Council adopted the resolution establishing the mission for the international security presence to be provided by the NATO-led Kosovo Force (KFOR) and the international civilian presence known as the UN Interim Administration Mission in Kosovo (UNMIK).

KFOR
Forces entered Kosovo from Macedonia on 12 June 1999 with six multinational brigades totalling 20,000 troops.

UNMIK
Once KFOR secured the province, the Civil Authority was established. It comprises four sections: humanitarian (UNHCR); administration (UN), institution building (OSCE) and reconstruction (EU).

KFOR
Commander (initial)	Lieutenant General Sir Michael Jackson (British Army)
Commander after 8.10.99	General Dr Klaus Reinhardt (German Army)
28 troop-contributing nations	42,500 troops

UNMIK
UN Special Representative of the Secretary-General	Dr Bernard Kouchner
Deputy UNKSG (humanitarian)	Dennis McNamara
Number of civilian police	5,100 (target figure)

--- multi-national brigade boundaries

Russian areas of responsibility

designated gateways for Yugoslav forces' phased withdrawal

routes used by advancing KFOR troops

SERBIA

FEDERAL REPUBLIC OF YUGOSLAVIA

MONTENEGRO

ALBANIA

FYROM

Air Security Zone (20km)
Ground Security Zone (5km)

Kumanovo
Gnjilane
Blace
Skopje
Podujevo
Pristina
Main KFOR HQ
Russian base
Russian Logistics base
Kosovo Polje
Pristina Airport
Urosevac
Kacanik
Glavica
Vucitrn
Srbica
Kosovska Mitrovica
Malesevo
Orahovac
Prizren
Dragas
Djakovica
Junik
Peć

0 10km
0 5 miles

IISSmaps

Europe *Kosovo: the refugee crisis*

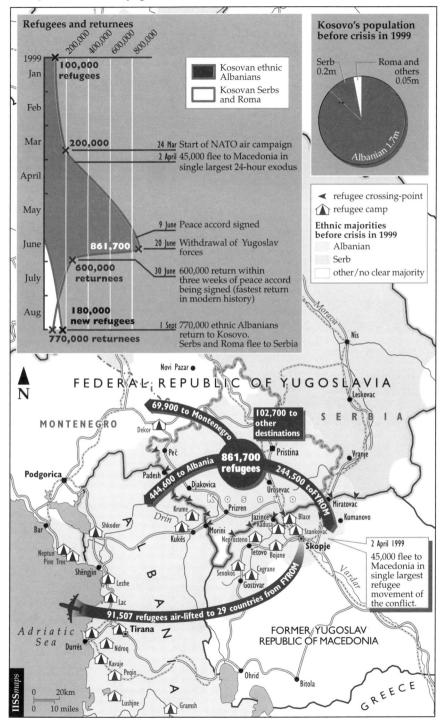

Refugees and returnees

200,000 400,000 600,000 800,000

1999
Jan — **100,000 refugees**

Feb

Mar — **200,000**
24 Mar Start of NATO air campaign
2 April 45,000 flee to Macedonia in single largest 24-hour exodus

April

May

June — **861,700**
9 June Peace accord signed
20 June Withdrawal of Yugoslav forces

July — **600,000 returnees**
30 June 600,000 return within three weeks of peace accord being signed (fastest return in modern history)

Aug — **180,000 new refugees**
770,000 returnees
1 Sept 770,000 ethnic Albanians return to Kosovo. Serbs and Roma flee to Serbia

Kosovan ethnic Albanians
Kosovan Serbs and Roma

Kosovo's population before crisis in 1999

Serb 0.2m
Roma and others 0.05m
Albanian 1.7m

◄ refugee crossing-point
⌂ refugee camp

Ethnic majorities before crisis in 1999
Albanian
Serb
other/no clear majority

N

Novi Pazar ●

FEDERAL REPUBLIC OF YUGOSLAVIA
Leskovac

MONTENEGRO
Dekor

69,900 to Montenegro

102,700 to other destinations

S E R B I A

Peć
Pristina
Vranje

Podgorica
Padesh
444,600 to Albania
Djakovica

861,700 refugees

244,500 to FYROM

Urosevac
Miratovac

Bar
Shkoder
Drin
Krume
Prizren
Jazince Radusa
Blace
Kumanovo

Kukës
Morini
Neprosteno
Stankovac

Neptun Pine Tree
Tetovo Bojane
Skopje

Shëngjin
Senokos
Cegrane

Lezhe
Gostivar
FYROM

Lac

91,507 refugees air-lifted to 29 countries from FYROM

Adriatic Sea
Durrës
Tirana

Ndroq

Kavaje

Peqin

FORMER YUGOSLAV REPUBLIC OF MACEDONIA

Ohrid
Bitola

Lushjne
Gramsh

2 April 1999
45,000 flee to Macedonia in single largest refugee movement of the conflict.

Vardar

Morava

Nis

G R E E C E

0   20km
0   10 miles

IIS*Ssnaps*

Europe *Fissile materials in Russia*

Naval site 49

Murmansk
(naval site/refuelling/icebreaker fleet)

Severodvinsk (refuelling/shipyard)

St Petersburg

Salaspils

Ignalina

Dubna

Minsk

BELARUS

Moscow

Podolsk

Obninsk

Avangard

Arzamas-16
(Sarov)

Dmitrov

Penza-19 (Zarechnyy)

Yekaterinbu

Kiev

Kharkov

MOLDOVA

Konstantinovsk

Sevastopol

Black Sea

Aktau

GEORGIA

Tbilisi

*Caspian
Sea*

ARMENIA **AZERBAIJAN**

T U R K M

Site with weapon-useable fissile material*

defence-   civilian and
related site   regulatory site

                  with more than one ton

                  with less than one ton

site with no weapon-useable fissile material*

site upgraded by 1 January 2000

site upgrade ongoing

nuclear states of the former Soviet Union

non-nuclear states of the former Soviet Union

*   either highly enriched uranium (HEU) or any
       form of plutonium

Norilsk

Petropavlovsk
(naval site)

■ **Moscow**

RUSSIAN FEDERATION

KAZAKSTAN

Vladivostok
(naval site/refuelling)

*Lake
Baikal*

rdlovsk-44 (Novouralsk)
Sverdlovsk-45

Zlatoust-36 (Trekhgornyy)

Beloyarsk
Sverdlovsk

Tomsk

Tomsk-7 (Seversk)

Krasnoyarsk-26 (Zheleznogorsk)
Krasnoyarsk-45 (Zelenogorsk)

Novosibirsk

Chelyabinsk-65 (Ozersk)
Chelyabinsk-70-(Snezhinsk)

MONGOLIA

Semipalatinsk

Ust-Kamenogorsk

CHINA

K A Z A K S T A N

Almaty

U Z B E K I S T A N

Tashkent

K Y R G Y Z S T A N

TAJIKISTAN

ISTAN

TAN

This map describes selected sites in the
former Soviet Union cooperating with
the US nuclear material protection,
control and accounting (MPC&A)
programme. The programme is intended
to reduce the threat of nuclear
proliferation and nuclear terrorism by
improving the security of nuclear
material in the states of the former Soviet
Union. Russia and the other newly
independent states inherited 650 metric
tons of highly enriched uranium and
plutonium from the Soviet Union.

The MPC&A programme began in 1993.
Since then, the US Department of Energy
has spent $481.2m on its activities. By
February 2000, around 50 tons of nuclear
material had been stored in secured
buildings. By 2006, 400 tons – 60% of
the inherited total – is scheduled to have
been secured.

The Middle East *The peace process: West Bank and Gaza*

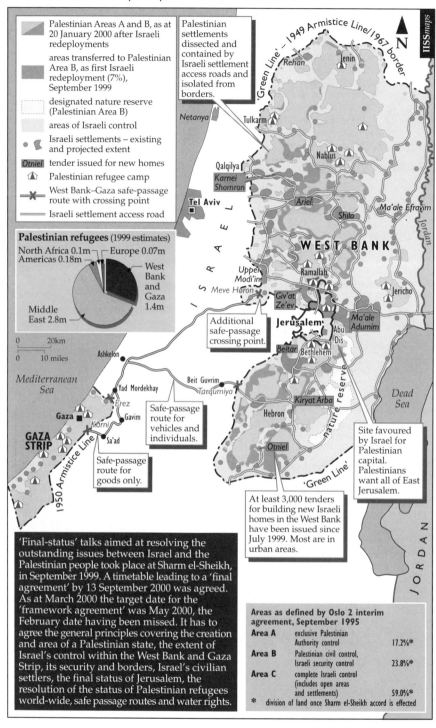

Palestinian Areas A and B, as at 20 January 2000 after Israeli redeployments

areas transferred to Palestinian Area B, as first Israeli redeployment (7%), September 1999

designated nature reserve (Palestinian Area B)

areas of Israeli control

Israeli settlements – existing and projected extent

Otniel tender issued for new homes

Palestinian refugee camp

West Bank–Gaza safe-passage route with crossing point

Israeli settlement access road

Palestinian settlements dissected and contained by Israeli settlement access roads and isolated from borders.

Palestinian refugees (1999 estimates)
North Africa 0.1m — Europe 0.07m
Americas 0.18m
West Bank and Gaza 1.4m
Middle East 2.8m

0   20km
0   10 miles

Additional safe-passage crossing point.

Safe-passage route for vehicles and individuals.

Safe-passage route for goods only.

Site favoured by Israel for Palestinian capital. Palestinians want all of East Jerusalem.

At least 3,000 tenders for building new Israeli homes in the West Bank have been issued since July 1999. Most are in urban areas.

'Final-status' talks aimed at resolving the outstanding issues between Israel and the Palestinian people took place at Sharm el-Sheikh, in September 1999. A timetable leading to a 'final agreement' by 13 September 2000 was agreed. As at March 2000 the target date for the 'framework agreement' was May 2000, the February date having been missed. It has to agree the general principles covering the creation and area of a Palestinian state, the extent of Israel's control within the West Bank and Gaza Strip, its security and borders, Israel's civilian settlers, the final status of Jerusalem, the resolution of the status of Palestinian refugees world-wide, safe passage routes and water rights.

Areas as defined by Oslo 2 interim agreement, September 1995

Area A	exclusive Palestinian Authority control	17.2%*
Area B	Palestinian civil control, Israeli security control	23.8%*
Area C	complete Israeli control (includes open areas and settlements)	59.0%*

* division of land once Sharm el-Sheikh accord is effected

The Middle East *The Golan Heights*

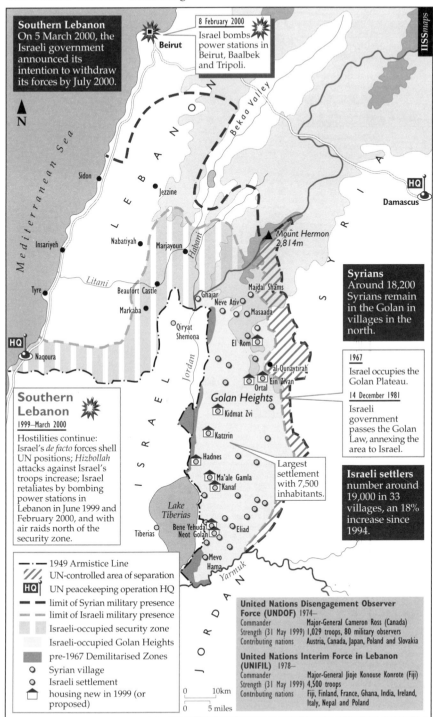

Southern Lebanon
On 5 March 2000, the Israeli government announced its intention to withdraw its forces by July 2000.

8 February 2000
Israel bombs power stations in Beirut, Baalbek and Tripoli.

N

Syrians
Around 18,200 Syrians remain in the Golan in villages in the north.

1967
Israel occupies the Golan Plateau.

14 December 1981
Israeli government passes the Golan Law, annexing the area to Israel.

Israeli settlers number around 19,000 in 33 villages, an 18% increase since 1994.

Southern Lebanon
1999–March 2000
Hostilities continue: Israel's *de facto* forces shell UN positions; *Hizbollah* attacks against Israel's troops increase; Israel retaliates by bombing power stations in Lebanon in June 1999 and February 2000, and with air raids north of the security zone.

Largest settlement with 7,500 inhabitants.

Beirut · Sidon · Jezzine · Insariyeh · Nabatiyah · Marjayoun · Tyre · Beaufort Castle · Markaba · Ghajar · Neve Ativ · Majdal Shams · Masaada · Qiryat Shemona · El Rom · al-Qunaytirah · Ein Zivan · Ortal · Golan Heights · Kidmat Zvi · Katzrin · Hadnes · Ma'ale Gamla · Kanaf · Lake Tiberias · Bene Yehuda · Neot Golan · Eliad · Tiberias · Mevo Hama · Naqoura · Damascus

Mediterranean Sea · Bekaa Valley · Litani · Hasbani · Jordan · Mount Hermon 2,814m · Yarmuk

LEBANON · SYRIA · ISRAEL · JORDAN

Mount Hermon 2,814m

Legend:
- 1949 Armistice Line
- UN-controlled area of separation
- **HQ** UN peacekeeping operation HQ
- limit of Syrian military presence
- limit of Israeli military presence
- Israeli-occupied security zone
- Israeli-occupied Golan Heights
- pre-1967 Demilitarised Zones
- ○ Syrian village
- ○ Israeli settlement
- ⌂ housing new in 1999 (or proposed)

0   10km
0   5 miles

United Nations Disengagement Observer Force (UNDOF) 1974–
Commander   Major-General Cameron Ross (Canada)
Strength (31 May 1999) 1,029 troops, 80 military observers
Contributing nations   Austria, Canada, Japan, Poland and Slovakia

United Nations Interim Force in Lebanon (UNIFIL) 1978–
Commander   Major-General Jioje Konouse Konrote (Fiji)
Strength (31 May 1999) 4,500 troops
Contributing nations   Fiji, Finland, France, Ghana, India, Ireland, Italy, Nepal and Poland

IISSmaps

Central Asia and the Caucasus *Conflict and trouble-spots in Central Asia*

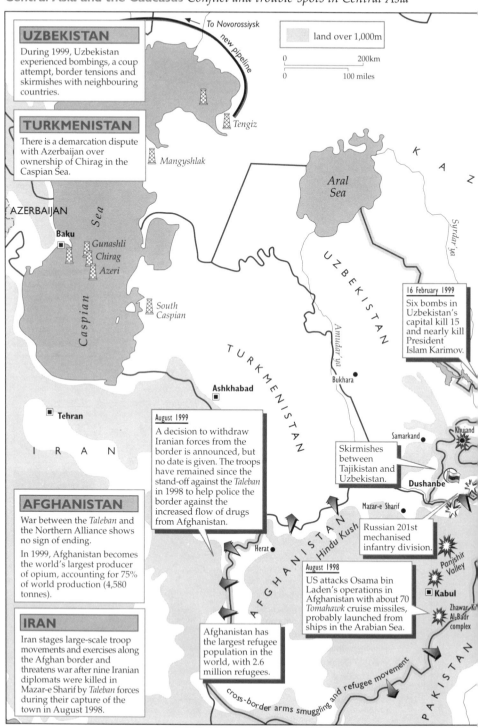

UZBEKISTAN

During 1999, Uzbekistan experienced bombings, a coup attempt, border tensions and skirmishes with neighbouring countries.

TURKMENISTAN

There is a demarcation dispute with Azerbaijan over ownership of Chirag in the Caspian Sea.

land over 1,000m

0   200km
0   100 miles

To Novorossiysk

new pipeline

Tengiz

Mangyshlak

Aral Sea

AZERBAIJAN

Baku

Gunashli
Chirag
Azeri

South Caspian

Caspian Sea

Syrdar'ya

U Z B E K I S T A N

Amudar'ya

16 February 1999

Six bombs in Uzbekistan's capital kill 15 and nearly kill President Islam Karimov.

Bukhara

T U R K M E N I S T A N

Ashkhabad

Samarkand   Khujand

Tehran

I   R   A   N

August 1999

A decision to withdraw Iranian forces from the border is announced, but no date is given. The troops have remained since the stand-off against the *Taleban* in 1998 to help police the border against the increased flow of drugs from Afghanistan.

Skirmishes between Tajikistan and Uzbekistan.

Dushanbe

AFGHANISTAN

War between the *Taleban* and the Northern Alliance shows no sign of ending.

In 1999, Afghanistan becomes the world's largest producer of opium, accounting for 75% of world production (4,580 tonnes).

IRAN

Iran stages large-scale troop movements and exercises along the Afghan border and threatens war after nine Iranian diplomats were killed in Mazar-e Sharif by *Taleban* forces during their capture of the town in August 1998.

Herat

Hindu Kush

Mazar-e Sharif

Russian 201st mechanised infantry division.

Panjshir Valley

August 1998

US attacks Osama bin Laden's operations in Afghanistan with about 70 *Tomahawk* cruise missiles, probably launched from ships in the Arabian Sea.

Kabul

A F G H A N I S T A N

Zhawar Kili Al-Badr complex

Afghanistan has the largest refugee population in the world, with 2.6 million refugees.

cross-border arms smuggling and refugee movement

P A K I S T A N

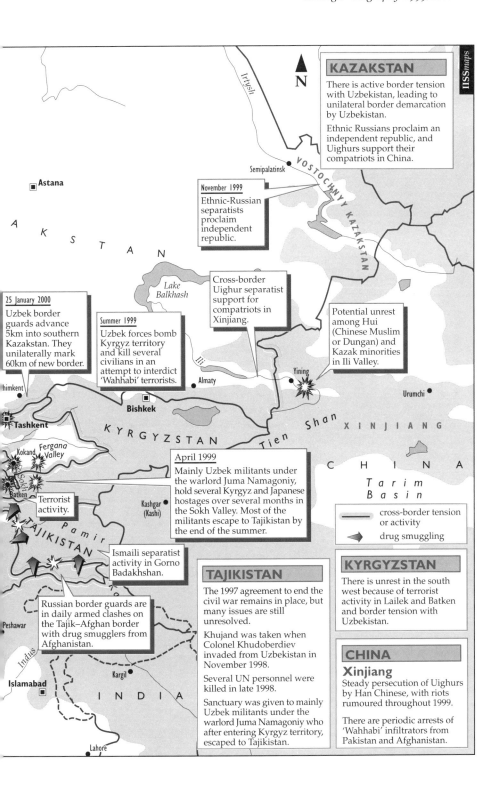

KAZAKSTAN

There is active border tension with Uzbekistan, leading to unilateral border demarcation by Uzbekistan.

Ethnic Russians proclaim an independent republic, and Uighurs support their compatriots in China.

November 1999
Ethnic-Russian separatists proclaim independent republic.

25 January 2000
Uzbek border guards advance 5km into southern Kazakstan. They unilaterally mark 60km of new border.

Summer 1999
Uzbek forces bomb Kyrgyz territory and kill several civilians in an attempt to interdict 'Wahhabi' terrorists.

Cross-border Uighur separatist support for compatriots in Xinjiang.

Potential unrest among Hui (Chinese Muslim or Dungan) and Kazak minorities in Ili Valley.

April 1999
Mainly Uzbek militants under the warlord Juma Namagoniy, hold several Kyrgyz and Japanese hostages over several months in the Sokh Valley. Most of the militants escape to Tajikistan by the end of the summer.

Terrorist activity.

Ismaili separatist activity in Gorno Badakhshan.

Russian border guards are in daily armed clashes on the Tajik–Afghan border with drug smugglers from Afghanistan.

cross-border tension or activity

drug smuggling

TAJIKISTAN

The 1997 agreement to end the civil war remains in place, but many issues are still unresolved.

Khujand was taken when Colonel Khudoberdiev invaded from Uzbekistan in November 1998.

Several UN personnel were killed in late 1998.

Sanctuary was given to mainly Uzbek militants under the warlord Juma Namagoniy who after entering Kyrgyz territory, escaped to Tajikistan.

KYRGYZSTAN

There is unrest in the south west because of terrorist activity in Lailek and Batken and border tension with Uzbekistan.

CHINA

Xinjiang
Steady persecution of Uighurs by Han Chinese, with riots rumoured throughout 1999.

There are periodic arrests of 'Wahhabi' infiltrators from Pakistan and Afghanistan.

Central Asia and the Caucasus *Conflict in the Caucasus*

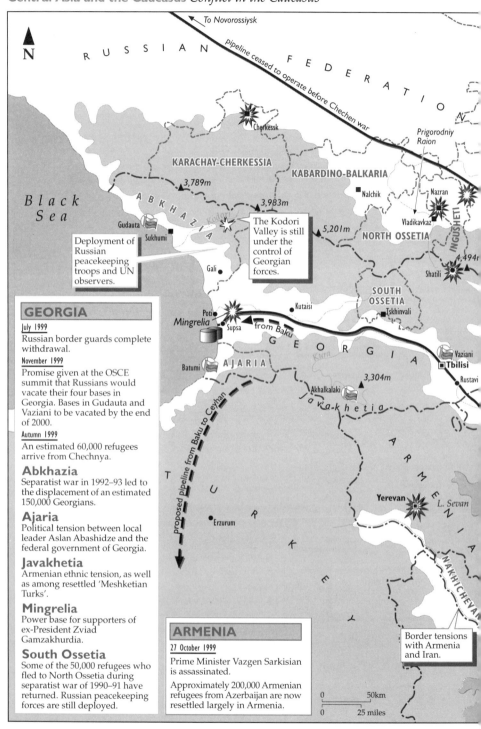

N

To Novorossiysk

R U S S I A N

Pipeline ceased to operate before Chechen war

F E D E R A T I O N

Prigorodniy Raion

Cherkessk

KARACHAY-CHERKESSIA

3,789m

KABARDINO-BALKARIA

■ Nalchik

Nazran

Black Sea

A B K H A Z I A

Kodori

3,983m

5,201m

Vladikavkaz ■

NORTH OSSETIA

INGUSHETI

Gudauta

Sukhumi ■

> The Kodori Valley is still under the control of Georgian forces.

4,494m

> Deployment of Russian peacekeeping troops and UN observers.

Gali ●

Shatili ▲

SOUTH OSSETIA

Kutaisi

Tskhinvali ■

GEORGIA

July 1999
Russian border guards complete withdrawal.

November 1999
Promise given at the OSCE summit that Russians would vacate their four bases in Georgia. Bases in Gudauta and Vaziani to be vacated by the end of 2000.

Autumn 1999
An estimated 60,000 refugees arrive from Chechnya.

Abkhazia
Separatist war in 1992–93 led to the displacement of an estimated 150,000 Georgians.

Ajaria
Political tension between local leader Aslan Abashidze and the federal government of Georgia.

Javakhetia
Armenian ethnic tension, as well as among resettled 'Meshketian Turks'.

Mingrelia
Power base for supporters of ex-President Zviad Gamzakhurdia.

South Ossetia
Some of the 50,000 refugees who fled to North Ossetia during separatist war of 1990–91 have returned. Russian peacekeeping forces are still deployed.

Mingrelia
Poti ●

Supsa from Baku

G E O R

Kura

Vaziani

Batumi ●

AJARIA

3,304m

■ Tbilisi

Rustavi ●

Akhalkalaki

J a v a k h e t i a

Proposed pipeline from Baku to Ceyhan

T U R K E Y

● Erzurum

A R M E N I A

Yerevan

L. Sevan

NAKHICHEVAN

ARMENIA

27 October 1999
Prime Minister Vazgen Sarkisian is assassinated.

Approximately 200,000 Armenian refugees from Azerbaijan are now resettled largely in Armenia.

> Border tensions with Armenia and Iran.

| 0 | 50km |
| 0 | 25 miles |

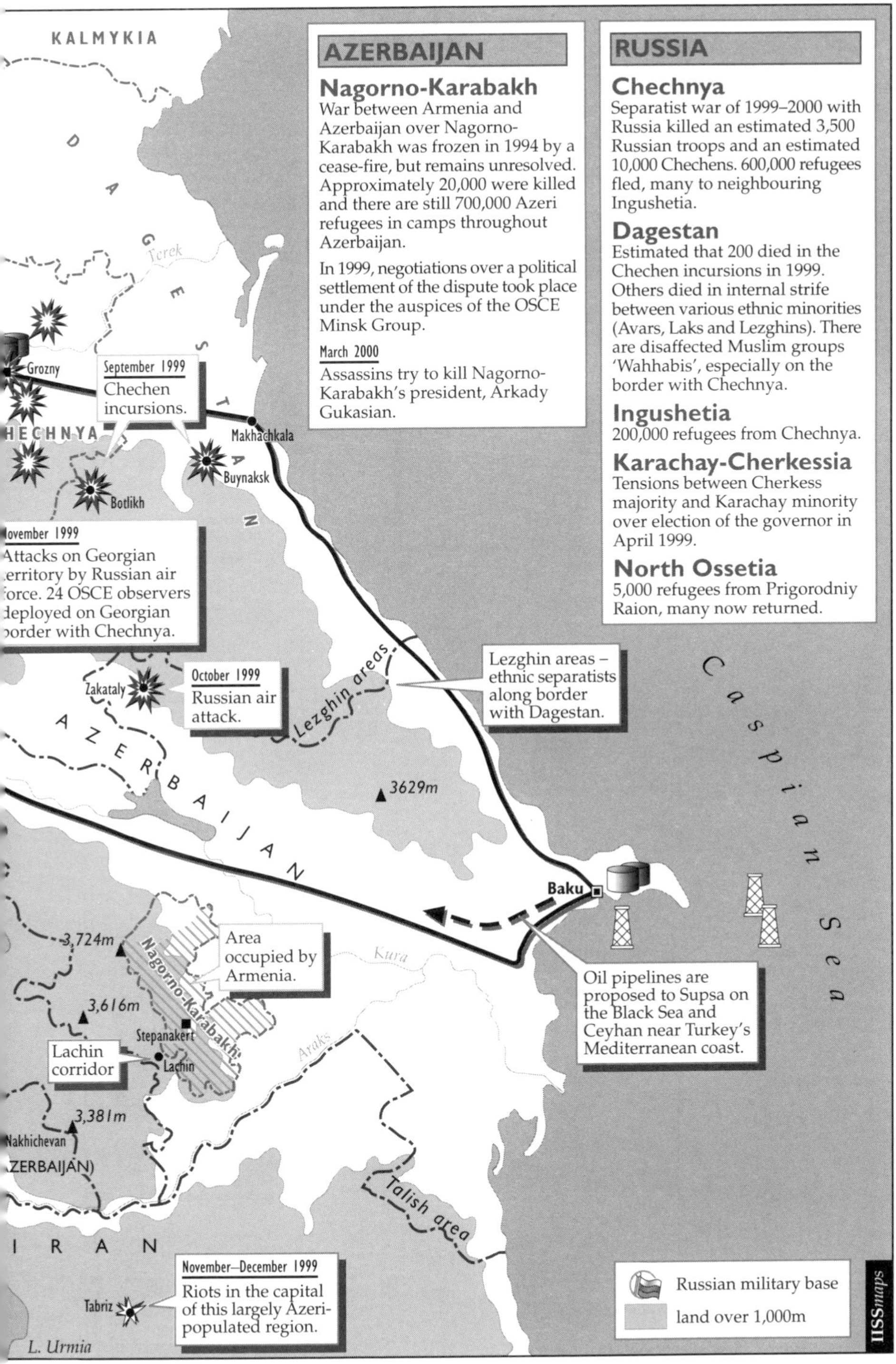
KALMYKIA
DAGESTAN
Terek
Grozny
CHECHNYA
Makhachkala
Buynaksk
Botlikh
AZERBAIJAN
Nagorno-Karabakh
War between Armenia and Azerbaijan over Nagorno-Karabakh was frozen in 1994 by a cease-fire, but remains unresolved. Approximately 20,000 were killed and there are still 700,000 Azeri refugees in camps throughout Azerbaijan.
In 1999, negotiations over a political settlement of the dispute took place under the auspices of the OSCE Minsk Group.
March 2000
Assassins try to kill Nagorno-Karabakh's president, Arkady Gukasian.
RUSSIA
Chechnya
Separatist war of 1999–2000 with Russia killed an estimated 3,500 Russian troops and an estimated 10,000 Chechens. 600,000 refugees fled, many to neighbouring Ingushetia.
Dagestan
Estimated that 200 died in the Chechen incursions in 1999. Others died in internal strife between various ethnic minorities (Avars, Laks and Lezghins). There are disaffected Muslim groups 'Wahhabis', especially on the border with Chechnya.
Ingushetia
200,000 refugees from Chechnya.
Karachay-Cherkessia
Tensions between Cherkess majority and Karachay minority over election of the governor in April 1999.
North Ossetia
5,000 refugees from Prigorodniy Raion, many now returned.
September 1999
Chechen incursions.
ovember 1999
Attacks on Georgian erritory by Russian air orce. 24 OSCE observers leployed on Georgian order with Chechnya.
October 1999
Russian air attack.
Zakataly
Lezghin areas
Lezghin areas – ethnic separatists along border with Dagestan.
Caspian Sea
3629m
Baku
Oil pipelines are proposed to Supsa on the Black Sea and Ceyhan near Turkey's Mediterranean coast.
Kura
3,724m
Area occupied by Armenia.
3,616m
Stepanakert
Lachin corridor
Lachin
Araks
3,381m
Nakhichevan
ZERBAIJAN)
Talish area
IRAN
November–December 1999
Riots in the capital of this largely Azeri-populated region.
Tabriz
L. Urmia
Russian military base
land over 1,000m
IISSmaps

Central Asia and the Caucasus *The Chechen war*

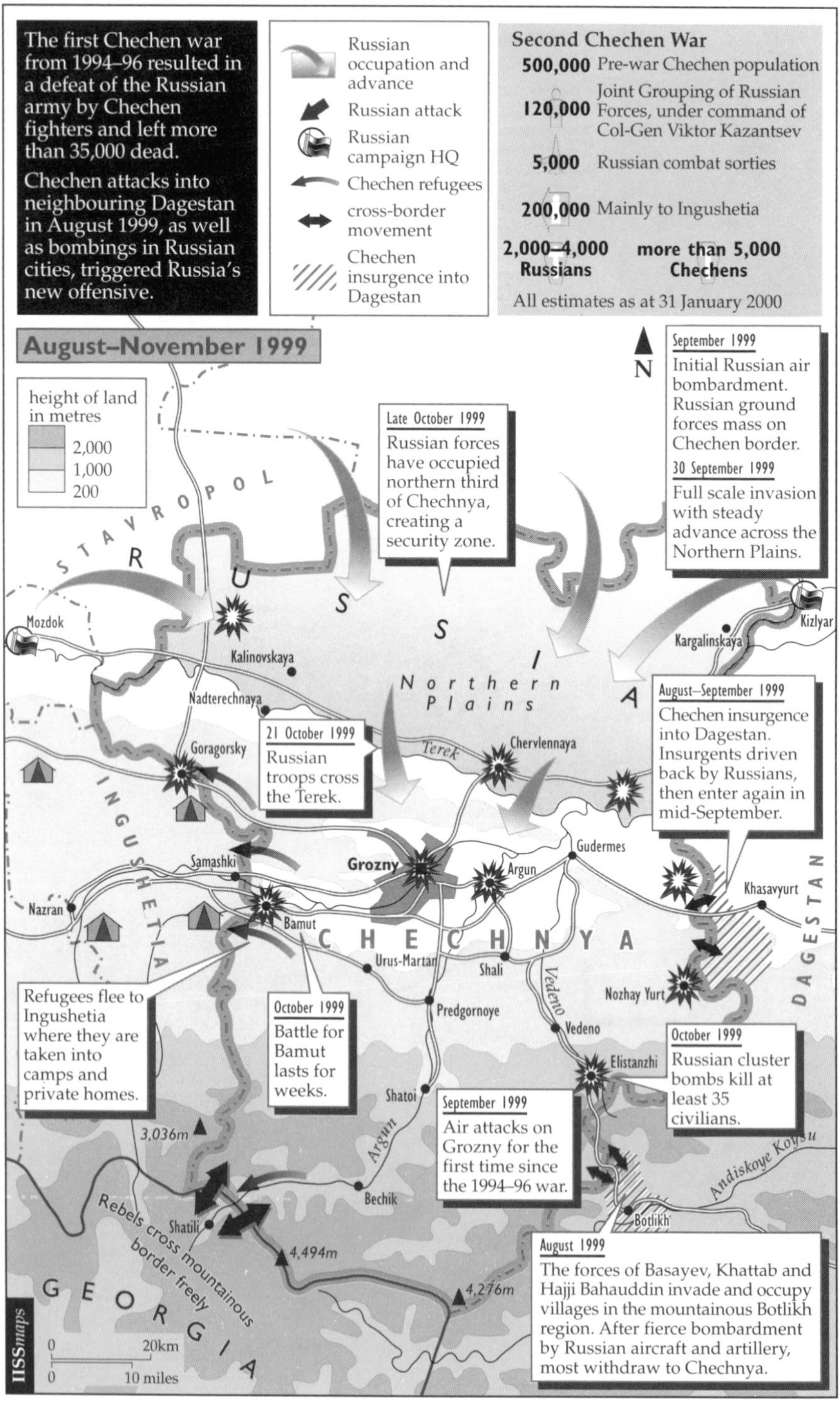
The first Chechen war from 1994–96 resulted in a defeat of the Russian army by Chechen fighters and left more than 35,000 dead.
Chechen attacks into neighbouring Dagestan in August 1999, as well as bombings in Russian cities, triggered Russia's new offensive.
Russian occupation and advance
Russian attack
Russian campaign HQ
Chechen refugees
cross-border movement
Chechen insurgence into Dagestan
Second Chechen War
500,000 Pre-war Chechen population
120,000 Joint Grouping of Russian Forces, under command of Col-Gen Viktor Kazantsev
5,000 Russian combat sorties
200,000 Mainly to Ingushetia
2,000–4,000 Russians
more than 5,000 Chechens
All estimates as at 31 January 2000
August–November 1999
height of land in metres
2,000
1,000
200
N
September 1999
Initial Russian air bombardment. Russian ground forces mass on Chechen border.
30 September 1999
Full scale invasion with steady advance across the Northern Plains.
Late October 1999
Russian forces have occupied northern third of Chechnya, creating a security zone.
STAVROPOL
RUSSIA
Mozdok
Kalinovskaya
Kizlyar
Kargalinskaya
Northern Plains
Nadterechnaya
21 October 1999
Russian troops cross the Terek.
Goragorsky
Terek
Chervlennaya
August–September 1999
Chechen insurgence into Dagestan. Insurgents driven back by Russians, then enter again in mid-September.
INGUSHETIA
Samashki
Grozny
Argun
Gudermes
Khasavyurt
Nazran
Bamut
CHECHNYA
DAGESTAN
Urus-Martan
Shali
Vedeno
Nozhay Yurt
Predgornoye
Vedeno
Refugees flee to Ingushetia where they are taken into camps and private homes.
October 1999
Battle for Bamut lasts for weeks.
Elistanzhi
October 1999
Russian cluster bombs kill at least 35 civilians.
Shatoi
September 1999
Air attacks on Grozny for the first time since the 1994–96 war.
3,036m
Argun
Andiskoye Koysu
Bechik
Botlikh
Rebels cross mountainous border freely
Shatili
4,494m
4,276m
August 1999
The forces of Basayev, Khattab and Hajji Bahauddin invade and occupy villages in the mountainous Botlikh region. After fierce bombardment by Russian aircraft and artillery, most withdraw to Chechnya.
GEORGIA
0 20km
0 10 miles
IISSmaps

Central Asia and the Caucasus *The battle for Grozny*

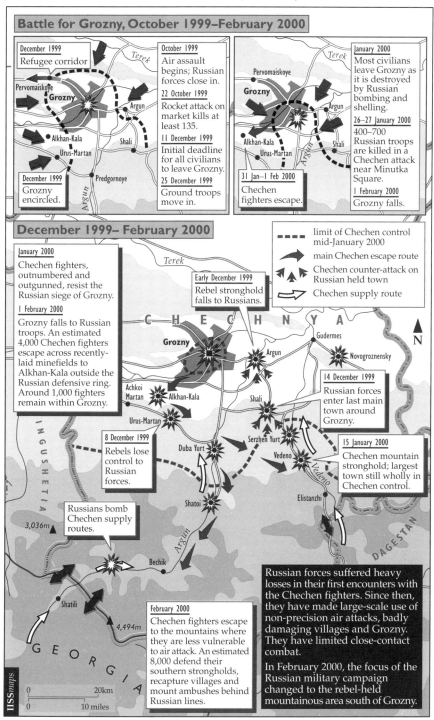

Battle for Grozny, October 1999–February 2000

December 1999
Refugee corridor

October 1999
Air assault begins; Russian forces close in.

22 October 1999
Rocket attack on market kills at least 135.

11 December 1999
Initial deadline for all civilians to leave Grozny.

25 December 1999
Ground troops move in.

December 1999
Grozny encircled.

January 2000
Most civilians leave Grozny as it is destroyed by Russian bombing and shelling.

26–27 January 2000
400–700 Russian troops are killed in a Chechen attack near Minutka Square.

31 Jan–1 Feb 2000
Chechen fighters escape.

1 February 2000
Grozny falls.

December 1999– February 2000

January 2000
Chechen fighters, outnumbered and outgunned, resist the Russian siege of Grozny.

1 February 2000
Grozny falls to Russian troops. An estimated 4,000 Chechen fighters escape across recently-laid minefields to Alkhan-Kala outside the Russian defensive ring. Around 1,000 fighters remain within Grozny.

Early December 1999
Rebel stronghold falls to Russians.

14 December 1999
Russian forces enter last main town around Grozny.

8 December 1999
Rebels lose control to Russian forces.

15 January 2000
Chechen mountain stronghold; largest town still wholly in Chechen control.

Russians bomb Chechen supply routes.

February 2000
Chechen fighters escape to the mountains where they are less vulnerable to air attack. An estimated 8,000 defend their southern strongholds, recapture villages and mount ambushes behind Russian lines.

- - - - limit of Chechen control mid-January 2000

main Chechen escape route

Chechen counter-attack on Russian held town

Chechen supply route

Russian forces suffered heavy losses in their first encounters with the Chechen fighters. Since then, they have made large-scale use of non-precision air attacks, badly damaging villages and Grozny. They have limited close-contact combat.

In February 2000, the focus of the Russian military campaign changed to the rebel-held mountainous area south of Grozny.

IISSmaps

0   20km
0   10 miles

Asia *The Kashmir dispute*

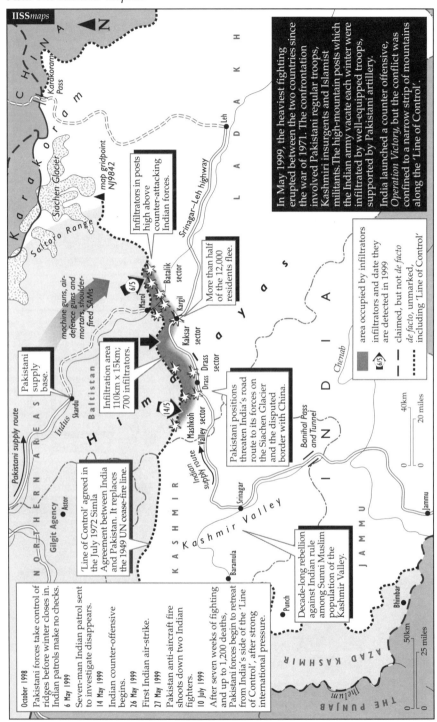

IISS*maps*

map gridpoint NJ9842

Infiltrators in posts high above counter-attacking Indian forces.

More than half of the 12,000 residents flee.

machine guns, air-defence guns and mortars, shoulder-fired SAMs

Pakistani supply base.

Infiltration area 110km x 15km; 700 infiltrators.

Pakistani positions threaten India's road route to its forces on the Siachen Glacier and the disputed border with China.

'Line of Control' agreed in the July 1972 Simla Agreement between India and Pakistan. It replaces the 1949 UN cease-fire line.

Decade-long rebellion against Indian rule among Sunni Muslim population of the Kashmir Valley.

In May 1999, the heaviest fighting erupted between the two countries since the war of 1971. The confrontation involved Pakistani regular troops, Kashmiri insurgents and Islamist militants. The high-mountain posts which the Indian army vacate each winter were infiltrated by well-equipped troops, supported by Pakistani artillery. India launched a counter offensive, *Operation Victory*, but the conflict was confined to a narrow strip of mountains along the 'Line of Control'.

area occupied by infiltrators

infiltrators and date they are detected in 1999

claimed, but not *de facto de facto*, unmarked, including 'Line of Control'

October 1998
Pakistani forces take control of ridges before winter closes in. Indian patrols make no checks.

6 May 1999
Seven-man Indian patrol sent to investigate disappears.

14 May 1999
Indian counter-offensive begins.

26 May 1999
First Indian air-strike.

27 May 1999
Pakistan anti-aircraft fire shoots down two Indian fighters.

10 July 1999
After seven weeks of fighting and up to 1,200 deaths, Pakistani forces begin to retreat from India's side of the 'Line of Control', after strong international pressure.

Karakoram Pass

C H I N A

Siachen Glacier

Saltoro Range

K a r a k o r a m

Leh

L A D A K H

Srinagar–Leh highway

Batalik sector

Kargil

Marol

6/5

Kaksar sector

Drass sector

Drass

Mashkoh Valley sector

14/5

H i m a l a y a s

Chenab

N O R T H E R N   A R E A S

Pakistani supply route

Skardu

Indus

Baltistan

Gilgit Agency

Astor

K A S H M I R

Kashmir Valley

Indian route supply

Srinagar

Baramula

Banihal Pass and Tunnel

Jammu

I N D I A

J A M M U

Punch

Bhimbar

A Z A D   K A S H M I R

Jhelum

T H E   P U N J A B

40km

20 miles

50km

25 miles

Asia *Sri Lanka's civil war*

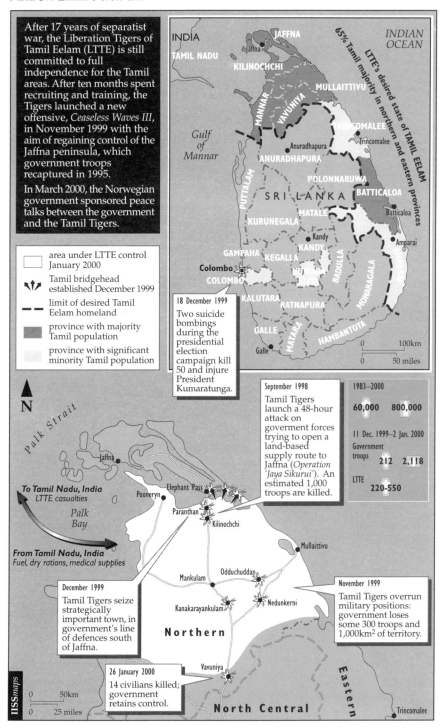

After 17 years of separatist war, the Liberation Tigers of Tamil Eelam (LTTE) is still committed to full independence for the Tamil areas. After ten months spent recruiting and training, the Tigers launched a new offensive, *Ceaseless Waves III*, in November 1999 with the aim of regaining control of the Jaffna peninsula, which government troops recaptured in 1995.

In March 2000, the Norwegian government sponsored peace talks between the government and the Tamil Tigers.

area under LTTE control January 2000

Tamil bridgehead established December 1999

limit of desired Tamil Eelam homeland

province with majority Tamil population

province with significant minority Tamil population

65% Tamil majority in northern and eastern provinces

LTTE's desired state of TAMIL EELAM

INDIA

TAMIL NADU

INDIAN OCEAN

JAFFNA, Jaffna, KILINOCHCHI, MULLAITTIVU, MANNAR, VAVUNIYA, TRINCOMALEE, Trincomalee, Anuradhapura, ANURADHAPURA, POLONNARUWA, BATTICALOA, Batticaloa, PUTTALAM, SRI LANKA, MATALE, KURUNEGALA, Kandy, KANDY, Amparai, GAMPAHA, KEGALLA, BADULLA, MONARAGALA, Colombo, COLOMBO, KALUTARA, RATNAPURA, GALLE, MATARA, HAMBANTOTA, Galle

Gulf of Mannar

18 December 1999
Two suicide bombings during the presidential election campaign kill 50 and injure President Kumaratunga.

September 1998
Tamil Tigers launch a 48-hour attack on goverment forces trying to open a land-based supply route to Jaffna (*Operation 'Jaya Sikurui'*). An estimated 1,000 troops are killed.

1983–2000
60,000   800,000

11 Dec. 1999–2 Jan. 2000
Government troops 212   2,118
LTTE   220-550

N

Palk Strait

To Tamil Nadu, India
LTTE casualties

Palk Bay

From Tamil Nadu, India
Fuel, dry rations, medical supplies

Jaffna, Pooneryn, Elephant Pass, Paranthan, Kilinochchi, Mullaittivu, Mankulam, Odduchuddan, Kanakarayankulam, Nedunkerni

December 1999
Tamil Tigers seize strategically important town, in government's line of defences south of Jaffna.

November 1999
Tamil Tigers overrun military positions: government loses some 300 troops and 1,000km² of territory.

Northern

26 January 2000
14 civilians killed; government retains control.

Vavuniya

Eastern

North Central

Trincomalee

IISSmaps

0   50km
0   25 miles

0   100km
0   50 miles

Asia *Indonesia: sources of instability*

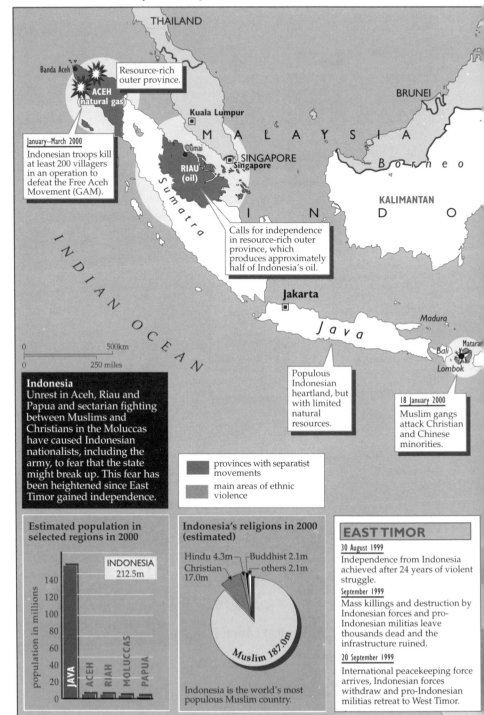

THAILAND

Banda Aceh

ACEH
(natural gas)

Resource-rich
outer province.

January–March 2000
Indonesian troops kill
at least 200 villagers
in an operation to
defeat the Free Aceh
Movement (GAM).

Kuala Lumpur

M A L A Y S I A

BRUNEI

Dumai

SINGAPORE
Singapore

RIAU
(oil)

B o r n e o

KALIMANTAN

I N D O

Sumatra

Calls for independence
in resource-rich outer
province, which
produces approximately
half of Indonesia's oil.

I N D I A N   O C E A N

Jakarta

Madura

J a v a

Bali
Lombok

Mataram

0   500km
0   250 miles

Indonesia
Unrest in Aceh, Riau and
Papua and sectarian fighting
between Muslims and
Christians in the Moluccas
have caused Indonesian
nationalists, including the
army, to fear that the state
might break up. This fear has
been heightened since East
Timor gained independence.

Populous
Indonesian
heartland, but
with limited
natural
resources.

18 January 2000
Muslim gangs
attack Christian
and Chinese
minorities.

provinces with separatist
movements

main areas of ethnic
violence

**Estimated population in
selected regions in 2000**

INDONESIA
212.5m

140
120
100
80
60
40
20
0

population in millions

JAVA
ACEH
RIAH
MOLUCCAS
PAPUA

**Indonesia's religions in 2000
(estimated)**

Hindu 4.3m — ┌Buddhist 2.1m
Christian ─   └ others 2.1m
17.0m

Muslim 187.0m

Indonesia is the world's most
populous Muslim country.

EAST TIMOR

30 August 1999
Independence from Indonesia
achieved after 24 years of violent
struggle.

September 1999
Mass killings and destruction by
Indonesian forces and pro-
Indonesian militias leave
thousands dead and the
infrastructure ruined.

20 September 1999
International peacekeeping force
arrives, Indonesian forces
withdraw and pro-Indonesian
militias retreat to West Timor.

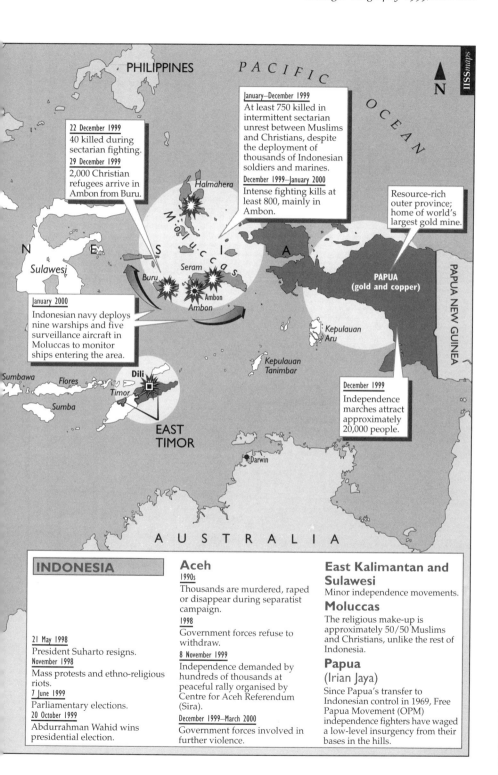

22 December 1999
40 killed during sectarian fighting.
29 December 1999
2,000 Christian refugees arrive in Ambon from Buru.

January–December 1999
At least 750 killed in intermittent sectarian unrest between Muslims and Christians, despite the deployment of thousands of Indonesian soldiers and marines.
December 1999–January 2000
Intense fighting kills at least 800, mainly in Ambon.

Resource-rich outer province; home of world's largest gold mine.

January 2000
Indonesian navy deploys nine warships and five surveillance aircraft in Moluccas to monitor ships entering the area.

December 1999
Independence marches attract approximately 20,000 people.

PHILIPPINES · PACIFIC OCEAN · N · IISS*maps*
Halmahera · Sulawesi · Buru · Seram · Ambon · PAPUA (gold and copper) · PAPUA NEW GUINEA · Kepulauan Aru · Kepulauan Tanimbar · Sumbawa · Flores · Dili · Timor · Sumba · EAST TIMOR · Darwin · AUSTRALIA · MOLUCCAS

INDONESIA

21 May 1998
President Suharto resigns.
November 1998
Mass protests and ethno-religious riots.
7 June 1999
Parliamentary elections.
20 October 1999
Abdurrahman Wahid wins presidential election.

Aceh
1990s
Thousands are murdered, raped or disappear during separatist campaign.
1998
Government forces refuse to withdraw.
8 November 1999
Independence demanded by hundreds of thousands at peaceful rally organised by Centre for Aceh Referendum (Sira).
December 1999–March 2000
Government forces involved in further violence.

East Kalimantan and Sulawesi
Minor independence movements.
Moluccas
The religious make-up is approximately 50/50 Muslims and Christians, unlike the rest of Indonesia.
Papua
(Irian Jaya)
Since Papua's transfer to Indonesian control in 1969, Free Papua Movement (OPM) independence fighters have waged a low-level insurgency from their bases in the hills.

Asia *The crisis in East Timor*

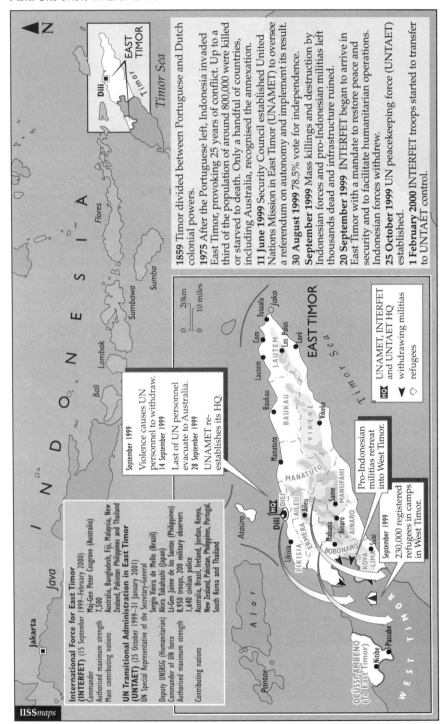

1859 Timor divided between Portuguese and Dutch colonial powers.

1975 After the Portuguese left, Indonesia invaded East Timor, provoking 25 years of conflict. Up to a third of the population of around 800,000 were killed or starved to death. Only a handful of countries, including Australia, recognised the annexation.

11 June 1999 Security Council established United Nations Mission in East Timor (UNAMET) to oversee a referendum on autonomy and implement its result.

30 August 1999 78.5% vote for independence.

September 1999 Mass killings and destruction by Indonesian forces and pro-Indonesian militias left thousands dead and infrastructure ruined.

20 September 1999 INTERFET began to arrive in East Timor with a mandate to restore peace and security and to facilitate humanitarian operations. Indonesian forces withdrew.

25 October 1999 UN peacekeeping force (UNTAET) established.

1 February 2000 INTERFET troops started to transfer to UNTAET control.

September 1999
Violence causes UN personnel to withdraw.
14 September 1999
Last of UN personnel evacuate to Australia.
28 September 1999
UNAMET re-establishes its HQ.

Pro-Indonesian militias retreat into West Timor.

September 1999
230,000 registered refugees in camps in West Timor.

International Force for East Timor (INTERFET) (15 September 1999–February 2000)
Commander — Maj-Gen Peter Cosgrove (Australia)
Authorised maximum strength — 7,500
Main contributing nations — Australia, Bangladesh, Fiji, Malaysia, New Zealand, Pakistan Philippines and Thailand

UN Transitional Administration in East Timor (UNTAET) (25 October 1999–31 January 2001)
UN Special Representative of the Secretary-General — Sergio Vieira de Mello (Brazil)
Deputy UNSRSG (Humanitarian) — Akira Takahashi (Japan)
Commander of UN force — Lt-Gen Jaime de los Santos (Philippines)
Authorised maximum strength — 8,950 troops, 200 military observers
— 1,640 civilian police
Contributing nations — Australia, Brazil, Ireland, Jordan, Kenya, New Zealand, Pakistan, Philippines, Portugal, South Korea and Thailand

Key:
HQ UNAMET, INTERFET and UNTAET HQ
▼ withdrawing militias
◇ refugees

0 20km
0 10 miles

EAST TIMOR

OCUSSI-AMBENO (To East Timor)

IISSmaps

Africa *Angola: a new upsurge in fighting*

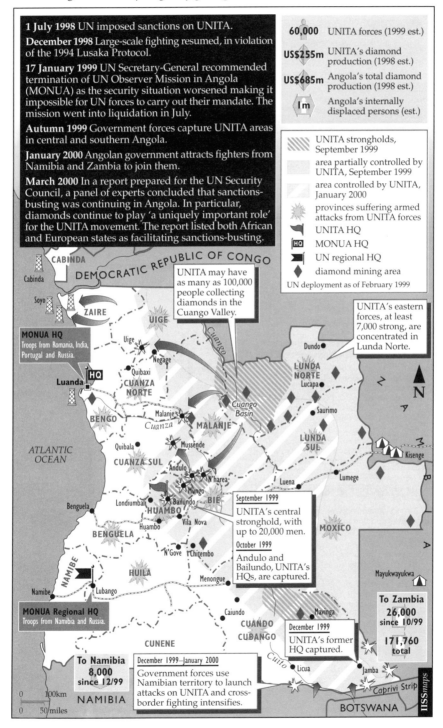

1 July 1998 UN imposed sanctions on UNITA.

December 1998 Large-scale fighting resumed, in violation of the 1994 Lusaka Protocol.

17 January 1999 UN Secretary-General recommended termination of UN Observer Mission in Angola (MONUA) as the security situation worsened making it impossible for UN forces to carry out their mandate. The mission went into liquidation in July.

Autumn 1999 Government forces capture UNITA areas in central and southern Angola.

January 2000 Angolan government attracts fighters from Namibia and Zambia to join them.

March 2000 In a report prepared for the UN Security Council, a panel of experts concluded that sanctions-busting was continuing in Angola. In particular, diamonds continue to play 'a uniquely important role' for the UNITA movement. The report listed both African and European states as facilitating sanctions-busting.

60,000	UNITA forces (1999 est.)
US$255m	UNITA's diamond production (1998 est.)
US$685m	Angola's total diamond production (1998 est.)
1m	Angola's internally displaced persons (est.)

UNITA strongholds, September 1999

area partially controlled by UNITA, September 1999

area controlled by UNITA, January 2000

provinces suffering armed attacks from UNITA forces

UNITA HQ

MONUA HQ

UN regional HQ

diamond mining area

UN deployment as of February 1999

UNITA may have as many as 100,000 people collecting diamonds in the Cuango Valley.

UNITA's eastern forces, at least 7,000 strong, are concentrated in Lunda Norte.

MONUA HQ Troops from Romania, India, Portugal and Russia.

September 1999 UNITA's central stronghold, with up to 20,000 men.

October 1999 Andulo and Bailundo, UNITA's HQs, are captured.

MONUA Regional HQ Troops from Namibia and Russia.

December 1999 UNITA's former HQ captured.

To Zambia	
26,000	since 10/99
171,760	**total**

To Namibia	
8,000	since 12/99

December 1999–January 2000 Government forces use Namibian territory to launch attacks on UNITA and cross-border fighting intensifies.

CABINDA
Cabinda
DEMOCRATIC REPUBLIC OF CONGO
Soyo
ZAIRE
UIGE
MONUA HQ
Uige
Cuango
Dundo
Negage
LUNDA NORTE
Lucapa
Quibaxi
Luanda HQ
CUANZA NORTE
BENGO
Malanje
Cuango Basin
Saurimo
Cuanza
MALANJE
ATLANTIC OCEAN
Quibala
Mussende
LUNDA SUL
Kisenge
CUANZA SUL
Andulo
Lumege
N'harea
Luena
Mungo
Bailundo
BIE
Londiumbali
HUAMBO
Benguela
Vila Nova
MOXICO
Huambo
BENGUELA
N'Gove
Chitembo
Mayukwayukwa
HUILA
Menongue
Namibe
Lubango
Caiundo
Mavinga
CUANDO CUBANGO
CUNENE
Cuito
Licua
Jamba
NAMIBIA
Caprivi Strip
BOTSWANA

0 100km
0 50 miles

N

IISSmaps

Africa *Horn of Africa: war, conflict and refugees*

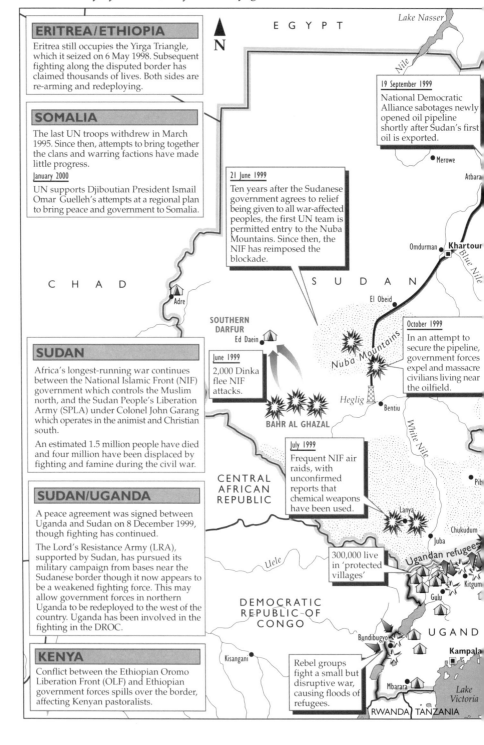

ERITREA/ETHIOPIA

Eritrea still occupies the Yirga Triangle, which it seized on 6 May 1998. Subsequent fighting along the disputed border has claimed thousands of lives. Both sides are re-arming and redeploying.

SOMALIA

The last UN troops withdrew in March 1995. Since then, attempts to bring together the clans and warring factions have made little progress.

January 2000

UN supports Djiboutian President Ismail Omar Guelleh's attempts at a regional plan to bring peace and government to Somalia.

SUDAN

Africa's longest-running war continues between the National Islamic Front (NIF) government which controls the Muslim north, and the Sudan People's Liberation Army (SPLA) under Colonel John Garang which operates in the animist and Christian south.

An estimated 1.5 million people have died and four million have been displaced by fighting and famine during the civil war.

SUDAN/UGANDA

A peace agreement was signed between Uganda and Sudan on 8 December 1999, though fighting has continued.

The Lord's Resistance Army (LRA), supported by Sudan, has pursued its military campaign from bases near the Sudanese border though it now appears to be a weakened fighting force. This may allow government forces in northern Uganda to be redeployed to the west of the country. Uganda has been involved in the fighting in the DROC.

KENYA

Conflict between the Ethiopian Oromo Liberation Front (OLF) and Ethiopian government forces spills over the border, affecting Kenyan pastoralists.

E G Y P T

Lake Nasser

19 September 1999

National Democratic Alliance sabotages newly opened oil pipeline shortly after Sudan's first oil is exported.

● Merowe

Atbara

21 June 1999

Ten years after the Sudanese government agrees to relief being given to all war-affected peoples, the first UN team is permitted entry to the Nuba Mountains. Since then, the NIF has reimposed the blockade.

C H A D

Adre

S U D A N

El Obeid ●

Omdurman **Khartoum**

Blue Nile

SOUTHERN DARFUR

Ed Daein ●

June 1999

2,000 Dinka flee NIF attacks.

Nuba Mountains

October 1999

In an attempt to secure the pipeline, government forces expel and massacre civilians living near the oilfield.

Heglig ● Bentiu

BAHR AL GHAZAL

White Nile

July 1999

Frequent NIF air raids, with unconfirmed reports that chemical weapons have been used.

CENTRAL AFRICAN REPUBLIC

Lanya

Pib

Chukudum

Juba

Uele

300,000 live in 'protected villages'

Ugandan refugees

Kitgum

DEMOCRATIC REPUBLIC OF CONGO

Gulu

Bundibugyo

U G A N D

Kisangani ●

Rebel groups fight a small but disruptive war, causing floods of refugees.

Mbarara

Kampala

Lake Victoria

RWANDA TANZANIA

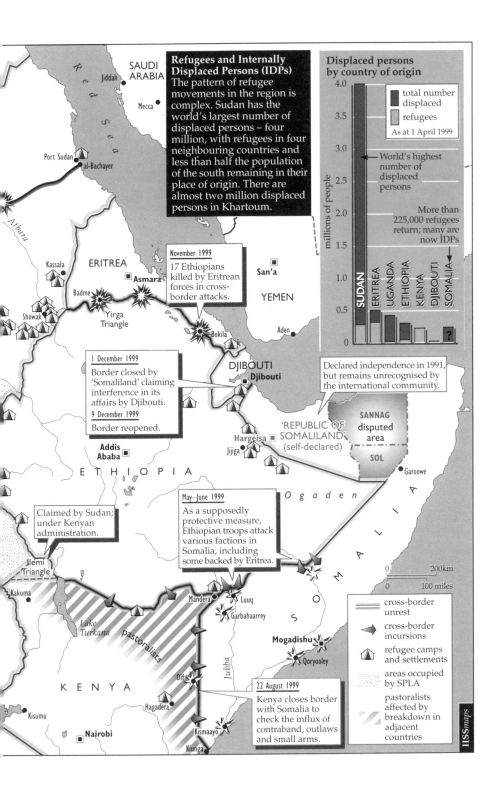

Refugees and Internally Displaced Persons (IDPs)
The pattern of refugee movements in the region is complex. Sudan has the world's largest number of displaced persons – four million, with refugees in four neighbouring countries and less than half the population of the south remaining in their place of origin. There are almost two million displaced persons in Khartoum.

Displaced persons by country of origin

millions of people

- ■ total number displaced
- □ refugees

As at 1 April 1999

← World's highest number of displaced persons

More than 225,000 refugees return; many are now IDPs

SUDAN ERITREA UGANDA ETHIOPIA KENYA DJIBOUTI SOMALIA

November 1999
17 Ethiopians killed by Eritrean forces in cross-border attacks.

1 December 1999
Border closed by 'Somaliland' claiming interference in its affairs by Djibouti.
9 December 1999
Border reopened.

Declared independence in 1991, but remains unrecognised by the international community.

SANNAG disputed area

'REPUBLIC OF SOMALILAND' (self-declared)

SOL

Claimed by Sudan; under Kenyan administration.

May–June 1999
As a supposedly protective measure, Ethiopian troops attack various factions in Somalia, including some backed by Eritrea.

22 August 1999
Kenya closes border with Somalia to check the influx of contraband, outlaws and small arms.

SAUDI ARABIA
Jiddah
Mecca
Port Sudan
al-Bachayer
Red Sea
Atbara
Kassala
ERITREA
Asmara
Badme
Showak
Yirga Triangle
Bokila
San'a
YEMEN
Aden
DJIBOUTI
Djibouti
Addis Ababa
ETHIOPIA
Hargeisa
Jijiga
Ogaden
Garoowe
SOMALIA
Ilemi Triangle
Kakuma
Lake Turkana
pastoralists
Mandera
Luuq
Garbahaarrey
Mogadishu
Qoryooley
Jubba
Dif
KENYA
Hagadera
Kismaayo
Kiunga
Kisumu
Nairobi

0 ___ 200km
0 ___ 100 miles

- ═══ cross-border unrest
- ➤ cross-border incursions
- ⛺ refugee camps and settlements
- ░░░ areas occupied by SPLA
- ▧ pastoralists affected by breakdown in adjacent countries

IISSmaps

Latin America *Violence and insurgency in Colombia*

The Revolutionary Armed Forces of Colombia (FARC) and the smaller National Liberation Army (ELN) are militarily stronger than at any time in the last 30 years. Since autumn 1997, the rebels have consistently defeated government troops in major engagements and now operate in over 60% of the country.

During 1998, President Andrès Pastrana's administration negotiated a three-month cease-fire (subsequently extended) and a demilitarised zone as a prerequisite to enable peacetalks. Despite this, FARC continued to launch offensives throughout 1999. Peace talks resumed on 13 January 2000 in the demilitarised zone.

The government also has to contend with the 4,000-strong, right-wing paramilitary forces, organised since 1966 as the Colombian United Self-Defence Forces (AUC).

In October 1999, the US announced that it is to establish an intelligence centre to fight drug production and trafficking.

During the past two decades, over 50,000 people have been killed in the political conflict, an estimated 50% of them by the paramilitaries. An estimated 500,000 have died through criminal and social violence.

January 2000
ELN attacks 23 electricity pylons in Antioquia. It has attacked a total of 267 and oil and gas installations and staged several mass kidnappings. The ELN is demanding a demilitarised zone in southern Bolívar and equal status with FARC in the peace talks.

12 December 1999
FARC attacks naval base, killing about 25 marines.

16 January 2000
Nearly 50 killed in FARC attack.

Likely location for US-funded drug intelligence centre.

The escalation in FARC violence during 1999 has raised concerns that the demilitarised zone is being used as a haven for at least 4,000 guerrillas to re-equip and train.

7 November 1998
Armed forces and police withdraw from 42,000 km², creating a demilitarised zone as demanded by FARC.

recent FARC and ELN attacks
demilitarised zone
area where FARC/ELN operate at will
areas of AUC activity
coca-producing areas

0   200km
0   100 miles

IISS*maps*

Global Trends *The IT 'revolution'*

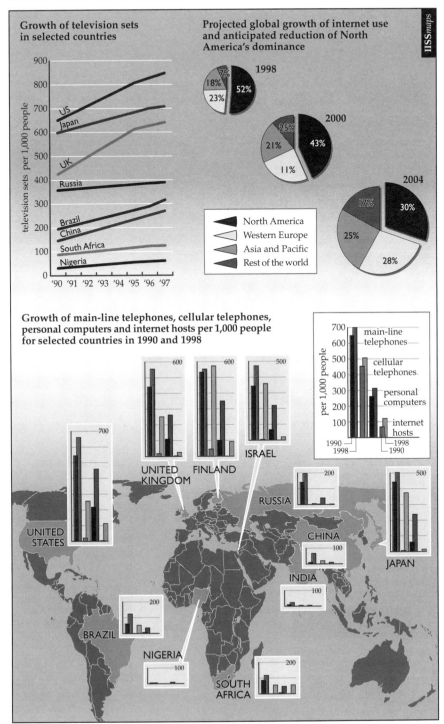

Growth of television sets in selected countries

Projected global growth of internet use and anticipated reduction of North America's dominance

IISS*maps*

1998
7%
18%
23%
52%

2000
25%
21%
43%
11%

2004
17%
30%
25%
28%

North America
Western Europe
Asia and Pacific
Rest of the world

Growth of main-line telephones, cellular telephones, personal computers and internet hosts per 1,000 people for selected countries in 1990 and 1998

main-line telephones
cellular telephones
personal computers
internet hosts

1990
1998

1998
1990

UNITED KINGDOM
FINLAND
ISRAEL
RUSSIA
CHINA
INDIA
JAPAN
UNITED STATES
BRAZIL
NIGERIA
SOUTH AFRICA

Global Trends *Transfers of technology related to nuclear-capable missiles since 1991*

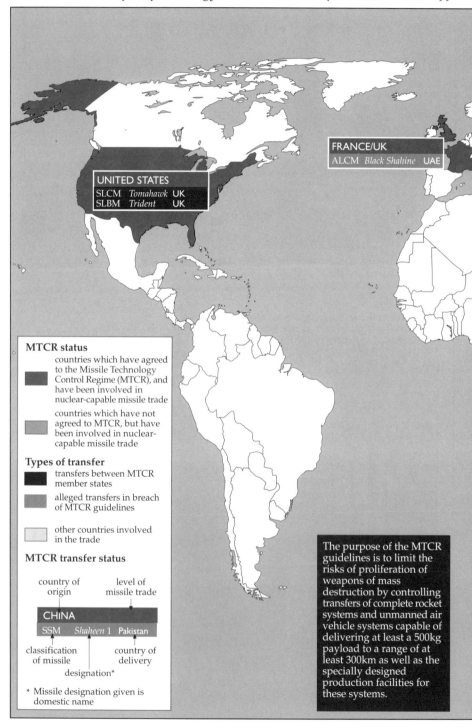

FRANCE/UK
ALCM *Black Shahine* UAE

UNITED STATES
SLCM *Tomahawk* UK
SLBM *Trident* UK

MTCR status

countries which have agreed to the Missile Technology Control Regime (MTCR), and have been involved in nuclear-capable missile trade

countries which have not agreed to MTCR, but have been involved in nuclear-capable missile trade

Types of transfer

transfers between MTCR member states

alleged transfers in breach of MTCR guidelines

other countries involved in the trade

MTCR transfer status

country of origin

level of missile trade

CHINA
SSM *Shaheen* 1 Pakistan

classification of missile

country of delivery

designation*

* Missile designation given is domestic name

The purpose of the MTCR guidelines is to limit the risks of proliferation of weapons of mass destruction by controlling transfers of complete rocket systems and unmanned air vehicle systems capable of delivering at least a 500kg payload to a range of at least 300km as well as the specially designed production facilities for these systems.

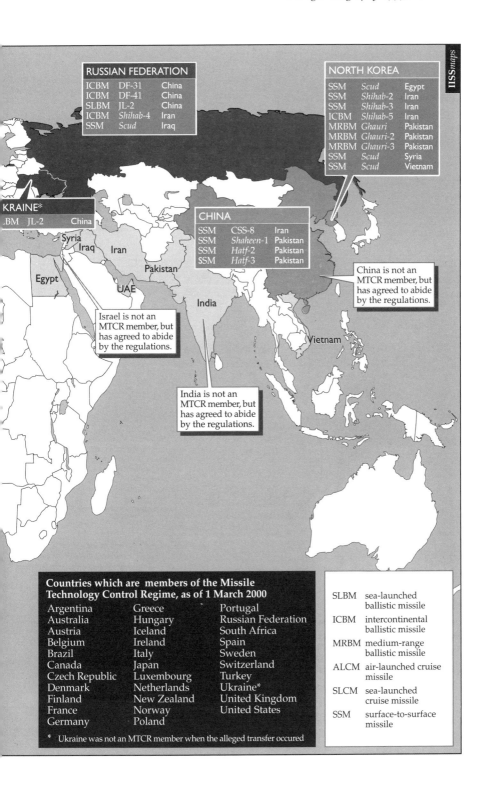

IISS*maps*

RUSSIAN FEDERATION

ICBM	DF-31	China
ICBM	DF-41	China
SLBM	JL-2	China
ICBM	*Shihab*-4	Iran
SSM	*Scud*	Iraq

NORTH KOREA

SSM	*Scud*	Egypt
SSM	*Shihab*-2	Iran
SSM	*Shihab*-3	Iran
ICBM	*Shihab*-5	Iran
MRBM	*Ghauri*	Pakistan
MRBM	*Ghauri*-2	Pakistan
MRBM	*Ghauri*-3	Pakistan
SSM	*Scud*	Syria
SSM	*Scud*	Vietnam

KRAINE*

.BM	JL-2	China

CHINA

SSM	CSS-8	Iran
SSM	*Shaheen*-1	Pakistan
SSM	*Hatf*-2	Pakistan
SSM	*Hatf*-3	Pakistan

China is not an MTCR member, but has agreed to abide by the regulations.

Israel is not an MTCR member, but has agreed to abide by the regulations.

India is not an MTCR member, but has agreed to abide by the regulations.

Countries which are members of the Missile Technology Control Regime, as of 1 March 2000

Argentina	Greece	Portugal
Australia	Hungary	Russian Federation
Austria	Iceland	South Africa
Belgium	Ireland	Spain
Brazil	Italy	Sweden
Canada	Japan	Switzerland
Czech Republic	Luxembourg	Turkey
Denmark	Netherlands	Ukraine*
Finland	New Zealand	United Kingdom
France	Norway	United States
Germany	Poland	

* Ukraine was not an MTCR member when the alleged transfer occured

SLBM	sea-launched ballistic missile
ICBM	intercontinental ballistic missile
MRBM	medium-range ballistic missile
ALCM	air-launched cruise missile
SLCM	sea-launched cruise missile
SSM	surface-to-surface missile

Global Trends *Small arms and light weapons*

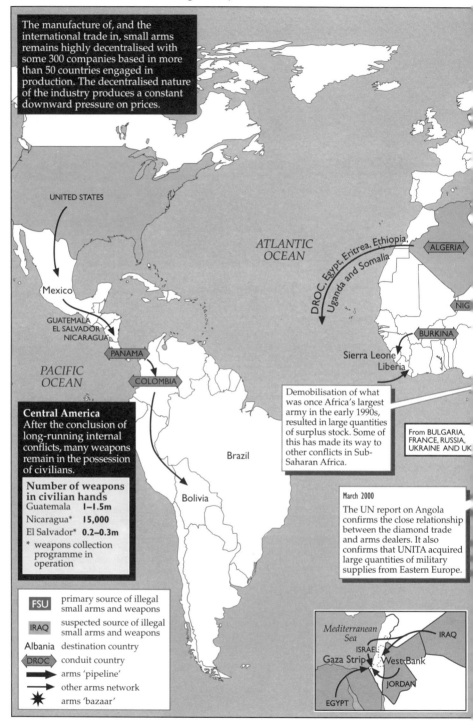

The manufacture of, and the international trade in, small arms remains highly decentralised with some 300 companies based in more than 50 countries engaged in production. The decentralised nature of the industry produces a constant downward pressure on prices.

UNITED STATES

ATLANTIC OCEAN

ALGERIA

Mexico

NIG

GUATEMALA
EL SALVADOR
NICARAGUA

BURKINA

PANAMA

Sierra Leone
Liberia

PACIFIC OCEAN

COLOMBIA

DROC, Egypt, Eritrea, Ethiopia, Uganda and Somalia

Brazil

Demobilisation of what was once Africa's largest army in the early 1990s, resulted in large quantities of surplus stock. Some of this has made its way to other conflicts in Sub-Saharan Africa.

From BULGARIA, FRANCE, RUSSIA, UKRAINE AND UK

Central America
After the conclusion of long-running internal conflicts, many weapons remain in the possession of civilians.

Number of weapons in civilian hands
Guatemala   1–1.5m
Nicaragua*   15,000
El Salvador*   0.2–0.3m
* weapons collection programme in operation

Bolivia

March 2000

The UN report on Angola confirms the close relationship between the diamond trade and arms dealers. It also confirms that UNITA acquired large quantities of military supplies from Eastern Europe.

FSU   primary source of illegal small arms and weapons
IRAQ   suspected source of illegal small arms and weapons
Albania   destination country
DROC   conduit country
⟶   arms 'pipeline'
⟶   other arms network
✳   arms 'bazaar'

Mediterranean Sea
IRAQ
ISRAEL
Gaza Strip   West Bank
JORDAN
EGYPT

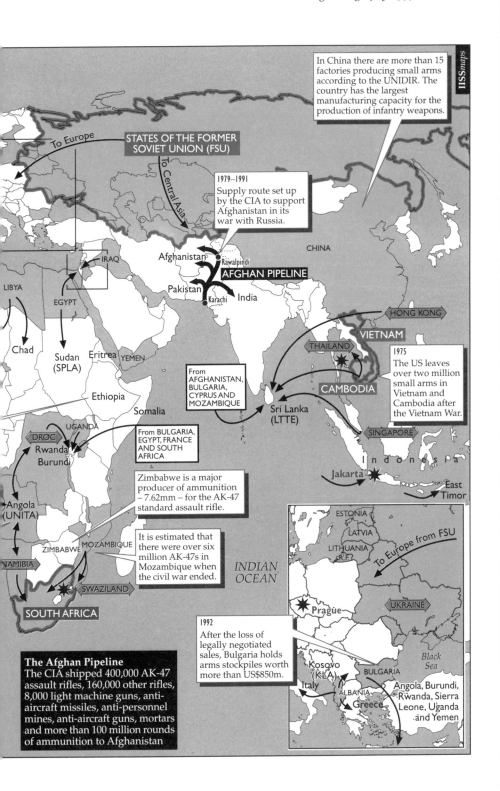

In China there are more than 15 factories producing small arms according to the UNIDIR. The country has the largest manufacturing capacity for the production of infantry weapons.

STATES OF THE FORMER SOVIET UNION (FSU)

1979–1991
Supply route set up by the CIA to support Afghanistan in its war with Russia.

To Europe

To Central Asia

CHINA

Afghanistan   Rawalpindi
AFGHAN PIPELINE
Pakistan   Karachi   India

HONG KONG

VIETNAM

THAILAND

1975
The US leaves over two million small arms in Vietnam and Cambodia after the Vietnam War.

CAMBODIA

IRAQ
LIBYA
EGYPT
Chad   Sudan (SPLA)   Eritrea YEMEN
Ethiopia
Somalia

From AFGHANISTAN, BULGARIA, CYPRUS AND MOZAMBIQUE

Sri Lanka (LTTE)

SINGAPORE

I n d o n e s i a

Jakarta   East Timor

UGANDA
DROC
Rwanda
Burundi

From BULGARIA, EGYPT, FRANCE AND SOUTH AFRICA

Zimbabwe is a major producer of ammunition – 7.62mm – for the AK-47 standard assault rifle.

Angola (UNITA)

It is estimated that there were over six million AK-47s in Mozambique when the civil war ended.

ZIMBABWE MOZAMBIQUE
NAMIBIA
SWAZILAND
SOUTH AFRICA

INDIAN OCEAN

ESTONIA
LATVIA
LITHUANIA
R.F.

To Europe from FSU

Prague

UKRAINE

Black Sea

1992
After the loss of legally negotiated sales, Bulgaria holds arms stockpiles worth more than US$850m.

Kosovo (KLA)
Italy
ALBANIA
Greece
BULGARIA

Angola, Burundi, Rwanda, Sierra Leone, Uganda and Yemen

The Afghan Pipeline
The CIA shipped 400,000 AK-47 assault rifles, 160,000 other rifles, 8,000 light machine guns, anti-aircraft missiles, anti-personnel mines, anti-aircraft guns, mortars and more than 100 million rounds of ammunition to Afghanistan

IISS*maps*

Global Trends *Selected financial and economic indicators*

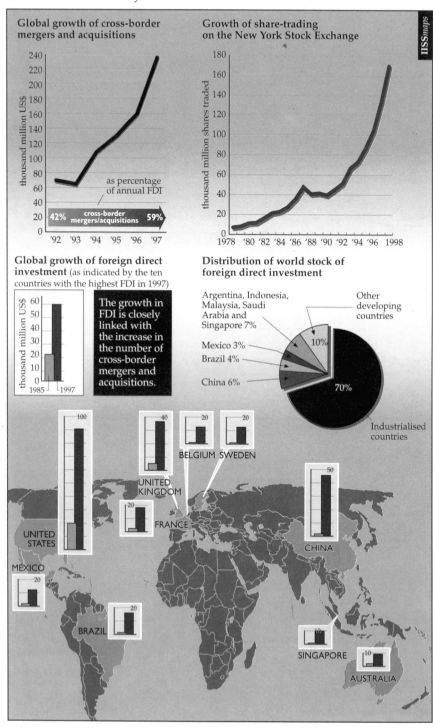

Global growth of cross-border mergers and acquisitions

thousand million US$

as percentage of annual FDI

42%   cross-border mergers/acquisitions   59%

'92 '93 '94 '95 '96 '97

Growth of share-trading on the New York Stock Exchange

thousand million shares traded

1978 '80 '82 '84 '86 '88 '90 '92 '94 '96 1998

IISS*maps*

Global growth of foreign direct investment (as indicated by the ten countries with the highest FDI in 1997)

thousand million US$

1985   1997

The growth in FDI is closely linked with the increase in the number of cross-border mergers and acquisitions.

Distribution of world stock of foreign direct investment

Argentina, Indonesia, Malaysia, Saudi Arabia and Singapore 7%

Mexico 3%

Brazil 4%

China 6%

Other developing countries

10%

70%

Industrialised countries

UNITED KINGDOM

BELGIUM SWEDEN

FRANCE

UNITED STATES

MEXICO

BRAZIL

CHINA

SINGAPORE

AUSTRALIA